Certificate in Business Accounting

Paper C05

Fundamentals of Ethics, Corporate Governance and Business Law

CIMA Study Text

KAPLAN

PUBLISHING

FOULKS LYNCH

British Library Cataloguing-in-Publication Data

A catalogue record for this book is available from the British Library.

Kaplan Publishing Foulks Lynch

Unit 2

Business Centre

Molly Millars Lane

Wokingham

Berkshire RG41 2QZ

ISBN 1 84390 928 6

978 1 84390 928 6

© FTC Kaplan Limited, 2006

Printed and bound in Great Britain.

Acknowledgements

We are grateful to the Chartered Institute of Management Accountants, the Association of Chartered Certified Accountants and the Institute of Chartered Accountants in England and Wales for permission to reproduce past examination questions. The answers have been prepared by Kaplan Publishing Foulks Lynch.

INTRODUCTION

This is the first edition of this Study Text, under the new CIMA Certificate syllabus.

Our aim was to produce a syllabus-tailored, exam-focused and student-friendly range of publications. To achieve this we have worked closely with numerous CIMA tutors and experts, and we are confident that this Study Text forms the best resource for your exam preparation.

It covers all syllabus topics to the required depth, and contains a wealth of exam-style and practice questions. Throughout the text you will find plenty of relevant examples, activities, diagrams and charts. These will put the subject matter in context and help you absorb the material easily.

The following points explain some of the concepts we had in mind when developing the layout of this book:

DEFINITION

KEY POINT

- **Definitions** – the text defines key words and concepts, placing them in the margin with a clear heading, as on the left. The purpose of including these definitions is to focus your attention on the point being covered.

- **Key points** – also in the margin, you will see key points at regular intervals. The purpose of these is to summarise concisely the key material being covered.

- **Activities** – the text involves you in the learning process with a series of activities designed to catch your attention and make you concentrate and respond. The feedback to activities is at the end of each chapter.

- **Self-test questions** – at the end of each chapter there is a series of self-test questions. The purpose of these is to help you revise some of the key elements of the chapter. All the answers to these questions can be found in the text.

- **End-of-chapter questions** – at the end of each chapter we include examination-type questions. These will give you a very good idea of the sort of thing the examiner will ask and will test your understanding of what has been covered.

Good luck with your studies!

KAPLAN PUBLISHING

CONTENTS

KAPLAN PUBLISHING

SYLLABUS AND LEARNING OUTCOMES

Syllabus outline

The syllabus comprises:

Topic and study weighting		
A	Ethics and Business	15%
B	Ethical conflict	10%
C	Corporate Governance	10%
D	Comparison of English Law with Alternative Legal Systems	10%
E.	The Law of Contract	20%
F.	The Law of Employment	10%
G	Company Administration and Finance	25%

Learning aims

This syllabus aims to test the student's ability to:

- discuss the framework of professional values, ethics and attitudes for exercising professional judgement and acting in an ethical manner, which is in the best interests of society and the profession

- explain the need to comply with the CIMA and IFAC *Codes of Ethics for Professional Accountants*

- explain the importance of good corporate governance and the evolution of good practice

- explain fundamental aspects of the organisation and operation of the English legal system and compare and contrast it with other legal systems

- explain the elements of the tort of negligence and the manner in which the tort impacts upon professional advisers

- explain the essential elements of a simple contract, what is regarded as adequate performance of the simple contract, and the remedies available to the innocent party in the event of a breach

- explain the essential differences between sole traderships, partnerships and companies limited by shares

- explain the way in which companies are administered, financed and managed

- apply legal knowledge to solve business problems.

Note: Unless specifically mentioned, the English legal system will be the context for those parts of this syllabus that relate to the study of business law.

Assessment strategy

There will be a computer-based assessment of two hours duration, comprising 75 compulsory questions, each with one or more parts.

A variety of objective test question styles and types will be used within the assessment.

Learning outcomes and indicative syllabus content

A.   Ethics and Business – 15%

Learning outcomes

On completion of their studies students should be able to:

- apply the values and attitudes that provide professional accountants with a commitment to act in the public interest and with social responsibility

- explain the need for a framework of laws, regulations and standards in business and their application

- explain the nature of ethics and its application to business and the accountancy profession

- identify the difference between detailed rules-based and framework approaches to ethics

- explain the need for continual personal improvement and lifelong learning

- explain the need to develop the virtues of reliability, responsibility, timeliness, courtesy and respect

- explain the ethical principles of integrity, objectivity, professional competence, due care and confidentiality

- identify the concepts of independence, scepticism, accountability and social responsibility

- explain the reasons why CIMA and IFAC each have a *Code of Ethics for Professional Accountants.*

Indicative syllabus content

- Values and attitudes for professional accountants

- Legal frameworks, regulations and standards for business

- The nature of ethics and its relevance to business and the accountancy profession

- Rules-based and framework approaches to ethics

- Personal development and lifelong learning

- Personal qualities of reliability, responsibility, timeliness, courtesy and respect

- Ethical principles of integrity, objectivity, professional competence, due care and confidentiality

- Concepts of independence, scepticism, accountability and social responsibility

- The CIMA and IFAC *Codes of Ethics for Professional Accountants*

B.   Ethical Conflict – 10%

Learning outcomes

On completion of their studies students should be able to:

- explain the relationship between ethics, governance, the law and social responsibility

- describe the consequences of unethical behaviour to the individual, the profession and society

- identify situations where ethical dilemmas and conflicts of interest occur

- explain how ethical dilemmas and conflicts of interest can be resolved.

Indicative syllabus content

- The relationship between ethics, governance, the law and social responsibility

- Unethical behaviour

- Ethical dilemmas and conflicts of interest

C.   Corporate Governance – 10%

Learning outcomes

On completion of their studies students should be able to:

- define corporate governance

- explain the interaction of corporate governance with business ethics and company law

- describe the history of corporate governance internationally

- explain the effects of corporate governance on directors' behaviour and their duties of skill and care

- explain different board structures, the role of the board and corporate governance issues

- describe the types of policies and procedures that 'best practice' companies introduce

- explain the regulatory governance framework for companies.

Indicative syllabus content

- The role and key objectives of corporate governance in relation to ethics and the law.

- The development of corporate governance internationally

- The behaviour of directors in relation to corporate governance and the duty of care towards their stakeholders

- The role of the board in establishing corporate governance standards

- Types of board structures and corporate governance issues

- Policies and procedures for 'best practice' companies

- Rules-based and principles-based approaches to governance

- The regulatory governance framework

D.   *Comparison of English Law with Alternative Legal Systems – 10%*

Learning outcomes

On completion of their studies students should be able to:

- explain the manner in which behaviour within society is regulated by the civil and the criminal laws

- identify and explain the sources of English law

- illustrate the operation of the doctrine of precedent by reference to the essential elements of the tort of negligence and its application to professional advisers

- compare and contrast the elements of alternative legal systems, Sharia law and the role of international legal regulations.

Indicative syllabus content

- The sources of English law

- The system of judicial precedent

- The essential elements of the tort of negligence, including duty, breach and damage/loss/injury and the liability of professionals in respect of negligent advice

- Alternative legal systems, including codified (civil law) systems, Sharia law and international legal regulations

E.   *The Law of Contract – 20%*

Learning outcomes

On completion of their studies students should be able to:

- identify the essential elements of a valid simple contract and situations where the law requires the contract to be in a particular form

- explain how the law determines whether negotiating parties have reached agreement and the role of consideration in making that agreement enforceable

- explain when the parties will be regarded as intending the agreement to be legally binding and how and agreement may be avoided because of misrepresentations

- explain how the contents and the terms of a contract are established and the possible repercussions of non-performance

- explain how the law controls the use of unfair terms in respect of both consumer and non-consumer business agreements

- explain what the law regards as performance of the contract, and valid and invalid reasons for non-performance

- explain the type of breach necessary to cause contractual breakdown and the remedies that are available for serious and minor breaches of contract.

Indicative syllabus content

- The essential elements of a valid simple contract

- The legal status of statements made by negotiating parties: enforceable offers and acceptances, and the application of the rules to standard form contracts using modern forms of communication and the role of consideration

- The principles for establishing that the parties intend their agreement to have contractual force and how a contract is affected by a misrepresentation

- Incorporation of express and implied terms, conditions and warranties

- The main provisions of sale of goods and supply of services legislation

- The manner in which the law controls the use of exclusion clauses and unfair terms in consumer and non-consumer transactions

- The level of performance sufficient to discharge contractual obligations

- Valid reasons for non performance by way of agreement, breach by the other party and frustration

- The remedies of specific performance, injunction, rescission, and requiring a contract party to pay the agreed price

- Causation and remoteness of damages, and their quantification

F.   The Law of Employment – 10%

Learning outcomes

On completion of their studies students should be able to:

- explain the difference between employees and independent contractors and how the contents of a contract of employment are established

- explain the distinction between unfair and wrongful dismissal

- demonstrate an awareness of how employers and employees are affected by health and safety legislation, including the consequences of a failure to comply.

Indicative syllabus content

- The tests used to distinguish an employee from an independent contractor

- The express and implied terms of a contract of employment

- Unfair and wrongful dismissal

- An outline of the main rules relating to health and safety at work, sanctions on employers for non-compliance, and remedies for employees

G.   *Company Administration and Finance – 25%*

Learning outcomes

On completion of their studies students should be able to:

- explain the essential characteristics of the different forms of business organisations and the implications of corporate personality

- explain the differences between public and private companies and establishing a company by registration or purchasing 'off the shelf'

- explain the purpose and legal status of the memorandum and articles of association

- explain the ability of a company to contract

- explain the main advantages and disadvantages of carrying on business through the medium of a company limited by shares

- explain the use and procedure of board meetings and general meetings of shareholders

- explain the voting rights of directors and shareholders and identify the various types of shareholder resolutions

- explain the nature of different types of share, the procedure for the issue of shares, and acceptable forms of payment

- explain the maintenance of capital principle and the procedure to increase and reduce share capital, including the repercussions of issuing shares for an improper purpose

- explain the ability of a company to take secured and unsecured loans, the different types of security and the registration procedure

- explain the procedure for the appointment, retirement, disqualification and removal of directors and their powers and duties during office

- explain the rules dealing with the possible imposition of personal liability upon the directors of insolvent companies

- identify and contrast the rights of shareholders with the board of a company

- explain the qualifications, powers and duties of the company secretary.

Indicative syllabus content

- The essential characteristics of sole traderships/practitionerships, partnerships, companies limited by shares and corporate personality

- 'Lifting the corporate veil' both at common law and by statute

- The distinction between public and private companies

- The procedure for registering a company, the advantages of purchasing a company 'off the shelf', and the purpose and contents of the memorandum and articles of association

- Corporate capacity to contract

- Board meetings: when used and the procedure at the meeting

- Annual and Extraordinary General Meetings: when used and the procedure at the meeting including company resolutions and the uses of each type of resolution

- The rights attaching to the different types of shares and the purposes and procedures for issuing shares

- The maintenance of capital principle, the purposes and rules for which shares may be issued, redeemed or, purchased and the provision of financial assistance for the purchase of its own shares

- The ability of a company to borrow money and the procedure to be followed

- Unsecured loans, and the nature and effect of fixed and floating charges

- The appointment, retirement and removal of directors and their powers and duties during office

- Fraudulent and wrongful trading, preferences and transactions at an under-value

- The division of powers between the board and the shareholders

- The rights of majority and minority shareholders

- The qualifications, powers and duties of the company secretary

HELPING YOU WITH YOUR STUDIES

Take control

Create favourable conditions and a positive attitude

- Plan to study at specific times each week. Devise a schedule and set goals.

- Choose a location where you can concentrate.

- Ask questions to be an active learner and to generate interest.

- Continually challenge yourself.

Study

Develop good learning techniques

- Use the **SQR3** method – it works with reading accountancy and management subjects. **Survey** (get an overall picture before studying in detail), **Question** (important things to learn are usually answers to questions), **Read** actively (to answer your questions), **Recite** (recall what you have read and connect topics) and **Review** (what you have covered and accomplished).

- Use the **MURDER** method – **Mood** (set the right mood), **Understand** (issues covered and make note of any uncertain bits), **Recall** (stop and put what you have learned into your own words), **Digest** (go back and reconsider the information), **Expand** (read relevant articles and newspapers), **Review** (go over the material you covered to consolidate the knowledge).

- Create **associations** and analogies to relate new ideas to what you already know and to improve understanding.

Practise

Practise under exam conditions

- **Practise** as much as possible – go through exam-style and standard questions under exam conditions.

Prepare for the exam

Develop exam technique

Be familiar with the structure of your exam and know how to approach and answer the questions.

KAPLAN PUBLISHING

THE EXAMINATION

Format of the examination:

This examination is computer-based and must be sat at a computer-based assessment centre.

There are 75 compulsory questions, each with one or more parts.

Total time allowed: two hours   100 marks

Computer-based assessment (CBA)

When sitting a CBA make sure that you are fully familiar with the software before you start answering the questions. If in doubt, ask the assessment centre staff to explain it to you.

With CBAs the questions are displayed on the screen and answers are entered using the keyboard and mouse. All the questions are of the objective-testing type, the most common of which being multiple choice. Other types of objective-testing questions include true/false, matching pairs of text and graphic, sequencing and ranking, labelling diagrams and numeric entry. Answer every question – if you dc not know the answer, you do not lose anything by guessing. Don't panic if you realise you answered a question incorrectly – you can always go back and change the answer. At the end of the assessment, if you are successful, you will be given a 'certificate of achievement' and your exam status will automatically be updated to reflect your success. If you are unsuccessful, you will receive performance feedback to help you identify areas of the syllabus where you need better understanding.

You can take a CBA at any time during the year – you do not need to wait for May and November exam sessions. However, do not attempt a CBA until you have completed all the study material relating to it. Do not skip parts of the syllabus.

For a CBA demo and the list of CIMA-accredited CBA centres, see the CIMA website at www.cimaglobal.com.

Chapter 1

THE ENGLISH LEGAL SYSTEM: SOURCES OF LAW

Syllabus content

Comparison of English law with alternative legal systems

- The sources of English law

  The law that relates to England and Wales derives from three main sources: case law (common law and equity), legislation (e.g. Acts of Parliament) and law from the European Union.

Contents

1   Classifications of English law

2   Common law and equity

3   Legislation and delegated legislation

4   The European Union as a source of law

1 Classifications of English law

1.1 Introduction

The term 'English legal system' incorporates the law of England and Wales. Within the United Kingdom both Scotland and Northern Ireland have different legal systems, although many Acts of Parliament may also apply to these jurisdictions.

In any community, laws are essential in order to be able to regulate and guide the actions of its citizens. If these rules are broken, penalties and other sanctions can be imposed.

1.2 Public law and private law

Public law governs the relationship between the individual and the state. Examples of public law are international law, constitutional and administrative law and the criminal law.

Private law governs the relationship of individuals between themselves. Examples of private law are company law, the law of tort and the law of contract.

If a private person wishes to take an action against another private person, say for breach of contract, it will fall under private law. Private individuals include legal persons such as companies.

1.3 Civil law and criminal law

A crime is an act or omission prohibited and punishable by law. The major differences between civil and criminal law include:

Purpose

Civil proceedings assist individuals to recover property or enforce obligations owed to them. Criminal proceedings are taken to suppress crime and punish the offenders, and are largely controlled by the state.

Civil law aims to provide individuals with compensation for their loss. Criminal law, on the other hand, is rarely compensatory but is to punish or to deter wrongdoers and in principle to correct and reform the offenders.

Procedure

Civil and criminal cases are normally dealt with in separate courts.

Criminal proceedings are usually brought by the Crown (through the Crown Prosecution Service). This is known as a prosecution, which may result in conviction and sentence (for example, a fine or imprisonment) if the accused is found guilty, or an acquittal if the case against him is not proved. The parties are known as the prosecution and the accused or defendant, and the court hearing is called a trial. The case against the accused must be proved beyond reasonable doubt.

A civil action is brought by an individual (the claimant) who sues another individual (the defendant) to obtain redress, usually in the form of damages, for a wrong done to him personally. The primary purpose of the action is to compensate the injured party (or confirm the existence of the injured party's rights), and not to punish the offender. The court hearing is called litigation. The case against the defendant must be proved on a balance of probabilities.

Certain acts or omissions may be both civil and criminal wrongs. Since the courts are divided into two distinct hierarchies, this usually means that separate proceedings must be brought in different courts. If A steals property from B, B can sue A in the civil courts for the tort of conversion and recover compensation for their loss. The compensation is called damages (a sum of money payable by A to B). Alternatively, or in addition, the state may bring criminal proceedings against A for theft. The result may well be a fine (a sum of money paid to the state by A).

Activity 1

Alan drives home from the pub in his friend Suzie's car. He has been drinking and has a level of alcohol in his blood that exceeds the legal limits. He drives in a reckless fashion and has an accident. The accident causes damage to Suzie's car.

In the subsequent civil legal action:

(a)   Who are the parties?

(b)   How will they have to discharge their burden of responsibility in order to prove Alan's liability?

Feedback to this activity is at the end of the chapter.

2   Common law and equity

2.1   The common law

KEY POINT

The common law is that which applies throughout England and Wales, declared by judges on the basis of fundamental legal principles.

The common law is that which applies throughout England and Wales, declared by judges on the basis of fundamental legal principles. It developed through customs and case law.

It provides a degree of continuity and predictability. Decisions are recorded and the laws become unified by the doctrine of judicial precedent. This doctrine states that where a decision has been made it shall be followed, where possible, in later cases.

KEY POINT

The doctrine of judicial precedent states that where a decision has been made it shall be followed, where possible, in later cases.

The main problem with the common law is that the only remedy available was damages (literally, money paid in compensation for loss). If a person wanted to stop a person doing something (such as not to light fires close to their house) or force another person to perform an act (such as to comply with the conditions of an agreement) there was nothing that the common law could provide.

2.2   Equity

DEFINITION

Equity is the body of discretionary rules and remedies devised by the courts on the basis of fairness and good conscience to remedy the defects of the common law.

Equity is the body of discretionary rules and remedies devised by the courts on the basis of fairness and good conscience to remedy the defects of the common law.

Equity began as the moral conscience of the law. The general principles of fairness that were laid down have been embodied in the maxims (or sayings) of equity. These maxims will feature many times in the laws of tort and contract and it is important to understand them:

- **Equity will not suffer a wrong to be without a remedy** – the only common law remedy is damages, but this is often not adequate or appropriate. Equity provides other remedies such as injunction, specific performance and rescission.

- **He who comes to equity must come with clean hands** – in order to expect and get a remedy based on fairness, claimants must themselves be fair. This means that they should not have been guilty of any improper or inequitable conduct.

- **Delay defeats equity** – also known as the doctrine of laches. Claimants must commence their case within a reasonable time of the breach or incident concerned; they should not have unduly delayed.

2.3   Comparison of common law and equity

Common law and equity may be compared as follows:

Common Law	Equity
Traditionally, the common law was rigid and inflexible. It was bound by rules of bureaucracy. (This is less true than was once the case.)	Equity is based on fairness, conscience and a moral code. This allows greater flexibility.
The common law is a complete system. It was first in time and was intended to be all encompassing.	Equity supplements the common law. It is often regarded as adding a gloss to the common law by recognising principles of fairness.
The only remedy available under the common law is damages.	Equity has many different remedies, each appropriate to the given situation.
There are set time limits under which an action must be brought under the common law. The Limitation Acts impose limits on the commencement of proceedings. The limit is usually six years, but can be as short as one year.	There are no strict time limits for bringing an action in equity, although the principle 'delay defeats equity' applies to impose the overall burden of reasonableness on the claimant.

The court will always have discretion as to whether to grant an equitable remedy rather than damages under the common law. However, if there is a conflict between the two sources of law equity will always prevail.

Activity 2

Charles and Sharon have been married for two years. They live at 14 Allerton Road. Their neighbour, Ben, insists upon lighting large bonfires at the bottom of his garden just in front of Charles and Sharon's shed, which contains two expensive motor bikes and Sharon's pottery-making equipment.

Charles and Sharon have, on many occasions, asked Ben to stop lighting the bonfires in that position but he has refused.

They eventually decide to move down the road to 28 Allerton Road. They have exchanged contracts on the purchase of number 28 and are to complete the move the next day when the vendor says that he will not move after all. They have to cancel the carpet laying at number 28 and they lose their deposit. That night Ben lights a huge bonfire and it sets light to the shed.

They seek legal advice on their problems. They are told that they can get damages for the burnt shed and lost equipment, an injunction to stop Ben lighting further fires, specific performance in respect of the move to number 28 and damages for the lost deposit.

Of the remedies they might seek, which originate at common law and which in equity?

Feedback to this activity is at the end of the chapter.

3 Legislation and delegated legislation

3.1 Introduction

Legislation is the law created by Parliament and other bodies to whom it has delegated authority.

There are two main forms of legislation: Acts of Parliament and delegated legislation. Parliament has the ability to make any laws that it sees fit and it is unable to legislate (make a law) so as to prevent a future Parliament from changing the law. However, since the United Kingdom entered the European Community (EC) in 1973, Parliament has lost some of its overall sovereignty. The United Kingdom has adhered to the Treaty of Rome and agreed to conform to European Union (EU) law. It can no longer be said that Parliament has sovereignty over the making of all laws.

Parliament consists of the House of Commons and the House of Lords.

3.2 Acts of Parliament

An Act of Parliament, or statute, is binding on everyone in the jurisdiction. It is the highest source of law and will supersede both common law and equity.

An Act may be passed to:

- **Create new law** – new law might amend existing law (whether existing legislation or case law) or cancel existing law (by repealing old legislation or overruling case law).

- **Authorise taxation** – a Finance Act is passed each year after the Chancellor of the Exchequer has published the Government's budget. This Act will then authorise the levying of taxes.

- **Codify existing law** – this is a way of putting all the existing sources of law on a particular topic into one statute.

- **Consolidate existing statutes** – this is where an Act brings together in a single statute all of the provisions on a particular topic previously contained in several statutes.

3.3 Delegated legislation

The process of enacting a Bill can be a lengthy one. Parliamentary time is very precious and it would not be possible to debate and consider in full all of the minute details required, for example, for welfare and finance legislation.

Delegated legislation is used to save Parliamentary time. It means that Parliament is given the time and the opportunity to do the job that it was elected to do, i.e. debate the principles of the legislation and the detail can be input by another body. Legislation-making powers are quite literally delegated to bodies outside Parliament.

DEFINITION

Legislation is the law created by Parliament and other bodies to whom it has delegated authority.

DEFINITION

Parliament consists of the House of Lords and the House of Commons.

DEFINITION

Acts of Parliament, or statutes, are legislation made by Parliament itself.

KEY POINT

An Act of Parliament, or statute, is binding on everyone in the jurisdiction. It is the highest source of law and will supersede both common law and equity.

This legislation is sometimes called subordinate or secondary legislation. It means that certain types of legislation can become part of the body of laws in the United Kingdom without having to endure the lengthy procedure necessary to enact an Act of Parliament.

3.4 Types of delegated legislation

There are different types of delegated legislation.

(a) **Orders in Council** – technically these are orders made by the Crown by and with the advice of Her Majesty's Privy Council. They are usually only used in times of national emergency, for example to mobilise the Armed Forces on the outbreak of hostilities.

(b) **Statutory Instruments (variously called Rules, Regulations and Orders)** – These are made by persons (e.g. a Minister) to whom the power has been delegated by Parliament. Parliament will do this by passing an Act of Parliament, or section of an Act, enabling a specified person to make laws within set limits. The Act is called an enabling Act. Statutory Instruments are used in three main situations:

  (i) to make detailed rules, often of a technical nature

  (ii) to alter monetary and other limits

  (iii) to make Commencement Orders to bring Acts of Parliament (wholly or partly) into operation on specified date(s).

(c) **Bye-laws** – these are made by local authorities or other bodies and are binding on all persons who come within their scope. In the same way as Statutory Instruments, there will be an 'enabling' Act of Parliament delegating the power to the local authority, etc.

The major difference between a bye-law and all other forms of legislation is that a bye-law has limited territorial scope, i.e. it is a local law.

3.5 Advantages of delegated legislation

In a complex and fast-moving society the law needs to keep up with changes and growth. The system of delegated legislation enables the process to be effective. Its main advantages are:

-   Parliamentary time is saved. There is simply not the time in the Parliamentary calendar to debate in detail all of the matters that require legislation. It allows Members of Parliament (MPs) to concentrate on key issues.

-   Due to changing society, regulations have to be adapted and changed, sometimes quite frequently. This is the case, for example, in welfare law where conditions and limits have to be altered to reflect increases in inflation and changes in the needs of society. It would be inefficient to do this in Parliament.

-   Matters such as tax law, defence and medical matters may require expertise. MPs could not understand such details and there is a need for expert input into legislation. This leaves Parliament free to consider and debate the underlying principles.

-   In an emergency there is insufficient time to resort to the processes of Parliament. Statutory Instruments and Orders in Council can be brought into force much more quickly than statutes.

3.6 Controlling delegated legislation

There has been some criticism of the system of delegated legislation. It has been claimed that it is unconstitutional, in that important rules and regulations are made without recourse to the proper elected authority, the House of Commons.

This argument can be countered by setting out the methods of controlling delegated legislation:

(a) Parliament can withdraw the powers that have been delegated to the body concerned. Also Ministers are answerable to Parliament for the rules and regulations (made by way of statutory instruments) made by their departments. Where Parliament is not happy with a Statutory Instrument (SI) as it stands, the Minister will have to withdraw it and start again.

SIs are subjected to the scrutiny of Parliament either before or after coming into force. They must be laid before Parliament and will cease to be operative if either House so resolves within 40 days of their being submitted. The more important SIs will not become operative at all unless they have been approved by both Houses of Parliament. A Joint Committee on Statutory Instruments scrutinises all general SIs laid before Parliament.

(b) The Department proposing to make the SI often takes steps to ensure that the various interests affected by the proposal are consulted. Some Acts of Parliament make this obligatory.

(c) The courts can challenge the validity of a SI. Challenges generally raise one of the following points:

(i) the content of the Instrument is outside the scope of the enabling Act of Parliament, i.e. the body passing it acts outside of its powers (it is said to have acted *ultra vires*)

(ii) the correct procedures were not followed in making the SI

(iii) the content of the SI is incompatible with 'Convention rights' under the Human Rights Act 1998.

In reviewing Statutory Instruments and Regulations the court will look to see if the person or body making the SI has acted unreasonably.

4 The European Union as a source of law

4.1 Introduction

The European Community (now called the European Union) was set up in 1957 by the Treaty of Rome: the immediate aim being to create a common market so as to eliminate trading boundaries between each member state.

The UK is bound by EU legislation relating to social, economic and industrial matters. As a consequence certain types of EU law are given direct legal effect within the UK's legal system, without the need for further enactment by Parliament. In addition, the Treaty of Rome gives the EU power to direct member states to alter their national laws.

If there is a conflict between EU law and national law, then EU law must be preferred.

4.2 Forms of EU legislation

(a) **Regulations** – when a regulation is made it is a law directly applicable in all the member states. There is no need to pass any legislation at national level. This is known as 'self executing'. If the passing of a regulation causes conflict with a member state's existing legislation, the regulation automatically overrides it.

(b) **Directives** – as the title suggests, directives are not self executing but are issued to certain member states requiring them within a certain period of time to alter their national laws. It is a way of bringing member states' laws into line.

Until the directive has been brought into force by the passing of a national statute it will not affect the rights and obligations of that country's citizens. Of itself, therefore, it is not a law.

However, there are two possible consequences where a member state fails to alter its laws in compliance with a directive.

(i) The member state commits a breach of the Treaty of Rome and it could be the subject of legal action in the European Court of Justice (ECJ) brought by:

- the European Commission. The ECJ will make a declaration that the state has failed to implement the directive

- any citizen who has suffered by the state's failure. The ECJ could order the state to pay damages to that person.

(ii) A citizen may rely on the terms of a directive, as a law, when bringing (or defending) legal proceedings against (or by) the state (but not a private individual) in a national court.

(c) **Decisions** –These are made by the Council of Ministers and the European Commission. A decision will be addressed to a particular member state or to an individual within that state and is a law automatically binding on the recipient. If the recipient is a member state, legislation may need to be passed to bring the decision into effect.

4.3 Principal institutions of the European Community

The most important institutions are:

(a) **The Council of Ministers** – this consists of one representative from each member state and it has law making powers.

(b) **The European Commission** – this is a non-elected secretariat based in Brussels. It makes policy proposals that must either be accepted by the Council of Ministers or rejected. The European Commission also implements EU policy when it has been agreed.

(c) **The European Parliament** – this is an elected body based in Strasbourg. Every member state elects a number of representatives to the European Parliament. Directives are debated here before being passed for final consideration to the Council of Ministers. Its powers are limited and it is mainly a consultative body. It does, however, have the power to dismiss members of the European Commission and it can reject the Community Budget.

(d) **The European Court of Justice (ECJ)** – this is the court of the European Union. It is located in Luxembourg and is staffed by senior judges (or other distinguished lawyers) on secondment from each member state. They are assisted by a permanent court officer called an Advocate-General. The ECJ's jurisdiction includes:

(i)   Actions between the Commission (and the other institutions) and member states where it is alleged that a member state has failed to comply with its obligations as laid down in the Treaty of Rome.

(ii)   The giving of rulings on the interpretation of EU law or national laws passed to implement directives. The cases reach the ECJ on a reference by a national court where it is asked by either party to the proceedings. Where a case reaches the highest legal authority in the member state (in the UK this is the Judicial Committee of the House of Lords) that court must make the reference if requested: other courts have discretion. The national court will then suspend the hearing until the ECJ has ruled on the point of law.

It is important to appreciate that a reference is made from a national court to the ECJ: not an appeal. The ECJ does not actually decide who wins or loses the case (that is for the national court): the ECJ's ruling merely states the meaning of a point of EU law, which the national court will then apply to the facts before it.

Every ruling of the ECJ is binding on all national courts of all member states.

The ECJ is an important driving force in EU law and its decisions have had a considerable impact on UK domestic law. For example:

- In 1976 the ECJ upheld the right of a national of a member state to stay in any other member state.

- In 1979 the ECJ ruled that any product legally manufactured in a member state must be allowed on the market of another member state.

- In 1990 the ECJ ruled that in a private occupational pension scheme, the imposition of an age condition that differs according to sex, for the purpose of entitlement to a pension, is not permissible.

Summary

On completion of their studies students should be able to:

- explain the manner in which behaviour within society is regulated by the civil and the criminal law

- identify and explain the sources of English law.

Self-test questions

Classifications of English law

1 State the different purposes of criminal law and civil law. (1.3)

2 What is the burden of proof in civil cases? (1.3)

Common law and equity

3 What is the only remedy available under the common law? (2.3)

Legislation and delegated legislation

4 Name the three types of Statutory Instrument. (3.4)

5 What is the main criticism of delegated legislation? How is this criticism overcome? (3.6)

The European Union as a source of law

6 What is the difference between a regulation and a directive? (4.2)

Multiple-choice questions

Question 1

In the event of conflict between law made by different bodies or persons, which type of law prevails?

A   European Union law

B   Statute law

C   Judicial precedent

D   Statutory Instrument

Question 2

What is meant by the *ratio decidendi* of a case?

A   The facts that the court found to be relevant in deciding the case

B   The legal principle on which the judicial decision was based

C   All statements of legal principles made by the court

D   Arguments advanced by counsel in support of their legal case

Question 3

A Statutory Instrument is:

A   A type of statute

B   A type of delegated legislation

C   Another word for a bye-law

D   A section in an Act of Parliament

For the answers to these questions, see the 'Answers' section at the end of the book.

Practice question

Jane

Suppose that a regulation is made by the Secretary of State under the Health and Safety at Work Act 1974 in response to a European Union directive. The regulation provides that 'no person may interfere with any fire escape, fire safety door, fire extinguisher, fire blanket, or other article'. For a joke Jane set off a fire alarm. She is told that she is to be prosecuted in court for this.

You are required:

(a)   to explain whether the court proceedings against Jane will be civil or criminal

(b)   to explain the meaning of 'Act', 'regulation' and 'directive' and the relationship between them

(c)   to explain whether or not Jane can require the case to be taken to the European Court of Justice.

For the answer to this question, see the 'Answers' section at the end of the book.

Feedback to activity

Activity 1

(a)   In the civil action Suzie will be the claimant (as her car has been damaged in the incident). Alan will be the defendant.

(b)   Suzie will have to prove that Alan's negligent driving caused damage to her car on a balance of probabilities.

Activity 2

Damages for the shed/equipment and the lost deposit – common law. Injunction and specific performance – equity.

Chapter 2

THE ENGLISH LEGAL SYSTEM: ALTERNATIVE LEGAL SYSTEMS

Syllabus content

Comparison of English law with alternative legal systems

- Alternative legal systems, including codified (civil law) systems, Sharia law and international legal regulations

Contents

1   Civil (codified) law

2   Sharia law

3   International legal regulations

1 Civil (codified) law

1.1 Common law

The previous chapter explained that the English legal system is a common law system. This means that it has developed as a result of judges deciding cases based on the doctrine of judicial precedent.

Common law systems tend to be found in countries with strong historical links to the UK, such as the United States, and countries that were once part of the British Empire.

Under the English system, trials are adversarial. Each party is represented by their own lawyers, who take the lead in questioning witnesses. The judge essentially acts as a referee. In cases involving a jury, the judge instructs the jury on the law, but the jury decides the facts. Appeals are usually only possible on questions of law.

1.2 Civil law

The other main type of legal system in the world today is civil law. This is sometimes referred to as codified law as, under this type of system, there are comprehensive written codes setting out the law. These codes are intended to set out the entire law on a particular topic.

Civil law systems tend to be found in Continental Europe, Latin America and large parts of Africa.

Under a civil law system, court decisions are not regarded as binding sources of law. However, they are persuasive. Court proceedings are conducted in a very different manner to those held under a common law system:

- there tends to be a series of court hearings over an extended period, rather than one continuous trial

- the judge actively investigates the case and conducts the questioning of witnesses

- the judge's notes and findings of fact comprise the record of the proceedings, whereas under a common law system a verbatim record of proceedings is kept

- documents play a more important role than witness testimony

- jury trials are almost unknown

- appeals are permitted on both questions of fact and law and new evidence can be received.

2 Sharia law

2.1 Definition

The term 'Sharia law' refers to an Islamic religious code for living that governs all elements of life. It is adopted by most Muslims to a certain extent as a matter of personal conscience, but it has also been formally instituted as law by certain countries and enforced by the courts. It is considered to be divine.

2.2　Sources

The primary sources of Sharia law are:

* the Koran (Qur'an) – the Muslim holy book, and
* the Hadith – the sayings and conduct of the prophet Mohammed.

However, Sharia law is also derived from:

* Scholarly consensus – the agreement of all Muslim scholars
* Legal analogy – a tool to derive rulings for new matters. For example, drugs are deemed impermissible, through legal analogy from the prohibition of alcohol in the Koran.

2.3　Actions

The Sharia regulates all human actions and puts them into five categories. The ultimate worth of an action is based on the individual's intention and sincerity.

* Obligatory actions – these are actions which must be performed and, when performed with good intentions, are rewarded.

* Forbidden actions – these are the opposite of an obligatory action.

* Recommended (meritorious) actions – a recommended action is that which should be done.

* Disliked (reprehensible) actions – these are the opposite of a recommended action.

* Permitted actions – a permitted action is that which is neither encouraged nor discouraged. Most human actions fall in this last category.

2.4　The operation of Sharia law

The way in which Sharia law is applied varies from country to country:

* In some countries it is considered acceptable to punish wrongdoers by stoning or amputating hands.

* Criticism of the Prophet Mohammed is usually forbidden.

* The eating of pork is prohibited, whilst animals that may be eaten must usually be killed in a specific way.

3　International legal regulations

3.1　Introduction

International law relates to the dealings between different nations.

The force of international law comes from the pressure that states put upon one another to behave consistently and to honour their obligations. Violations of international law are frequently overlooked. If they are addressed, it is usually through diplomacy or the adoption of sanctions, such as the severance of economic or diplomatic ties.

3.2 Sources

International law is derived from a number of sources:

- International treaties/conventions – these are obligations that states expressly and voluntarily accept between themselves.

- Custom – this is derived from the consistent practices of states. Judgments of international tribunals and scholarly works are persuasive sources of custom.

- General principles of law – these refer to those principles that are commonly recognised by the major legal systems of the world.

- International bodies – these may establish collective agreements on defined areas, for example the Internation Federation of Accountants.

3.3 Arbitration

The International Court of Justice (ICJ) is situated in the Hague and was established in 1945. States can mutually agree to submit disputes to the ICJ for arbitation. ICJ judgments are binding, but the ICJ has no means to enforce its rulings. The ICJ may also give an advisory opinion on any legal question referred to it.

Summary

On completion of their studies, students should be able to:

- compare and contrast the elements of alternative legal systems, Sharia law and the role of international legal regulations.

Self-test questions

Civil (codified) law

1   Which parts of the world tend to have civil law systems? (1.2)

2   Give three examples of ways in which a trial under a civil law system tends to differ from a trial under a common law system. (1.2)

Sharia law

3   State three of the sources of Sharia law. (2.2)

4   What are the five categories of actions? (2.3)

International legal regulations

5   Which court can arbitrate on matters of international law? (3.3)

Chapter 3

THE ENGLISH LEGAL SYSTEM: NEGLIGENCE AND THE DOCTRINE OF PRECEDENT

Syllabus content

Comparison of English law with alternative legal systems

- The system of judicial precedent
- The essential elements of the tort of negligence, including duty, breach and damage/loss/injury and the liability of professionals in respect of negligent advice

Negligence is the breach of a legal duty to take care that results in damage by the defendant to the claimant. In order to establish negligence the claimant must prove that the defendant owed the claimant a duty of care, that there was a breach of that duty and that the claimant thereby suffered loss or damage.

Contents

1   The doctrine of judicial precedent

2   The court structure

3   The tort of negligence

4   Duty of care

5   Breach of duty of care

6   Resultant loss

7   Negligent mis-statements

1 The doctrine of judicial precedent

1.1 Introduction

Common law and equity developed through a series of judge-made decisions. These decisions were recorded and a huge number of rules evolved. Judges created law in this way and it became essential to provide consistency. If the legal system was to be just, it had to be fair and consistent.

The system adopted by the judges of following previous decisions is called the doctrine of judicial precedent. Some precedents are binding (meaning they must be followed in later cases) whereas others are merely persuasive (meaning that a judge in a later case may choose to follow it but is not bound to do so).

There are three factors to be considered when differentiating between a binding precedent and a persuasive precedent:

- *ratio decidendi* and *obiter dicta*
- the hierarchy of the courts (in general lower courts are bound by precedents set by the higher courts, but not vice versa)
- the material facts of the cases.

1.2 Ratio decidendi and obiter dicta

DEFINITION

Ratio decidendi (literally: the reason for the decision) is the statement of law on which the judge based their decision.

It is this part of the judgement which forms a binding precedent. *Ratio decidendi* (literally the reason for the decision) is the statement of law on which the judge based their decision.

It is important to realise that the *ratio decidendi* has nothing to do with the facts of the case, it is a statement of law that is carried down to later decisions.

DEFINITION

Obiter dicta (literally: other things that were said) are other statements of law that did not form the basis of the decision.

Obiter dicta (literally: other things that were said) are other statements of law that did not form the basis of the decision. *Obiter dicta* are not binding on future judges. However, such statements may assist judges in the future if they are relevant and based on good sense. As such they are persuasive authority.

1.3 Material facts

In order for a precedent to be binding on a judge in a later case, the material facts of the two cases must be the same. If the facts are merely similar judges are not bound by the existing precedent: they may choose to apply it (i.e. it was persuasive) or they may refuse to apply it (i.e. they have distinguished the two cases on their facts).

1.4 Is a precedent always binding?

A precedent will not be binding if:

- it has been overruled by a higher court. This will not reverse the actual decision in the case but it will change the law for future cases.
- it has been overruled by statute. An Act of Parliament is the highest legal authority.
- it was made *per incuriam* (through lack of care).
- the facts of the case currently before the court can be materially distinguished from the facts of the earlier case.
- the *ratio decidendi* is obscure and so cannot be clearly identified. This may apply where the judges in the same case reach the same conclusion but for different reasons, in effect giving several *ratios*.

2 The court structure

2.1 Civil cases

The two main civil courts of first instance are the County Court and the High Court. (A court of 'first instance' is where the matter will be heard in full for the first time.)

The High Court is split into three divisions:

(a) The Queen's Bench Division (QBD) deals mainly with claims for damages and equitable remedies as a result of breaches of contract and torts.

(b) The Chancery Division deals in matters of partnership and company law, together with trusts, certain revenue matters and important property issues.

(c) The Family Division deals in matrimonial disputes (such as defended divorces) and children cases (such as custody issues).

2.2 Criminal cases

All criminal cases start in the Magistrates Court. If the magistrates are of the opinion that the case is serious, they will transfer it to the Crown Court where it will be held by a judge and jury.

2.3 Appeals

It is usually only possible to appeal on a point of law, rather than on a question of fact. Appeals generally lie to the Court of Appeal (civil division or criminal division, as applicable).

Appeal from the Court of Appeal is, with leave, to the House of Lords.

From the House of Lords cases can be referred to the European Court of Justice.

Note that it is sometimes possible to appeal direct from the High Court to the House of Lords. This is known as the 'leap-frog' procedure. In order to leap frog:

- permission must be obtained from the trial judge

- the appeal must be on a point of law of general public importance

- the point of law must be the subject of an existing Court of Appeal binding precedent or a point of statutory interpretation

- the House of Lords must grant leave.

KEYPOINT

Appeal from the Court of Appeal is, with leave, to the House of Lords.

2.4 The hierarchy of the courts

Precedent has developed by the process that the *ratio decidendi* of a case must be applied in any case heard in a court, which is on the same level, or below the level in the hierarchy, of the court originally making the decision.

The hierarchy of courts is as follows:

The House of Lords

This court is the highest court in England and Wales and its decisions are binding on all other courts. However, the Lords are not bound by their own decisions if they consider, in exceptional circumstances, that they do not want to follow the *ratio decidendi* laid down.

The Court of Appeal

The Court of Appeal's decisions are binding on all courts except for the House of Lords. It is generally bound by its own previous decisions.

The High Court of Justice

A single High Court judge is bound by the decisions of higher courts (e.g. the House of Lords and the Court of Appeal). However, a single High Court judge is not bound by the decision of another single High Court judge. When two or more High Court judges are sitting together (as a Divisional Court) their decisions are binding on any other Divisional Court of that division and upon a single High Court judge.

Other courts (Crown Courts, County Courts and Magistrates' Courts)

Decisions of these courts are not usually reported (so they are not part of the system of precedent). They are bound by the decisions of higher courts. Decisions by these courts do not bind any courts.

3 The tort of negligence

3.1 Introduction

The word tort is derived from Norman French and means harm or wrong. The claimants' claims are that they have suffered loss, e.g. damage to property, as a result of the wrong that was done to them by the defendant. The defendant should pay them money as compensation for the loss suffered.

3.2 What is a tort?

DEFINITION

A 'tort' can be defined as a breach of a legal duty or infringement of a legal right, arising independently of contract, which gives rise to a claim for unspecified damages.

- A breach of a legal duty or infringement of a legal right – there is no liability in tort unless the law recognises that a legal duty or right exists that has been breached.

- Arising independently of contract – no contractual relationship need exist for a claim to be made (but the existence of a contract does not preclude liability in tort).

- Claim for unspecified damages – the compensation for the loss is determined by the courts.

3.3 Essential elements

The tort of negligence has three essential elements:

(a) The existence of a duty of case

(b) Breach of that duty

(c) Loss arising as a result of that breach

4 Duty of care

4.1 To whom is it owed?

'You must take reasonable care to avoid acts or omissions which you can reasonably foresee would be likely to injure your neighbour. Who then is my neighbour? The answer seems to be persons who are so closely and directly affected by my act that I ought reasonably to have them in contemplation as being so affected when I am directing my mind to the acts or omissions which are called in question'. Lord Atkin in *Donoghue v Stevenson.*

Donoghue v Stevenson (1932)

Facts: Mrs Donoghue went to a cafe with a friend. The friend bought her a bottle of ginger beer, which Mrs Donoghue drank and then allegedly discovered that there was a decomposed snail in the bottom of the opaque bottle. Mrs Donoghue found this sight so upsetting that she suffered physical illness. She sued the manufacturer, claiming that they were under a duty to see that such outside bodies did not get into the beer.

Held: there was a duty on behalf of the manufacturer to take reasonable care in the manufacture of products. The manufacturer owes a duty to the consumer to take reasonable care to prevent injury.

Note that the word 'reasonable' appears twice in the quoted passage from Lord Atkin's judgement. In general, it denotes the objective standard of an ordinary person (as distinct from any personal standard of the individual involved).

The importance of the neighbour principle is that it can impose a duty of care towards persons with whom the party at fault has no contractual relationship and of whose identity he was previously unaware.

In Donoghue's case, the soft-drink manufacturer was held to owe a duty of care towards any person who might consume its product. This was because the manufacturer could foresee that if it put its product on the market in an impure state and in a closed and opaque container, injury to the consumer was likely to result.

4.2 Restrictions

The court is not prepared to find that a duty of care exists in all situations where the acts or omissions of the defendant cause a foreseeable loss or injury. In addition, **the claimant must be sufficiently proximate**. A claimant will be sufficiently proximate if they (or the class to which they belong, e.g. pedestrians) could have been expected by a reasonable person to be adversely affected by a want of care on the defendant's part. In addition, the court may refuse to find a duty of care even if the claimant was foreseeable and proximate, if it is not fair, just or reasonable to impose a duty on the defendant.

5 Breach of duty of care

5.1 Introduction

The second element of negligence is that there has been a breach of that duty of care.

'Negligence is the omission to do something which a reasonable man, guided upon the considerations which ordinarily regulate the conduct of human affairs, would do, or doing something which a prudent and reasonable man would not do.'

The claimant generally must show that the defendant failed to take the degree of care that a reasonable man would have taken in the circumstances.

5.2 The standard of care

The reasonable man is sometimes described as 'the man in the street' or 'the man on the Clapham omnibus'.

There are some general rules on the standard applied to determine whether a person has acted as a 'reasonable man'.

Professional man

The reasonable man is not expected to be skilled in any particular trade or profession. However, if they act or purport to act in a professional capacity, they must show the care and skill of an ordinary person of that profession.

The skill of an ordinary person of that profession will depend on the profession and the standards and practices existing at the time.

Roe v Minister of Health (1954)

Facts: the claimant was injured when contaminated anaesthetic was administered to him during an operation. This contamination occurred because of invisible cracks in the container, the possibility of which was not known to the medical profession at that time.

Held: the defendant was not liable in negligence as his behaviour was to be judged in the light of medical knowledge current at the time of the incident.

Amateur

An amateur who undertakes the job of an expert will be judged by expert standards.

Nettleship v Weston (1971)

Facts: a learner driver was in a collision.

Held: The standard of care required was that of a reasonable driver, and not that of a reasonable learner driver.

Accountants

The standard used to judge whether accountants have exercised sufficient care and skill in their work will depend on the actual work undertaken, and:

– Any statutory provisions or professional codes or guidelines setting out what the accountant must do or not do in carrying out that particular work. Failure to follow any such provision or code would be evidence of failure to meet the required standard.

– General practice and knowledge of the profession as a whole. This will include any professional code, but will also cover areas where there is no such agreed code or where the code itself is outmoded or not followed.

In *JEB Fasteners v Marks Bloom* (1982) there were various allegations of negligence:

– Various sales were omitted – there was no justification for the omission and the accountants were in breach of their duty.

– Various purchases were omitted – this was due to the delay of the accountants in making enquiries and failing to make exhaustive enquiries and they were, therefore, in breach of their duty.

- Various expenses were understated – the individual items were small, but there was a number of them. Given that it is accepted that there will be some small errors in even the most carefully audited accounts, the accountants were not found to be in breach of their duty in making these errors.

- The stock was wrongly described and consequently overvalued. The accountants had not followed normal accountancy practice. They were, therefore, in breach of their duty. This was the major finding of negligence as it most drastically affected the true financial position of the company.

6 Resultant loss

6.1 Introduction

In negligence there is no liability unless damage is shown to have resulted from the breach of the duty of care. The claimant must establish a causal link between the defendant's conduct and the damage that has been incurred.

The defendant's conduct must have been an effective **cause** of the claimant's loss.

Once causation has been proved, the claimant must then prove that the loss is not too remote in law.

6.2 Cause of loss

A test used to describe liability is referred to as the 'but for' test. If the claimant's loss would not have occurred **but for** the defendant's conduct then the defendant has caused the loss. If, however, the claimant would have suffered the loss regardless of the defendant's conduct then the defendant has not caused the loss.

JEB Fasteners Ltd v Marks, Bloom & Co (1982)

Facts: The defendant accountants audited the accounts of X Co. The audit report was negligently prepared. The claimant then took over X Co.

Held: The defendants did owe the claimant company a duty of care because they knew the claimant company was considering taking over X Co and thus were likely to rely on the audited accounts. However, the claimant company's action for damages failed because they had taken over the company not on the basis of the accounts but in a desire to obtain the services of two of X Co's directors. But for this motive no take over would have been made. Therefore the breach did not cause the loss suffered.

It is normally up to the claimant to prove that the defendant's breach caused their loss. However, sometimes there appears to be no other explanation for the claimant's loss. This is known as *res ipsa loquitur* (the thing speaks for itself). In such cases, the courts may reverse the burden of proof and require the defendant to prove that they were not negligent.

6.3 Remoteness of damage

The court will have to determine the extent of the loss for which the claimant is entitled to recover damages. The defendant will not be liable for damage that, legally, is too remote a consequence of their conduct.

Whether the damage is too remote or not depends on the 'reasonable foreseeability' test. A loss is not too remote if a reasonable man would have foreseen the *type* of injury, loss or damage.

The Wagon Mound (No.1) (1961)

Facts: due to the defendants' negligence, oil was spilled and accumulated around the claimant's wharf. The oil ignited and the wharf suffered fire damage.

Held: the defendants were held not liable since, while damage to the wharf by oil pollution was foreseeable, damage by fire was not.

6.4 Contributory negligence

If the claimant is partly responsible for their own injuries, the defendant can plead the defence of contributory negligence. The court may then reduce any damages it awards to the claimant, depending on the degree to which they are judged responsible for their loss.

7 Negligent mis-statements

7.1 Introduction

In *Hedley Byrne*, the House of Lords created a new duty situation by recognising liability for negligent statements causing economic loss made in circumstances where there exists a special relationship between the parties. Previously, damages for pecuniary loss were recoverable only if the loss arose from a wilful or reckless false statement, i.e. the tort of deceit.

Hedley Byrne & Co Ltd v Heller & Partners Ltd (1963)

Facts: the appellants (Hedley Byrne) were advertising agents, who had contracted to place adverts for their client's (Easipower) products. As this involved giving Easipower credit, they asked the respondents, who were Easipower's bankers, for a reference as to the creditworthiness of Easipower.

Heller gave favourable references (but stipulated that the information was given without responsibility on their part). Relying on this information, the claimants extended credit to Easipower and lost over £17,000 when the latter, soon after, went into liquidation. The claimants sued Easipower's bankers for negligence.

Held: the respondents' disclaimer was adequate to exclude the assumption by them of the legal duty of care, but, in the absence of the disclaimer, the circumstances would have given rise to a duty of care in spite of the absence of a contract or fiduciary relationship. Thus, but for the disclaimer, the bank was liable on its misleading statement. ***Note:*** nowadays the disclaimer might be invalidated under Unfair Contract Terms Act (UCTA) 1977.

7.2 Special relationship

KEY POINT

For an action for a negligent mis-statement, there must be a special relationship between the parties that has been established in an appropriate context.

For an action for a negligent mis-statement, there must be a special relationship between the parties that has been established in an appropriate context.

In *Hedley Byrne,* Lord Morris expounded the formulation of a special relationship in these terms:

'... it should now be regarded as settled that if someone possessed of a special skill undertakes, quite irrespective of contract, to apply that skill for the assistance of another person who relies on such skill, a duty of care will arise ...

... furthermore, if, in a sphere in which a person is so placed that others could reasonably rely on his judgement or his skill or his ability to make careful enquiry, a person takes it on himself to give information or advice to be passed on to another person who, as he knows or should know, will place reliance on it, then a duty of care will arise ...'

The concept of 'special relationship' has now been redefined by the House of Lords in the leading case of:

Caparo Industries plc v Dickman and others (1990)

Facts: In this case Caparo owned shares in F plc and, after receiving the audited accounts, which showed a profit for the year, it purchased more shares in F plc and then made a successful takeover bid for F plc. After the take over Caparo sued the auditors alleging that the accounts were misleading in that they showed a profit when in fact there had been a loss. The House of Lords in determining the existence and scope of the duty of care recognised the difficulty in setting a single general principle that could be applied to every situation. However, it did set out three criteria that must be fulfilled to give rise to a duty of care:

Foreseeability of damage – this appears to be the standard test of foreseeability in the tort of negligence.

Proximity – the court accepted that it was difficult to precisely define proximity. It was clear that there are circumstances where, although damage is foreseeable, there will be no duty of care because there is insufficient proximity. The court was anxious to differentiate between:

- the situation where an expert advises a known person who relies on the statement for a known purpose (as in *Hedley Byrne*)

- the situation where a statement made by an expert is

  generally made available and could foreseeably be relied on for a number of purposes of which the statement maker had no reason to know.

If a duty of care were owed in the second situation to anyone who read the statement, this would create for the statement maker 'liability in an indeterminate amount for an indeterminate time to an indeterminate class' or, looking at it the other way, would give the general public an entitlement to use expert knowledge, unknown to the expert, for its own purposes and hold the expert liable if it were wrong. Thus, the second criteria of proximity limits the duty to circumstances where the defendant knew the statement would be communicated to the claimant, either as an individual or a member of an identifiable class, in respect of transactions of a particular kind and that the claimant would rely on the statement in considering whether to undertake that particular kind of transaction. Thus, one must look at:

- the purpose for which the statement was made
- the statement maker's knowledge of the person relying on the statement
- the type of transaction in which it was used.

Whether it is just and reasonable that a duty of care should be imposed in the sense that to impose liability is not contrary to public policy. Again the court acknowledged that it was difficult to set out precisely a definition of this.

Held: Auditors of a public company owe no duty of care to the public at large who rely on the accounts when purchasing shares in the company. Nor is any duty owed to existing individual shareholders who purchased additional shares as they are in no better position than a member of the public.

KEY POINT

There are three criteria that must be met to give rise to a duty of care – foreseeability of damage, proximity and whether it is just and reasonable for a duty to be imposed.

There are numerous cases that illustrate the *Caparo* three-fold test for the existence of a special relationship.

Al Saudi Banque v Clarke Pixley (1989)

Facts: in reliance on accounts audited by Clarke Pixley, A1 Saudi Banque loaned money to a company called Gallic Credit International Ltd. Later Gallic went into insolvent liquidation. It was alleged that Gallic's accounts had been negligently audited.

Held: Auditors owe no duty of care to a bank that lends money, regardless of whether the bank is an existing creditor making further advances or is only a potential creditor making new advances, because in such circumstances there is no proximity between existing or potential creditors of a company and its auditors.

Esso Petroleum v Mardon (1976)

Facts: During pre-contractual negotiations for the three-year lease of a petrol filling station, L (an expert with over 40 years' experience acting on behalf of Esso) forecast the throughput of the station by the third year as 200,000 gallons. Mr Mardon suggested that 100,000 gallons might be more realistic, but his doubts were quelled by L's expertise and experience and Mardon took the lease. In the event the throughput in the third year was only 86,000 gallons and Mr Mardon lost all his capital. Esso sued Mr Mardon for arrears of rent and Mr Mardon counterclaimed for damages in the tort of negligence.

Held: The action in tort for negligent mis-statement succeeded. A duty of care existed because there was a special relationship between the parties based on proximity and reasonable foreseeability. (Breach of duty and resultant loss were also proved.)

In *Caparo* the House of Lords was of the opinion, *obiter*:

- that a duty of care might be owed to the shareholders as a body (in effect meaning a duty of care would be owed to the company). The purpose of the statutory audit report is to provide the general meeting with an independent view as to the truth and fairness of the accounts prepared by the directors so that the general meeting can reward (or otherwise) the directors – thus the proximity test would be established.

- that if during the audit the auditor was told that a particular person intended to rely on the accounts for a stated purpose, the auditors would owe a duty of care to that person in respect of that purpose.

Two contrasting cases concerning the proximity test are *Morgan Crucible v Hill Samuel* (1991) and *James McNaughten Paper v Hicks Anderson* (1991).

Morgan Crucible v Hill Samuel (1991)

Facts: MC made a bid for FCE plc, which then issued circulars containing profit records and forecasts recommending its shareholders not to accept the bid. The circulars expressly referred to the 1984 and 1985 audited accounts. Eventually MC increased its bid and, on the FCE board recommending acceptance, MC's bid succeeded. Subsequently MC discovered that the accounts and the profit forecasts grossly overstated FCE's profits and that FCE was worthless. Had MC known the true facts it would never have made the bid, let alone increased it. So MC sued FCE's merchant bank, directors and accountants in the tort of negligence in respect of circulars issued after the bid was first made.

Held: *Caparo* could be distinguished because here it is alleged the claimants knew MC would rely on the circulars for the particular purpose of deciding whether or not to make an increased bid and intended that they should. Thus there might be proximity.

Note: The full trial of the action was never heard: this was an interlocutory proceeding to decide whether there was any cause of action. (In legal procedures a case can be 'struck out' before it comes to trial if, on the facts alleged, there is no law on which the claimant could possibly succeed.) Presumably the parties eventually settled out of court.

James McNaughten Paper v Hicks Anderson (1991)

Facts: JMP entered into negotiations with MK Paper for an agreed take-over of MK. The chairman of MK asked its accountants, HA, to prepare draft accounts as quickly as possible for use in the negotiations. The accounts when prepared were shown by MK to JMP. After the take-over was completed, JMP discovered certain discrepancies in the accounts. JMP brought an action against MK's accountants in the tort of negligence.

Held: that no duty of care was owed because of lack of proximity between JMP and HA. The prime reasons for lack of proximity included:

- the accounts were produced for MK's use in negotiations not for JMP's
- draft accounts are not intended to be relied on as if they were final accounts.

7.3 References

Spring v Guardian Assurance (1994)

Facts: Guardian Assurance gave an unfavourable reference about their employee, Spring, to his potential new employer. Because of the reference Spring did not get the new job.

Held: By the House of Lords (reversing the Court of Appeal) that an employer owes a duty of care in the tort of negligence to the subject of a reference.

Note: The House of Lords recognised, *obiter*, that a duty of care might be owed to the recipient of the reference.

Summary

On completion of their studies, students should be able to:

- illustrate the operation of the doctrine of precedent by reference to the essential elements of the tort of negligence and its application to professional advisers.

Self-test questions

The doctrine of binding precedent

1 What is the *ratio decidendi* of a case? (1.2)

2 Are *obiter dicta* binding in future cases? (1.2)

3 State three circumstances in which a precedent will not be binding. (1.4)

The court structure

4 What are the three divisions of the High Court? (2.1)

5 If a person is dissatisfied with judgement in the County Court, to where can the appeal be made? (2.3)

6 Is the House of Lords bound by its own decisions? (2.4)

The tort of negligence

7   What are the three essential elements of the tort of negligence? (3.3)

Breach of duty of care

8   What standard of care is required? (5.2)

Resultant loss

9   What is the test for remoteness of damage in tort? (6.3)

Negligent mis-statements

10   In *Caparo Industries v Dickman* what three factors were held relevant to the establishment of a duty of care? (7.2)

Multiple-choice questions

Question 1

Pattie sued Dave Builders Ltd for damages for faulty workmanship relating to an extension to Pattie's house. The amount claimed was £10,000 and the judge in the County Court found for the defendant. Pattie wishes to appeal. What is the position?

A   She cannot appeal – the judge's decision in such a case is final

B   She may appeal to the Crown Court for a re-trial

C   She may appeal to the Court of Appeal

D   She may appeal to the High Court

Question 2

Which of the following is not an essential element of the tort of negligence?

A   Duty of care

B   Breach of contract

C   Breach of duty

D   Resultant loss

Question 3

Breach of duty of care in negligence is defined in law as:

A   Acting recklessly or without consideration of the consequences

B   Doing something a reasonable person would not do or not doing something a reasonable person would do

C   Doing something intentionally that a reasonable person would not do carelessly

D   Acting carelessly without considering the effect on those people who are affected by the actions

Question 4

If, in the tort of negligence, the defendant is able to establish that the breach of duty of care did not cause any loss or injury to the plaintiff:

A   The claimant may recover nominal damages only

B   The claimant may recover damages in respect of physical injury but not financial loss

C   The defendant is not liable

D   The defendant is fully liable as the duty of care has been broken

For the answers to these questions, see the 'Answers' section at the end of the book.

Practice question

Bernice

Andrew is driving his car home late one night; he is tired and not concentrating properly. Bernice steps from the pavement into his path; she is drunk and did not look first. Andrew does not notice her until it is too late and knocks her down. Bernice's lost earnings from her injuries are estimated to be £75,000.

Required:

(a)   Fill in the gaps and complete the sentence.

A personal injury claim such as this is likely to be heard in the ………………..
before a ……………………….. The issues must be proved … *(Your answer must not exceed 5 words.)*   **(4 marks)**

(b)   Fill in the gap and complete the sentence.

Bernice would need to prove that Andrew was ……………….. ; she would need to show that he owed her …   *(Your answer must not exceed 20 words.)*   **(5 marks)**

(c)   Delete as appropriate, fill in the gap and complete the sentence.

This area of law is largely based on *case law/statute* and relies on the doctrine of ……………………….. . It is determined whether Andrew has breached his duty of care by … *(Your answer must not exceed 20 words.)*   **(6 marks)**

(d)   Explain any defence Andrew may have and the effect it would have on Bernice's claim if successful. *(Your answer must not exceed 20 words.)*   **(5 marks)**

For the answers to these questions, see the 'Answers' section at the end of the book.

Chapter 4

CONTRACT: THE NATURE OF A CONTRACT

Syllabus content

The law of contract

•   The essential elements of a valid simple contract

Contracts are a central feature of modern life: the purchase of a drink in a public house; the boarding of a bus; the ordering of goods; the booking of a course of study – all constitute contracts. The law of contract is therefore of fundamental importance to the activities of virtually all kinds of business. A contract is in effect a mini legal system, in that its provisions govern the rights and obligations of the parties. This and the next seven chapters deal with the detail of this mini legal system.

Contents

1   What is a contract?

2   Outline of contract law

3   Basic principles and definitions

1 What is a contract?

A contract is an agreement between two or more parties that is enforceable by law.

Although all contracts are agreements, not all agreements are contracts. This is because some agreements we might make are not enforceable at law. For example if two friends agree to go out to dinner together this is not a contract: neither could sue the other in court should one of them back out.

2 Outline of contract law

The law of contract is concerned with three basic questions:

(a) Is there a contract? The answer to this question lies in the rules relating to **formation** of a contract. In order for a legally binding contract to exist, the following elements must be satisfied:

    (i) **Agreement, i.e. offer and acceptance** – there must be a clear agreement between the parties. Generally this is established by finding an offer by one party that the other accepts without qualification. For example, if John offers to sell his car for £500 to Bill by word of mouth and Bill verbally accepts, then a contract exists, provided the other essential elements are satisfied.

    (ii) **An intention to create legal relations** – the agreement must be intended to be subject to an action in a court of law if a dispute arises between the parties, as opposed to a mere domestic or social arrangement.

    (iii) **Consideration** – this means that each party to the contract must 'buy' the agreement of the other party. This may be shown by one party suffering a loss or detriment, in return for the benefit received. For example, in a contract of sale the buyer acquires the goods and pays the price, whilst the seller receives the price in return for the goods handed over. The law enforces bargains made by the parties, not gratuitous promises.

    (iv) **Capacity** – each party must have the legal power to bind itself contractually to the agreement concluded. For example, the Crown, corporations, persons under the age of eighteen (minors) and persons of unsound mind or under the influence of drink have limitations on their power to contract.

    (v) **Form** – some contracts are required to be made in a particular form such as writing. For most contracts, however, there is no special requirement and an oral agreement is just as much binding in law as a written agreement.

(b) Is the agreement one that the law should recognise and enforce? Some contracts will be wholly or partly invalid at law because of a vitiating factor such as mistake, misrepresentation or undue influence.

(c) When do the obligations of the parties come to an end and what are the remedies for breach of contract? The most common method of termination of a contract is when each party performs his contractual obligations and this necessarily requires knowledge of exactly what each party undertook to do, i.e. the terms of the contract. Remedies for breach of contract include monetary compensation (called damages), an action for the price, and the court orders of specific performance and injunction.

3 Basic principles and definitions

3.1 General principles

(a) **Freedom of contract** – the essence of contract is bargain. The parties are free to make their own bargain and the terms of the contract must be decided on by the parties to the contract. There are, in practice, some restrictions on this principle.

  (i) **Standard form contracts** where a person faced with a standard form cannot usually bargain. He must take it or leave it, e.g. conditions of rail travel.

  (ii) **Implied terms** where the parties have failed to express all the terms of their contract, the court may imply terms into the agreement based on the presumed but unexpressed intention of the parties. Sometimes, such terms are implied by statute, e.g. implied conditions as to fitness and quality in sale of goods and implied conditions as to periods of notice in contracts of employment.

  (iv) **Prohibitions** for example on clauses excluding liability in certain transactions (the Unfair Contract Terms Act 1977) or on unfair terms in consumer contracts (Unfair Terms in Consumer Contract Regulations 1999).

  Despite these restrictions, the principle of freedom of contract is still important, especially in commercial transactions where parties who negotiate are on an equal footing.

(b) **Sanctity of contract** – the agreement of the parties cannot be interfered with either by the parties themselves, by the court or by third parties. Once the parties have made their agreement each must abide by it, unless released by the other, even though circumstances change so as to affect their expectations. The parties may make a good or a bad bargain – the courts will not interfere and renegotiate the terms for them. The fact that a party is not in any way at fault does not excuse it from its obligation to perform the contract. Thus, in a contract for the sale of goods, a shop is under a contractual obligation to sell goods that are of satisfactory quality. If the goods are defective, the customer has an action against the shop for breach of contract. It is no excuse for the shop to plead that the defect was the fault of the person who manufactured the goods.

  There are some restrictions on the application of this principle of sanctity of contract:

  (i) restrictive interpretation is placed on exemption clauses in contracts

  (ii) lawful excuses for non-performance of a contractual obligation, e.g. frustration.

3.2 Definitions

(a)   **Specialty/simple** – a contract made by deed is called a specialty contract. In order to make a contract in the form of a deed

- it must be in writing
- it must state on its face that it is a deed
- it must be signed by each party
- each party's signature must be witnessed
- the witness must also sign, and
- it must be delivered.

It is normal, although not necessary, to employ a solicitor to draw up a contract in the form of a deed.

Any contract that is not a specialty contract is a simple contract.

You will see that these two types of contract are treated differently:

(i)   in order for a specialty contract to exist consideration is not necessary

(ii)   the time limit (called the limitation period) for suing for breach of contract is 6 years for simple contracts and 12 years for specialty contracts.

(b)   **Bilateral/unilateral** – a contract whereby both parties make promises and are bound is a bilateral contract (the usual type of contract, e.g. a contract for sale of something, where the seller promises to transfer legal title to the buyer and the buyer promises to pay).

A contract whereby one party makes promises and the other party is free to perform or not as it chooses is a unilateral contract. Once the party chooses to perform, the party making the promise is bound. This is a reward type situation, where one person promises to pay another if the other does something as in *Carlill v Carbolic Smoke Ball Company* (1893) (see Chapter 5).

(c)   **Void/voidable** – a contract may be vitiated (flawed) by a number of factors, e.g. misrepresentation, illegality, in which case the contract is either void or voidable.

Void: a void contract has no legal effect on either party – it is as if there is no contract. Any property that is transferred under a void contract must be handed back to the transferor, who remains the owner of it; if the transferee keeps the goods the real owner could sue for wrongful detention of goods, i.e. conversion.

Voidable: a voidable contract exists unless and until it is brought to an end at the option of one of the parties, usually at the option of the innocent party. The act by which the innocent party avoids a voidable contract is called rescission.

Summary

On completion of their studies students should be able to:

* identify the essential elements of a valid simple contract and situations where the law requires the contract to be in a particular form.

Self-test questions

Outline of contract law

1   List the five essential elements necessary for the formation of a contract. (2)

2   State two vitiating factors. (2)

Basic principles and definitions

3   How is a deed made? (3.2)

4   Distinguish between a void contract and a voidable contract. (3.2)

Chapter 5

CONTRACT: OFFER AND ACCEPTANCE

Syllabus content

The law of contract

- The legal status of statements made by negotiating parties. Enforceable offers and acceptances, and the application of the rules to standard form contracts using modern forms of communication.

This chapter covers the first essential element in the formation of a contract: that of agreement. Generally, the two components of agreement are that an offer has been made by one party (called the offeror), which the other party (called the offeree) has accepted.

Contents

1   The offer

2   Situations where there is no offer

3   Acceptance

1 The offer

An offer is a definite and unequivocal statement of willingness to be bound by contract.

DEFINITION

An offer is a definite and unequivocal statement of willingness to be bound by contract.

1.1 Form of the offer

- The offeror can make the offer expressly. This is where a person makes the offer orally or in writing.

- The offeror can make the offer impliedly (i.e. by conduct). This is where a person's behaviour implies the offer. An example of this would be a person filling their tank with petrol at a petrol station. It is implicit in their behaviour that they are offering to buy the petrol.

In order to be valid the offer must have certain elements. Without these elements the offer does not legally exist and so cannot be accepted.

The requirements of a valid offer are set out below.

1.2 Definite and unequivocal

The offer must be a definite and unequivocal statement of willingness to be bound in contract. It cannot be vague or uncertain in its interpretation. So, an offer to sell someone a particular car for £5,000 will be an offer. But a statement that a person will sell: '... one of my cars for about £5,000' will not be an offer; it is uncertain and vague.

1.3 Clear intention to be bound

There must be a clear intention of present willingness to be bound by the offer. The offeror must not merely be negotiating. All the offeree has to do is to accept the terms as laid down by the offeror and the contract will be complete.

1.4 Persons to whom an offer may be made

The offer can be made to a particular person, to a class of persons or even to the whole world.

An example of an offer made to the whole world arose in the leading case of *Carlill v Carbolic Smokeball Co* (1893).

Facts: he manufacturers of a medicinal 'smokeball' advertised in a newspaper that anyone who bought and used the ball properly and nevertheless contracted influenza would be paid a £100 reward. Mrs Carlill used the ball as directed and did catch flu. The manufacturers claimed that they did not have to pay her the £100 as an offer could not be made to the whole world.

Held: that an offer could be made to the whole world, that the wording of the advert amounted to such an offer, and that Mrs Carlill had accepted it by properly using the smokeball.

Another example of an offer to the world at large is a more typical advert for reward, say when someone has lost their cat and they offer a financial incentive for the finder to return it.

1.5 Communication of the offer

The offer must actually reach the person to whom it was made to be capable of acceptance. In other words the offeree must know of it.

1.6 Termination of an offer

The offer must be open, i.e. still in force, when the offeree accepts it. It is important to note that when an offer has been terminated it can no longer be accepted.

(a) **Revocation of offer** – one of the most important ways in which an offer can be terminated is by revocation by the offeror.

An offer can be revoked by the offeror or a person authorised to act on their behalf at any time before it has been accepted by the offeree. The revocation may be by express words or it may be implied from the offeror's conduct.

(i) The critical thing to note for examination questions is that the revocation will not take effect until the revocation has been received and clearly understood by the offeree. Until then, it remains open, and can be accepted.

Byrne v Leon Van Tienhoven (1880)

Facts: an offer was posted by the defendant in Cardiff on 1 October. It was received by the claimant in New York on 11 October. He at once cabled an acceptance (effectively accepting on this date). In the meantime the defendant had changed his mind and had sent a letter of revocation from Cardiff on 8 October. This letter of revocation reached New York on 15 October. The question before the court was whether the offer had been accepted or revoked.

Held: the revocation was not complete until it had been communicated to the offeree. This was on 15 October. In the meantime, however, the offer had been accepted. As a result, the revocation was ineffective and the contract did exist. The defendant was therefore liable under the contract.

(ii) The revocation can be communicated by the offeror or by a reliable third party who has or can be assumed to have the power to revoke the offer.

Dickinson v Dodds (1876)

Facts: the defendant, on 10 June, gave the claimant a written offer to sell a house for £800, to be left open until 12 June at 9.00am. On 11 June the defendant sold the house to a third party for £800, and that evening the defendant's brother-in-law told the claimant of the sale. Before 9.00am the next day the claimant accepted the offer.

Held: as the claimant knew that the defendant was no longer in the position to sell the property to him, the defendant had validly withdrawn his offer. If a reasonable person would have been aware of this withdrawal the offer is withdrawn.

(iii) The rule that an offer can be revoked at any time before acceptance applies even though the offeror has stated that he will keep the offer open for a stated time.

Routledge v Grant (1828)

Facts: Grant offered to buy Routledge's horse and gave him six weeks to decide whether or not to accept. Before the six weeks had elapsed, Grant withdrew his offer.

Held: in the absence of Routledge already having accepted, Grant was entitled to revoke his offer.

To safeguard their position in such a situation, the offeree might choose to pay the offeror to keep the offer open. This, an option, is a separate binding contract. Thus, if during the period of the option, the offer is revoked the offeror commits a breach of contract for which damages are recoverable by the offeree.

DEFINITION

A counter offer is an offer made in response to an offer. This has the effect of rejecting the original offer and the original offer is therefore no longer capable of acceptance.

(b)   **Rejection of an offer** – an offer can be terminated by a rejection. This is the action of the offeree turning down the offer. This is either outright, by the offeree stating that they will not accept it, or by a counter offer.

A counter offer is an offer made in response to an offer. An example of a counter offer is where the offeree offers a lower price or in any other way barters with the offeror. This counter offer terminates the original offer in the same way as an outright rejection, terminates the original offer.

Hyde v Wrench (1840)

Facts: Wrench offered to sell Hyde a farm for £1,000. Hyde made a counter offer, by offering £950. Wrench rejected this. Later Hyde came back and said that he now accepted the original offer of £1,000. Wrench rejected it.

Held: Hyde could no longer accept the original offer. It had been terminated by the counter offer and was no longer capable of acceptance. His 'acceptance' was merely a fresh offer which Wrench was free to turn down.

(c)   **Lapse of an offer** – an offer can also be terminated by lapse.

(i)   If the offer is stated only to be open for a specific time period, it will end after the expiration of this time. If there is no specific period of time mentioned by the offeror the offer will lapse after a reasonable length of time. If there is a dispute about the time period the court will decide what is reasonable. It is a question of fact to be decided in each case.

(ii)   If the offer was made subject to a condition, it will lapse on failure of that condition. An example of this would be an offer to supply an establishment with alcohol as long as it had a licence to sell alcohol. If the establishment for any reason lost its licence, the offer would lapse and would no longer be capable of acceptance.

(iii) If the offeror dies, the offer can no longer be accepted once the offeree knows of the death.

(iv)   If the offeree dies, the offer cannot be accepted by their personal representatives.

Activity 1

Gail offers to sell Clare her dog for £10. Clare is not sure and wants to check with her husband first. She gives Gail £1 on Gail's promise to keep the offer open for two days. Before the two days have elapsed Gail sells the dog and tells Clare.

Advise Clare.

Activity 2

P offers to sell his car to Q.

(a)   Q accepts P's offer and then dies.

(b)   Q dies and his executors purport to accept P's offer.

In each situation, is there a binding contract?

Feedback to these activities is at the end of the chapter.

1.7   Summary

In order to be valid, the offer must be:

- clear, definite and unequivocal

- one that the offeror intends to be bound by

- made to a person, a group of persons or to the whole world

- communicated to the offeree

- open when it is accepted.

Until all of these conditions are present the offer will not be valid and so cannot be accepted.

2   Situations where there is no offer

2.1   Introduction

When considering an examination question it is vital to decide whether or not the facts amount to an offer. Not all statements amount to an offer and only an offer can be accepted, so leading to a contract. It is vital to distinguish the offer from the other possibilities in the exam question.

2.2   Invitation to treat

DEFINITION

An invitation to treat is not an offer in itself but is an invitation to others to make an offer.

An invitation to treat is often the starting point of the negotiations.

Shop displays

Pharmaceutical Society of Great Britain v Boots Cash Chemists (1953)

Facts: statute requires that the sale of certain pharmaceuticals must be carried out under the supervision of a qualified pharmacist. Boots operated a store where the drugs were sold on a self-service basis and the customers paid at a cash desk for the goods they had selected. A pharmacist was present at the cash desk but not at the shelves where the goods were displayed with a price tag. The Pharmaceutical Society claimed that the statute was being contravened.

Held: the display of goods in a shop was not an offer but an invitation to treat. It was the customer who made the offer and Boots could either accept or reject this offer at the cash desk (in the presence of a qualified pharmacist). The act constituting the acceptance is the ringing up of the price on the till by the cashier and at that moment a binding contract of sale is made.

Fisher v Bell (1960)

Facts: the Restriction of Offensive Weapons Act 1959 creates a criminal offence of 'offering for sale' certain offensive weapons. A shopkeeper was prosecuted under this statute for displaying a flick knife in his shop window.

Held: a window display was not an offer of sale but only an invitation to treat. So the display did not infringe the law.

Advertisements

Sometimes an advertisement is an offer, sometimes it is an invitation to treat.

The general position is that it will be an invitation to treat because further negotiations are intended or expected.

Partridge v Crittenden (1968)

Facts: the appellant inserted an advertisement in a periodical 'Bramblefinch cocks and hens, 25s each'. It was held this was an invitation to treat not an offer.

It will be an offer if no further negotiations are intended or expected. This is the position with rewards – *Carlill v Carbolic Smokeball* (1893).

Catalogues and prospectuses

These are invitations to treat, not offers.

2.3 A mere statement of intention

An offer must be distinguished from a mere statement of intention.

Harris v Nickerson (1873)

Facts: an auction sale of furniture was advertised in a newspaper. A London broker saw the advert and travelled up to attend the sale in order to bid for various lots. Unknown to him the items had been withdrawn from the sale before he arrived. He claimed that his actions of turning up at the auction sale amounted to an acceptance of the offer contained in the advertisement. As a result he claimed that the auctioneers had breached the contract in not selling the items of furniture. He then sued for damages to cover his loss.

Held: the advertisement did not amount to an offer.

- It was not clear, definite or unequivocal from the advertisement that the auctioneers wanted to sell the items of furniture to the broker.

- The auctioneers had no intention to be bound to this broker.

Accordingly, the critical pre-requisites for an offer were not all present and this advertisement was a mere statement of intention.

2.4 A statement of price

An offer must be distinguished from a mere supplying of information.

The statement of a price in answer to an enquiry is not necessarily an offer to sell at that price.

Harvey v Facey (1893)

Facts: a telegram was sent by Harvey to Facey asking: 'Will you sell us Bumper Hall Pen? Telegram lowest cash price'. Bumper Hall Pen was a piece of land owned by Facey. A telegram was sent in reply stating: 'Lowest cash price for Bumper Hall Pen £900'. Harvey responded by sending a further telegram stating: 'We agree to buy Bumper Hall Pen for £900 asked by you'. There were no further communications and Harvey then claimed that Facey was bound by an enforceable contract to sell the land for £900.

Held: that a concluded contract had not been negotiated. The first telegram was a request for information and the second telegram was merely an answer to the question posed in the first telegram. The final telegram embodied an offer to buy the land for £900, but the offer was not accepted by the landowner to bring a contract of sale into existence.

Activity 3

John sees a car displayed on a garage forecourt with a sticker on the windscreen 'For Sale. £999'. He walks in and says to the manager that he is buying the car for £999. The manager refuses to sell it to him. Has John a contractual right to the car?

Feedback to this activity is at the end of the chapter.

3 Acceptance

3.1 Introduction

Acceptance is the unconditional assent to all the terms of the offer.

If an offeree attempts to change the terms of the offer or qualify it in any way it will terminate the offer and be classed as a counter-offer. It is only when the offeree has accepted the offer unconditionally that the parties can be said to be in agreement.

Not all enquiries about the terms of the contract will amount to a counter offer by the offeree. The offeree may only be enquiring about delivery times or other less essential terms of the contract. Only that which amounts to a complete rejection of the terms suggested by the offeror will terminate the offer, rendering it incapable of acceptance. However, an enquiry about the price will almost certainly be a counter offer.

3.2 Form of acceptance

- As a general rule, any form of acceptance is valid whether it be oral, written or merely inferred from the conduct of the parties.
- However, if the offeror stipulates a mandatory method of acceptance (e.g. by stating that acceptance must be in writing) then no other form of acceptance would be valid.

If the offeror makes the stipulation as a request, any other equally advantageous form of acceptance is valid.

Yates Building v R J Pulleyn & Sons (1975)

Facts: the offeror asked for the offer to be accepted by registered or recorded delivery letter. The offeree accepted by an ordinary letter, which arrived promptly.

Held: the offeror had suffered no disadvantage in the way that the offer had been accepted. As the offeror had not specified that the acceptance could only be made by recorded or registered letter the acceptance was valid.

- An offeror may not stipulate that silence shall amount to acceptance.

Felthouse v Bindley (1863)

Facts: F wrote to his nephew offering to buy the nephew's horse for £30 15s and adding 'If I hear no more about him, I consider the horse mine at that price'. The nephew never replied.

Held: there was no contract: an offeror cannot impose contractual liability on an offeree merely by proclaiming that silence shall be deemed acceptance.

The modern day format of the *Felthouse v Bindley* principle is 'inertia selling' as where a tradesman sends unsolicited goods to a customer accompanied by a letter stating that if the goods are not returned within ten days it will be assumed they are bought. The common law decision in *Felthouse v Bindley* is that the customer cannot have a contract imposed on them in this way. The Unsolicited Goods and Services Act 1971 takes matters further by providing that if unsolicited goods are sent with the intention that the recipient shall either purchase or hire them from the sender then the recipient may keep the goods as an unconditional gift provided six months have elapsed and the sender has not taken steps to retrieve the goods. The Act also makes it a criminal offence to demand payment for unsolicited goods.

3.3 Communication of acceptance

- Acceptance is not effective until and unless it is communicated to the offeror. Silence is not acceptance.

- *Brogden v Metropolitan Railway* (1877) The communication must be carried out by the offeree or by their authorised agent.

Powell v Lee (1908)

Facts: at a meeting the managers of a school decided to accept Lee's offer to be headmaster. Acting on his own initiative one of the managers informed Lee of the decision.

Held: there was no contract because there had been no communication of the acceptance by the managers as a body nor communication by a person authorised by them.

There are two exceptions to the rule that acceptance must be communicated:

- dispensation by the offeror
- the postal rule.

3.4 Dispensation by the offeror

The offeror may expressly or impliedly dispense with the need for communication. Offerors may dispense altogether with communication or merely dispense with communication to themselves.

- **Express dispensation** – for example, an offeror may, if they so wish, ask for a message of acceptance to be left on their telephone answering machine. It would seem that a contract exists from the moment such a message is left and even if the offeror never plays back their messages.

  Alternatively, the offeror could say 'if you accept there is no need to tell me'.

- **Implied dispensation** – the terms of the offer may imply that communication of acceptance is unnecessary. This will be the case in unilateral contracts such as *Carlill v Carbolic Smokeball* (1893).

3.5 The postal rule

The postal rule states that the communication of acceptance will be complete and effective when the letter is posted or placed into the hands of the relevant postal authorities.

The postal rule will only apply when acceptance by post is either the chosen, obvious or reasonable method of acceptance.

- It will be the chosen method of acceptance where the offeree has stipulated that posting the acceptance is the only acceptable method.

- It will be the obvious method of acceptance in a standard business situation or where the parties are communicating at a distance and the offeror requires a record of the reply.

- Where the offer was by letter, it will be the reasonable method of acceptance if an ordinary person, looking at all the circumstances would assume that to reply by post was the proper way.

The offeror can expressly or impliedly reject the postal rule.

Household Fire Insurance v Grant (1879)

Facts: Grant applied for shares in a company. The company posted a letter of allotment (i.e. accepting his offer) to Grant. He never received it. Later, the company went into liquidation and Grant was sued for the balance owing on the shares.

Held: the acceptance was complete as soon as the letter of acceptance was posted. As a result Grant was liable under the contract to pay the existing balance.

Holwell Securities v Hughes (1974)

Facts: Holwell Securities had been granted an option by Hughes to purchase some property. This option was to be exercised by 'notice in writing' by a given date. Holwell Securities sent Hughes a letter giving notice of their intention to exercise the option. This letter was delayed in the post until after the specified date.

Held: the words notice in writing mean that the notice must actually be received and that posting it was not enough in this instance.

The letter must be properly stamped addressed and posted. Handing a letter to a postman who is authorised to deliver is not equivalent in law to posting a letter.

Activity 4

Alan accepted a business offer, which had been made by letter, by posting a letter in a post box in the country. He knew, by reading the local paper, that the postal service in his area had been suspended due to the ill health of two of the postal workers. The letter never arrived at the premises of the offeror.

Was the offer accepted by Alan's actions?

Feedback to this activity is at the end of the chapter.

Summary

In order for a legally binding contract to exist there must be both offer and acceptance. Together they amount to an agreement.

In order to be valid an offer must be:

- clear, definite and unequivocal

- one that the offeree intends to be bound by

- made to a person, a group of persons or to the world

- communicated to the offeree

- open when it is accepted.

An offer should be distinguished from an invitation to treat, a mere statement of intention and a statement of price. No offer occurs in these situations and so they are not capable of acceptance.

In order to be valid an acceptance must:

- be an unconditional assent to all the terms of the offer (and not amount to a counter offer)

- be made either verbally, in writing or by conduct

- be made in the way that the offeror has expressly stipulated or in a way that is equally quick, efficient and reliable

- be clearly communicated to the offeror by the offeree. However the **postal rule** will render the acceptance complete once the letter of acceptance has been posted. The rule will **only** apply where acceptance by letter is within the contemplation of the parties as a means of communication.

On completion of their studies students should be able to:

- explain how the law determines whether negotiating parties have reached agreement.

Self-test questions

The offer

1   Define an offer. (1)

2   At what point in time will a revocation terminate an offer? (1.6)

3   What effect will a counter offer have on an offer? (1.6)

Situations where there is no offer

4   What is an invitation to treat? (2.2)

Acceptance

5   Define an acceptance. (3.1)

6   In what different ways can an acceptance be validly made? (3.2)

7   State the two exceptions to the rule that acceptance must be communicated. (3.3)

8   When will the postal rule apply? What is the rule? (3.5)

Practice questions

1   Mark and Daniel

Mark wants to stay in Daniel's hotel for three nights. Daniel explains that he only has one room left for that particular period and that he will let Mark have the room under two conditions. Firstly, that Mark pays him £75 per night and secondly, that Mark accepts this offer in writing by first class post to be received by the next day.

Advise the parties on the following:

(a)   Is Daniel's offer valid? What are the prerequisites for a valid offer?

(b)   What would happen if Mark arrived the next day with a written acceptance which he delivers to Daniel but Daniel informs him that he sent a fax purporting to revoke the offer the previous day? Mark never received the fax.

(c)   What if Mark sends his acceptance on the same day that the offer is made but the letter gets lost in the post? Would your answer be the same if a postal strike had started on the day the offer was made?

(d)   What if there is no postal strike but Mark sends the letter of acceptance by second class post, which does not arrive until the day after the one specified by Daniel?

2   A – sale of car

A advertised his car for sale for £5,000 in a local newspaper. B saw the advertisement and telephoned A offering him £4,500 for the car. A eventually offered to sell B the car for £4,800 and B said he would need to drive the car before he could agree such a price. They agreed a time to meet at A's house at the weekend for a test-drive. On Friday A sold the car to X for £4,500.

Is there a binding contract between A and B?

For the answers to these questions, see the 'Answers' section at the end of the book.

Feedback to activities

Activity 1

Clare cannot accept Gail's offer to sell to the dog because the offer has been terminated by an effective revocation. However, Clare can sue Gail for damages for breach of the collateral contract to keep the offer open.

Activity 2

(a)   Q made a binding contract before he died. Therefore Q is contractually bound to buy the car from P. (Since Q is dead it is his personal representatives who will have to carry out his pre-death obligations and actually buy the car.)

(b)   Q's death causes P's offer to lapse. There is therefore no offer that Q's executors can accept and accordingly no binding contract.

Activity 3

No. The display of the car is not an offer. His statement that he will buy is therefore not an acceptance, it is an offer that the manager has chosen to reject. There is no binding contract.

Note: Under criminal law it is an offence for a business to display goods for a price at which it is unwilling to sell. It is likely then that the garage here could be prosecuted and fined. This does not, however, have any bearing on the law of contract which is civil law.

Activity 4

No. The postal rule will not apply in this situation as it is not a reasonable method of acceptance. As Alan knows of the suspension in the postal service he cannot reasonably state that he considered this an acceptable way to reply.

As a result the usual rules on acceptance apply and as Alan's letter never reached its destination it was never accepted. No contract.

Chapter 6

CONTRACT: CONSIDERATION

Syllabus content

The law of contract

- The role of consideration

This chapter introduces and explains the second pre-requisite for a contract – consideration. Consideration is a highly examinable topic and should be carefully learnt.

Contents

1   Nature of consideration

2   The rules

3   The part-payment problem

1 Nature of consideration

1.1 The basic rule

Every simple contract must be supported by consideration.

1.2 Specialty contracts

Contracts made by deed (known as speciality contracts) do not require consideration.

1.3 Definition of consideration

Consideration is the price paid by each party to the contract for the other party's promise.

The case of *Currie v Misa* (1875) laid down the accepted definition of consideration. It can be defined as: 'some right, interest, profit or benefit accruing to one party, or some forbearance detriment, loss or responsibility given, suffered or undertaken by the other'.

It is essentially where one person (being a party to the contract) does something, omits to do something or promises to do or omit something in exchange for another person (the other party) doing, omitting or promising something.

It must be an exchange. A simple everyday example is where a person purchases a drink from a vending machine. One party inserts the money into the machine and in exchange for this receives the canned drink. Both parties are receiving a benefit (the person inserting the money, takes the canned drink, and the vending machine company takes the money), and simultaneously they are each being detrimented. The purchaser is losing the purchase price and the drinks company the can that has been vended.

A more modern definition, and one that reflects more the importance of respective promises, rather than the concept of benefit/detriment is: 'consideration is an act or forbearance (or the promise of it) on the part of one party to a contract as the price of the promise made to him by the other party to the contract': *Dunlop v Selfridge* (1915).

1.4 Executed and executory consideration

Executed consideration is given where a promise is made in return for the performance of an act. For example, where an offer of reward is made one party promises to pay if and when another performs the specified act: *Carlill v Carbolic Smokeball Co Ltd* (1893).

Executory consideration is given where there is an exchange of promises to do something in the future. Executory means 'yet to be done'. There is a contract even though at the time it is concluded or agreed neither of the parties has actually done the thing that they have promised to do.

An example is where you get into a taxi and ask to be taken to a particular destination. You have given your promise to pay the fare when you arrive at your destination and the taxi driver has promised to take you there.

2 The rules

2.1 Consideration need not be adequate but must be valuable

In law, the parties to a contract are free to conclude their bargain on whatever terms they think are appropriate. The courts will not question the adequacy of the consideration agreed upon by balancing the commercial value of the respective promises or acts of the parties, but they must be satisfied that there is something of real value provided by the parties. As long as the parties are of equal bargaining power and there is no duress they will not investigate the motives behind the transaction or check the value of the consideration given.

Valuable consideration means money or money's worth, that is to say something upon which a monetary value can be placed such as rendering a service.

The consideration provided must be valuable in the sense that it must have some value, however slight. In *Thomas v Thomas* (1842) a promise to convey a house to a widow on her promise to pay £1 per year rent and keep the house in repair was binding.

Chappell & Co v Nestle Co Ltd (1960)

Facts: Nestle offered records for sale to the public for 1s 6d (7½p) and three chocolate wrappers each.

Held: the chocolate wrappers were part of the consideration even though they were of minimal value and, in fact, thrown away by Nestle as soon as received.

However, where the consideration for a transaction is highly inadequate it may raise a suspicion of fraud, duress or undue influence on the part of the person gaining the advantage.

2.2 Consideration must be sufficient

The consideration provided must be sufficient in the sense that it must be something the law recognises as consideration.

(a) **Performance of existing duty imposed by law** – where a person has to do something by law, the discharge of that duty will not amount to consideration and cannot support a contract.

Collins v Godefroy (1831)

Facts: a witness, subpoenaed (legally required) to attend court, was promised payment if he would attend court and give evidence. He attended court and sued for the payment promised.

Held: he had not provided consideration, as he was legally obliged to attend under the subpoena.

However, if an act is performed over and above that required by law or public duty, that act is sufficient consideration for any promise to confer a benefit in return.

Glasbrook Brothers Ltd v Glamorgan County Council (1925)

Facts: Glasbrook Brothers Ltd promised to pay the police authority if it stationed police officers on company premises to protect that property from damage during a miners' strike. The company had rejected a recommendation by the superintendent in charge that a mobile force moveable to any trouble spot constituted an adequate safeguard.

Held: the police authority was entitled to payment of the promised remuneration. The police have a public duty to provide only that degree of protection that is reasonably necessary in the circumstances of the individual case. A permanent force of policemen on company property was an additional protection which provided the consideration necessary to enforce the promise to pay.

(b) **Performance of an existing contractual duty owed to the other party to the contract** – if a person is obliged to perform an act under an existing contract and the other party then promises to pay an additional sum of money to ensure that the work is finished on time, there will be no new contract in respect of the extra sum of money unless there is some practical benefit to the party offering the extra money.

This is because the person doing the work has provided no new consideration. No more work has been done than the person was already obliged to do under the pre-existing contract. Without this consideration there can be no contract and so it cannot be claimed that this new contract has been breached.

Stilk v Myrick (1809)

Facts: a ship's captain, unable to replace two deserting seamen from the crew, promised those remaining that if they completed the voyage the wages of the deserters would be divided amongst them, in addition to their contractually agreed wage.

Held: the extra payment need not be paid since the remaining seaman, by completing the voyage did no more than they were originally contractually obliged to do.

The following case is rather difficult to reconcile with *Stilk v Myrick*.

Williams v Roffey Brothers (1990)

Facts: Williams agreed to do some carpentry in a block of flats for Roffey at a fixed price of £20,000. There was an agreed date by which the work was to be completed. The work ran late and Roffey agreed to pay an extra £10,000 to ensure that the work was completed on time. If the work was not completed on time Roffey would have suffered a penalty in his own contract with the owner of the flats.

Held: the Court of Appeal decided that even though Williams was in effect doing nothing over and above the original agreement to complete the work by the agreed time, there was a new contract here for the £10,000. The court decided that both Williams and Roffey benefited from the new contract. Two reasons were given:

(i)   the consideration given by Williams was enabling Roffey to avoid the penalty sum due to the owner of the flats if the work was delayed (and not merely finishing the work on time). As such he had provided something new.

(ii)   Roffey's promise to pay the extra £10,000 had not been extracted by fraud or pressure. (It was Roffey who had approached Williams and had volunteered the extra money.) It would be inequitable to go back on his promise.

Obviously, if more than the original work was provided there is sufficient consideration.

Hartley v Ponsonby (1857)

Facts: a high number of desertions from a merchant ship rendered the vessel unseaworthy since it was now undermanned. Extra pay was offered to the crew if they remained loyal.

Held: the promise of extra money was recoverable by the seamen who remained loyal since they were now working in a dangerous situation not contemplated by their original contractual undertaking, (i.e. they were doing more than required by their original contract).

(c)   **Past consideration** – the act or promise of one party and the act or promise of the other must constitute one single transaction. One party must do something because the other party is doing something. If one party makes a promise in return for an act or promise that has already been performed unilaterally, the two promises are not a response to one another and do not support a contract. Past consideration is insufficient.

Re McArdle (1951)

Facts: a man and his wife spent £488 on improvements to a bungalow in which they resided with the husband's mother. When the mother died the house would become the joint property of the husband, and his brothers and sisters. The man attempted to enforce a promise to repay the cost of the improvements, made by the brothers and sisters after completion of the work.

Held: since all the work had been carried out before the promise was made, this past consideration could not support the later promise to reimburse the cost so as to bring a binding obligation into existence. Past consideration is no consideration.

However, there are exceptions to the rule that consideration must not be past:

(i)   Bills of exchange can be supported by past consideration, so a cheque issued in payment for work already done will be enforceable.

(ii)   Past consideration is sufficient to support a written acknowledgement of a debt in order to re-start time running for the purposes of the Limitation Act 1980.

(d)   **Illegal consideration** – the doing of, or promise of doing, an illegal act is insufficient to amount to consideration.

2.3 Consideration must move from the promisee

A person wishing to enforce a contract must show that they personally provided consideration. It is not enough that someone else provided consideration to the party being sued. For example, Alan services Brian's car in return for Brian's promise to pay the agreed charge of £20 to Colin. If Alan completes the service, Colin cannot sue for payment of the £20 since he did not personally supply consideration to Brian. Only Alan can sue Brian.

This principle is often confused with the rule called 'privity of contract' that only a party to a contract can enforce it, but, although interconnected, the two rules operate independently of each other.

Tweddle v Atkinson (1861)

Facts: the claimant's father and father-in-law agreed with each other to pay the claimant £100 and £200 respectively in consideration of his then intended marriage. After the marriage had taken place they confirmed their agreement in writing. The £200 was not paid and the claimant sued his father-in-law's executor to recover this sum.

Held: his action failed because he had not provided consideration.

3 The part-payment problem

3.1 The rule in Pinnel's case

The rule in *Pinnel's case* (1602) states that payment of a lesser sum in satisfaction of a greater sum cannot be any satisfaction for the whole sum. This rule is an illustration of the fact that performing an existing contractual promise cannot be consideration for a further contract with the promisor.

Foakes v Beer (1884)

Facts: Mrs Beer obtained a judgement against Dr Foakes for a sum of £2,090 with interest. She agreed to payment of the debt in instalments and also promised that further proceedings on the judgement would not be taken. After receiving the £2,090, Mrs Beer sued for £360 interest on the judgement debt which Dr Foakes refused to pay.

Held: the interest was recoverable. Payment of the debt and costs, a smaller sum, was not consideration for the promise to accept this amount in satisfaction of a debt, interest and costs, a greater sum. The debtor had not provided any consideration for the promise not to claim interest.

A creditor who agrees to accept £50 from a debtor in payment and satisfaction of a debt for £100, does not receive any benefit for their promise not to claim the balance; consequently the creditor's promise is unenforceable at common law. The creditor cannot be restrained from breaking their promise and taking legal action to recover the balance of the debt still unpaid.

But note:

- The rule only applies to specified claims, i.e. claims for fixed amounts, e.g. the price of goods, and not for unspecified amounts, such as damages for defective goods.

- The rule only applies to undisputed claims; where the claim is disputed in good faith, the value is again uncertain. Unless this were so, all legal actions compromised to avoid litigation could be reopened at a later stage.

It seems unfair that a party can apparently dupe another party into accepting a smaller sum in full and final settlement of their claim and then go back and sue for the full amount. So the law has found ways around the problem.

3.2 Exceptions

(a) **Variation of terms at the creditor's request (accord and satisfaction** – where the payment of a lesser sum in discharge of a greater debt is accompanied by the introduction of some new element at the creditor's request, the new element is sufficient consideration to support the creditor's promise not to claim the balance of the debt still unpaid. This is often called accord and satisfaction. The accord is the agreement to accept less and the satisfaction is the new consideration.

The new element introduced at the creditor's request, which is the consideration received for not claiming the balance, may take a number of forms, for example:

(i) payment of the debt on a date earlier than that originally agreed

(ii) payment at a different place to that stipulated in the agreement

(iii) payment of a smaller sum accompanied by the transfer of another item (e.g. £10 plus a book in satisfaction of a £15 debt).

D&C Builders v Rees (1966)

Facts: the defendant owed £482 to the claimant (a building company) for work carried out. The defendant, knowing the claimant was in desperate need of money to stave off bankruptcy, offered £300 by cheque in settlement of the debt saying that if the claimant refused it would get nothing. The claimant accepted the £300 reluctantly in settlement.

Held: the claimant could successfully sue for the balance. Several reasons contributed to the court's decision, amongst them were:

(i) in view of the pressure put on the claimant and the claimant's reluctance there was no true accord

(ii) payment by cheque and cash are, in these circumstances, no different. Therefore the payment by cheque did not amount to consideration: it conferred no benefit over and above payment in cash.

If the promise to accept less than is owed, or nothing at all, is made by deed it will be binding. Remember that an agreement made by deed does not require consideration.

(b) **Equitable doctrine of promissory estoppel** – Another way around the part-payment problem is to apply the principle of equity or fairness.

The equitable concept of estoppel, referred to as promissory estoppel, may operate to prevent a person going back on his promise to accept a lesser amount, at least for a period of time. The promise that the claimant is prevented by equity from resiling from is a promise relating to their future conduct.

Central London Property Trust Ltd v High Trees House Ltd (1947)

Facts: in 1937, the claimant company ('the lessor') let a block of flats in London to the defendant company ('the lessee') on a 99-year term, at a ground rent of £2,500 per year. During the war the lessor agreed to reduce the rent by one-half. By 1945, all the flats had been let and the lessor claimed full rent for the last two quarters of 1945.

Held: the lessor's claim should be allowed since the wartime conditions giving rise to the promise to reduce the rent had now ended and the agreement was no longer operative.

Although the claimants were not claiming the full rent during the war the court commented on whether they could have claimed it. (This was *obiter dicta.*) The lessee had not provided any consideration for the lessor's promise to reduce the rent, but if payment of full rent had been demanded for the years during which the flats were unoccupied, then the equitable doctrine of promissory estoppel would have barred any such claim. The promise not to claim the full rent was 'intended to be acted upon, and in fact acted upon, is binding so far as its terms properly apply. It is binding as covering the period down to 1945, and from that time full rent is payable.' In this way Lord Denning let promissory estoppel in through the back door of *obiter dicta*.

It must be clear that one party has made an unequivocal representation whether by words or conduct, upon which it is intended that the other party should rely.

Activity 1

Bev offers to sell Raman her car for £12,000. Raman accepts and promises to pay in two instalments; the first instalment due in three months and the balance after a further three months. Raman pays the first instalment but then loses his job and he realises that he will be unable to pay the balance.

He approaches Bev and asks her if she will accept a further £4,000 in full and final settlement of all of her claims. She agrees and he pays her a cheque.

The next day Bev issues proceedings in the County Court for the outstanding £2,000. Her action is based on the original contract. Raman serves a defence upon her that is based upon the fact that the money is not, in fact, owed at all. He claims that there is a new contract in which she has agreed to accept £10,000 in full and final settlement of all claims. Raman says that this is contractually binding.

Write a brief summary of the competing contractual claims in this situation concentrating upon the matters surrounding the mutual consideration.

Feedback to this activity is at the end of the chapter.

Summary

On completion of their studies, students should be able to:

- explain the role of consideration making the agreement enforceable.

Self-test questions

Nature of consideration

1 Give a definition of consideration. (1.3)

2 What is the difference between executory and executed consideration? (1.4)

The rules

3 In the case of *Nestle v Chappell* why was it held that three chocolate wrappers could be regarded as consideration? (2.1)

4 What were the two key reasons as to why it was decided that Roffey should be paid the extra £10,000 by Williams even though it appears on the facts of the case that he in fact provides nothing new? (2.2)

The part-payment problem

5 What is the rule in *Pinnel's* case? (3.1)

6 What was the name of the case in which Lord Denning introduced the concept of promissory estoppel? (3.2)

Practice question

Paul

Explain whether Paul is required by the law of contract to fulfil his promises in the following situations:

(a) He promises to sell an expensive car to Arthur for £10.

(b) He returns home to find that his house windows have been cleaned by Bernard and he promises to pay Bernard £1 for his work.

(c) He agrees to pay Charles £100 for painting his house within three weeks and he later promises a further £20 if Charles finishes the job on time.

(d) He promises to deliver goods to David in return for a payment to him of £50 by Eric.

(e) He promises to release Frank from a debt of £500 if Frank pays him £400.

For the answer to this question, see 'Answers' section at the end of the book.

Feedback to activity

Activity 1

Bev claims that there is no consideration for the new contract:

- Raman did not offer her anything other than that which he was contractually obliged to do (i.e. pay money under the existing contract)

- as a result there was insufficient consideration to support the new contract and it did not exist

- the case of *Stilk v Myrick* applies: Raman has not exceeded his existing contractual duty and so is still bound by the original contract.

Raman is claiming that there is a new contract. He can support this claim by paying the smaller sum early so he has provided new consideration (under the rules of 'accord and satisfaction'). Being paid earlier is valuable and so it will be regarded as sufficient consideration.

Chapter 7

CONTRACT: INTENTION, CAPACITY, FORM, ILLEGALITY

Syllabus content

The law of contract

- The principles for establishing that the parties intend their agreement to have contractual force

This chapter introduces and explains the three final pre-requisites for a contract – intention to create legal relations, capacity and form.

Even if all five of the essential elements of a contract are present, the agreement will nevertheless be void if it is illegal.

Contents

1 Intention to create legal relations

1.1 Introduction

Some agreements are not intended to be legally enforceable, their nature being such that a reasonable person viewing the words and conduct of the parties objectively would not conclude that they intended to create legal relations. For example, a reasonable person would not expect an enforceable legal obligation to spring from a mere social engagement, such as an invitation to lunch, despite the presence of all the other essential elements necessary to create a binding agreement.

1.2 Domestic and social arrangements

In domestic and social arrangements there is a rebuttable presumption that there was no intention that the agreement be legally binding. Arrangements in a domestic or social context include agreements made between members of a family and between friends. A presumption means that the claimant in the action need not prove certain matters on a balance of probabilities; the court presumes that they exist.

Balfour v Balfour (1919)

Facts: the defendant, who was about to go abroad, promised to pay his wife £30 per month in consideration of her agreeing to support herself without calling on him for any further maintenance. The wife contended that the defendant was bound by his promise.

Held: there was no legally binding contract between the parties. As it was a domestic agreement it was presumed the parties did not intend to be legally bound.

However, this presumption may be rebutted. Thus the court may reach a contrary conclusion after examining the words used and the surrounding circumstances.

Simpkins v Pays (1955)

Facts: Pays and her grand-daughter, together with Simpkins, a paying lodger, submitted an entry each week in a fashion competition appearing in the Sunday Empire News. All three devised a separate solution to the competition, but they were submitted on one coupon only, in Pays' name. The entry fees and postage were shared equally. The granddaughter made a correct forecast and Pays received a prize of £750. Simpkins claimed a one-third share of the prize money.

Held: although this was an arrangement in a domestic context the presumption was rebutted: it was a legally enforceable joint enterprise and the parties clearly intended to share any prize money. 'There was mutuality in the arrangements between the parties and an intention to create legal relations.' It was decided that on the facts this went beyond a mere friendly agreement and became a joint enterprise.

The usual presumption that agreements between spouses living happily together are not legally enforceable does not apply when they are about to separate, or have already separated.

Merritt v Merritt (1970)

Facts: a husband, separated from his wife, wrote and signed a document stating that, in consideration of the wife paying off the outstanding mortgage debt of £180 on their matrimonial home, he would transfer the house standing in their joint name into her sole ownership. The wife implemented her promise, but the husband refused to transfer title in the house to her, alleging that his promise was a domestic arrangement not giving rise to legal relations.

Held: the husband's promise was enforceable, the agreement having been made when the parties were not living together amicably. A legal relationship is contemplated where a husband deserts his wife and an agreement is concluded on ownership of the matrimonial home occupied by the wife and children.

1.3 Commercial agreements

In the case of ordinary commercial dealings, e.g. buying goods in a shop, there is a strong presumption that the parties intended it to be legally binding. This presumption can be rebutted if a contrary intention is clearly expressed in the agreement itself, but the courts are reluctant to rebut the presumption.

Jones v Vernon's Pools Ltd (1938)

Facts: Jones contended that he had forwarded a winning entry to the defendant company of football pools promoters, but they denied having received it. In order to deal with this type of eventuality, a clause was printed on the pools coupon, which Jones had signed, stating that 'any agreement … entered into … shall not … give rise to any legal relationship … but … is binding in honour only'.

Held: a contract did not exist between the parties, since the wording of the agreement clearly negated any such intention. Jones could not, therefore, sue the pools company for breach of contract.

Activity 1

Is there an intention to create legal relations in the following circumstances?

(a) Sally agrees that her cousin can come and stay with her whilst she is in the UK on a holiday from her home in Australia. A week before her cousin arrives in the UK, Sally asks her boyfriend to move in with her and the room is no longer available.

(b) Phillippe goes into a cycle repair shop to get a small puncture mended. The repair work only takes three or four minutes but the shop charges him £5. Phillippe does not want to pay because he claims that the person who did his repair was on his lunch break.

(c) Christine promises to pay her estranged husband £50 per day to childmind their 18-month old son. The son is living with Christine.

(d)   Edward commissions his uncle, who is a professional artist, to paint a portrait of his mother. He gives him some fairly precise instructions but does not want to pay the fee of £150 that his uncle later asks him for.

Feedback to this activity is at the end of the chapter.

2 Capacity to contract

In order for a contract to be valid the parties must have the legal capacity or ability to contract.

Those who are deemed incapable by the law to contract include:

- minors (in certain situations)
- the mentally disordered
- drunkards.

3 Form of a contract

3.1 Common law rule

The general rule is that a contract may be in any form whatsoever. Thus a contract is valid whether it is made orally, in writing or even by conduct.

In practice, the parties will choose to put important contracts in writing so that there can be no argument as to their terms.

3.2 Statutory exceptions

(a)   **Contracts that must be by deed**

Examples include:

(i)   a conveyance of land

(ii)   a lease (where the lease is for three years or more).

(b)   **Contracts that must be in writing**

Examples include:

(i)   bills of exchange, e.g. a cheque, and promissory notes, e.g. a bank note

(ii)   regulated consumer credit agreements, e.g. a hire purchase agreement

(iii) legal assignments of debts

(iv)   contracts for the sale or other dispositions of land.

3.3 Land

The stages in the sale of land are:

- **The precontractual stage** – when the owner of land advertises its sale, they are making an invitation to treat. They are not making an offer to sell at the price stated.

  On a sale of land, preliminary communications and statements of intention are usually expressly stated to be subject to contract. This means that neither party wishes to be bound by any statement made until a formal and binding contract has been drawn up. The parties are given an opportunity to reflect on the proposed transaction before being finally committed to it.

- **Exchange of contracts** – eventually each party signs a copy of the contract of sale and the parties then exchange contracts. The buyer has a copy of the contract with the seller's signature and vice versa. At this stage the purchaser usually pays a deposit. The contract states that the seller will transfer title and the buyer will pay the balance of the purchase money on the completion date.

  The contract for the sale of land must, by the Law of Property (Miscellaneous Provisions) Act 1989, be made in writing and must incorporate all the terms expressly agreed. The document(s) must be signed by or on behalf of each party to the contract. If this required form is not used the contract is unenforceable.

- **Completion** – completion of the transaction takes place when the purchaser hands over the balance of the agreed price and the seller hands over a conveyance or transfer deed to the purchaser together with the title deeds to the property or the land certificate.

  This stage, being a conveyance of the land, must be in the form of a deed – Law of Property Act 1925. If this required form is not used the conveyance is invalid, i.e. ownership does not vest in the transferee.

Activity 2

Jane orally agrees to sell her house to John with completion to be in a month's time.

Jane is now refusing to sign a deed conveying ownership to John. Can John compel her to do so?

Feedback to this activity is at the end of the chapter.

4 Illegality

In this context, the term 'illegal' is not confined to what is criminally illegal. Some agreements are declared illegal by statute or common law. They are a nullity, i.e. absolutely void of legal effect and therefore no action can be based on them.

4.1 Contracts illegal at common law

A contract is illegal at common law, as being harmful to the interests of society, if it offends against the concepts of public policy. Examples include:

- An agreement knowingly made to further a sexually immoral purpose: *Pearce v Brooks* (1866) (a contract to hire a horse-drawn carriage to a prostitute where it was known she would use it to attract clients).

- Where the direct or indirect object is to commit a crime or a tort, such as attempts to defraud HM Revenue and Customs.

- A contract that tends to promote corruption in public affairs: *Parkinson v College of Ambulance* (1925) (money donated to charity in return for a promised knighthood).

- Contemplated actions in a friendly foreign country that violate its law thereby disrupting international goodwill: *Foster v Driscoll*

(1929) (smuggling alcohol into the USA during the prohibition era).

- Contracts with enemy aliens: *Daimler Co Ltd v Continental Tyre & Rubber Co (GB) Ltd* (1916) (purchase of tyres during the First World War from a German-owned company).

- Interference with the administration of justice: *John v Mendoza* (bribery of a creditor to desist from bankruptcy proceedings against his debtor).

4.2 Contracts illegal under statute

A statute or a statutory instrument may expressly or impliedly declare a certain type of contract or other transaction to be illegal.

The particular statute will often state the precise effects of illegality. An example, from company law, is s151 Companies Act 1985 which states that it is illegal for a company to give financial assistance for the acquisition of its own shares. If the assistance is given, for example, by way of a 'loan contract' the company cannot sue on the contract to recover its money. As we shall see though, there are other legal principles that can be relied on in order to enable the company to recover.

Summary

On completion of their studies students should be able to:

- explain when the parties will be regarded as intending the agreement to be legally binding.

Self-test questions

Intention to create legal relations

1   What is the presumption in respect of intention to contract in a situation between husband and wife? (1.2)

2   What facts in the case *Simpkins v Pays* distinguished it from other cases that have held that agreements between friends are not generally legally enforceable? (1.2)

Form of a contract

3   What is the general common law rule regarding the form of a contract? (3.1)

4   Name the Act of Parliament that requires a contract for the sale of land to be in writing. (3.3)

5   What does the Law of Property Act 1925 require to be in the form of a deed? (3.3)

Illegality

6   What, in general, is the effect of an illegal contract? (4)

Multiple-choice question

Which of the following statements is incorrect?

A   If an agreement is of a commercial nature, it is presumed that the parties intend legal relations.

B   If an agreement is of a commercial nature, the parties cannot argue that there was no intention to create legal relations.

C   Even if an agreement is of a commercial nature, it is open to the parties to show that legal relations were not intended.

D   Even if a commercial agreement is in writing, it is open to the parties to show that legal relations were not intended.

For the answer to this question, see the 'Answers' section at the end of the book.

Feedback to activities

Activity 1

(a)   No: they are family and this appears to be a promise from one family member to another. There is no evidence to rebut the presumption that they do not intend to be legally bound.

(b)   Yes: this is a commercial situation and the presumption is that an intention exists. There are no persuasive rebutting factors here.

(c)   Yes: this is a domestic situation but the couple is estranged and so the presumption of no intention is rebutted by the situation.

(d)   Yes: although the parties are relatives this agreement appears to have been made in a business or commercial context. *Note:* The indicative words 'commissions' and 'professional'. The presumption is that the parties intend to be legally bound.

Activity 2

No. The contract, being an oral contract for the sale of land, is unenforceable – Law of Property (Miscellaneous Provisions) Act 1989.

Chapter 8

CONTRACT: MISREPRESENTATION

Syllabus content

The law of contract

- How a contract is affected by a misrepresentation

This chapter looks at the meaning of misrepresentation and what effect it will have on the formation of a contract.

Examination questions in this area tend to require you to recognise that one of the parties is claiming that a misrepresentation was made to him and the remedies that are being sought as a result.

Contents

1   Misrepresentation

2   Types of misrepresentation and remedies

3   Rescission

4   Damages for misrepresentation

1 Misrepresentation

1.1 Definition of misrepresentation

A misrepresentation may be defined as a false statement of material fact made by one of the contracting parties before or at the time of entering into the contract, which was intended to and did induce the other party to make the contract.

The definition of misrepresentation can be broken down. It must be:

- a statement

- of fact

- which is false

- made by one contracting party

- and it induced the contract.

1.2 Statement

The representation may be express or implied by conduct. The general rule is that silence does not constitute a misrepresentation. However, there are exceptions to this general rule and a party can be liable for what they did not say:

- Where silence distorts a positive representation: a half truth may be false because of what it leaves unsaid.

Nottingham Patent Brick v Butler (1886)

Facts: the potential purchaser of a house asked if there were any restrictive covenants in relation to the property. (A restrictive covenant in this context is an agreement attaching to the title of the property, which, for example, would not allow for any further building works on the land.) The solicitor replied that he was not aware of any such covenants. This was a true statement because the solicitor had not actually looked for any covenants when he had searched the title, i.e. checked the title deeds, etc. He should have done this type of search and if he had done so he would have discovered certain restrictions.

Held: this statement amounted to a misrepresentation because it was a misleading statement in the context it was given.

- Where a party makes a representation during the course of negotiations that is true, but which becomes false before the making of the contract is concluded, they are under a duty to disclose this fact to the other party. If they do not the original statement has become a misrepresentation.

With v O'Flanagan (1936)

Facts: O'Flanagan correctly told With that his medical practice produced an income of £2,000 a year, but when With bought it some four months later it was practically worthless, owing to neglect while O'Flanagan was ill during that period.

Held: failure to correct his earlier statement amounted to a misrepresentation.

- In contracts of utmost good faith (*uberrimae fidei*) where one party only is in possession of vital information, it must be communicated to the other party so that they can assess the advisability of entering into a contractual relationship.

Insurance contracts are an example of a contract of utmost good faith. The person who takes out a buildings insurance or life insurance contract possesses full knowledge of the material facts. These facts, such as defects in the house or the history of their health, are used by the insurance company to calculate the risk.

The person taking out the insurance (the insured) must make full disclosure to the insurer of every material circumstance known to them that would influence the judgement of a prudent insurer in determining whether to accept the risk. Failure to do so renders the policy voidable at the instance of the insurer and it is immaterial that no loss has been suffered as a result of non-disclosure. (A voidable contract is one that can be rescinded by one of the parties.)

- A fiduciary relationship is a relationship of trust and confidence. In some fiduciary relationships the nature of the relationship imposes a duty to make full disclosure, e.g. partners, promoters of a company and the company, principal and agent, and in arrangements between members of a family. Equity imposes the duty of disclosure in order to prevent abuse of confidence.

DEFINITION

A voidable contract is one that can be rescinded by one of the parties.

DEFINITION

A fiduciary relationship is a relationship of trust and confidence.

DEFINITION

The effect of rescission is to restore the parties to their original positions.

1.3 Statement of fact – not law, opinion or intention

- **Law** – a statement of law is not a statement of fact and thus a false statement of law will not amount to a misrepresentation.

- **Opinion** – a statement of opinion is not a statement of fact.

Bisset v Wilkinson (1927)

Facts: Bisset agreed to buy a farm from Wilkinson, allegedly relying on a representation that the farm would support about 2,000 sheep if properly worked. In fact, to the knowledge of both parties, the farm had never been used for this particular purpose. Bisset claimed rescission on ascertaining that the farm would not support anywhere near the suggested number of sheep. (The effect of rescission is to restore the parties to their original positions.)

Held: rescission could not be granted since there had not been any misrepresentation. Although the seller's erroneous assertion induced the contract, it was not a statement of fact but a mere opinion.

- **Intention** – like a statement of opinion, a statement of a person's intention is not a statement of fact. A genuinely stated intention therefore cannot amount to a misrepresentation if it is not adhered to.

However, a false statement of an intention that is not genuinely held is considered to be a misrepresentation of fact.

Edgington v Fitzmaurice (1885)

Facts: the directors of a company invited loans from the public stating that the money would be used to improve the company's business. The directors' real intention was to pay off the company's existing debts.

Held: the statement of intention was also a statement of fact. The directors had made a mis-statement of their present intention as to their future conduct. This was a misrepresentation of fact as they were stating an intention that they did not, in reality, hold.

- **Advertising puff** – a tradesman's praise of their wares is usually regarded as a mere puff and not a representation, e.g. 'this product washes clothes whiter than white'.

Dimmock v Hallet (1866)

Facts: an auctioneer described some land as 'fertile and improvable' when it was in part useless and abandoned.

Held: this was not a misrepresentation but merely a 'flourishing description'. (Note however that legislation now requires estate agents to describe property accurately.)

1.4 False

A statement is false not only if it is untrue, but also where it is true but misleading in the context.

1.5 Made by one contracting party

The statement must be made by the contracting party or their agent. A statement made by a contracting party that reaches the other party indirectly is actionable provided the misrepresentor intended it to reach the misrepresentee.

1.6 Inducement

The misrepresentation must have induced the other party to enter the contract. Thus, the innocent party cannot avoid the contract if:

- it was made after the contract had been entered into
- they did not know of the misrepresentation.

Horsfall v Thomas (1862)

Facts: Horsfall made a gun for Thomas which had a defect that Horsfall concealed. However, Thomas did not examine the gun before paying for it.

Held: as Thomas was unaware of the misrepresentation (the concealment of the defect) it had not induced him to enter into the contract.

- they knew the statement was false.
- they did not rely on the statement, e.g. he ignored it or made his own independent investigation.

Attwood v Small (1838)

Facts: Small, who was interested in purchasing a mine and iron works from Attwood, made inquiries concerning its earning capacity. Attwood's reply was an exaggeration of the true position, but Small appointed his own agents to make a survey, and they confirmed the view already expressed by the seller. On discovering the inaccuracy six months after completing the sale, Small attempted to rescind the contract.

Held: the buyer was not entitled to rescind the sale since he had not relied upon the seller's misrepresentation, but on his own independent investigation.

It is important to note that even if the misled party had the means to discover the falseness of the representation, they are not required to use those means. They are entitled to rely on the representation made by the other party, if they choose to do so, instead of making their own enquiries.

Redgrave v Hurd (1881)

Facts: a solicitor advertised for a partner. The advertisement described the practice as moderate with extensive connections in a populous town. Another solicitor answered the advertisement and at an interview the advertiser stated that the business was worth about £300 pa. No accounts had been kept but the prospective partner inspected various papers, which showed that the business produced a gross income of £200 pa and an agreement was concluded. In fact the practice was worthless.

Held: the new partner was entitled to rescission as he had been induced to enter into a contract by representation that turned out to be untrue. It was not an answer to his claim to say that if he had exercised due diligence he would have discovered the real situation.

Activity 1

Which of the following would amount to a misrepresentation?

(a)   Michael is applying for motor vehicle insurance. He states that he has no penalty points on his driving licence: a true statement. However, before the policy is issued he gets stopped by the police and the Magistrates' Court convicts him of careless driving. He has five penalty points endorsed on his licence but he does not inform the insurance company.

(b)   Lesley bought a hover mower on the basis that she saw an advertisement for the mower, which said that it was equally effective whatever the weather. She now discovers that although not completely useless the mower is, in fact, much more effective when mowing her lawn when it is dry.

(c)   Jim bought a car from Ron. Ron told Jim that the mileage on the odometer was absolutely genuine, even though it was unusually low for a car of that age. The truth is that Ron had interfered with the car's instrumentation and he knew that he was telling a lie. Unbeknown to Ron, Jim had known the previous owner and knew that, in fact, the mileage must be higher than Ron was admitting to.

Feedback to this activity is at the end of the chapter

2   Types of misrepresentation and remedies

2.1   Fraudulent misrepresentation

A misrepresentation is fraudulent if the person making the statement did not honestly believe it to be true, either because they knew it to be false or because they made it recklessly, not caring whether or not it was true.

Derry v Peek (1889)

Facts: a tramways company was authorised to make certain tramways by special Act of Parliament, which provided that the carriages might be moved by animal power and, with the consent of the Board of Trade, by steam or any mechanical power. The company issued a prospectus stating that it had the right to use steam or mechanical power, instead of horses. The claimant bought shares on the faith of this advertisement, but the Board of Trade afterwards refused their consent to the use of steam power and the company was wound up. At the time of issuing the prospectus the company honestly believed the consent would be granted as a matter of course.

Held: the statement contained in the prospectus was not a fraudulent misrepresentation since the company entertained an honest belief that it was true.

Remedies for fraudulent misrepresentation are:

- rescission of the contract (although the injured party may elect not to rescind but rather to affirm the contract). Rescission is an equitable remedy. It puts the parties back into their exact precontractual positions.

- a claim for damages based on the common law tort of deceit.

2.2 Negligent misrepresentation

Section 2(1) Misrepresentation Act 1967 provides that a misrepresentation is made negligently when the person making the statement (the misrepresentor) cannot prove they both believed the statement to be true and that they had reasonable grounds for that belief. This should be considered in an examination question when the misrepresentor is in a position of trust (such as a professional person or someone who is regarded as an expert) and makes a statement without properly and fully checking the facts.

Remedies for negligent misrepresentation are:

(a) at common law, rescission of the contract (although the injured party may elect not to rescind but rather to affirm the contract). Note that s2(2) Misrepresentation Act 1967 authorises the court to award damages instead of rescission if it would be equitable to do so (i.e. if it would be too severe a penalty to impose rescission on a person guilty of a relatively minor negligent misrepresentation)

(b) a claim for damages under s2(1) Misrepresentation Act 1967.

The misled party is more likely to bring an action for negligent rather than fraudulent misrepresentation as the latter is much easier to prove, the onus being on the representor to disprove negligence.

A misrepresentation may also give risk to a claim for damages at common law in the tort of negligence.

2.3 Innocent misrepresentation

In this case the representor had reasonable grounds for their statement but it was nonetheless untrue.

The sole remedy for innocent misrepresentation is rescission of the contract, although the injured party may elect not to rescind but rather to affirm the contract. Affirmation is any act by a party entitled to rescind, which has the effect of showing their continuing intention to be bound, e.g. voting with shares bought under a voidable contract.

Note that due to s2(2) Misrepresentation Act 1967, the court may award damages in lieu of rescission (as for negligent misrepresentation). However, the court has no power under s2(2) Misrepresentation Act 1967 to award damages in lieu of rescission where the right to rescission has been lost. Thus if rescission is not available, e.g. because the parties cannot be restored to their original position or because the contract has been affirmed, there is no remedy available for an innocent misrepresentation.

DEFINITION

Affirmation is any act by a party entitled to rescind, which has the effect of showing their continuing intention to be bound, e.g. voting with shares bought under a voidable contract.

---

3 Rescission

3.1 What is rescission?

Rescission is an equitable remedy that restores the parties to their exact pre-contractual position. Rescission can mean a formal order of the court or the act of a party cancelling or 'avoiding' the contract.

Car & Universal Finance v Caldwell (1964)

Facts: a man was induced by fraud to sell his car to a crook called Norris, who paid by cheque. His cheque was dishonoured and he disappeared. The seller notified the police and the Automobile Association immediately and asked them to try to find the car.

Held: he had successfully rescinded the contract as he had done all that he could in the circumstances.

Note: where a party pays by cheque this is a representation that the cheque will be paid.

3.2 The bars to rescission

Rescission is an equitable remedy. It is lost in the following circumstances:

- **Affirmation** – this is where a party, knowing of the misrepresentation, shows an intention nevertheless to continue with the contract.

Affirmation may also be inferred where a claimant, who has discovered the misrepresentation, does nothing to exercise their rights to rescind.

- **Lapse of time** – all equitable remedies must be sought within a reasonable time. What is a reasonable time will vary according to the circumstances.

Leaf v International Galleries (1950)

Facts: five years had elapsed before the purchaser discovered that the painting he had bought was not, as he had been led to believe, by Constable.

Held: he was barred from rescission by lapse of time.

Note: the misrepresentor had made an innocent misrepresentation and since damages are not available where the misrepresentation is innocent Leaf was left with no remedy in the law of misrepresentation.

It is likely that lapse of time is not a bar to fraudulent misrepresentation.

- **Restitution is impossible** – the parties can no longer be restored to their original position, e.g. the goods have been consumed or deteriorated.

- **Intervention of innocent third party rights** – a third party has acquired rights that would be prejudiced by rescission, e.g. if they have bought the contract goods from the party who made the misrepresentation.

Lewis v Averay (1972)

Facts: L offered his car for sale. A rogue agreed to buy it and induced L to accept his cheque by claiming to be a well-known actor. The rogue sold the car to A who took it in good faith. The rogue's cheque 'bounced' and L sought to recover the car from A.

Held: the first contract was voidable for fraudulent misrepresentation but A had purchased the car before L took steps to rescind the contract. A kept the car.

4 Damages for misrepresentation

4.1 Fraudulent misrepresentation

Where a misrepresentation has been made fraudulently, the injured party can obtain damages to put them in the position they would have been in had the misrepresentation not been made. The misrepresentator is liable for all losses caused by their fraud.

4.2 Negligent misrepresentation

There is some uncertainty as to the method of assessing damages for negligent misrepresentation. The Court of Appeal has held that the same method should be used as that applicable to fraudulent misrepresentation.

4.3 Summary of remedies

The remedies for misrepresentation can be summarised as follows:

- **fraudulent misrepresentation** – the misrepresentee can rescind the contract and/or claim damages under the tort of deceit

- **negligent misrepresentation** – the misrepresentee can rescind the contract and/or claim damages under s2(1) Misrepresentation Act 1967 or under the tort of negligence

- **innocent misrepresentation** – the misrepresentee can rescind the contract

- if (whatever the type of misrepresentation) the contract is still executory, i.e. yet to be carried out, the misrepresentee may refuse to perform it

- sometimes a representation will also be a term of the contract, in which case the innocent party will not only have remedies for misrepresentation but also remedies for breach of contract. This matter is covered in the later chapter 'Contract Terms'.

Activity 2

Susan goes into an Indian restaurant. She says that she will only purchase a curry if the staff can assure her that all of the ingredients are fresh that day. She is assured that they are.

She orders her meal on the basis of this statement and when she is half way through eating it she starts to feel ill and discovers that some of the food has gone off. She says that she intends to rescind the contract. Can she?

Feedback to this activity is at the end of the chapter

Summary

On completion of their studies, students should be able to:

- explain how an agreement may be avoided because of misrepresentations.

Self-test questions

Misrepresentation

1   What is the definition of a misrepresentation? (1.1)

2   Can silence ever constitute a misrepresentation? (1.2)

3   How does a statement of fact differ from a statement of intention or opinion? (1.3)

Types of misrepresentation and remedies

4   Define fraudulent misrepresentation. (2.1)

5   If a person is found liable for a negligent misrepresentation, under what section of the Misrepresentation Act 1967 can the misrepresentee claim for damages? What tort is also available? (2.2)

Rescission

6   What are the four bars to rescission? (3.2)

Multiple-choice questions

Question 1

A fraudulent misrepresentation will render the contract:

A   Void

B   Voidable

C   Unenforceable

D   Executed

Question 2

Amos, a sheep farmer, told Gullable that his farm, in his opinion, had sufficient grazing for 3,000 cows. Gullable knew the land had never been used for dairy farming. Gullable purchased the farm, but, as he can only graze 1,000 cows on it, he wants to rescind the sale contract. What is the position?

A   Amos's statement is one of opinion and is therefore a misrepresentation

B   Amos's statement is one of opinion but is treated as one of fact because of his special knowledge

C   Amos's statement is one of fact

D   Amos's statement is one of opinion and is therefore not a misrepresentation

Question 3

A Ltd has been induced to enter into a contract with B Ltd by the latter's innocent misrepresentation.

Which of the following is correct?

A   A Ltd may sue B Ltd for damages in the tort of negligence

B   A Ltd may sue B Ltd for damages under the Misrepresentation Act 1967

C   A Ltd may request rescission of the contract or damages in lieu of rescission under the Misrepresentation Act 1967

D   A Ltd may treat the contract with B Ltd as void

For the answers to these questions, see the 'Answers' section at the end of the book.

Practice question

Misrepresentations

Mort completed a proposal form for a life assurance policy. In answer to a question asking what other such proposals he had made he stated that one had been accepted. This was correct, but he omitted to mention that three other proposals had been turned down. Mort has now died and his widow is claiming on the policy.

To what extent is she likely to succeed?

For the answer to this question, see the 'Answers' section at the end of the book.

Feedback to activities

Activity 1

(a)   Yes – this is a contract of utmost good faith. When the facts changed the driver should have told the insurance company as the risk had changed.

(b)   No – this is almost certainly mere advertising puff. It was more of a description than a representation.

(c)   No – the statement must induce the misrepresentee to enter into the contract. Here Jim knew of the lie that Ron had told and so could not be said to have entered into the contract due to this attempted inducement.

Activity 2

Rescission is only available where the parties can be returned to their exact pre-contractual position. As she has eaten part of her meal this is no longer possible.

She can claim damages if the misrepresentation was either fraudulent or negligent. However, if the misrepresentation was completely innocent and the restaurant genuinely and reasonably believed that the food was fresh, as rescission is no longer possible she can get no remedy in misrepresentation. (Later you will see that Susan will have a remedy for breach of an implied term of the contract.)

Chapter 9

CONTRACT: TERMS

Syllabus content

The law of contract

- Incorporation of express and implied terms, conditions and warranties
- The main provisions of sale of goods and supply of services legislation
- The manner in which the law controls the use of exclusion clauses and unfair terms in consumer and non-consumer transactions

Now that the contract has been formed and is valid, it is important to look at what its contents are. The contents of the contract are its terms and it is these that will dictate the parties' legal obligations. The terms can include simple things such as price and date of delivery, but they can also be complicated references to the passage of title in the goods and the exclusion of liability in the event of a breach of contract.

Terms can be implied into a contract or they can be expressly inserted by either or both of the parties. The most usual example of an examination question on express terms is on exclusion (sometimes known as exemption) clauses. The most usual implied terms are inserted by the Sale of Goods Act 1979.

Contents

1   Terms of a contract

2   Contractual terms and mere representations

3   Express terms

4   Implied terms

5   Conditions, warranties and intermediate terms

6   Sale of Goods Act 1979 implied terms

7   Supply of Goods and Services Act 1982 implied terms

8   Exclusion clauses

1 Terms of a contract

1.1 Introduction

In determining the contents of a contract (i.e. the terms) there are a number of areas that need to be considered:

- whether a statement made in negotiations has become a term of the contract or not

- the need for certainty of essential terms of the agreement

- what, if any, terms will be implied into a contract

- the importance of any particular term and what happens if it is broken

- whether a term in a contract excluding or limiting a party's liability for breach is effective.

2 Contractual terms and mere representations

2.1 Introduction

A statement, written or oral, made during negotiations leading to a contract, may be a term of the subsequent contract or merely a representation inducing the contract.

It is important to ascertain whether a statement becomes a term of the contract or remains a mere representation, because the remedies available to a wronged party will differ depending on whether there is a breach of a contractual term or merely a misrepresentation.

- If the representation is subsequently included in the contract as one of its terms and if it is then later found to be untrue, the party misled has remedies for breach of the term, as well as for misrepresentation.

- If, however, the representation does not become a term of the contract, the party misled will have remedies only for misrepresentation.

2.2 Intention of the parties

Whether a statement becomes a term of the contract or not depends on the intention of the parties. The test of the parties' intentions is objective and will depend on what was said and the circumstances in which the statement was made. In deciding whether a statement is a term or a representation the following are relevant guidelines:

- When the statement was made – the greater the interval of time between making the statement and making the contract the more likely that it will be a representation.

- Whether the statement was reduced to writing after it was made – if it was it is more likely to be a term of the contract.

- The importance of the statement to the recipient, e.g. where a statement on the quality of the goods being sold is the whole basis upon which the contract is made as far as the buyer is concerned it will be a term.

Bannerman v White (1861)

Facts: a buyer of hops asked the seller whether sulphur had been used in the treatment and added that if it had he would not buy. The sellers assured him that sulphur had not been used. Sulphur had been used.

Held: the court decided that as the use of sulphur was a vital part of the contract, around which the whole deal revolved, it was a term.

- The strength of the statement by the maker is important. Where a party negotiating the contract suggests that the other party should check the accuracy of their assertions before finally concluding the contract, e.g. suggesting to a potential house purchaser that a survey should be made and a report of the probable defects in the structure to be given, the statement will probably not be a term.

However, it has been held to be a term where a forceful or emphatic assertion suggests that a potential buyer need not bother to check its accuracy.

Schawel v Reade (1913)

Facts: Schawel was examining a horse that he was considering buying for stud purposes. The seller stated: 'You need not look for anything, the horse is perfectly sound. If there was anything the matter with the horse I should tell you'. Schawel then ceased his examination. A few days later a price was agreed upon and three weeks later Schawel bought the horse relying on the seller's statement. The horse proved to be unsuitable for stud purposes.

Held: the seller's statement was a contractual term. It was obvious from the words and actions of the parties that it was intended that in the purchase the responsibility for the soundness of the horse should rest upon the vendor.

- Whether the person making the statement had special knowledge or skill, e.g. where goods are sold by an expert who guarantees to the buyer that they have stated qualities which, in fact, they lack, the statement has been held to be a term of the contract.

Dick Bentley Productions Ltd v Harold Smith (Motors) Ltd (1965)

Facts: Bentley was interested in purchasing a Bentley car with an ascertainable history. The defendant, a car dealer, persuaded Bentley to purchase a car, which was described as having a replacement engine and gearbox with only 20,000 miles on the odometer since replacement. The assertion relating to the mileage was false.

Held: the dealer's statements became a term of the contract of sale, for breach of which damages were recoverable. The special skill and knowledge of the car dealer placed him in a stronger position than the purchaser, consequently the court could more easily infer that the statements relating to the condition of the car formed the basis of a contractual term rather than a mere representation.

However, where a layman who does not normally deal in the kind of goods being disposed of makes an assertion to an expert, the statement is unlikely to be a term of the contract.

Oscar Chess Ltd v Williams (1957)

Facts: Williams, on selling a car to the claimant company of car dealers, asserted that it was a 1948 model. The registration book appeared to confirm this statement, but it had been altered by a previous owner and the car was in fact a 1939 model.

Held: the statement was an innocent misrepresentation but not a term of the contract. The seller, who was not a car dealer with expert knowledge, did not intend to be bound contractually by his statement concerning the age of the vehicle. The dealers should have checked the engine and chassis numbers to verify the date of manufacture.

A representation is something that is said by the offeror in order to induce the offeree to enter into the contract. It only later becomes a term of that contract if it becomes formalised, e.g. written down and inserted into a written agreement, or can be said to be a very important part of the contract, for example, a statement on which the other party relies.

If what is said is merely a representation and is untrue, the innocent party's action is for misrepresentation.

If what is said is not only a representation but also becomes a term of the contract and is untrue, the innocent party may sue for misrepresentation and/or breach of contract at their choice.

Activity 1

Which of the following would be regarded as terms and which would be merely representations?

(a)   A potential purchaser viewed a property. The owners made several comments about the soundness of the foundations. The sale fell through at the time when the potential purchaser lost her job. One year later the sale was re-activated without any further comments about the foundations being made. It turns out that the foundations were unsound.

(b)   A purchaser of a car made it clear they wanted to buy a particular model due to its rarity value. It turns out that the car was in fact a much later model.

(c)   When buying diving equipment, the purchaser expressed doubt as to whether a particular model of wet suit would withstand conditions in very cold water. The seller was insistent that the suit would be ideal in those conditions and asserted that it was designed specifically with that in mind.

(d)   An art dealer spotted what he considered was a rare painting through the window of someone's private house. He went into the house to enquire if he could buy the painting from the owner and was convinced to buy it when the owner confirmed that the painting was definitely by that particular artist.

Feedback to this activity is at the end of the chapter.

3   Express terms

DEFINITION

Express terms may be written or oral or partly written and partly oral. (Normally, an oral contract is as enforceable and as valid as a written contract.) Express terms are terms specifically inserted into the contract by either or both of the parties.

Express terms may be written or oral or partly written and partly oral. (Normally an oral contract is as enforceable and valid as a written contract.) Express terms are terms specifically entered into the contract by either or both of the parties.

3.1   Certainty of terms

Note that an agreement can only be enforced as a contract if its terms are clear and complete on all essential points. Thus the terms of the contract must be complete and certain of meaning and, if they are not, an agreement that was made by the parties will be incapable of enforcement.

Scammell v Ouston (1941)

Facts: an agreement provided for the balance of the price ... 'on hire purchase terms over a period of two years'.

Held: the words 'hire purchase terms' was considered too imprecise and there was no contract.

It would however be sufficient if the agreement provided that the price under the contract should be the price ruling in an existing market on the completion date or that a dispute over price should be decided by an arbitrator or valuer.

The course of dealing between the parties or the custom of their trade may suffice to indicate the missing term that they intended to adopt but did not express.

The parties may have included meaningless words in their contract; this is particularly likely to happen when they use standard printed conditions not adapted to their transaction. If the words are unnecessary they may be disregarded: *Nicolene v Simmonds (1953)* ('usual conditions of acceptance apply' – but there were none – contract construed without them). If, however, the words used are essential but imprecise then the contract is unenforceable.

4 Implied terms

4.1 Introduction

DEFINITION

Implied terms are terms that are not expressly included by the parties, but which nevertheless are still part of the workings of the contract. They can be implied by:
- the nature of the contract
- Acts of Parliament
- custom and usage.

Implied terms are terms that are not expressly included by the parties, but which nevertheless are still part of the workings of the contract. They can be implied by:

- the nature of the contract
- Acts of Parliament
- custom and usage.

As a general rule, implied terms bow to the express provisions of the contract. However, some of the statutory implied terms cannot be excluded even by express provision or can only be excluded to a limited extent.

4.2 Terms implicitly required by the nature of the contract

The courts can imply terms that are required by the contractual relationship. These terms may be implied into all similar contractual relationships, unless excluded or inconsistent with the express terms.

The courts may imply a term where the parties have failed to cover a particular matter which, unless remedied, makes the agreement unworkable. Such implied terms are based on the presumed but unexpressed intention of the parties.

4.3 Terms implied by Acts of Parliament

Examples are the Sale of Goods Act 1979; the Supply of Goods and Services Act 1982; the Partnership Act 1890; and a number of employment Acts. Many of these implied terms are only effective in the absence of contrary agreement. Others, however, are automatically included in the contract and cannot be excluded. The most important example here is the Sale of Goods Act 1979. This is discussed in detail later in this chapter.

4.4 Terms implied by custom and usage

Any contract may be deemed to incorporate any relevant custom of the market, trade or locality in which it is made, unless the custom is inconsistent with the express terms or the nature of the contract.

A term may be implied on the basis of what the particular parties have done in the past – this is called usage.

Activity 2

Consider each of the following terms and decide in each case whether they are express or implied.

(a)   A contract for the sale of 15 tractors is written down. The delivery date is to be decided later. The purchaser later faxes through the delivery date.

(b)   When buying a second-hand car from a private seller, Jimmy fails to ask whether the person selling actually owns the vehicle in question.

(c)   A holiday company reserves the right to change the destination and date of its customers' destinations.

Feedback to this activity is at the end of the chapter.

5 Conditions, warranties and intermediate terms

5.1 Importance of the distinction between conditions and warranties

DEFINITION

A condition is a vital term of the contract, breach of which may be treated by the innocent party as a substantial failure to perform a basic element of the agreement.

A condition is a vital term of the contract, breach of which may be treated by the innocent party as a substantial failure to perform a basic element of the agreement. The innocent party has the choice of either treating the contract as repudiated (or ended) and claiming damages for any loss suffered, or merely claiming damages for the breach.

The individual circumstances of the case will usually indicate quite clearly which of these two alternatives is more appropriate. For example, James may buy a washing machine from Bernard, with the intention of using it in his launderette. If the washing machine is defective, James may wish to treat the contract as repudiated for breach of condition, by refusing to accept the machine and seeking a refund of the purchase price. He may also claim damages for business lost by being unable to hire out the machine to customers. Alternatively, after a complete overhaul by a mechanic, James may decide to affirm the contract, keep the washing machine, but claim damages for the inconvenience, expenses and loss of profits incurred.

DEFINITION

A warranty is a less-important term that is incidental to the main purpose of the contract. Failure to observe it does not cause the whole agreement to collapse: consequently the innocent party may claim damages for its breach but not treat the contract as repudiated.

A warranty is a less-important term that is incidental to the main purpose of the contract. Failure to observe it does not cause the whole agreement to collapse: consequently the innocent party may claim damages for its breach but not treat the contract as repudiated.

If the washing machine supplied to James in the example quoted above works but looks shoddy because of damage to the exterior casing caused during delivery by Bernard, a claim for damages may take the form of a reduction in the purchase price, probably by mutual agreement between the two parties.

Compare the following two cases:

Poussard v Spiers (1876)

Facts: a soprano, Madame Poussard, agreed to sing in a series of operas for Spiers. She failed to appear on the opening night and Spiers refused her services for subsequent nights.

Held: the obligation to appear on the opening night was a condition. Since Madam Poussard was in breach of this condition, Spiers was entitled to treat the contract as at an end and was therefore not himself in breach by refusing her services for the remaining nights.

Bettini v Gye (1876)

Facts: a tenor, Bettini, who agreed to sing in a series of concerts and to attend six days of rehearsals beforehand failed to appear for the first four rehearsal days. Gye in consequence refused Bettini's services for the balance of the rehearsals and performances.

Held: the obligation to appear for rehearsals was a warranty and therefore Bettini's breach did not entitle Gye to treat the contract as at an end. Gye was accordingly in breach of contract when he refused Bettini's services for the remainder of the contract.

5.2 How the distinction is made

Whether a term is a condition or a warranty depends on a number of factors.

- Statute may declare the category of the term. For example the Sale of Goods Act 1979 implies a term into every contract for the sale of goods to the effect that the seller has a right to sell and the Sale of Goods Act states that the term is a condition.

- The parties may expressly declare that a term is to be a condition, as when for example time is declared to be the essence of the contract. But mere use of the word condition or warranty is not of itself conclusive.

- The court considers, in the light of the circumstances existing when the contract was made, whether the parties regarded the term as a vital one going to the root of the contract or whether it was a term of lesser importance collateral to the main purpose of the contract. This will be a question of fact in each case.

5.3 Innominate terms

The courts have recognised an intermediate category of terms (innominate or intermediate terms) which are neither conditions nor warranties. Within this category the courts then consider whether the nature and effect of a breach is to deprive the injured party of substantially the whole benefit of the contract. If this is the effect of a breach, sometimes called a fundamental breach, then the injured party is entitled to terminate the contract. If the effect of a breach is not serious, the innocent party may not terminate the contract: they may only claim damages.

The Hansa Nord (1976)

Facts: citrus pulp pellets were sold for £100,000. One of the conditions of the contract was: 'shipment to be made in good condition'. On arrival not all of the pellets were in good condition, and their market value was reduced by £20,000. However, even if all the goods had been sound the market value, which had fallen between sale and delivery, was only £86,000. The buyers rejected the goods, which were later sold and eventually re-acquired by the original buyers for £34,000 (and used by them for the original purpose).

Held: on the question of whether the buyers' rejection had been justified, the provision as to shipment in good condition was neither a condition nor a warranty, but an intermediate stipulation. The effect of the breach was not sufficient to justify treating the contract as discharged. The buyers' only remedy was in damages, i.e. the difference in value of the sound goods and the defective goods.

Unless a term is clearly a condition, modern cases tend to treat all terms as innominate and just consider the seriousness of the breach.

The question of classification of terms only arises if the injured party wishes to end the contract; if the injured party wants damages alone there is no need to consider the status of the term broken.

6 Sale of Goods Act 1979 implied terms

6.1 Scope of the Sale of Goods Act 1979

DEFINITION

A contract for the sale of goods is defined in the Sale of Goods Act 1979 as a contract whereby the seller transfers or agrees to transfer the property in goods to the buyer for a money consideration called the price.

The provisions of the Sale of Goods Act 1979 apply only to a contract for the sale of goods. This is defined in the Sale of Goods Act 1979 as a contract whereby the seller transfers or agrees to transfer the property in goods to the buyer for a money consideration called the price.

Activity 3

Annabel agrees to sell her house to Bernard.

Is this contract governed by the Sale of Goods Act 1979?

Activity 4

Charles agrees with Diana to swap his CD player for her television.

Is this contract governed by the Sale of Goods Act 1979?

Activity 5

Edward agrees to hire a car from F Rentals Ltd.

Is this contract governed by the Sale of Goods Act 1979?

Activity 6

Gerry takes his car to H Garage plc for its annual service.

Is this contract governed by the Sale of Goods Act 1979?

Feedback to these activities is at the end of the chapter.

6.2 **Title**

Whatever a contract may say, there is a deemed condition that the seller has a right to sell the goods; or in the case of an agreement to sell, that, when the property is to pass, they will have a right to sell the property: s12(1) Sale of Goods Act 1979.

Rowland v Divall (1923)

Facts: a claimant who had bought and used a car, discovered that it had been stolen and returned it to the actual owner. *Note:* The law requires him to return it to the true owner.

Held: in an action against the seller, the claimant recovered the full purchase price as being money paid on a consideration that had wholly failed. The defendant's argument that the claimant had accepted the goods and so could only sue for damages as if it were a breach of warranty was rejected. The defendant's argument that the claimant had received a benefit (the several months use of the car) also failed.

6.3 **Description**

Introduction

In a sale by description the contract includes some description of the goods and the buyer contracts in reliance on that description. If it is a sale by description, there is an implied condition that the goods correspond with the description.

What is a sale by description?

Most sales involve some description, if only to identify the goods.

* Where the buyer has not seen the goods, the contract is necessarily a sale by description.

* A sale is not prevented from being a sale by description only because, being exposed for sale or hire, the goods are selected by the buyer.

Beale v Taylor (1967)

Facts: a car was described as a Herald 1200 in an advertisement and the car had a plate saying 'Herald 1200' on it. The buyer saw the car and agreed to buy it. It transpired that the car was only partly a Herald 1200: part of another, older, model had been welded on to it.

Held: this was a sale by description notwithstanding the buyer had seen the car. Since the car was not a Herald 1200, the condition of compliance with description had been breached.

Why is it important?

In a sale of goods by description, there is an implied condition that the goods correspond with the description: s13 Sale of Goods Act 1979.

Moore and Co & Landauer and Co (1921)

Facts: a contract provided for the sale of a consignment of 3,000 tins of fruit packed in cases of 30 tins each, but some of the tins were actually packed in cases of 24 tins.

Held: the buyer was allowed by s13 to reject the whole consignment.

6.4 Satisfactory quality and fitness for purpose

Introduction

The most important of the conditions implied by the Sale of Goods Act 1979 are in s14:

(a) that the goods supplied are of a satisfactory quality except in respect of:

  (i) defects specifically drawn to the buyer's attention before the contract is made

  (ii) defects that any examination actually carried out by the buyer before the contract ought to reveal. The buyer is not obliged to make any examination at all and therefore, the more detailed the examination, the more the buyer restricts their rights.

(b) in a case where the buyer, expressly or by implication, makes known to the seller any particular purpose for which the goods are being bought, that the goods supplied are reasonably fit for the purpose, whether or not it is a purpose for which such goods are commonly supplied, except where either the buyer does not rely, or it is unreasonable for them to rely, on the skill or judgement of the seller.

In the course of business

The s14 terms are only implied into contracts made in the course of a business. 'Business' is defined in s61 Sale of Goods Act 1979 as including a profession and the activities of any government department or local or public authority. Similar terminology is used in the Unfair Contract Terms Act 1977 and has been interpreted to mean that there must be some regularity of dealing in those kinds of goods or the transaction must be an integral part of the business. Thus, for example, an accountant selling their stereo would not be selling in the course of business. However, s14 Sale of Goods Act 1979 makes it clear that where a private person sells through a professional agent, e.g. an auctioneer, they sell in the course of business unless the buyer knew the seller was a private person or reasonable notice was given to the seller of this fact.

Satisfactory quality: s14(2) Sale of Goods Act 1979

Goods are of a satisfactory quality if they meet the standard that a reasonable person would regard as satisfactory, taking account of any description of the goods, the price (if relevant) and all other relevant circumstances such as:

(a) fitness for all the purposes for which goods of the kind in question are commonly supplied

(b) appearance and finish

(c) freedom from minor defects

(d) safety

(e) durability.

Thus, a buyer must not expect very cheap goods to be of the same quality as more expensive ones. Other relevant considerations might be that the goods are secondhand, or were made or acquired at great speed to comply with the buyer's special request. Goods used in the way or ways in which goods of that class are normally used and that do not work properly or fail after an unreasonably short time, or which are unsafe or injurious are clearly not of satisfactory quality. So too are goods that though originally sound are damaged through having been badly packed by the seller with the knowledge of the kind of journey they

---

DEFINITION

Goods are of satisfactory quality if they meet the standard that a reasonable person would regard as satisfactory, taking account of any description of the goods, the price (if relevant) and all other relevant circumstances.

---

would have to make. They are defective in quality notwithstanding that the damage occurs after the buyer has taken them away.

Fitness for purpose: s14(3) Sale of Goods Act 1979

Whether goods are as fit for the purpose(s) that goods of that kind are commonly supplied is an aspect of the question as to whether they are of satisfactory quality. However, where the buyer may explain to the seller a particular purpose for which they require the goods, then if the seller contracts with them, the seller is in general liable under s14(3) if the goods are not fit for that purpose.

Griffiths v Peter Conway Ltd (1939)

Facts: the buyer was allergic to a Harris tweed coat, which was perfectly fit for a normal person.

Held: there was no breach of condition of fitness for purpose as the buyer had not told the seller of the special circumstances, i.e. her sensitivity to such fabric.

If the buyer does rely on the seller's judgement, it is unlikely that a court will find it was unreasonable for them to do so, even if both parties trade in the same business. Even a retail shopkeeper can be relied on in this way since they are expected to select their stock with skill and judgement. It is not necessary that the buyer rely exclusively on the seller's skill and judgement, provided that the matter complained of arises from that aspect of the goods for which the buyer did rely on the seller.

Comparing: s14(2) and s14(3) Sale of Goods Act 1979

S14(2) gives the buyer protection against shoddy goods; s14(3) gives them protection against unsuitable goods. Sometimes, however, both are available. They are invaluable in the field of consumer protection since liability is strict. The shopkeeper does not have to be shown to be at fault.

Activity 7

B buys a car from S, an accountant. The next day the car breaks down and B discovers that the engine is completely worn out. Can B return the car to S and recover his money on the basis of breach of either s14(2) or s14(3) Sale of Goods Act 1979?

Feedback to this activity is at the end of the chapter.

6.5 Sales by sample

Introduction

DEFINITION

A sale by sample occurs when the buyer is given the opportunity of examining a small part only of the goods to be bought, but such as to be typical of the whole, in this context usually called the bulk of the goods.

A sale by sample occurs when the buyer is given the opportunity of examining a small part only of the goods to be bought, but such as to be typical of the whole, in this context usually called the bulk of goods.

Thus, corn, toys, pianos or parrots might all be sold by sample if the bulk of the goods was large enough to justify the method. A contract of sale is by sample if, and only if, there is a term in the contract, express or implied, to that effect: s15 Sale of Goods Act 1979.

A contract of sale is not by sample merely because part of the goods was shown to the buyer during the negotiations preceding the contract: both parties must accept as a contract term that the sale is by sample. Trade usage may, of course, raise the necessary presumption without any express agreement to that effect, but if the contract is written it will normally be treated as a sale by sample only if stated to be so.

Why is it important?

In a contract for sale by sample there are implied conditions:

(a)   that the bulk shall correspond with the sample in quality

(b)   that the buyer shall have a reasonable opportunity of comparing the bulk with the sample

(c)   that the goods shall be free from any defect rendering them unsatisfactory, which would not be apparent on reasonable examination of the sample: s15 Sale of Goods Act 1979.

The test is one of reasonable examination of the sample and not one of thorough examination.

Godley v Perry (1960)

Facts: a boy of six bought a catapult from the defendant's newsagency shop and damaged his eye when it broke in his hands as a result of having been indifferently manufactured. The catapult was part of a quantity bought by sample from a wholesaler and the defendant's wife had tested the sample beforehand by pulling back its elastic.

Held: while the defendant was liable to the boy in damages for the catapult being neither fit for its purpose nor of satisfactory quality (s14(2);(3)), the defendant could also himself claim against the wholesaler because the defect of the goods could not be discovered by reasonable examination of the sample (s15).

Reasonableness is the statutory yardstick. The Act does not even speak of carrying out practicable tests on the goods concerned, but of reasonable examination.

If the bulk does not correspond with the sample, the buyer is not prevented from rejecting the bulk merely because they have made payment in full. Whenever the bulk does not correspond with the sample, the buyer can either reject the whole or retain the whole, or retain some of the goods and reject the rest.

6.6   Non-consumer contracts

The terms implied into contracts for the sale of goods by sections 13, 14 and 15 Sale of Goods Act 1979 are all conditions. Normally, if breached, the buyer would be allowed to treat the contract as discharged, reject the goods and claim damages. However, where the buyer is a non-consumer, i.e. they are acting in the course of their business, they will be unable to treat the contract as discharged and reject the goods if the breach is so slight that it would be unreasonable for them to reject the goods. They will only be able to claim damages.

Activity 8

Rosemary purchased a second-hand computer for her business from a private seller. She bought it in a telephone conversation having seen an advertisement for a 'XXX 123 model'. Rosemary already used XXX 123 models and was delighted to acquire another. A short while after the computer was delivered it broke down and the engineer discovered that it was a WWW 789 model that was now obsolete. What rights does Rosemary have?

Feedback to this activity is at the end of the chapter.

7 Supply of Goods and Services Act 1982 implied terms

7.1 Scope of the Supply of Goods and Services Act 1982

The Act concerns contracts for the supply of services, contracts of hire and contracts of exchange.

The only part of the Act that is examinable is the law concerning contracts for the supply of services. The law is dealt with below.

7.2 The Supply of Goods and Services Act 1982

Introduction

The Act deals with contracts for the supply of services. Problems tend to arise because in many service industries the consumer has little idea of what is involved in providing the service and is, therefore, not in a good position to judge whether a good service has been provided or whether a reasonable charge made. In addition, there is the problem that many people who provide services, e.g. accountants, do not quote the price for providing the service at the commencement of the contract.

The Act covers contracts for the supply of a service under which a person, the supplier agrees to carry out a service. The Act does not cover contracts of employment, apprenticeship, services of an advocate in a court or tribunal or of a company director to their company.

Implied terms

S13 implies a term into a contract for the supply of a service where the supplier is acting in the course of business, that **the supplier will carry out the service with reasonable care** and skill.

S14 implies a term into a contract for the supply of a service where the supplier is acting in the course of business where the time for the service to be carried out is not fixed by the contract, nor left to be fixed in a manner agreed by the parties nor by a course of dealing, that **the supplier will carry out the service within a reasonable time**.

S15 implies a term into a contract for the supply of a service where the consideration for the service is not determined by the contract, nor left to be determined in a manner agreed by the parties nor a course of dealings, that **the party contracting with the supplier will pay a reasonable charge.**

8 Exclusion clauses

8.1 Definition and effect

The term exclusion clause (or exemption clause) is applied both to clauses that totally exclude one party from the liability that would otherwise arise from some breach of contract,and to clauses that restrict liability in some way.

The tendency of modern statutes is to prevent the use of exclusion clauses, especially in dealing with private citizens who frequently do not read or do not understand the effect of the printed document put before them for acceptance.

8.2 Validity of exclusion clauses

In order to be valid, the exclusion clause must pass three separate tests:

(a)   The common law test – this test is broken down into two sub-parts:

   (i)   the clause must be incorporated into the contract and not added after the contract is complete

   (ii)   the clause must be clear and precise; any vagueness will be construed against the party who is attempting to rely on it.

(b)   The statutory test laid down by the Unfair Contract Terms Act 1977.

(c)   The test set out in the Unfair Terms in Consumer Contracts Regulations 1999.

Note that if the exclusion clause does not pass the first test it need not be subjected to the rigours of the Unfair Contract Terms Act 1977 or the Unfair Terms in Consumer Contracts Regulations 1999.

8.3 The common law test – incorporation into the contract

It must be shown that the party who is to be bound by the clause did in fact agree to it.

If they signed a contractual document in which the clause is included, they will generally be treated as having agreed to it even if they did not read the document.

L'Estrange v Graucob (1934)

Facts: the proprietress of a cafe bought a cigarette vending machine and signed a contract of sale, which she did not read, that contained a clause: 'Any express or implied condition statement or warranty statutory or otherwise not stated herein is hereby excluded.' The machine was defective.

Held: she was unable to recover the price or obtain damages because she was bound by the clause as she had signed the contract.

However, a signatory is not bound by an exclusion or limiting clause where their signature to the document was induced by fraud or misrepresentation by the other party, or their agent.

Curtis v Chemical Cleaning Co (1951)

Facts: the claimant took a white satin wedding dress to the defendants for cleaning. She was asked to sign a document that contained a clause: 'that the dress is accepted on condition that the company is not liable for any damage howsoever arising' but, before she signed, she was told that the effect of the document that she was about to sign was to exclude liability for damage to beads or sequins. Without reading all the terms of the document the claimant then signed as she was asked. The dress was stained due to the negligence of the defendants.

Held: the defendants were liable and could not rely on the exclusion clause because of the misrepresentation as to the extent of the exemption clause.

If the document was not signed (as most contracts will not be) then the offeree is not bound if it can be shown that they did not know that the document contained (or incorporated by reference) terms of the contract or that reasonable notice of those terms was not given to them, e.g. by stating where the terms could be read. Most of the 'railway ticket' case law is on the application of this principle.

KEY POINT

An exclusion clause cannot be introduced into a contract after it has been made unless the other party agrees.

An exclusion clause cannot be introduced into a contract after it has been made unless the other party agrees. Examples include the following cases:

Olley v Marlborough Court (1949)

Facts: a notice in a hotel room excluded liability for loss or damage to guests' property.

Held: this was ineffective because the contract for accommodation had been made at the reception desk.

J Spurling Ltd v Bradshaw (1966)

Facts: the defendant had dealt with the claimant for a number of years. On the contract in question he had delivered four full barrels to the claimant to store. As usual, he later received a document that both acknowledged receipt and contained a clause excluding liability for negligence by the claimant. The barrels were empty when he collected them. The defendant refused to pay and the claimant sued.

Held: the exclusion clause had been incorporated into the contract through previous course of dealings whereby he had been sent copies of documents containing the clause, even though he had never read the clause.

8.4 Common law test – construction of the clause

The party relying on an exemption clause to relieve them from some or all of the consequences flowing from their breach of contract must prove that it was a term which, when properly construed, covered the loss or damage suffered by the other party.

A case law example of a clause that passed the common law test of construction is the House of Lords decision in:

Photo Productions Ltd v Securicor (1980)

Facts: the claimant, a company that owned a factory, entered into a contract with the defendant, a security company, by which the defendant was to provide security services at the factory, including night patrols. While carrying out a night patrol at the factory an employee of the defendant deliberately lit a fire and as a result the factory and stock inside, together valued at £615,000, were completely destroyed. The claimant sued the defendant for breach of contract and in their defence the defendant pleaded an exemption clause the relevant wording of which was: '...under no circumstances shall (Securicor) be responsible for any injurious act or default by any employee of (Securicor) unless such act or default could have been foreseen and avoided by the exercise of due diligence on the part of (Securicor) as his employer...' No negligence was alleged against the defendant for employing the employee.

Held: even such a fundamental breach could be excluded. The exemption clause was clear and unambiguous and protected the defendant from liability.

Note: The facts of this case arose before the Unfair Contract Terms Act 1977 became law.

8.5 Unfair Contract Terms Act 1977

This Act relates to contracts made in the course of business and provides the most important limitations on the validity of exemption clauses. If the clause passes the common law test, it must still satisfy this statutory test.

The Act restricts the extent to which a person can exclude or limit their liability for negligence, for breach of contract and for misrepresentation.

Liability for negligence: s2 Unfair Contract Terms Act 1977

Negligence includes any express or implied term of a contract to take reasonable care and the common law duty in the tort of negligence to take reasonable care.

The Act provides that:

- a person in business cannot exclude or restrict liability for death or personal injury resulting from negligence (defined in s1), by contract or any notice – s2 Unfair Contract Terms Act 1977, i.e. a total prohibition on such terms

- a person in business cannot exclude or restrict liability for negligence causing loss other than death or personal injury unless it is reasonable – s2 Unfair Contract Terms Act 1977, i.e. provisions subject to the requirement of reasonableness.

Liability for breach of the Sale of Goods Act 1979 implied terms: s6 Unfair Contract Terms Act 1977

- Any exclusion of the s12 Sale of Goods Act 1979 implied term as to title is void.

- The Sale of Goods Act 1979 implied terms as to description (s13), satisfactory quality (s14(2)), fitness for purpose (s14(3)), and sample (s15):

  - cannot be excluded or restricted by reference to a contract term, as against a person dealing as a consumer

  - as against any other person, such liability can only be excluded or restricted in so far as the term satisfies the requirement of reasonableness.

Note: Unlike most of Unfair Contract Terms Act 1977, s6 can apply even where it is a non-business attempting to exclude liability, but in most non-business sales there is no implied term as to quality.

Note: s6 also applies, in the same way, to the equivalent terms implied by the Supply of Goods and Services Act 1982.

Liability for other breaches of contract

A term in a standard term contract or in any consumer contract purporting to exclude or restrict liability for a breach is effective only if it is reasonable: s3 Unfair Contract Terms Act 1977. However the precise meaning of s3 is uncertain.

Overland Shoes Ltd v Schenkers Ltd (1998)

Facts: Schenkers Ltd were worldwide freight carriers. They entered into a contract with Overland Shoes Ltd to transport a consignment of shoes that Overland was importing from China. The contract incorporated the standard trading conditions of the freight carriers' trading association, which included an exclusion clause. A dispute arose and Schenkers relied on the exclusion clause.

Held: the exclusion clause was reasonable under the Unfair Contract Terms Act 1977. The clause formed part of a set of standard trading terms used by many trading associations throughout the world, which were carefully balanced, and which had long been recognised as fair and reasonable.

Liability for misrepresentation

S3 Misrepresentation Act 1967 (as inserted by Unfair Contract Terms Act 1977) states that if a contract contains a term that would exclude or restrict liability for pre-contractual misrepresentations that term shall have no effect except in so far as it satisfies the requirement of reasonableness.

The following definitions are contained in the Unfair Contract Terms Act 1977.

(a)   Standard term contracts

Standard term contracts arise where the exemption clause is contained in a contract setting out in writing that party's standard terms of business.

(b)   Consumer contracts: s12 Unfair Contract Terms Act 1977

A party deals as a consumer in relation to another party if:

(i)   they neither make the contract in the course of a business nor hold themselves out as doing so

(ii)   the other party does make the contract in the course of a business

(iii)   the goods (if any) passing under or in pursuance of the contract are of a type ordinarily supplied for private use or consumption.

It is for those claiming that a party does not deal as a consumer to show that they do not.

(c)   The requirement of reasonableness

The burden of proving reasonableness is on the party wishing to rely on the clause. To be reasonable the term must be a fair and reasonable one to be included having regard to the circumstances that were, or ought reasonably to have been, known to or in the contemplation of the parties when the contract was made.

By way of a supplement to the test, Schedule 2 Unfair Contract Terms Act 1977 lists five guidelines indicating which matters in particular are to be taken into account. These are:

(i)   the strength of the bargaining positions of the parties relative to each other, taking into account (among other things) alternative means of supplying the buyer's requirements

(ii)   whether the buyer received an inducement to agree to the term, or in accepting it had an opportunity of making a similar contract lacking such a term with other persons

(iii)   whether the buyer knew or ought to have known of the existence and the extent of the term, having regard to trade custom and any previous course of dealing between the parties

(iv)   whether it was reasonable to expect that when the contract was made it would be practical for the buyer to comply with a condition such that liability of the seller would be excluded or restricted if they did not

(v)   whether the goods were manufactured, processed or adapted to the special order of the customer.

These guidelines are specifically applied by Unfair Contract Terms Act 1977 to ascertain reasonableness in the context of contracts for the sale of goods and other transfers of goods, e.g. hire or exchange. However, they are also used when ascertaining the reasonableness of exemption or limitation clauses in relation to other breaches of contract.

Where the clause is attempting to limit (rather than exclude) liability the courts must have regard to the resources that that party could expect to be available to them for the purpose of meeting the liability should it arise and how far it was open to them to cover themselves by insurance.

(d)   Unfair Terms in Consumer Contracts Regulations 1999

The Unfair Terms in Consumer Contracts Regulations 1999 are aimed at unfair terms generally, including exclusion clauses. The rules apply only to standard form contracts for the supply of goods or services. A number of contracts, e.g. employment contracts and partnership contracts, are not covered by the regulations. The contract must be between a seller or supplier and a consumer, not a business.

An unfair term in a contract is covered by the regulations if it '…contrary to the requirement of good faith causes a significant imbalance in the parties' rights and obligations under the contract to the detriment of the consumer'.

The regulations specify that written terms should be in plain and intelligible language.

To decide whether a term satisfies the requirement of good faith, the regulations specify a number of factors:

(i)   the strength of the bargaining position of the parties
(ii)   whether the consumer had any inducements to agree to the term
(iii)   whether the goods or services were supplied to the special order of the consumer
(iv)   the extent to which the seller had dealt fairly and equitably with the consumer.

If a clause is held to be unfair, the clause is not binding on the consumer. The Regulations allow the Office of Fair Trading to challenge unfair terms on behalf of consumers. For example, a statement on a company's invoices included a declaration that a company would not be liable for damage caused as a result of its work on customers' property. This was considered to be unfair since the exclusion covered any liability on the part of the company for its own negligence or failure to exercise reasonable care. The company agreed to delete the term.

Activity 9

Will the following exclusion clauses be valid or invalid?

(a)   Sharon buys a fire extinguisher and a week later receives the guarantee for the product. On the guarantee there is a clear exclusion clause.

(b)   Dominic enters a car park. At the entrance, before he buys his ticket, there is a clear sign excluding all liability for injury done to any of the car park's users by falling masonry from building work being carried out on the building.

(c)   Lola gets on a train without a ticket. She buys one on the train and the conductor informs her that the train has had to change destinations due to some signalling work. He explains to her that the terms and conditions of travel exclude the train company from liability for any resulting breach of contract and that these can be seen at any railway station.

(d)   Company A has been dealing with Company B for two years. Each time the contract has included an exclusion clause, exempting Company B from liability for delay in shipping the products to Company A. On this occasion the contract has mistakenly omitted the clause and the goods are delayed due to the closure of the Suez Canel. Company B attempts to exclude liability.

Feedback to this activity is at the end of the chapter.

Summary

On completion of their studies, students should be able to:

- explain how the contents and the terms of a contract are established and the possible repercussions of non-performance

- explain how the law controls the use of unfair terms in respect of both consumer and non-consumer business agreements.

Self-test questions

Contractual terms and mere representations

1 What is the importance of the difference between a representation and a term? (2.1)

Implied terms

2 State three ways in which terms can be implied into a contract. (4.1)

Conditions, warranties and intermediate terms

3 What are the differences between conditions and warranties? (5.1)

4 What is an innominate term? (5.3)

Sale of Goods Act 1979 implied terms

5 What condition does s12 Sale of Goods Act 1979 imply? (6.2)

6 What is a sale by description? (6.3)

7 Does s14 Sale of Goods Act 1979 apply to private sales? (6.4)

8 Define satisfactory quality. (6.4)

9 Distinguish s14(2) and s14(3) Sale of Goods Act 1979. (6.4)

Supply of Goods and Services Act 1982 implied terms

10 What are the three 'reasonable' terms implied by the Supply of Goods and Services Act? (7.2)

Exclusion clauses

11 What is the purpose of an exclusion clause? (8.1)

12 If a contract is signed, when will an exclusion clause contained in that contract not be valid at common law? (8.3)

Multiple-choice questions

Question 1

Tee Ltd has broken one of the terms of its contract with Vee Ltd. If that term is a condition, which of the following is correct?

A   Vee Ltd is entitled to sue for damages only

B   Vee Ltd may repudiate the contract and sue for damages

C   Vee Ltd is entitled either to repudiate the contract or sue for damages

D   Vee Ltd is only entitled to repudiate the contract

Question 3

A Ltd has broken one of the terms of its contract with B Ltd. If that term is a warranty, which of the following is correct?

A   B Ltd may repudiate the contract and claim damages

B   B Ltd may repudiate the contract and apply for rescission

C   B Ltd is entitled to damages only

D   B Ltd is entitled to damages and rescission

Question 3

The Unfair Contract Terms Act 1977 provides that an attempt by any person to exclude or restrict their liability for death or personal injury resulting from negligence in any contract is:

A   Void unless reasonable

B   Effective only in a non-consumer transaction

C   Void

D   Valid if the other party to the contract knows of the exclusion clause or has been given reasonable notice of it

For the answers to these questions, see the 'Answers' section at the end of the book.

Practice question

F and W – Toaster

F purchased an electric toaster from a shop owned by W. A week later, while she was using the toaster, she suffered a relatively severe electric shock and the toaster ceased to function. F took the toaster back to the shop and demanded a refund of her money from W. W informed her she should complain to the manufacturers as the shop was not responsible for a manufacturing fault.

After F had left the shop, W looked at the conditions of sale that he had agreed with the manufacturers of the toaster. He discovered the agreement included a clause that excluded the manufacturers from liability for any express or implied conditions or warranties concerning the quality and fitness of the toasters they had supplied to him.

Advise F and W in the law of contract.

For the answer to this question, see the 'Answer' section at the end of the book.

Feedback to activities

Activity 1

(a)   Mere representation

(b)   Representation and term

(c)   Representation and term

(d)   Mere representation

Activity 2

(a)   Express

(b)   Implied – there is an implied term of ownership in all contracts where one person (being in business or not) sells goods to another (s12 Sale of Goods Act 1979).

(c)   Express

Activity 3

No: a house is land, not goods.

Activity 4

No: the price must be money (either wholly or partly). This contract (called a contract of exchange or barter) is governed by the Supply of Goods and Services Act 1982.

Activity 5

No: 'property' in goods means ownership, not possession. This is a contract of hire (governed by the Supply of Goods and Services Act 1982).

Activity 6

No: the main purpose of this contract is the provision of a service (i.e. supplying skills and labour), not the sale of goods. The contract is governed by the Supply of Goods and Services Act 1982.

Activity 7

No. This is a private sale (presumably) and therefore s14(2) and s14(3) do not apply to protect the buyer. Thus the position is, at common law, *caveat emptor* ('let the buyer beware'). If the car has been bought by the firm and used by members of it, the sale might be in the course of business.

Activity 8

This would appear to be a sale by description. There is an implied condition, from s13 Sale of Goods Act 1979, that goods sold by description shall correspond to that description. The breach of this condition gives Rosemary the right to terminate the contract and recover the purchase price. Since Rosemary bought from a private seller neither s14(2) satisfactory quality, nor s14(3) fitness for purpose, apply.

Activity 9

(a)   Invalid – not incorporated at common law.

(b)   Void – under s2 Unfair Contract Terms Act 1977 (assuming the injury arises negligently).

(c)   Valid – if reasonable under s3 Unfair Contract Terms Act 1977. Valid if in good faith under Unfair Terms in Consumer Contracts Regulations 1999.

(d)   Valid

Chapter 10

CONTRACT: DISCHARGE

Syllabus content

The law of contract

- The level of performance sufficient to discharge contractual obligations

- Valid reasons for non-performance by way of agreement, breach by the other party and frustration

This chapter examines the termination of a contract. To discharge a contract is to end it. If a contract has been discharged, neither party has further obligations under it.

Discharge of a contract is a popular examination area and the main questions that are asked tend to be in the areas of:

- performance of a contract

- frustration.

Contents

1   Methods of discharge

2   Performance

3   Agreement

4   Breach

5   Frustration

1 Methods of discharge

A contract imposes obligations on the parties from which they may be discharged in various ways:

- **Performance** – when a party has done what is required of them under the contract they no longer have any obligations under it.

- **Agreement – the parties may agree to terminate unfulfilled obligations.** That agreement must itself be a contract subject to the usual rules, especially consideration.

- **Breach** – breach of contract is the inexcusable failure by a party to a contract to fulfil some or all of their obligations under it or a defective performance of those obligations. If one party commits a breach of contract the other may in some cases, at their option, elect to treat the contract as at an end with the result that their own obligations are discharged. They are accepting that the other's repudiatory breach terminates the contract.

- **Frustration** – in certain cases a contract that becomes impossible to perform is thereby discharged.

DEFINITION

Breach of contract is the inexcusable failure by a party to a contract to fulfil some or all of their obligations under it or a defective performance of those obligations.

---

2 Performance

2.1 General rule

The general rule is that a contract is discharged by performance only when both parties have complied fully and exactly with the terms of the contract.

Re Moore & Landauer (1927)

Facts: contract for tinned fruit to be delivered packed in cases of 30 tins each. The correct number of tins was delivered, but in cases varying between 24 and 30 tins each.

Held: the contract was not performed even though the market value was the same. The buyer could reject all the goods and not pay.

From this general rule it has sometimes been held that if a single price has been agreed for performance of the contract, no part of the price is payable unless and until the entire contract has been exactly performed.

Cutter v Powell (1795)

Facts: the defendants agreed to pay Cutter thirty guineas 'provided he proceeds, continues and does his duty as second mate' on a voyage from Jamaica to Liverpool. Cutter died before the end of the journey. His administrator sought to recover a proportion of the agreed wage.

Held: she was unable to succeed as Cutter had not performed his part of the contract. (But note that nowadays the doctrine of frustration would apply to the contract.)

2.2 Exceptions

The general rule that performance must be complete, accurate and exact to be effective could lead to injustice if it is complete performance of the contract that is required (as in *Cutter v Powell* above). It has been modified by the common law and by equity to make the rule fairer.

KEY POINT

The general rule is that a contract is discharged by performance only when both parties have complied fully and exactly with the terms of the contract.

2.3 Severable or divisible contracts

Cutter v Powell is an example of an 'entire' contract. However, most contracts will be treated as divisible into distinct and separate obligations, e.g. a contract for a consignment of goods will be regarded as several obligations, to deliver goods, of appropriate quality, in the right amount etc. Whether a contract is 'entire' or severable will depend on construction of the contract and the intention of the parties.

If the parties can be deemed to have intended to divide their contract into two or more separate contracts, each individual contract may be discharged separately. For example, in a contract to deliver a consignment of goods by instalments, the buyer may agree to pay for each instalment when delivered.

If the first instalment delivered conforms with the terms of the contract, the buyer cannot refuse to pay for it on the grounds that the second delivery is defective in some respect, although payment for the second instalment may be validly refused. Such contracts are called severable or divisible contracts.

Where a contract is divisible, the court will treat non- (or defective) performance of an obligation as a breach of contract – the effect will depend on the type of breach.

2.4 Performance prevented by one party

DEFINITION

Quantum meruit is a claim for the value of work done or services rendered, rather than for the contract price. The words literally mean 'as much as is merited'.

One party may be prevented from fully carrying out their contractual duties because of some act or omission by the other party that effectively prevents the contract being duly performed as anticipated. In such cases the party partially implementing the agreed terms may sue on a *quantum meruit*, or for damages for breach of contract, in order to recover compensation for the amount of work actually completed. *Quantum meruit* is a claim for the value of work done or services rendered, rather than for the contract price. The words literally mean 'as much as is merited'.

Planché v Colburn (1831)

Facts: Planché agreed to write a book for a series of books to be published by Colburn, but the series was discontinued before completion of the work by the author.

Held: the original contract had been discharged by the defendant's breach, but reasonable remuneration was recoverable on a *quantum meruit* basis, independently of the original contract.

2.5 Acceptance of partial performance

Where a party accepts the benefit conferred on them by the other party's partial performance, the court may infer a promise to pay for the benefit received and grant the other party a right to recover a reasonable price on a *quantum meruit* claim.

For example, a seller may agree to deliver 40 bottles of a specified wine to a buyer. If only 20 bottles are tendered, the buyer may refuse to accept delivery; but if they accept the 20 bottles they must pay a reasonable price for them. However, if they had no choice but to accept partial performance, then no payment can be claimed.

Sumpter v Hedges (1898)

Facts: Sumpter contracted to erect buildings on Hedges' land, but abandoned the work when it was only partially completed. Hedges took possession of the land and buildings and completed the work himself, using materials which Sumpter had left behind. Sumpter sued on a *quantum meruit* to recover compensation for the value of the work done prior to his abandonment of the job.

Held: Sumpter could not recover a reasonable price for his work. It could not be presumed from his conduct that Hedges voluntarily accepted partial performance. He had no other option open to him than to accept the half-completed buildings and finish the work himself, or employ another builder to do so. (However, Sumpter was allowed to recover the value of the materials used, because it was open to Hedges to choose whether or not to use those particular materials in completing the building.)

2.6 Substantial performance

A party that has substantially performed their contractual duties in the manner stipulated may recover the agreed price, less a deduction by way of a claim for damages in respect of duties not properly executed. This is an equitable exception to the rule of full performance.

Hoenig v Isaacs (1952)

Facts: the claimant, an interior decorator, agreed to decorate and furnish the defendant's flat for a sum of £750 payable as the work proceeded and the balance on completion. When the job was done the defendant moved in but complained of faulty design and bad workmanship and would not pay the £350 balance.

Held: in a contract for work and labour for a lump sum the employer cannot repudiate liability on the ground that the work, when substantially performed and when he has taken the enjoyment of it, is in some respects not in accordance with the contract. The term that required completion was not a condition; hence, the defendant should pay for the work, less a sum in damages for breach of warranty.

If the defects are so extensive that it cannot be said that the contract has been substantially performed, then no part of the contract price can be recovered unless the contract is severable when there may be partial recovery.

Bolton v Mahadeva (1972)

Facts: the claimant agreed to install central heating in the defendant's house for £1,560. His work was defective: the system did not produce adequate heat, and it gave off fumes. It would have cost £174 to put the defects right.

Held: the plumber could not recover £1,560 less £174 – he could not rely on the doctrine of substantial performance; this was an entire contract.

The doctrine of substantial performance raises the question of the distinction between conditions and warranties. All terms that are conditions must be strictly performed, i.e. there is no scope for substantial performance. In respect of 'intermediate' terms, the test of substantial performance is whether the party has received substantially the whole benefit as intended under the contract.

If the party abandons the contract the doctrine cannot be relied upon. It is an equitable doctrine and to abandon work in this way would be unfair.

2.7 Time for performance

When a contract does not specify the time of performance of the obligations, they must be performed within a reasonable time.

When a contract does specify the time of performance of the obligations, the question arises as to whether 'time is of the essence', i.e. a condition of the contract. In such cases, if there is a delay in performance the injured party may treat this delay as breach of condition and pay nothing (and also refuse to accept late performance if offered).

The parties may expressly agree in their contract that time shall be of the essence. Even if they do not so provide and there is delay, the injured party may then make time of the essence of the contract by serving a notice requiring performance within a specified but reasonable additional period.

Charles Rickards Ltd v Oppenheim (1950)

Facts: the contract was for delivery of a custom-built Rolls Royce car within seven months; the buyer agreed to wait three months more and then gave four weeks' notice to complete.

Held: at the expiry of his notice he could cancel the order as by serving notice he had made time of the essence, although he could not have done so immediately the original delivery period expired (as he had waived his right).

In absence of any such explicit provision, the question of whether time is to be treated as of the essence depends on the nature of the contract. For example:

- In commercial contracts and any others where lapse in time could materially affect the value of the subject matter, time is of the essence unless there is evidence to the contrary.

- In contracts where specific performance might be ordered, the court (applying equitable principles) will be inclined to treat the time of performance as not of the essence. In particular, time is not of the essence in completion of the sale of land, i.e. if the vendor fails to effect a transfer of the land at the agreed date they may hold the purchaser to accepting it at a later date (unless, of course, time has been made of the essence). The purchaser must satisfy themselves with their action for damages.

Time for payment of the contract price is not of the essence unless so agreed.

DEFINITION

Specific performance is an equitable remedy whereby the court orders a person to complete their obligations under a contract. It is usually only available in contracts for the transfer of land or goods (not work or services).

3 Agreement

3.1 By terms in the existing agreement

The original contract may contain some terms that allow the parties to discharge the contract. As this is part of the original contract, no new consideration is required to discharge the contract.

3.2 By a new agreement

The parties may agree to discharge, i.e. end, the contract. This agreement will be binding only if it is under seal or supported by consideration. The discharge may be bilateral or unilateral.

- **Bilateral discharge** – discharge will be bilateral where both parties still have contractual obligations to perform. Any agreement to discharge the contract relieves both parties from further performance. Each party's promise to release the other party from further performance is their consideration for the release from their own obligations.

- **Unilateral discharge** – discharge will be unilateral where one party has performed all their obligations but the other has not. Any promise by the party that has performed their obligation to release the other ('accord') will not be binding on them unless the other party has given consideration ('satisfaction') or the agreement to discharge is made by deed.

Where fresh consideration is given, e.g. a cancellation fee, there is 'accord', i.e. agreement by which the obligation is discharged, and 'satisfaction', i.e. the consideration that makes the agreement effective.

The parties may agree to discharge the original contract and substitute a new one in its place (novation), e.g. a contract to supply a colour television replaced by a contract to supply a radio.

They may agree to vary the original contract, e.g. a contract to deliver a carpet in January is varied by extending the delivery date to March.

4 Breach

DEFINITION

A breach of contract occurs:

- when a party fails to perform, or performs defectively, an obligation under the contract (actual breach)

- when, before the time fixed to perform an obligation, a party shows an intention not to perform (anticipatory breach)

A breach of contract occurs:

- when a party fails to perform, or performs defectively, an obligation under the contract (actual breach)

- when, before the time fixed to perform an obligation, a party shows an intention not to perform (anticipatory breach).

4.1 Discharge by acceptance of breach

If one party commits a breach of condition, or a substantial breach of an intermediate term, or totally renounces the contract, the breach does not automatically terminate the contract but the other party may then at their option:

- treat the contract as terminated (discharged) and claim damages for any loss suffered, or

- treat the contract as operative and claim damages for any loss suffered.

In the first case their outstanding obligations are discharged by the breach followed by the election to terminate, but in the second case the parties continue to be bound by the contract since the contract remains in existence.

A breach of warranty will not entitle the innocent party to treat their outstanding obligations under the contract as discharged by the breach: they may claim damages only.

See the cases of *Poussard v Spiers* (1876) and *Bettini v Gye* (1876) (Chapter 9).

4.2 Actual breach

Actual breach occurs where one party is in breach of a condition or improperly repudiates (ends) the contract, (see *Bettini v Gye*), or if they make it impossible to perform, or prevent completion of the contract by the other party.

If the contract is an entire one in which the obligations are interdependent or concurrent, then the contract is discharged by such a breach, e.g. purchase of an item that does not work. Breach of condition by the seller discharges the buyer from their duty to pay.

If the contract is a divisible one, or if the obligations are independent of each other, then the innocent party's only remedy is to sue for damages for the breach; they cannot treat themselves as discharged from their own contractual obligations by the other party's breach of performance.

If the innocent party does have the right to treat themselves as discharged from their contractual obligations and wishes to exercise that right, they must, as a general rule, communicate that decision to the party in breach for otherwise silence may be construed as evidence that they waive their right to treat themselves as discharged.

4.3 Anticipatory breach

A contract is discharged by anticipatory breach when one party expressly or impliedly repudiates the obligations imposed on them by the contract before the arrival of the time fixed for performance.

In any such case the injured party has a choice of action:

(a) They can, by notifying the other party of their decision, accept the repudiation and treat the contract as immediately discharged and even commence proceedings for breach. This is known as 'accepting' the breach.

Thus the party repudiating the contract may be sued immediately for breach of contract, even though the date has not yet arrived for the repudiating party to perform their obligations under the contract.

Hochester v De La Tour (1853)

Facts: the defendant, who had agreed to engage the claimant as a courier as from 1 June 1852, wrote a letter on 11 May repudiating the contract of employment. On 22 May the claimant brought an action claiming damages for breach of contract.

Held: damages were recoverable. It was not necessary to wait until 1 June 1852, the date when his duties as courier were to begin, before suing for breach of contract.

(b) Alternatively, the injured party can affirm the contract in the hope that performance will be rendered. They must then wait until the time for performance arrives before they can sue.

In this case the party in default can escape liability if they in fact perform the contract at the due date or if their obligation to do so is meanwhile discharged, e.g. by frustration.

Avery v Bowden (1855)

Facts: the charterers of a ship declared in advance that they did not require her; the ship owners refused to accept the repudiation and affirmed the contract by sending the ship to the port of loading (Odessa). However, before she arrived there, the contract was frustrated by the outbreak of the Crimean War, as civilian shipping was barred from the theatre of war. The owners now sued.

Held: the contract had not been discharged by the breach because the owners had not accepted the breach; but the frustrating event discharged it rendering the ship owners unable to sue for breach.

5 Frustration

5.1 Introduction

The general rule is that, unless otherwise agreed, a party who fails to perform their contractual obligations is in breach of contract and liable for damages. This is the position whatever the reason given in excuse.

Paradine v Jane (1647)

Facts: a tenant was sued for rent of premises of which he had been dispossessed for three years by the King's enemies.

Held: he was nevertheless liable for the rent.

KEY POINT

A contract is frustrated where, although possible to perform when made, it subsequently becomes impossible through the happening of a supervening event that was the fault of neither party.

The doctrine of frustration was developed to mitigate the severity of this rule where performance of a contract subsequently becomes impossible through the happening of a supervening event that occurred through the fault of neither party. Later cases have extended the doctrine beyond strict 'impossibility' to situations where circumstances have so changed that performance would now be so radically different as to destroy the commercial purpose of the contract.

If a contract is frustrated, it is automatically discharged with the result that both parties are lawfully excused from further performance.

The doctrine is narrowly applied and the following cases show the limits of the doctrine.

5.2 Application of the doctrine

Frustration has been held to apply in the following circumstances:

Destruction of the subject matter

Taylor v Caldwell (1863)

Facts: the claimants entered into an agreement with the defendants for the hire of a certain music hall for the purpose of giving a series of concerts. Before the series was due to begin, the hall was destroyed by accidental fire.

Held: the claimants could not recover damages. The destruction of the hall excused both parties from the performance of their promises.

Destruction of the essential object need not be complete; it suffices if the damage is so extensive that the commercial purpose of the agreement is thwarted.

Non-occurrence of the event on which the contract was based

Krell v Henry (1903)

Facts: Henry hired a room from Krell for two days. Both parties knew that the room would be used as a position from which to view the coronation procession of Edward VII, but the contract itself made no reference to that intended use. The King's illness caused a postponement of the procession.

Held: the contract was frustrated. Henry was excused from paying rent for the room. The necessary inference to be drawn from the circumstances surrounding the conclusion of the contract was that the holding of the procession on the dates planned was regarded by both parties as basic to performance of the contract.

Herne Bay Steamboat Co v Hutton (1903)

Facts: the claimant company agreed to hire out a steamboat to the defendant for a fee of £250 for a period of two days, for the purpose of taking passengers to Spithead to cruise round the fleet and see the naval review on the occasion of Edward VII's coronation. The review was cancelled, but the boat could still have been used to cruise round the assembled fleet. The defendant refused to use the boat or pay the balance of the agreed fee still outstanding, and the claimant company sued for payment.

Held: the claimant company was entitled to sue. The contract was not frustrated. The holding of the naval review was not the only event upon which the intended use of the boat was dependent. The other object of the contract was to cruise around the fleet and this remained capable of fulfilment.

Incapacity where the contract requires personal performance

A prime example of a contract of personal service is the contract of employment and such a contract is always frustrated by the death of the employee. The position is the same where illness or injury renders them permanently incapable of performing the contract.

Where the illness (or other incapacity such as internment, conscription and, possibly, imprisonment) is temporary, much depends on whether resumed performance after the incapacity would be radically different commercially from what was envisaged by the contract.

A factor relevant here is the probable length of the contract. For example, a day's illness would not frustrate a contract of employment of no fixed duration whereas in:

Condor v The Barron Knights (1966)

Facts: the drummer in a pop group ordinarily employed for seven nights a week was advised by his doctor not to work for more than four nights.

Held: his contract had been frustrated because it was not commercially feasible to employ a second part-time drummer.

The courts and tribunals dealing with contracts of employment are today very reluctant to find frustration of the contract, because in doing so they would deprive the employee of their right to claim unfair dismissal.

Impossibility caused by some change in the law or by action taken under statutory authority

Re Shipton, Anderson & Co (1915)

Facts: could a contract for the sale of wheat stored in a warehouse be frustrated when the government requisitioned it under its emergency wartime powers?

Held: yes it could. The war was a 'supervening event' that over-rode the original contract.

An extensive interruption that alters performance

An extensive interruption to performance may make any further execution of the contract fundamentally impracticable or essentially different to performance as originally contemplated by the contracting parties.

Metropolitan Water Board v Dick Kerr & Co Ltd (1918)

Facts: Kerr & Co agreed to construct a reservoir for the water board within a period of six years, subject to an extension of time if the work should be unduly delayed or impeded, however occasioned. During the First World War the Minister of Munitions ordered work to stop and the plant to be sold.

Held: although the event that occurred was literally within the delay clause and seemingly precluded frustration, nonetheless the contract has been frustrated. The interruption to the work was of such a character and duration that it vitally and fundamentally changed the conditions of the contract. If performance was resumed it would be essentially different to the type of performance as originally envisaged.

5.3 When frustration will not apply

A contract is not frustrated:

- If it merely becomes more difficult or expensive to perform in a different way.

Tsakiroglou v Obleé Thorl (1960)

Facts: a contract was entered into for the sale of groundnuts. The contract price included shipment from the Sudan to Hamburg in Germany. The seller costed the contract on the basis of the shortest shipping route (via the Suez Canal) although this was not an express term of the contract, nor would the court allow it to be an implied term. After the making of the contract the Suez Canal was unexpectedly closed. As this would have meant a 2½ times longer journey around the Cape of Good Hope, the seller alleged that the contract was discharged by frustration.

Held: the contract was not impossible to perform, it was merely more expensive for the seller and therefore not frustrated.

Davis Contractors v Fareham UDC (1956)

Facts: the claimant contracted to build a number of houses for the defendant for £94,000 over a specified period. Due to labour shortages it took much longer and cost the claimant £110,000. They pleaded that the contract had been frustrated and were therefore entitled to claim on a *quantum meruit* basis for the benefit conferred.

Held: the undue delay that caused extra expense did not amount to frustration.

- If one party has expressly undertaken that they will do something that they later find they cannot achieve – since there is no change of circumstances, merely a realisation of impossibility, there is no frustration

- If one party by their own choice induces impossibility that could have been avoided ('self-induced' frustration) this is not frustration.

Maritime National Fish v Ocean Trawlers (1935)

Facts: a contract for hire of a trawler that required a trawler licence was claimed to be frustrated when the owner obtained insufficient trawler licences for all its boats and failed to allocate one to the trawler that had been hired.

Held: the contract was not frustrated. The person claiming the frustration had caused the event themselves and so could not rely upon the doctrine. The owner remained liable to the hirer.

5.4 Effects of frustration

The position of the parties is governed by the Law Reform (Frustrated Contracts) Act 1943:

(a) All sums paid under the contract must be repaid. Any sums payable (whether overdue or due in the future) cease to be payable.

(b) If one party has incurred expenses under the contract they can deduct them from any sums that have to be repaid under paragraph (a), or claim them from any overdue sums, but if there are no such sums, they cannot recover such expenses from the other party.

(c) Where one party has received some benefit under the contract, they must pay for that benefit.

Summary

On completion of their studies students should be able to:

- explain what the law regards as performance of the contract, and valid and invalid reasons for non-performance.

Self-test questions

Methods of discharge

1   What are the four ways in which a contract can be discharged? (1)

Performance

2   What is the general rule about the performance of a contract? (2.1)

3   Is the doctrine of substantial performance a common law or an equitable doctrine? (2.6)

4   Give an example of a contract where time will be of the essence. (2.7)

Agreement

5   What is meant by bilateral discharge of a contract? (3.2)

Breach

6   Will a breach of warranty ever entitle the innocent party to accept the breach and end the contract? (4.1)

Frustration

7   Define frustration (5.1)

8   What is the position of a party who has incurred expenses under a frustrated contract? (5.4)

Multiple-choice question

Frustration discharges a contract when:

A   A contract is impossible to perform at the time it is made

B   An event occurs after the contract has been made rendering its performance more difficult and expensive to perform

C   An event occurs after the contract has been made rendering its performance impossible

D   A party expressly promises to do something which they later decide is not in their best interests.

For the answer to this question, see the 'Answers' section at the end of the book.

Practice questions

Question 1: E's series of concerts

D engages with E to sing in a series of concerts.

In both of the following situations, what is the legal position if, before the first concert can take place:

(a)   the theatre in which the concerts are to be held is seriously damaged by fire and the concerts are cancelled

(b)   E is found guilty of drug smuggling and sent to prison for two years?

Question 2: Seville publications plc

Seville publications plc agrees to pay Leporello £20,000 for writing a biography it would like to publish. They agree a time-scale for the writing of the book and Seville pays an immediate advance of £5,000 to Leporello. No formal contract is drawn up but Seville writes to Leporello and says 'As arranged at our meeting, we confirm that you are to write for us a biography of the late Don Giovanni called 'The Catalogue Song' for a fee of £20,000. We enclose a cheque for £5,000 by way of advance as agreed.'

Leporello begins work and three months later, when he has written 50,000 words, the publishers tell him that they have had a change of company policy and no longer intend to publish biographies. They ask for the return of the £5,000 advance.

Advise Leporello.

For the answers to these questions, see the 'Answers' section at the end of the book.

Chapter 11

CONTRACT: REMEDIES FOR BREACH

Syllabus content

The law of contract

- The remedies of specific performance, injunction, rescission, and requiring a contract party to pay the agreed price

- Causation and remoteness of damages, and their quantification

The preceding chapters considered whether or not a contract has been breached. This chapter considers the remedies available for breach of contract, comprising monetary remedies, e.g. damages and an action for the price and, where a monetary remedy would be inadequate, the court orders of specific performance and injunction.

An examination question in this area may require knowledge of the calculation of damages or the availability of the equitable remedies.

Contents

1   Summary of remedies

2   Damages

3   Unspecified damages

4   Measure of damages

5   Action for the price

6   Specific performance

7   Injunction

8   Limitation of actions

9   Privity of contract

1 Summary of remedies

In appropriate cases the party who has suffered a breach of contract may have any of the following remedies:

- damages
- action for price
- specific performance
- injunction.

2 Damages

2.1 Aim of damages

The aim of damages in contract is usually to put the injured party into the position they would have been in if the contract had been properly performed – often referred to as bargain loss. Thus in a contract for the sale of goods where the seller has failed to deliver goods, the buyer's measure of damages will be the difference between the agreed contract price and the price the buyer needed to pay in order to get the goods elsewhere, i.e. the prevailing market price. However, in some cases the courts award 'reliance losses', that is losses incurred in trying to perform the contract prior to the breach.

Damages are compensatory; they are not usually intended to be punitive. Thus damages are not usually affected by the motive or intention behind the breach of contract – whether good or bad.

2.2 Specified (liquidated) damages

The parties in the contract may include a term in the contract that states the amount of damages to be paid in the event of a breach of contract.

If the amount specified is a genuine attempt to pre-estimate the loss that will be suffered in the event of a breach of contract, the clause will be enforceable by either party to the contract.

However, if the amount that is specified is much greater than the greatest loss that the innocent party could suffer, and the intention is to deter a breach and to punish in the event of a breach, the clause will be void and unenforceable.

If the contract does not make any provision for damages, the court will determine the damages payable on the basis of the principles set out in paragraphs 3 and 4. They are unspecified damages.

3 Unspecified damages

3.1 Calculation of unspecified damages

KEY POINT

Damages is the common law remedy and is available as of right for every breach of contract.

Damages is the common law remedy and is available as of right for every breach of contract.

Two questions arise when the court is assessing a claim for unspecified damages:

- Remoteness of damage – what losses should be included in the claim?
- Measure of damages – what level of damages will compensate the party claiming?

3.2 Remoteness of damage

The basic rule is that damages are awarded to put the innocent party in the same position that they would have been in had the contract been properly performed. Thus damages are awarded for loss of bargain. However, some losses, albeit flowing from the breach, are nevertheless too remote and not recoverable.

Consider, for example, the following situation. A builder agrees to build a factory by a certain date. If erection of a new factory is delayed, the manufacturer may lose profits on their trade for the period of delay. They may have to buy products (which they could have made) in order to fulfil contracts to supply customers; they may have to pay interest charges on capital invested in raw materials which they cannot use or pay wages to employees for whom they have no work. Which of these indirect losses and expenses (loosely called consequential loss) can they recover from the builder as damages for breach of contract in failing to complete the factory on time?

Hadley v Baxendale (1854)

Facts: a carrier was given a mill-shaft to deliver to a plant manufacturer as a model for making a new shaft. The carrier delayed in delivery and, unknown to him, the mill stood idle during the period of delay.

Held: he was not liable for the loss of profit and the rule was formulated as follows: the loss should be such as may fairly and reasonably be considered either arising naturally, i.e. according to the usual course of things, from the breach of contract, or such as may reasonably be supposed to have been in the contemplation of both parties at the time they made the contract as the probable result of the breach of it.

So there are two types of loss for which damages may be recovered:

- that which arises naturally in the usual course of things – general damages, sometimes known as 'normal loss'

- that which does not occur naturally in the usual course of things but which both parties could foresee, when the contract was made, as the likely result of breach – special damages sometimes known as 'abnormal loss'.

3.3 Hadley v Baxendale applied

Both branches of the rule arising from the case of *Hadley v Baxendale* are based on a test of foresight and probability. In the first branch, the test is what would an outsider with no special knowledge of the circumstances regard as the likely consequence of a breach?

In *Hadley v Baxendale* it was held that without inside knowledge the carrier could not be expected to realise that delay on his part would keep the mill idle (in many cases mill owners were likely to have a spare shaft to use in an emergency).

The second branch of the rule starts from the special knowledge (if any) that the parties possessed when they made their contract and asks what, with that knowledge, should reasonably have been foreseen as the likely loss resulting from breach.

Victoria Laundry v Newman Industries (1949)

Facts: a laundry required a new boiler to enlarge its plant. There was delay in delivery of the boiler and as a result the laundry lost:

- a normal trading profit from delay in bringing the new plant into use

- an extra large profit on certain government contracts.

Held: the boiler manufacturer was held liable for the loss of normal profits; under the first branch of the rule, he or anyone else would know that an industrial boiler was essential to the operation of the plant, and, therefore, to earning normal profits from it. He was not liable for the loss of profit on the government contracts, of which he had no information. (If, of course, he had known of them he would have been liable under the second branch of the rule.)

Recovery of damages in contract is usually for financial loss (e.g. loss of profits) but other types of loss may be recoverable, e.g. personal injury and property damage. In an appropriate case damages can be recovered for mental distress and loss of enjoyment, but only if the contract was one designed to give pleasure or enjoyment.

Jarvis v Swan's Tours Ltd (1973)

Facts: the defendant's winter sports holiday brochure represented various facilities available at a ski resort. On the basis of these representations, the claimant booked a holiday. The advertised facilities were not available and the claimant was very disappointed. The claimant claimed damages for breach of contract to provide the holiday promised.

Held: the claimant was entitled to compensation for loss of entertainment and enjoyment. Damages for mental stress could also be recovered.

4 Measure of damages

4.1 General

DEFINITION

The measure of damages is the amount that will, so far as money can, put the claimant in the position in which they would have been had the contract been performed.

The measure of damages is the amount that will, so far as money can, put the claimant in the position in which they would have been had the contract been performed. Thus for example if a buyer bought goods for £50 that the seller refused to deliver, the buyer's damages would be the cost to them of acquiring the same goods from someone else. So if they had to pay £60 their damages would be £10 (plus the £50 if they had already paid that to the seller). If a buyer refused to accept goods, the seller's loss would be the difference between the contract price and the price they could actually sell for.

If the claimant has suffered no actual loss, they will be awarded only nominal damages.

Surrey County Council v Bredero Homes Ltd (1993)

Facts: SCC sold some land to BH and in the contract of sale BH covenanted to build no more than 72 houses on the plot. In deliberate breach of contract BH built 77 houses. SCC claimed damages equal to the profit BH had made on the extra houses.

Held: the remedy at common law for breach of contract was the award of damages to compensate the innocent party for their loss: it was not to transfer to them any benefit that the wrongdoer had gained by their breach of contract. Since SCC had not suffered any loss, it followed that the damages recoverable had to be nominal.

4.2 Difficulties of evaluation

The court's inability to evaluate the claimant's losses with mathematical accuracy is not sufficient reason for refusing to grant any compensation at all, even though the assessment of damages is almost a matter of guesswork.

Chaplin v Hicks (1911)

Facts: Chaplin agreed with Hicks, a theatrical manager, to attend an interview at which 12 girls would be chosen from 50 contestants to work in the theatre. Hick's failure to give Chaplin sufficient notice of the interview prevented her attendance. She claimed damages for loss of her chance of being selected. The defendant contended that Miss Chaplin was entitled to nominal damages only since it was impossible to determine objectively whether she would have been chosen.

Held: although assessment of her loss was problematic, since it could not be determined whether Chaplin would have been chosen, the claimant should nonetheless receive some compensation. Damages of £100 were awarded.

However, the claimant must provide some justification for their claim and cannot just pick a number.

4.3 Taxation

Sometimes the court will take into account the effect of taxation. This is particularly important in an action for wrongful dismissal where an employee is claiming loss of earnings. Their actual loss will not be their gross pay, but their net pay after taxation.

4.4 Mitigation

KEY POINT

An aggrieved party who has suffered from a breach of contract must take reasonable steps to mitigate, i.e. reduce, any losses caused by the breach of contract.

A duty is imposed upon a claimant to take all reasonable steps to mitigate any loss caused to them by the defendant's breach of contract. Compensation will not be awarded for any damage incurred that the claimant had a reasonable opportunity to avoid.

Brace v Calder (1895)

Facts: Brace was employed by a partnership for a fixed period of two years, but after only five months the partnership was dissolved, thereby prematurely terminating his contract of employment. He was offered identical employment with a reconstituted partnership, which was immediately formed to replace the previous one. He refused the offer and sued for wages he would have earned had his job continued for the agreed two-year period.

Held: Brace had not mitigated the loss he suffered by his employer's breach of contract, thus he could only recover nominal damages.

If there is an anticipatory breach and the innocent party elects to treat the contract as operative, they are under no duty to mitigate their loss and may continue with their own performance.

4.5 The available market rule

This special rule applies to contracts for the sale of goods where the breach is either the buyer wrongfully refusing to accept the goods or the seller wrongfully refusing to deliver the goods. By s51 Sale of Goods Act 1979, if an available market exists, the damages are deemed to be the difference between the contract price and the available market price as at the date of breach. An available market exists where goods of that type can be freely bought or sold at prices fixed by supply and demand.

Activity 1

S agrees to sell 100 barrels of crude oil to B at £20 per barrel, delivery on 1 May.

S refuses to deliver and B buys oil elsewhere at £25 per barrel. The 'spot' price (i.e. available market price) for crude on 1 May is £22 per barrel.

What is B's measure of damages?

Feedback to this activity is at the end of the chapter.

4.6 Date of assessment of damages

In most cases the loss must be assessed as at the date of the breach, and may include a claim for pre-contract expenditure reasonably incurred in anticipation of performance.

When calculating the amount of damages to be awarded the court will award an amount that, as far as possible, puts the injured party into the position that they would have been in had the contract been properly performed. Factors include:

- financial loss will be recovered but damages can also be awarded for stress, inconvenience and frustration

- even if the award cannot be mathematically calculated the court will award damages by the process of estimating the loss

- the party that suffered loss is under a duty to mitigate their loss and the damages awarded will reflect this.

5 Action for the price

Where the breach of contract is non-payment of the price, the seller sues for the price. This is an action for a specified sum – no question of remoteness or quantum arises. There is also no duty to mitigate.

6 Specific performance

This is an equitable remedy whereby the court orders the defendant to carry out their obligations under the contract. Like other equitable remedies, it is at the discretion of the court to grant it and it cannot be obtained as of right (contrast with damages, which is a common law remedy and is awarded as of right). It therefore follows that it is only given where it is just and equitable to do so. The main principles that determine when specific performance is ordered or refused are:

- Where damages are an adequate remedy, specific performance will not be ordered. On a sale of goods (unless they are unique) or an agreement to lend money, damages is an adequate remedy for the extra cost if the claimant can obtain similar goods or money elsewhere. By contrast, specific performance will often be ordered on a contract for sale of land: each piece of the earth's surface is unique.

- Where the court could not adequately supervise the performance of the contract, it will not order specific performance. Contracts for construction of buildings fall under this head.

- Specific performance will not be given where it would cause undue hardship. Thus specific performance will not be ordered of a contract of personal services, such as an employment contract, on the basis that it is contrary to public policy to compel an unwilling party to maintain continuous personal relations with another (also it would require constant supervision).

- The remedy will only be given on the basis of mutuality, i.e. the remedy will only be granted if both parties could, if necessary, seek the protection of the court. For this reason a minor cannot obtain an order for specific performance since the court would not be able to enforce such an order against them. (A minor is a person under 18 years of age. Minors have only limited power to contract in English law.)

- Specific performance will not be given to a party that has acted unfairly or improperly. This is expressed by the maxim 'He who comes to Equity must come with clean hands'. As with all equitable remedies, a party that wishes for specific performance must act promptly – 'Delay defeats the Equities'.

7 Injunction

An injunction is an order of the court that either requires a person to do something (mandatory injunction) or prohibits a person from doing something (prohibitory injunction). It is an equitable remedy and is granted on the same principles as specific performance.

The court will grant an injunction to restrain a party from committing a breach of contract.

Metropolitan Electric Supply v Ginder (1901)

Facts: the contract obliged the defendant to take all his electricity from the claimant; the obligation was in substance not to take electricity from another supplier.

Held: an injunction to that effect was issued.

An injunction will not be granted if it would have the effect of requiring specific performance in circumstances where the latter would be refused.

Page One Records Ltd v Britton (1967)

Facts: the Troggs (a pop group) agreed to employ P as their manager for five years and not to employ any other manager. The Troggs dismissed P, who consequently sought an injunction to restrain them from employing any other manager.

Held: the injunction was refused because if denied the services of another manager, the Troggs would in effect have had to employ P, since they could not do without a manager.

However, an injunction may be granted in circumstances such as the following.

Warner Brothers Pictures Inc v Nelson (1936)

Facts: the film star, Bette Davis (Miss Nelson) entered into a contract with the claimants, whereby she agreed that she would not undertake other film work without obtaining their written consent. The claimant sought an injunction to restrain her from doing film work for another company in breach of this agreement.

Held: the injunction would be granted since she could still earn her living as an actress, in other ways.

An injunction will be granted only where it is 'just and convenient to do so', and, if it is inappropriate, the court can award damages in lieu of the injunction.

8 Limitation of actions

KEY POINT

Normally time runs from the date on which the breach occurred. In the case of simple contracts the limitation period is six years and in the case of contracts by deed, 12 years.

The Limitation Act 1980 provides that any action on a contract is 'barred' if not brought within the requisite period. Normally time runs from the date on which the breach occurred. In the case of simple contracts the limitation period is six years and in the case of contracts by deed, 12 years. If the claim includes damages for personal injuries or death, however, the period is normally reduced to three years (however, the Act provides that the three-year period can be extended by the court if the injury does not become apparent within the period).

There are three instances where the limitation period may be extended:

KEY POINT

The Limitation Act 1980 only applies to common law remedies. In equity there is a more flexible doctrine known as **laches** which requires the claimant to bring their action within a reasonable time depending on all the circumstances.

- Where the claimant is a minor or of unsound mind when the cause of action accrued, time does not begin to run until the disability ceases.

- Where the cause of action is concealed by the defendant's fraud, time does not begin to run until such moment as the claimant should, with reasonable diligence, have discovered the breach.

- Where the defendant makes some acknowledgement in writing of their liability or makes a payment towards it, then time begins to run afresh from the date of such acknowledgement or payment. However, such acknowledgement or part payment made after the limitation period has expired will not start time running again. This rule applies only to claims for specified damages.

The Limitation Act 1980 only applies to common law remedies. In equity there is a more flexible doctrine known as **laches** (pronounced 'lay cheese') which requires the claimant to bring their action within a reasonable time depending on all the circumstances.

9 Privity of contract

DEFINITION

A contract creates a personal obligation and only the original contracting parties can acquire enforceable rights or be subject to legal liabilities under it.

9.1 The doctrine of privity

A contract creates a personal obligation and only the original contracting parties can acquire enforceable rights or be subject to legal liabilities under it.

Dunlop Pneumatic Tyre Co v Selfridge (1915)

Facts: D made and sold tyres to a distributor on condition that he would not resell the tyres at less than the list price (the Resale Prices Act 1976 would now invalidate such terms) nor resell them to a retailer without imposing the same conditions about retail price. The distributor resold to S who offered the tyres to the public at less than D's list price.

Held: D could not enforce the contract between the distributor and S because D was not a party to it.

9.2 Exception to the doctrine of privity

The Contract (Rights of Third Parties) Act 1999 states that a person who is not a party to the contract (a third party) may in their own right enforce a term of the contract if:

- the contract contains an express term which states that they can,
- the term confers a benefit on them
- the contract expressly identifies the third party either by name or by description.

Note: The third party need not be in existence at the time the contract is made. Therefore a contract can confer benefits on an unborn child, or on a company that is to be incorporated in the future.

Summary

On completion of their studies students should be able to:

- explain the type of breach necessary to cause contractual breakdown
- describe the remedies that are available for serious and minor breaches of contract.

Self-test questions

Damages

1   What is the aim of damages? (2.1)

Unspecified damages

2   Is damages a common law or an equitable remedy? (3.1)

3   State the rule in *Hadley v Baxendale*. (3.2)

Measure of damages

4   If a person cannot show actual loss as a result of a breach of contract what sort of damages will the court award? (4.1)

Specific performance

5   Why will specific performance not be ordered of a contract of employment? (6)

Limitation of actions

6   What is the limitation period in the case of simple contracts? (8)

Practice question

B Bros Ltd

B Bros Ltd is a company running a factory manufacturing four-wheel drive vehicles, some of which are sold to the military. The factory has an automated production line producing 10 vehicles per day. The line is controlled by a computer.

The computer develops a serious fault, which stops the line functioning. C Ltd offer a 24-hour call out service for such faults. The production manager telephones C Ltd, explaining the situation and C Ltd's engineer agrees to attend 'straight away'. In fact, he does not attend for three days during which time production is at a standstill.

A high-powered delegation from the Ozono Republic Ministry of Defence arrives on the second day to tour the factory and discuss an order for 1,000 vehicles and associated service contracts. Unimpressed, they award the contract to another company.

Ten vehicles had already been built to the Ozono Republic's specification and painted in their military colours in anticipation of the contract being awarded, which was seen as a mere formality. B Bros do not see the point in looking for an alternative buyer and scrap the vehicles.

Required:

(a)   Fill in the gaps and complete the sentence.

C Ltd are in breach of contract, the likely remedy is ……………………….. Under the rules first developed in ……………………… v ……………………… and applied in ……………………… v ……………………… C Ltd will be liable for … *(Your answer must not exceed 30 words.)*   **(7 marks)**

(b)   Explain what duty B Bros have in relation to the 10 vehicles produced and painted. *(Your answer must not exceed 20 words.)*   **(5 marks)**

(c)   Fill in the gaps and complete the sentence.

If war had been declared on the Ozono Republic, the contract between them and the other company would have been ……………………….. Any deposit paid by the Ozono Ministry of Defence would have been ……………………….. unless …. *(Your answer must not exceed 20 words.)*

     (3 marks)

(d)   If the contract had been granted to B Bros and contained a term that prevented them selling vehicles to the People's Republic of Bazami, if breached this would be enforced by an ……………………… which is an ……………………… remedy and as such is ……………………… Its effect would be …. *(Your answer must not exceed 15 words.)*   **(5 marks)**

For the answer to this question, see the 'Answers' section at the end of the book.

Feedback to activity

Activity 1

£200.

Chapter 12

EMPLOYMENT: THE CONTRACT OF EMPLOYMENT

Syllabus content

The law of employment

- The tests used to distinguish an employee from an independent contractor

- The express and implied terms of a contract of employment

Employment law is concerned with the law relating to individual contracts of employment (i.e. the law that affects employees). It is not generally concerned with the law relating to the self-employed, which is largely governed by consumer or commercial law. However, some provisions do affect both employees and the self-employed. Thus we first turn to the important distinction between these two types of employment and then consider the employment contract itself.

Contents

1   Types of contract

2   Tests used to distinguish between employee and independent contractor

3   Formation of the contract of employment

4   Written particulars of employment

5   Terms implied by the courts

6   Implied terms – other sources

1 Types of contract

1.1 Introduction

There are two types of working relationship:

Employee – a shop assistant who works for a large department store from nine to five, Monday to Friday, with specific holidays and wages will be an employee of the store.

Self-employed – an electrician who runs his own business and comes in to do a one-off rewiring job for the department store is not an employee, he is self-employed.

The legal distinctions between these two types of working relationship are important. In legal terminology, the shop assistant is an employee under a contract of service and the electrician is an independent contractor under a contract for services.

The distinction between a contract of service (an employee) and a contract for services (an independent contractor) is an absolutely critical one in the field of employment law.

1.2 Importance of distinction

The difference is important for a variety of reasons, the most important are:

- only employees are afforded protection under employment protection legislation

- only employees have implied into their contract certain common law duties of employer and employee

- only employees can make their employers vicariously liable for their torts

- only employees are given preferential rights to what they are owed on the insolvency of the employers

- only employees are entitled to certain state benefits such as jobseeker's allowance, statutory sick pay, and statutory maternity pay

- employees' tax is deducted through PAYE and is assessed under the employment income provisions. Independent contractors are assessed under the trading income provisions and are themselves responsible for payment of tax

- an employer must pay National Insurance contributions in respect of every employee, but not in respect of independent contractors. Employees must also pay an 'employees' contribution and this must be deducted from their wages by the employer. Independent contractors pay a 'self-employed' contribution and are themselves responsible for payment.

The two examples given above are fairly clear cut ones. However, it is not always easy to determine whether a person is an employee or an independent contractor, and the courts have developed a number of tests to make the distinction.

1.3 Vicarious liability of an employer

An employer will be vicariously liable for any tort committed by an employee if this act or omission occurred within the scope of the employment relationship.

Conditions

An employer will be liable for a tort of a worker if it is shown that:

- they are an employee and not an independent contractor

- the tort was committed by the employee in the course of their employment, and not whilst the employee was on a 'frolic of their own'.

Course of employment

Unless the employer has expressly authorised the conduct, they are vicariously liable only for those torts committed by their employee in the course of their employment.

A distinction is drawn between a wrongful way of doing something that the employee is authorised to do, and an act that the servant is not authorised to perform at all.

Limpus v London General Omnibus Co (1862)

Facts: the defendants' driver was forbidden to race with or obstruct other buses. He disobeyed these instructions and the claimant was injured.

Held: the company was held to be vicariously liable for his tort since he had merely done what he was authorised to do, albeit in an improper and unauthorised manner.

Beard v London General Omnibus Co (1900)

Facts: a bus conductor, on his own initiative, turned round a bus at a terminus and negligently injured a third party.

Held: he was not acting within the course of his employment as it was not his job to drive buses, merely to act as a conductor. He was on a frolic of his own.

2 Tests used to distinguish between employee and independent contractor

2.1 The control test

The sole test that was used until about the 1940-50s to determine whether a person was an employee or an independent contractor was the 'control' test. This was set out in *Yewens v Noakes (1880)* – 'a servant is a person subject to the command of his master as to the manner in which he shall do his work'.

Thus a person was an employee if the employer could tell them not only what to do but how to do it. The test was based on the fact that in an agricultural or early industrial society the employer did have more knowledge and skill than the employees.

However, with developing technology and specialisation the control test became inappropriate as employers would hire people for particular skills, e.g. a chemical engineer, which the employer did not have sufficient knowledge or skill to instruct the manner in which they carried out their work.

Therefore several other tests have been developed. There is now no single test and the operation of the various tests is far from satisfactory.

2.2 The integration test

This test provides that under a contract of service, the work done is an integral part of the business, whereas under a contract for services the work done is not integrated into it but only accessory to it and is being done by the worker as a person in business on their own account.

Cassidy v Minister of Health (1951)

Facts: was a doctor in a hospital an employee or an independent contractor?

Held: although the hospital did not control the manner of his work he was nevertheless an employee because he was part of the institution of the hospital.

Beloff v Pressdam (1973)

Facts: B was a regular contributor to a newspaper. She had no regular hours, wrote for other newspapers, and had leave to write books. However, she wrote regularly for this newspaper, including leaders and was an active member of the editorial staff, attending regular meetings and taking part in editorial decisions. Was she an employee?

Held: she was an employee: her work was an integral part of the business.

However the test is not satisfactory because it is sometimes difficult to ascertain what is integral and what is accessory and it does not deal with certain cases, for example, workers who provide their own equipment.

2.3 The economic reality test

The economic reality test tends to be the test that the courts use to establish whether a contract of service exists or not.

This is also sometimes called the multiple test. It looks at the economic reality behind the relationship.

Ready Mixed Concrete v Ministry of Pensions (1968)

Facts: the driver of a lorry had a contract with a company under which he drove his lorry only on company business, obeyed instructions of the foreman and wore company colours. He provided his own lorry, which he had obtained from the company on hire purchase and was painted company colours. He could employ a substitute driver. He was paid on the basis of mileage and quantity of goods delivered. He paid the expenses of repair and maintenance of the lorry and his own national insurance and income tax. The Minister of Pensions claimed that he was an employee and the company had therefore to make the employer's insurance contributions.

Held: although the employer exercised some control over his work, the other factors were not consistent with there being a contract of service. In particular the fact that he owned his own equipment and was operating at his own financial risk to a degree (i.e. was a small businessman) meant that he was an independent contractor.

Market Investigations Ltd v Minister of Social Security (1969)

Facts: a market research interviewer worked on and off under a series of contracts whereby she interviewed for a company in accordance with interview instructions issued by the company. She had to complete the work within a specified period but otherwise had no specified hours of work. There was no provision for holiday or sick pay and she was free to work for others while working for the company.

Held: the company did have some control over the manner in which she did her work and the terms of the contract were consistent with a contract of service. The court emphasised that she did not provide her own tools and took no risk. She was therefore not 'in business on her own account' and was an employee not an independent contractor. The court also emphasised that there was 'no exhaustive test compiled, nor strict rules laid down' as to the factors that identified a contract of service.

A list of factors that will be considered includes:

- The degree of control by the 'employer'.

- The degree to which the worker risks loss or stands to gain from profit.

- Ownership of tools and equipment.

- The degree to which the worker's work is an integral part of the business.

- Regularity and method of payment.

- Regularity of hours.

- Whether there is a mutuality of obligations, i.e. is the employer under a duty to provide work and the worker under a duty to accept it.

- The ability to provide a substitute, i.e. the ability to delegate the performance of the contract.

- The terms used by the parties – although it is a factor to be considered, it is not decisive. The court will consider the substance not the form, and will not be persuaded by a label that is clearly inconsistent with the facts of the relationship.

The court will weigh up the factors, giving such weight to each factor as is warranted in the circumstances.

No single test is really capable of determining employee status, therefore all of the above factors will be considered.

Note that the amount of work done is not a deciding factor. Thus a person who works part-time can be an employee or an independent contractor depending on which side of the line he or she falls on the above tests.

Activity 1

James employs a marketing advisor, Andrew. Andrew pays his own income tax and National Insurance contribution and works an agreed number of hours each week, but at times of his own choosing. Andrew also works for other employers provided that they are not competitors of James. What factors would need to be considered in order to decide whether Andrew's contract was one of service or for services?

Feedback to this activity is at the end of the chapter.

3 Formation of the contract of employment

3.1 Introduction

The employment relationship is a contractual one. The basic rules of contract will apply. There must be offer and acceptance, intention to create legal relations and consideration. Usually the offer comes from the employer and the acceptance from the employee: the consideration provided by the employer is their promise to pay the employee and the consideration of the employee is their promise to work for the employer.

Both parties must have capacity to contract. Generally an employment contract is binding on a minor only if it is on the whole for their benefit. The minimum age at which a minor may be employed is 13 and there are also statutory restrictions on employing children under 16.

Generally the contract may take any form. It can be oral or in writing, express or implied. Certain contracts, e.g. apprentices or seamen, must be in writing. There is also a duty on employers to provide a written statement of particulars.

The vitiating factors of misrepresentation and illegality will also apply to employment contracts. In a number of cases, attempts by the employer and employee to evade the payment of tax rendered the contract void for illegality. If the contract is void the employee will have no right to claim wages, redundancy, unfair dismissal etc.

Finally, the contract may be discharged by performance, agreement, frustration and breach. The remedies available will include the usual contractual remedies, plus the statutory remedies of unfair dismissal and redundancy.

3.2 Express terms of the contract

The employment contract will include terms **expressly** agreed between the parties.

3.3 Implied terms

Common law also implies terms into employment contracts. Terms may be implied by custom and practice of the trade or by usage over a period of time. Many employees will therefore have terms incorporated into their contracts of employment from collective agreements between the union and the employer.

3.4 Statutory provisions

KEY POINT

The contract of employment will be a mixture of implied terms, terms expressly agreed between the parties and statutory provisions.

Statute has impinged greatly on the ability of the employer and employee to set their own terms. The statutes were enacted partially in recognition of the employer's superior bargaining power to give some protection to the employee, partially to bring UK law into line with European Union law and partially through measures that apply to many situations to prevent discrimination.

- The Equal Pay Act 1970 implies terms, i.e. that persons have the same conditions of employment irrespective of sex or marital status.

- The Sex Discrimination Act 1975 prohibits discrimination on the basis of sex; the Race Relations Act 1976 prohibits discrimination on the basis of race; and the Trade Union and Labour Relations Act 1992 prohibits discrimination on grounds of a membership of a trade union; and the Employment Rights Act 1996 prohibits discrimination on grounds of health and safety complaints.

- Various statutes, in particular the Factories Act 1961, the Offices, Shops and Railway Premises Act 1963 and the Health and Safety at Work Act 1974 impose safety standards on employers and on employees.

- The Employment Rights Act 1996 gives employees certain rights, such as a right not to be unfairly dismissed, a right to a redundancy payment if made redundant and a right a minimum period of notice to terminate the contract.

- The Wages Act 1986 makes provision in respect of the manner of payment of wages and deductions.

- The Working Time Regulations 1998 limit the hours that a worker can be required to work to an average of 48 a week. It also gives the right to four weeks paid leave a year and one day off each week.

- The Employment Act 2002 gives parents of children under the age of six the right to request flexible working arrangements. The employer must give serious consideration to such a request and can only reject it for clear business reasons. The Act also introduced paternity and adoption leave.

- The Employment Equality (Age) Regulations 2006 make age-related discrimination and harassment unlawful. The regulations impose a default retirement age of 65. Compulsory retirement at an earlier age is still possible, but only if justifiable. Employees have the right to request to work beyond their normal retirement date. The employer is not legally bound to agree to these requests, but has to give them reasonable consideration.

Note that the Equal Pay Act 1970 actually implies a term into an employee's contract. However, the other statutory provisions do not imply terms but either make provisions in contracts invalid if they contravene the rights given or give employees a statutory right to make a claim over and above the provisions in their contract.

4 Written particulars of employment

4.1 Timing and content

S1 Employment Rights Act 1996 requires an employer to provide employees with a written statement of certain particulars of their employment within two months of the commencement of employment. The aim of the provision is to ensure that the employee knows what the employer believes to be their legal rights under the contract.

The statement must contain the following information:

- Names of the employer and employee.

- The date on which the employment began and the date on which the employee's period of continuous employment began, taking into account any employment with a previous employer that counts towards that period. (This is important for the employee to calculate their entitlement to many of the statutory rights.)

- The scale or rate of pay or method of calculating it, e.g. rates for piece work or overtime.

- Intervals of pay – weekly, monthly, etc.

- Hours of work.

- Holidays and holiday pay.

- Sick pay and sick leave.

- Pension and pension schemes and whether a contracting-out certificate in respect of the State Pension Scheme is in force.

- The job title or a brief description of work

- Place or places of work

- Any collective agreement affecting the employment

- Length of notice required by employer and employee to terminate a contract (or, if the employment is to be temporary or for a fixed term, the date it is to end).

- Details of any disciplinary or grievance procedure, specifying the person to whom the employee can apply if they have a grievance generally or are dissatisfied with any disciplinary decision relating to them and any further steps that follow from their application, e.g. an appeal procedure if the employee is not satisfied.

Any change in the particulars must be notified by written statement within one month.

4.2 Purpose of written statement

The statement is not the contract itself unless both the employer and employee acknowledge that it is such, e.g. if it is called a contract and both parties sign it. The statement is prepared by the employer and it is therefore generally seen by the courts as a unilateral declaration by the employer of their view of the terms. It is strong *prima facie* evidence of the terms but by no means conclusive and the court will allow evidence to determine what the terms are.

If an employer fails to provide a written statement or if the statement is incomplete, the employee can complain to an employment tribunal that can determine the terms that ought to have been included. It must attempt to discover what the parties in fact agreed. The effect of the determination is that the employer is deemed to have supplied a statement in the correct form. However, the tribunal cannot then enforce the terms. Because the remedy is so limited, applications on their own are rare. Generally the application will be coupled with one for unfair dismissal or redundancy.

4.3 Employees to whom statements need not be given

The written statement need not be given to the following categories of employees:

- where the employment continues for less than one month

- where the employment is wholly or mainly outside Great Britain, unless the employee ordinarily works in Great Britain for the same employer.

No statement need be given in respect of disciplinary procedures if at the start of employment there are fewer than 20 employees. However, details of grievance procedures must be given.

5   Terms implied by the courts

5.1   Introduction

If there is a gap in what the parties have expressly agreed in an employment contract, the common law may imply a term. Thus, the law has implied terms to give effect to the presumed but unexpressed intentions of the parties using the 'officious bystander' or 'business efficacy' test. These implied terms are sometimes called 'terms implied in fact'.

There are also terms implied in law that arise from the nature of the employment relationship. The employment relationship is based on one of obedience by the employee and the managerial prerogative of the employer.

If an employee is in breach of their contract (including breach of an implied term) the employer may sue them for damages to recover any loss. Moreover, if the employee commits a very serious breach of contract, the employer may elect to treat the contract as discharged, i.e. they may dismiss the employee without notice (called summary dismissal).

The same principles apply when an employer breaches their duties. When an employer commits a serious breach such that the employee is entitled to treat the contract as discharged, the effect is that the employee resigns and is treated as having been constructively dismissed.

5.2   Duties of the employee

(a)   Duty to obey lawful and reasonable orders

Pepper v Webb (1968)

Facts: a gardener refused to plant the plants where instructed by the employer.

Held: he was in breach of the duty of obedience and this, coupled with the fact that he was rude and surly, justified summary dismissal.

The order must be lawful. The employee need not obey an order that would result in the commission of a criminal offence.

Gregory v Ford (1951)

Facts: an employee refused to drive a vehicle that was not covered by insurance.

Held: this was not a breach of duty.

(b)   Duty of mutual co-operation (or the duty to perform the work in a reasonable manner)

The duty of the employer to give, and the employee to obey, lawful instructions is often expressed as the duty of mutual co-operation. The employer must not act in a manner calculated to damage the mutual trust and confidence and this is taken into account in considering the reasonableness of the order. The courts have interpreted the duty to obey lawful and reasonable orders as a duty not to frustrate the commercial objectives of the employer.

(c)   Duty to exercise reasonable care and skill

The employee must act with reasonable care in performing their duties. The standard of care will depend on the circumstances. It is generally accepted that a single act of negligence, unless it is gross negligence, will not justify summary dismissal. However, there are certain occupations, such as airline pilots, where a single act of negligence in performing essential duties may warrant dismissal.

Lister v Romford Ice & Cold Storage Co Ltd (1957)

Facts: an employee negligently drove a lorry into another employee who then sued the employer.

Held: the employer's insurance company sued the employee-driver who was held liable to pay. (In fact this right of indemnity is rarely enforced because the employer is insured and the insurance companies have generally agreed not to pursue this line.)

(d)   Duty of good faith – a duty to give honest and faithful service

This duty of fidelity covers a number of obligations and is based on the concept that the employment relationship is one of mutual trust and confidence.

(i)   Misappropriation of property or accounting for secret profits – the employee cannot use the employer's property as their own.

(ii)   Duty not to compete with their employer's business – the employees may do other work in their own time. However, the law imposes a duty not to do spare-time work that competes with their employer's and may cause them damage.

Hivac Ltd v Park Royal Scientific Instruments Ltd (1946)

Facts: two employees of a company that manufactured sophisticated components for hearing aids worked on weekends for a rival company.

Held: the court granted an injunction restraining them from breaching their duty even though there was no evidence of misuse of confidential information. The manner of making the devices was secret and there was a real risk that there might be a transfer of such information.

Nova Plastics Ltd v Froggatt (1982)

Facts: an odd job man worked for a competitor in his spare time.

Held: he was not in breach of contract.

The dividing line is not clear, but the test is probably whether the employee's spare time work results in a real danger of causing loss to the employer.

Note that if the employer wishes to restrain their employee from working for a competitor after leaving their employment, they must obtain a promise from the employee to that effect.

(iii)   Duty not to disclose trade secrets or misuse confidential information – many contracts will have an express term covering this area. However, even if there is no such express term, an employee must not disclose trade secrets to a third party nor misuse confidential information they have acquired in the course of their employment. This implied duty may continue after the employment has ceased. Clearly an employee who uses or sells secret processes such as chemical formulae or photocopies list of customers and sells them or uses them for their own purposes will be in breach.

Where a person invents or writes something as part of their employment, the right to the patent or copyright will generally belong to their employer.

British Syphon v Homewood (1956)

Facts: a syphon was designed by an employee at the request of the employer but patented in the employee's name.

Held: it belonged to the employer.

If it is produced outside work but the employee allows the employer to use it, the patent or copyright will belong to the employee. However, even if the employer is entitled to the invention, the employee may claim compensation if their employer has given them inadequate reward or it was of outstanding benefit.

The duty of confidentiality does not extend to information that there is a public duty to disclose, such as unlawful acts of the employer.

The real problem arises in drawing a line between trade secrets or confidential information and general knowledge and skill acquired by the employee in the course of their employment.

(e)   Duty to render personal service

Activity 2

Charlotte is employed as a junior clerk by a firm of accountants. She is asked by a friend, Beth, who runs her own dress design business, if she will do Beth's book-keeping in her spare time. Under employment law, will Charlotte be able to accept this offer?

Feedback to this activity is at the end of the chapter.

5.3   Duties of the employer

(a)   Duty to pay reasonable remuneration – in practice this implied duty rarely arises since most contracts of employment contain an express term regarding pay.

The employer is obliged to pay remuneration (whether under an express or implied term) even though there may be no work available.

(b)   Duty to indemnify the employee – the employer must indemnify their employee where the employee has incurred a legal liability whilst acting on the employer's behalf except where:

(i)   the employee knew they were committing an unlawful act
(ii)   the employee knew the employer had no right to give the order.

(c)   Duty to take reasonable care for the health and safety of their employees – there is a common law duty to provide safe plant and equipment, a safe system of work and competent staff. The standard of care required is the same as in the tort of negligence.

(d)   Duty to give reasonable notice of termination of employment – this implied duty rarely arises, since most contracts of employment contain express provisions.

(e)   Duty of mutual co-operation – the employer has a duty not to behave in a manner calculated to damage the relationship of trust and confidence.

Wares v Caithness Leather Products (1974)

Facts: an employer abusively reprimanded a female employee in foul language.

Held: he had broken the contract of employment.

5.4 Provision of work

There is no general common law duty to provide work. However, such a term may be implied where the particular circumstances show that failure to provide work would deprive the employee of a benefit contemplated by the contract. For example, where the contract expressly provides for remuneration on a piecework or commission basis, it may be possible to imply a duty on the employer to provide sufficient work to enable the employee to earn a reasonable sum.

5.5 Sick pay

There is no common law duty on the employer to pay an employee who is absent from work through sickness or injury.

5.6 Holidays and holiday pay

There is no common law duty on an employer to allow an employee a holiday (whether or not the so-called statutory or public holidays).

5.7 References

There is no common law duty on the employer to provide a reference, but if they do so:

- the employee may have an action in the tort of defamation where the reference is derogatory (subject to the defences of truth and qualified privilege)

- the employee (and perhaps also the recipient) may have an action in the tort of negligence.

6 Implied terms – other sources

6.1 Custom and practice

When an employee is given a job there may be little, if any, discussion of the terms of the contract. Few contracts of employment will cover all eventualities expressly or by use of implied terms. Many of the day-to-day matters will be governed by long-term practice within the business, e.g. whether overtime is paid for working Sundays.

6.2 Collective bargaining agreements

This is an agreement between the employer and a trade union. It covers a matters that are of direct concern to individual employees, for example, pay, hours and disciplinary procedures.

The collective agreement must be incorporated into individual employment contracts.

Conclusion

A contract of employment combines express terms agreed by both parties and terms implied by statute, common law, custom, collective agreements and work rules and notices. If these express or implied terms are breached by employer or employee then there may be a cause for legal action.

Summary

On completion of their studies, students should be able to:

- explain the difference between employees and independent contractors and how the contents of a contract of employment are established.

Self-test questions

Types of contract

1   What is the difference between a contract of service and a contract for services? (1.1 and 1.2)

Tests used to distinguish between employee and independent contractor

2   What is the alternative name for the economic reality test? (2.3)

Formation of the contract of employment

3   Which Act of Parliament implies terms into employment contracts? (3.4)

Written particulars of employment

4   Within what timescale must a written statement of particulars be issued to employees? (4.1)

5   List five of the required particulars of the written statement. (4.1)

Terms implied by the courts

6   What type of order is it an employee's duty to obey? (5.2)

7   Is an employer obliged to give a reference? (5.7)

Multiple-choice questions

Question 1

Which of the following statements is not correct?

A   Employees have a right not to be unfairly dismissed but this does not apply to independent contractors

B   Employers must deduct income tax and National Insurance contributions from the wages paid to their employees, but not from the amounts paid to independent contractors

C   Both employees and independent contractors can enforce contractual rights against their 'employer'

D   Both employees and independent contractors would rank as preferential creditors in respect of unpaid wages, if their 'employer' went into liquidation

Question 2

Which of the following statements is correct?

An employee is always entitled to:

A   Patent rights on any invention produced by them at their workplace

B   Use confidential information after the employment has ceased

C   Require their employer to give a reference if other work is being sought

D   Disobey an order from their employer if it is unreasonable

Question 3

Which of the following statements is correct?

An employer always has an implied duty:

A   To provide facilities for smokers

B   To give employees who leave a reference

C   To provide work

D   To behave reasonably and responsibly towards employees

For the answers to these questions, see the 'Answers' section at the end of the book.

Feedback to activities

Activity 1

(a)   The level of James's control over Andrew despite Andrew being free to work at whatever times he pleases.

(b)   Any financial risk that Andrew bears.

(c)   Whether Andrew provides any equipment or materials for the job.

(d)   The way in which James and Andrew view the contract. (The tax and national insurance position is evidence they view it as a contract for services.)

(e)   Is James under an obligation to provide work for Andrew?

Activity 2

The factors to consider are Charlotte's implied duty of loyalty to her employer and whether she has the capacity to harm the interests of her employer by working for Beth. Given Charlotte's junior status as a clerk and the fact that Beth's business is not in competition with the firm of accountants it would appear unlikely that this would be a problem.

Chapter 13

EMPLOYMENT: TERMINATION OF EMPLOYMENT

Syllabus content

The law of employment

- Unfair and wrongful dismissal

This chapter will consider the ways in which a contract of employment may be terminated. Examples of wrongful dismissal and unfair dismissal will be considered, together with the claims that are possible for employees in these situations.

Contents

1   Methods of termination of the employment contract

2   Breach of contract – wrongful dismissal at common law

3   Unfair dismissal

4   Remedies for unfair dismissal

1 Methods of termination of the employment contract

1.1 Termination without notice by the employer

Termination without notice by the employer is summary dismissal of the employee.

The general principle is that summary dismissal is justified if the conduct of the employee is such that it prevents further satisfactory continuance of the relationship, i.e. a serious breach of the contract of employment. For example:

- wilful disobedience of a lawful order

- misconduct such as dishonesty, the use of violence or disclosure of trade secrets

- habitual, serious and persistent neglect, carelessness, or laziness.

In contractual terms, the act of the employee must be such as to entitle the employer to repudiate the contract immediately, i.e. a very serious breach of contract.

If the employer unjustifiably terminates the contract, the employee may maintain an action for damages for wrongful dismissal.

1.2 Termination without notice by the employee

Termination without notice by the employee is where they repudiate the contract by leaving. This would normally mean a breach of contract by the employee.

Note, however, that the employee may leave in circumstances that warrant their doing so because of the behaviour of the employer. This will amount to constructive dismissal by the employer and the employee will have an action for wrongful dismissal.

1.3 Termination by notice

Notice can be by either party giving notice for the specified period. The period of notice may be:

- express – specified in the employment contract itself, but this must not be less than the statutory minimum

- implied by the courts into the contract on the basis of the presumed intention of the parties, i.e. reasonable notice.

1.4 Termination by agreement

Termination by agreement is when the parties to a contract of employment by agreement end their relationship at any time and upon any terms.

1.5 Termination by operation of law

- **Frustration** – this could be due to death, long illness, incapacity, or imprisonment.

- **Dissolution, winding up** – the dissolution of a partnership where the partners are the employers will terminate the contracts; similarly the compulsory liquidation of a company, where the company is the employer, will terminate employment contracts.

1.6 Possible claims

An employee who is dismissed may have one or both of the following claims:

- damages for wrongful dismissal at common law – this is for breach of the employment contract

- an order for reinstatement, re-engagement or a monetary award for unfair dismissal.

An employer will have a claim for breach of contract if the employee is in breach, e.g. they leave employment without proper notice (unless there has been constructive dismissal).

2 Breach of contract – wrongful dismissal at common law

2.1 Introduction

Where an employment contract is terminated not in accordance with the terms of the contract, there is a breach of contract and the innocent party will have a claim for damages. The court will not usually grant specific performance of an employment contract.

2.2 Employer's breach

The employer will be in breach of their contract with their employees if they terminate the contract without giving proper notice. The length of notice required will be determined by the contract, subject to the statutory minimum imposed by the Employment Rights Act 1996. Also note that where a fixed-term employment contract expires and is not renewed there is no breach of contract.

(a) **Summary dismissal** – this will be a wrongful dismissal unless:

    (i) the employee waives their rights, accepts payment in lieu or there is an agreement to discharge

    (ii) the employee has repudiated or is in fundamental breach of their own obligations, e.g.

- wilful refusal to obey lawful instructions, e.g. *Pepper v Webb (1968)*

- failure to show a professed skill

- serious or persistent negligence

- breach of duty of good faith, e.g. Hivac v Park Royal Scientific (1946)

- immorality or drunkenness (even when outside working hours if it is important to the job).

(b) **Constructive dismissal** – a serious breach of contract by the employer such as entitles the employee to treat the contract as discharged.

Western Excavation Ltd v Sharp (1978)
Facts: what conduct will amount to constructive dismissal?
Held: an employee is entitled to treat themselves as constructively dismissed if the employer is guilty of conduct that is a significant breach going to the root of the contract of employment, or that shows that the employer no longer intends to be bound by one or more of the essential terms of the contract. Whether the employee leaves with or without notice, the conduct must be sufficiently serious to entitle them to leave at once. However, they must act quickly, for if they continue for any length

of time without leaving, they will be regarded as having elected to affirm the contract and will lose their right to treat themselves as discharged.

Where such a repudiatory breach occurs, the employee resigns and will have an action against the employer for wrongful dismissal.

Donovan v Invicta Airways (1970)

Facts: the employer put pressure on the employee, an airline pilot, to take abnormal risks on a flight. The employer did this three times in rapid succession. Each time the employee refused. Relations with management deteriorated and he left.

Held: the employer had committed a serious breach of contract amounting to constructive dismissal. The employee succeeded in an action for wrongful dismissal.

2.3 Employee's remedies

The employee who has been dismissed has the following remedies at common law:

(a) If they are dismissed rightfully with proper notice they have no claim if they are paid for the full period of notice. (There is no breach of contract.)

(b) If they are dismissed rightfully without proper notice, they may claim for unpaid wages.

(c) If they are dismissed wrongfully, without proper notice, they may:

  (i) sue for wages accrued that are due, if any, and damages for wrongful dismissal, or

  (ii) sue for a declaration that the contract still subsists and for an injunction restraining breach. An injunction is an equitable remedy, granted at the discretion of the court, ordering a person to do, or to desist from doing, some act as a remedy for a breach of duty (contractual or otherwise). (However, an injunction would very rarely be granted in these circumstances.)

2.4 Damages

The damages that would be awarded will depend on the following principles:

(a) The contractual remoteness rule applies: *Hadley v Baxendale (1854)*.

(b) In practice, the measure is usually the net wages that the employee would have received over the normal notice period. (Remember, damages are designed to restore the claimant's position. They would have received net pay, i.e. after tax had their employment continued.)

(c) The following additional claims may be made:

  (i) loss of commission or tips and possibly pension rights

  (ii) lost prospects if the employee is an apprentice, but otherwise nothing for difficulty in getting a new job

  (iii) loss of the right to claim unfair dismissal if the wrongful dismissal prevents him from having the qualifying continuous employment to claim.

(d) Deductions may be made as follows:

  (i) for mitigation or for failure to do so (i.e. did, or should, the employee have found new work?)

DEFINITION

An injunction is an equitable remedy, granted at the discretion of the court, ordering a person to do, or to desist from doing, some act as a remedy for a breach of duty (contractual or otherwise).

(ii)   jobseekers allowance received.

There is no set limit on the amount of damages. (Unlike unfair dismissal compensation, which is subject to a set maximum amount.)

The usual statutory periods of limitation relating to claims for breach of contract apply (six years – simple contract; 12 years – contract by deed) so that an employee wrongfully dismissed will not be restricted by the three month limitation period imposed in cases of unfair dismissal.

Claims are made to the County Court or High Court. However, if the employee is also suing for unfair dismissal, both claims can be heard in an Employment Tribunal.

2.5   Employee's breach and employer's remedies

If the employee is in breach, an employer has the following remedies:

- Dismiss the employee without notice if the breach is serious enough to justify treating the contract as discharged.

- If the employee wrongfully leaves without notice, sue them for breach. This is rarely pursued because the damages awarded would be so small (unless the employee is on a very high salary and a long period of notice).

- Bring action to recover any secret profit or other loss caused by the breach of duty.

- Seek an injunction – generally, this will not be awarded to prevent an employee from leaving. However, it is often used to enforce the duty of confidentiality.

Activity 1

An employee is discovered to be accepting commissions unknown to her employer. Could the employee be summarily dismissed and on what grounds?

Feedback to this activity is at the end of the chapter.

3   Unfair dismissal

3.1   General points

- This is a statutory claim made under the Employment Rights Act 1996.

- The claim is taken to the Employment Tribunal. Appeal, on a point of law only, lies to the Employment Appeal Tribunal, then to the Court of Appeal, and finally to the House of Lords.

- The claim does not depend on a breach of contract, so the remedy is not damages. The possible remedies for unfair dismissal are reinstatement, re-engagement and a monetary award.

- Only employees can claim, not independent contractors.

- Employees in excluded classes of employment cannot claim. (An example of relevance to the examination is employees who ordinarily work outside Great Britain.)

3.2   Upper age limit

The claimant must be, at the effective date of termination, under the normal retiring age. This is whatever it might be for the job except that, for redundancy, it cannot exceed 65. If there is no normal retiring age, or if it is different for men and women, the normal retiring age is deemed to be 65.

(From 1 October 2006, when the Employment Equality (Age) Regulations come into effect, employees will be able to bring an unfair dismissal claim after the normal retirement age.)

3.3 Qualifying period of employment

Ending with the effective date of termination, the employee must have been continuously employed for one year.

The following absences do not break continuity:

- **sickness** or injury (up to 26 weeks)

- **pregnancy** (up to 26 weeks)

- maternity leave under the right to return to work provisions.

3.4 Dismissal

KEY POINT

The employee must prove they have been dismissed.

The employee must prove they have been dismissed. Under the Employment Rights Act 1996, an employee is dismissed if:

- the contract is terminated by the employer with or without notice

- a fixed term contract expires and is not renewed

- the employee was constructively dismissed.

(a) **Resignation is not dismissal** (unless in circumstances amounting to constructive dismissal)

Morton Sundour Fabrics v Shaw (1966)

Facts: an employee was warned that it was likely that he would be made redundant at some unspecified future date. He then left (because he had found another job).

Held: he had not been dismissed.

However, if an employee had actually been given notice of dismissal and leaves before the expiry of the notice, this is still treated as a dismissal.

A difficult case showing the very narrow borderline between dismissal and resignation is:

Saunders v Neale (1974)

Facts: the employees went on strike and were warned by the employer that if they did not return they would be dismissed. The employer did not actually dismiss them, but when the strike was over the employer refused to take them back as there was no work for them because his business had disappeared during the strike.

Held: on the facts the employees had dismissed themselves, i.e. they had not been dismissed by the employer, they had resigned.

(b) **Termination by mutual consent is not dismissal**

(c) **Frustration is not dismissal**

3.5 Effective date of termination

The effective date of termination varies according to the manner of termination:

- In relation to an employee whose contract is terminated by notice, whether their employer's or their own, it means the date on which that notice expires.

- In the case of an employee whose contract is terminated without notice, it means the date on which the termination takes effect.

- In circumstances where a fixed term contract expires without being renewed, it will be the date on which that term expires.

If the circumstances are such that the statutory period of notice required under the ERA 1996, if given, would have expired later than the effective date of termination as defined above, that later date is treated as the effective date of termination for the purposes of computing the qualifying period of employment. For example, an employee who has been continuously employed for one week short of a year and who is then dismissed without notice will be deemed to have been given the statutory notice to which they would otherwise have been entitled, that is one week, and hence will have the protection of the unfair dismissal legislation.

A part of a week is deemed to be a full week.

3.6 Unfair dismissal – what must be proved

It is for the employee to show that they have been dismissed, but once this has been done, or if it is accepted by all parties that there was a dismissal, it is for the employer to show:

- what was the reason or, if more than one, the principal reason for the dismissal

- that this reason related to one or more of the statutory fair reasons.

3.7 What was the reason?

An employer can only rely on a given reason where they knew of it at the date of the dismissal.

Devis v Atkins (1977)

Facts: the employer dismissed the employee and afterwards discovered that the employee had been guilty of dishonesty.

Held: dishonesty was not the reason for the dismissal and therefore the employer could not rely on it in order to justify the dismissal as fair.

Note that the position is different in a wrongful dismissal action: the employer may rely on facts discovered at a later date to defend an action for wrongful dismissal.

3.8 The statutory fair reasons for dismissal

There are five reasons on which the employer may rely in order to justify the dismissal as fair:

- The **capabilities or qualifications** of the employee (i.e. the lack of them) for performing work of the kind they were employed to do. Capability is to be assessed by reference to skill, aptitude, health or any other physical or mental quality; and qualification means any relevant degree, diploma or other academic, technical or professional qualification.

- The **conduct** of the employee, for example:

  Stevenson v Golden Wonder Ltd (1977)

  Facts: a technical manager took part in an unprovoked assault on another employee at a company social function held outside working hours in the company canteen.

Held: this was a fair reason for the dismissal.

Any breach of the employee's contractual duties (express or implied) would also be misconduct.

- The fact that the employee was **redundant.** A person will be redundant if their dismissal was attributable wholly or mainly to the fact that

  - the employer has ceased (or intends to cease) to carry on the business for the purposes of which or in the place where the employee was employed

  - the requirements of that business for employees to carry out work of a particular kind, or in a place where they were so employed, have ceased or diminished or are expected to cease or diminish.

  Vaux and Associated Breweries v Ward (1969)

  Facts: a quiet public house was modernised by installing a discotheque. The 57-year-old barmaid was dismissed in order to make way for a younger more glamorous barmaid.

  Held: Mrs Ward had not been dismissed for redundancy as there was no change in the nature of the particular work being done.

- The fact that the employee could not continue to work in the position which they held without **contravention of** a duty or restriction imposed by or under **statute**.

- **Some other substantial reason** of a kind such as to justify the dismissal of an employee from the position that the employee held. The reason need only be one that can possibly justify dismissal, not one which in the court's opinion of the facts does justify it. There is an element of objective judgement, thus excluding mere personal motives. Examples of some other substantial reasons are as follows:

  - conduct of the employee away from the employment where this impinges on the employment relationship, for example:

    Singh v London County Bus Services

    An employee in a position of trust was convicted of a criminal offence of dishonesty (which he committed off duty).

  - the dismissed employee was recruited as a temporary replacement for an employee disabled through injury or illness or pregnancy, provided this temporary status was set out in writing on engagement.

  The Employment Rights Act 1996 specifically states that industrial action pressure or union pressure is not 'other substantial reason'.

3.9 Reasonableness of employer

Once the employee has shown that they were dismissed and the employer has shown that it was for one or more of the five fair reasons, it is then for the tribunal to decide whether the dismissal was fair or unfair.

The Employment Rights Act 1996 states that the determination of this question 'depends on whether in the circumstances (including the size and administrative resources of the employer's undertaking) the employer acted reasonably or unreasonably in treating the reason given as a sufficient reason for dismissing the employee; and that question shall be determined in accordance with equity and the substantial merits of the case'.

Case law shows that this reasonableness test involves two questions:

- Whether the reason given was sufficiently serious to justify dismissal. Thus it is unlikely to be reasonable to dismiss for a minor isolated act of misconduct.

- Whether the employer adopted reasonable procedures both in coming to the decision to dismiss and in the manner of the dismissal.

The Arbitration, Conciliation and Advisory Service (ACAS) has issued Codes of Practice for procedures to be followed in coming to the decision to dismiss an employee, e.g. warnings, proper inquiry into alleged misconduct, etc., which the Employment Tribunal has regard to. These were illustrated by the House of Lords in *Polkey v AE Dayton Services (1987)* where it was stated that:

- in a case of incapability, the employer will normally not act reasonably unless he gives the employee fair warning and an opportunity to mend his ways and show he can do the job;

- that in a case of misconduct, the employer will normally not act reasonably unless he investigates the complaint fully and fairly and hears whatever the employee wishes to say in his defence or in explanation or mitigation;

- in a case of redundancy (this was the situation in *Polkey*) the employer will normally not act reasonably unless he warns and consults any employees affected or their representative, adopts a fair basis upon which to select for redundancy and takes such steps as may be reasonable to avoid or minimise redundancy by redeployment within his own organisation.

The Standard Dismissal Procedure

Statutory dismissal and disciplinary procedures were introduced with effect from 1 October 2004. The provisions apply to all employers who wish to dismiss or take action against an employee, except where:

(i)   the parties are exempt from the statutory procedures
(ii) the employee resigns (constructive dismissal)
(iii) the employee's conduct is gross misconduct (where the modified procedure applies).

The Standard Dismissal Procedure consists of the following three steps:

(i)   The employer must set out in writing for the employee the nature of their conduct and the basis of the complaint.

(ii) The employer must invite the employee to a meeting to discuss the issue. The employee should take all reasonable steps to attend. After the meeting, the employer must tell the employee of any decision and offer a right of appeal.

(iii) If the employee wishes to appeal they must tell the employer, who should invite them to a meeting to discuss the appeal. The final decision must be communicated to the employee.

The modified procedure applies where there is gross misconduct on the part of the employee, which entitles the employer to dismiss without notice, or where the employment cannot continue for reasons other than the employee's conduct or capability. The modified procedure applies after the employer has dismissed the employee.

(i)   The employer must set out in writing the nature of the alleged misconduct/reason for dismissal, the evidence for it and the right of appeal and send it to the employee.

(ii)   If the employee wishes to appeal they must tell the employer, who should invite them to a meeting to discuss the appeal. The final decision must be communicated to the employee.

3.10 Inadmissible reasons

The Employment Rights Act 1996 sets out a number of reasons on which the employer is not allowed to rely in order to justify the dismissal as fair, for example:

- Dismissal in health and safety matters, which includes the dismissal of any employee because they raise health and safety matters or refuse to work because of lack of health and safety

- Dismissal on the grounds of pregnancy or childbirth

- Assertion of a statutory right.

If the dismissal is for any of these reasons, it is automatically unfair and the qualifying conditions do not have to be satisfied. In addition, the monetary awards are substantially higher than for other reasons.

3.11 Complaint of unfair dismissal

As a general rule, a complaint of unfair dismissal must be presented to the Employment Tribunal within three months from the effective date of termination or within such further period as the tribunal considers reasonable. However, the tribunal will not extend the period unless it is satisfied that it was not reasonably practicable for the complaint to be presented within the initial three months period.

4   Remedies for unfair dismissal

4.1   Reinstatement or re-engagement

If a complaint of unfair dismissal succeeds, the tribunal must explain to the complainant its powers to order reinstatement or re-engagement.

Reinstatement means resumption of work as though there had been no break and nullifies totally the effect of the dismissal.

Re-engagement means re-employment under a new contract of employment.

In exercising its discretion, the tribunal must first consider reinstatement and if it decides not to make an order to this effect, it must then consider re-engagement. In both cases, however, it should take into account:

- the wishes of the complainant

- whether it is practicable for the employer to comply with such an order

- whether it would be just having regard to the conduct of the complainant.

Very few reinstatement or re-engagement orders are made, principally because generally employees do not wish it.

4.2   Monetary award

Where the Tribunal does not make an order for reinstatement or re-engagement it must make a monetary award. Sometimes it will exercise its discretion to make a monetary award even though there is reinstatement or re-engagement.

DEFINITION

Reinstatement means resumption of work as though there had been no break and nullifies totally the effect of the dismissal.

DEFINITION

Re-engagement means re-employment under a new contract of employment.

The monetary award has three components: the basic award, the compensatory award, and the special, additional or higher award.

If an employee is guilty of misconduct, it may be that they will have no claim at all. However if, despite their misconduct, their dismissal is nevertheless unfair, for example as a result of the employer's failure to give a warning or to comply with the practical guidance given in the Code of Practice, their compensation may be reduced by 100%. In these circumstances, a tribunal is not entitled to take account of misconduct subsequent to the dismissal in deciding the fairness or reasonableness of the dismissal, but it is nevertheless entitled in assessing compensation to have regard to subsequently-discovered misconduct and, if it thinks fit, to award nominal or nil compensation on this basis.

4.3 Basic award

The basic award depends on the age of the employee, their weekly pay and the length of their continuous employment.

For each year of employment, where the employee is wholly over the age of 41	$1\frac{1}{2}$ week's pay
For each year of employment, where the employee is below the age of 41 but over the age of 22	1 week's pay
For each year of employment, where the employee is below the age of 22	$\frac{1}{2}$ week's pay

There is a maximum of 20 years and a maximum of £290 weekly pay.

The tribunal may reduce this amount:

- by any redundancy payment awarded by the tribunal

- if the employee has caused or contributed to his dismissal.

However, it is payable regardless of actual loss.

4.4 Compensatory award

The second part of the award is within the tribunal's discretion and is known as a compensatory award, which will be of such amount as is just and reasonable having regard to the employee's losses and expenses through dismissal up to a maximum of £58,400. In assessing compensation, the tribunal will take into account immediate loss of wages based on net figures, the manner of dismissal, future loss of wages, loss of protection in respect of unfair dismissal and loss of pension rights, and will then deduct:

- money received from the employer

- state benefits

- any failure to mitigate loss (in terms of weeks or months)

- damages received for wrongful dismissal.

4.5 Additional award

An additional award of up to £15,080 is made:

- where an employer ignores an order for reinstatement or re-engagement

- where the dismissal was unfair because of unlawful race or sex discrimination

- where the reason for the dismissal was an inadmissible one.

Summary

On completion of their studies, students should be able to:

- explain the distinction between unfair and wrongful dismissal

Self-test questions

Methods of termination of the employment contract

1   What is summary dismissal? (1.1)

2   What is the remedy available to an employee wrongfully dismissed? (1.6)

Breach of contract – wrongful dismissal at common law

3   What is constructive dismissal? (2.2)

Unfair dismissal

4   How long must an employee have worked in order to qualify for unfair dismissal? (3.3)

5   What are the five reasons set out in the Employment Rights Act 1996 for fair dismissal? (3.8)

Remedies for unfair dismissal

6   What is reinstatement? (4.1)

7   What is re-engagement? (4.1)

Practice question

A, B, C & D

You are a solicitor and have been approached by the following clients about various problems relating to employment law.

Adrian has been dismissed without notice after one month's service for being five minutes late twice in one week.

Charlene has been dismissed for raising the fact that she has not been given a Statement of Particulars by her employer after three months.

Dennis has been dismissed from his job at a theme park. The management have decided that the park needs a younger image and Dennis is 48 years old. The theme park are arguing that he is redundant.

(a)   Fill in the gaps and delete as appropriate.

Adrian has been *wrongfully/unfairly* dismissed. His remedy is ...., specifically he has been dismissed .... The .... sets out the minimum notice period Adrian can expect as *one week/one month*.

(5 marks)

(b)   Fill in the gaps and delete as appropriate.

Charlene's dismissal is .... under the ....
She can have her case tried at *County Court/Employment Tribunal*, her period of
service *is/is not* relevant and she will receive a *higher/nominal* award.   **(5 marks)**

(c)   Dennis *is/is not* redundant and the case of .... is authority for
this. This is because .... *(Your answer must not exceed 15 words.)*

(3 marks)

For the answer to this question, see the 'Answers' section at the end of the book.

Feedback to activity

Activity 1

The employee could be summarily dismissed on the grounds of breach of the duty of
good faith.

Chapter 14

EMPLOYMENT: HEALTH AND SAFETY

Syllabus content

The law of employment

- An outline of the main rules relating to health and safety at work, sanctions on employers for non-compliance, and remedies for employees

This chapter concentrates on the legislative provisions that are intended to ensure that workplaces are safe and free from risks to health. It primarily deals with provisions of the criminal law, but also reviews civil liability in tort and contract.

Contents

1   Introduction

2   Factories Act 1961

3   The Offices, Shops and Railway Premises Act 1963

4   Working Time Regulations 1998

5   Health and Safety at Work Act 1974

1 Introduction

1.1 Overview

Employers must ensure safe and healthy working conditions for their employees. If they do not do so, they may be in breach of a common law or statutory duty enabling employees to make a civil claim against them. Alternatively, they may be guilty of a criminal offence under a statutory provision or under the common law and be open to prosecution by the Health and Safety Executive.

1.2 Civil liability

If an employee has been injured at work, they may have an action against their employer for damages:

- in the law of contract for breach of the common law implied term to take reasonable care for the health and safety of their employees

- in the tort of negligence for breach of the common law duty of care or for breach of the Occupiers Liability Act 1957

- in tort for breach of statutory duty, e.g. under the Health and Safety at Work Act 1974.

All these civil actions for damages will be brought in the County Court or High Court (Queen's Bench Division) as appropriate.

Every employer is required to insure against liability to employees for personal injury arising in the course of employment – Employer's Liability (Compulsory Insurance) Act 1969.

Under the Employment Rights Act 1996, an employee who has complained about safety at work and is consequently victimised or dismissed may take action against their employer in the Employment Tribunal.

1.3 Criminal liability

An employer (and sometimes employees) may be prosecuted, and on conviction fined and/or imprisoned, for criminal offences created by:

- the common law, e.g. manslaughter

- legislation (see below).

2 Factories Act 1961

The Factories Act 1961 imposes a general duty on the occupier of a factory to ensure healthy and safe working conditions so far as is reasonably practicable. The general duty is supplemented by a number of specific provisions, e.g. regarding cleanliness, temperature, ventilation, lighting, sanitary and washing facilities.

3 The Offices, Shops And Railway Premises Act 1963

This Act makes provision for the safety, health and welfare of persons in all offices and shops and most railway buildings near the railway. Offices and shops that are only part of a building used for other purposes, e.g. an office in a school, are covered. The duties on the occupier are virtually the same as those under the Factories Act 1961.

4 Working Time Regulations 1998

The Working Time Regulations govern entitlement to the 48-hour maximum working week, rest breaks and paid holidays for most groups of workers.

5 Health and Safety at Work Act 1974

5.1 Introduction

The Act provides general statutory duties relating to all places of work. Regulations are made under the Act imposing detailed and specific duties to different workplaces.

The examiner requires students to appreciate the existence of the regulations under the Health and Safety at Work Act 1974, the fact that they create criminal offences and may be the basis of civil proceedings in tort for breach of statutory duty.

Students are not required to know the detail of any of the regulations. They are required, however, to have knowledge of the provisions of the Health and Safety at Work Act 1974 itself.

5.2 Health and safety provisions of the Health and Safety at Work Act 1974

Employers' duties

(a) **The general duty to employees**– every employer has a general duty to ensure the health, safety and welfare at work of all their employees **so far as is reasonably practicable.**

This responsibility includes, in particular:

(i) The provision and maintenance of plant and systems of work that are safe and without risk to health.

(ii) Arrangements for ensuring safety and absence of risks to health in connection with the use, handling, storage and transport of articles and substances.

(iii) The provision of such instruction, training and supervision as is necessary to ensure the health and safety at work of their employees.

(iv) As regards any place of work under the employer's control, the maintenance of it in a condition that is safe and without risks to health and the provision and maintenance of means of access to and exit from it that are safe and without such risks.

(v) The provision and maintenance of a working environment for their employees that is safe, without risks to health, and adequate as regards facilities and arrangements for their welfare at work.

Note that the duty is to make particular provision 'so far as is reasonably practicable'. The court takes into account the degree of risk against the sacrifice involved. If the sacrifice is disproportionately heavy then it is not reasonably practicable.

(b)   **Written statement of policy** – unless otherwise prescribed, an employer must prepare a written statement of their general policy on health and safety at work for their employees and the organisation and arrangements that are in force for carrying out that policy and bring it to the notice of their employees. The statement may be revised from time to time as appropriate.

(c)   **Consultation** – it is the duty of the employer to consult representatives of the employees with a view to the making and maintenance of arrangements that will enable them and their employees to co-operate effectively in promoting and developing the health and safety at work of the employees and in making sure that the measures are effective.

Under the Safety Representatives and Safety Committee Regulations 1977, a recognised trade union may appoint safety representatives to represent the employees in discussions with management, investigate potential hazards, accidents and complaints and the workplace generally. (Note that these representatives are allowed time off with pay to carry out their duties.) An employer must appoint a safety committee where safety representatives have been appointed and request such a committee. The committee, composed of employer's representatives, safety representatives and trade union representatives, then monitors the safety, etc. of the workplace.

(d)   **Duty to persons other than employees** – the employer (and anyone who is self-employed) has a duty to conduct their undertaking in such a way as to ensure, so far as is reasonably practicable, that persons not in their employment are not exposed to risks to their health or safety.

Duties on persons controlling business premises

(a)   Any such person (including employers) must take such measures, so far as is reasonably practicable, to ensure that all means of access thereto or egress therefrom and any plant or substance in the premises is safe and without risks to health.

(b)   Any such person must use the best practicable means for preventing pollution.

Duties on manufacturers, etc

Any person who designs, manufactures, imports or supplies any articles for use at work must ensure, so far as is reasonably practicable, that it will be safe and without risks to health.

Employees' duties

Every employee must:

•   take reasonable care for the health and safety of themselves and of other persons who may be affected by their acts or omissions at work

•   as regards any duty or requirement imposed on their employer or any other person or under any of the relevant statutory provisions, co-operate with them so far as is necessary to enable that duty or requirement to be performed or complied with.

Duty on every person

No person shall intentionally or recklessly interfere with or misuse anything provided in the interests of health or safety.

5.3 Enforcement of health and safety legislation

The Health and Safety at Work Act 1974 contains detailed provisions for enforcing, by use of criminal proceedings, all of the duties imposed by all health and safety legislation.

The Health and Safety Commission has the general duty of monitoring health and safety at work and of proposing new legislation on specific measures to the Secretary of State who will then make the appropriate regulations by Statutory Instrument.

The Health and Safety Commission also has an executive arm, called the Health and Safety Executive, which monitors the health and safety of particular workplaces. Health and Safety Executive Inspectors have wide investigative powers. Thus, they have power to enter premises and make examinations and investigations, take pictures or samples, and require people to give information. Where appropriate, they serve notices on the employer to ensure that they carry out their duties under the legislation. The two types of notice are:

- **Improvement notice** – an inspector may serve such a notice calling for the remedying of contraventions within a specified period. During the period specified in such a notice, work may be carried on, but if at the end of a specified period of time the remedial work has not been done, the inspector may prosecute or serve a prohibition notice.

- **Prohibition notice** – an inspector may serve notice which will prevent any activities at all being carried on, should an employer contravene the relevant statutory provisions and involve the risk of serious personal injury.

Health and Safety Executive Inspectors also have the duty of instituting criminal proceedings against any person who fails to discharge their legislative duties (including failure to comply with an improvement or prohibition notice). The sanctions include fines and imprisonment and, in the case of directors and managers of companies, disqualification. Health and Safety Executive Inspectors may also prosecute common law offences such as manslaughter.

Activity 1

X, an employee, deliberately removes a guard from a dangerous machine that he is operating. Has he committed a criminal offence, and if so, who will bring the prosecution?

Feedback to this activity is at the end of the chapter.

Summary

On completion of their studies, students should be able to:

- demonstrate an awareness of how employers and employees are affected by health and safety legislation, including the consequences of a failure to comply.

Self-test questions

Introduction

1   List the three possible civil actions that an employee who is injured at work may have against their employer. (1.2)

Health and Safety at Work Act 1974

2   List the general duties of employers under the Health and Safety at Work Act 1974. (5.2)

3   What is an improvement notice? (5.3)

4   Who prosecutes for breach of health and safety legislation? (5.3)

Feedback to activity

Activity 1

He commits a criminal offence under the Health and Safety at Work Act 1974: 'No person shall intentionally or recklessly interfere with anything provided in the interests of safety.'

The prosecuting authority will be the Health and Safety Executive.

Chapter 15

COMPANY ADMINISTRATION AND FINANCE: LEGAL PERSONS

Syllabus content

Company administration and finance

*   The essential characteristics of sole traderships/practitionerships, partnerships, companies limited by shares and corporate personality

This chapter is designed to introduce you to the concept of legal personality and to form an underpinning for the next four chapters on registered companies.

Contents

1   Natural and legal persons

2   Types of business organisation

1 Natural and legal persons

1.1 The concept of legal personality

A legal person is an entity that the law recognises as having rights and as being subject to duties. Because rights and duties can only be enforced by legal proceedings, an alternative definition is: an entity that can sue (to enforce its rights) and be sued (for the enforcement of its duties).

The law recognises two types of legal person:

- All human individuals are legal persons – natural legal persons.

- The law also recognises certain types of associations of people as artificial legal persons, such as corporations. These are associations formed in a formal manner, i.e. incorporated and which, once formed, become independent legal persons. Such an incorporated body, having legal personality, may sue and be sued in its corporate name. An example of a corporation is a limited company.

1.2 Natural legal persons

The legal personality of human beings begins at birth. On death, all the deceased's rights and liabilities pass automatically to their personal representatives who may then sue and be sued in their name and on their behalf.

Although every human being is a legal person, minors and insane persons have restricted personality.

1.3 Artificial legal persons: corporations

A corporation is an artificial legal person. As such, a corporation exists independently of the individuals who at any given time are the members of the corporate body.

There are three possible methods of incorporation:

- **By royal charter granted by the Crown** – a body to whom a charter has been granted is called a chartered corporation. Royal charters are usually reserved for bodies such as the British Broadcasting Corporation (BBC) and the Institute of Chartered Accountants in England and Wales (ICAEW).

- **By Act of Parliament** – a corporation incorporated by its own particular Act of Parliament is called a statutory company. Many of the state-owned companies, i.e. the nationalised industries, were statutory companies until privatisation.

- **By registration under the Companies Acts** – a company incorporated by registration under the Companies Acts is called a registered company.

1.4 Unincorporated associations

Examples of unincorporated groups are partnerships, trade unions and many members' clubs. These are simply associations that have no separate existence in law. The main points to note are:

- **Ownership of land** – as the association is not a legal person it cannot own land in its own name. Usually a trust will be set up and the association will appoint trustees to hold the land for the benefit of the association.

- **Contracts** – a member of a club or other unincorporated association who makes a contract is usually personally liable; other members (or usually a committee or trustees) are liable only if they authorised it or ratified it later.

- **Torts** – a member of an unincorporated association who commits a tort will be personally liable. A committee or trustees who appointed that person may be vicariously liable if they authorised the act.

A partnership is an unincorporated association but because of its special nature there are special laws dealing with it.

1.5 Partnerships

Partnership law is largely codified by the Partnership Act 1890. The Act governs the relationship between partners and outsiders (third parties). These provisions of the Act cannot be excluded or modified by agreement between the partners themselves. The Act also lays down rules governing the relations between the partners themselves, but these provisions can be varied by express agreement between the partners: for example, the Partnership Act states that all partners shall share equally in profits, but it is extremely common in practice for the partners to agree a different profit sharing arrangement.

Definition of a partnership

Section 1 of the Partnership Act 1890 states: Partnership is the relationship which subsists between persons carrying on a business in common with a view of profit. Business is defined to include every trade, occupation or profession. The Companies Act 1985 generally prohibits partnerships of more than 20 persons, requiring them to register as a company. Exceptionally, certain professional partnerships such as solicitors and accountants may have more than 20 partners.

If a relationship falls within the above definition, the persons involved are partners even if they did not really wish to be.

Since a partnership is a relationship, it is not a separate legal entity – it is nothing more than each and every individual partner. For convenience, a partnership may choose to operate under a name other than the names of the individual partners: such a name is called a partnership or firm name. In practice, a third party wishing to sue the partners will sue using the firm name as the name of the defendant, but the effect in law is as if they had sued each and every partner individually.

Liability in contract

If a partner, acting on behalf of the firm, makes a contract with the third party and it is one that either the other partners have authorised or, if they have not, it is one that would appear to the third party to be the usual way of carrying on the type of business carried on by the partnership then the effect, by Section 5 of the Partnership Act 1890, is that each and every partner is bound to the contract. The end result is that the third party may choose to sue any one, some, or indeed all of the partners on the contract. If, for example, the third party chooses to sue just one of the partners, that partner is liable for the full amount of the judgement (not just their share). Once they have paid that full amount to the third party, they may then claim a contribution from their co-partners.

Liability for torts

If a partner commits a tort while acting within the ordinary course of the business, they and every other partner could be sued by the third party.

Thus each and every partner is personally liable for everything done either actually or purportedly on behalf of the firm, and, because the partnership is not a separate legal entity with its own assets and property, every partner's personal assets, e.g. their house, is available to pay business debts due to third parties. It is this, the personal liability of partners, which is the most significant disadvantage of carrying on business through the means of a partnership and has led to the development of the limited liability company.

The Limited Partnerships Act 1907 introduced the concept of a limited partnership. Limited partnerships are however extremely rare in the UK because under the Act any partner who wishes to limit their liability must be a sleeping or dormant partner, taking no part in the management of the business and there must be at least one general partner whose liability is always unlimited.

2 Types of business organisation

2.1 Sole trader

An individual human person may carry on business on their own as a sole trader. A sole trader is sometimes called a sole proprietor. Since they are the business and therefore own the assets, they are liable for all the debts. This unlimited personal liability of the sole trader means that this form of business organisation is inappropriate for any business involving a degree of risk or a business on more than a very modest scale.

2.2 Partnership

Partnerships are suitable for small businesses involving a relationship of mutual trust and confidence. Because of the unlimited personal liability of each and every partner, the partnership is not suitable for businesses involving any degree of risk.

2.3 Registered company

Larger businesses, particularly those involving some degree of business risk, will choose to incorporate as a registered company. A registered company is a legal entity in its own right and although it will obviously act through human agents, those agents are not held personally responsible for their acts, which are regarded as being the acts of the corporation itself. Thus, for example a member (or shareholder) of a company cannot, as a general rule, be sued by third parties for the company's debts.

2.4 Limited Liability Partnership

The Limited Liability Partnerships Act 2000 created a new form of business organisation, known as a Limited Liability Partnership (LLP).

Characteristics of an LLP

- It is an artificial person with unlimited capacity. This means it can do anything that a natural person can do.

- It can enter into contracts in its own name. Each member of the LLP is an agent of the LLP.

- It can own its own property.

- It will continue in existence despite any changes in membership.

- The members will be liable to contribute to its assets if it is wound up. The extent of their liability will be set out in its internal regulations.

Incorporation of an LLP

(a) To form an LLP, there must be at least two persons who are associated for the purpose of carrying on a lawful business with a view to profit and who subscribe their names to a document called an 'incorporation document'.

(b) The incorporation document must be delivered to the Registrar of Companies.

(c) The incorporation document must set out:

(i) the name of the LLP and must end with limited liability partnership or llp or LLP

(ii) the country in which the registered office is to be located and its full postal address

(iii) the names and addresses of the members of the LLP.

(d) The Registrar will issue a certificate that the LLP is incorporated by the name stated in the incorporation document.

The main purpose of creating an LLP is to combine the flexibility of a partnership with limited liability for its members. Note also that:

• Members of an LLP are not required to enter into a formal agreement amongst themselves about the internal affairs of the business. If they do, there is no requirement to publish any such agreement.

• The profits of an LLP will be taxed as if the business was carried on as a partnership.

Summary

On completion of their studies, students should be able to:

• explain the essential characteristics of the different forms of business organisations and the implications of corporate personality

Self-test questions

Natural and legal persons

1 Define a legal person. (1.1)

2 State the three methods of incorporation. (1.3)

3 Define a partnership. (1.5)

Multiple-choice questions

Question 1

Midas and Croesus, two philanthropists, decide to work together to co-ordinate their giving to various worthy causes.

What is the legal nature of the relationship?

A   A partnership under the Partnership Act 1890

B   An unlimited private company

C   A corporation aggregate

D   An unincorporated association

Question 2

Which of the following is/are a legal person?

(i)   The Crown

(ii)   Mary White

(iii)   Pace Whitehouse (a firm of accountants)

(iv)   Accountancy Ltd

A   (ii) only

B   (ii), (iii) and (iv) only

C   (i), (ii) and (iv) only

D   (i), (ii), (iii) and (iv)

Question 3

Which of the following is/are a **natural** legal person?

(i)   The Crown

(ii)   Mary White

(iii)   Pace Whitehouse (a firm of accountants)

(iv)   Accountancy Ltd

A   (ii) only

B   (ii), (iii) and (iv) only

C   (i) and (iii) only

D   (i), (ii), (iii) and (iv)

For the answers to these questions, see the 'Answers' section at the end of the book.

Chapter 16

COMPANY ADMINISTRATION AND FINANCE: NATURE AND FUNCTION OF COMPANIES, COMPANY REGISTRATION

Syllabus content

Company administration and finance

- The essential characteristics of sole traderships/practitionerships, partnerships, companies limited by shares and corporate personality

- 'Lifting the corporate veil' both at common law and by statute

- The distinction between public and private companies

- The procedure for registering a company, the advantages of purchasing a company 'off the shelf', and the purpose and contents of the memorandum and articles of association

The aim of this chapter is to build an understanding of the company registered under the Companies Act 1985.

Contents

1 Introduction

1.1 Background to company law

The present legislation on company law is contained mainly in the Companies Act 1985. However, at the time of going to print, the Companies Bill 2006 is working its way through Parliament.

The Bill will result in major changes to the legislation on company law as it not only amends and restates many of the provisions of the Companies Act 1985, but also repeals approximately two thirds of the Act. The Bill also codifies certain provisions that are currently found only in case law.

Much of the current company law originates from a time when the majority of companies were large companies with many shareholders. Today the majority of companies are small private companies with narrow share ownership and much of the current law is therefore irrelevant to them. Those parts that are relevant, such as the various exemptions offered to private companies, are often hard to find as they are mixed into the provisions that are only relevant to public companies.

The structure of the new law is intended to reverse the format of the current legislation. It is aimed initially at small private companies, with the parts relevant to large companies and public companies shown as additional provisions.

The Companies Bill 2006 began life as the Company Law Reform Bill in 2005. It has undergone a lengthy journey through Parliament, undergoing many revisions, and is expected to receive Royal Assent in November 2006. Some of its provisions will take effect immediately, but the majority will come into effect on a date ordered by the Secretary of State or the Treasury, probably around April 2007. As this examination can be sat at any time of the year, students should check with CIMA to confirm whether the new legislation is examinable at their chosen examination date.

1.2 Company and partnership compared

The essential difference between a company and a partnership is that a company is a legal person separate from its members, whereas a partnership is merely two or more persons in a particular form of relationship with each other; a partnership or firm is a group of partners but not a separate legal entity.

Advantages and disadvantages of using a company or a partnership to carry on business will often derive from special factors such as taxation and limited liability. Other points of comparison to be considered are:

	Company	Partnership
(a)	A company must have a written constitution, i.e. the memorandum and articles of association.	There need not be a written partnership agreement, though it is usual.
(b)	A company is a separate legal person and so it (as distinct from its members) may: • own property • contract in its own name • sue/be sued in its own name.	A partnership is not a separate person and so it is the partners personally who: • own property • are party to contracts • are liable if sued.

(c)	Shares in a company are in principle transferable, although the right of transfer may be restricted.	A partner cannot transfer their status as partner to someone else without the consent of all the other partners.
(d)	There is no maximum number of members.	The maximum number of partners is 20. However, most professional partnerships are not subject to a maximum.
(e)	The members of the company are, as such, neither its managers (directors) nor its agents.	The partners are entitled to share in its management and are agents of the firm for carrying on its business in the usual way.
(f)	Capital subscribed by members for their shares cannot ordinarily be returned to them, but they are not liable for the company's debts.	Partners may withdraw capital but are still liable without limit for the firm's debts to its creditors.
(g)	Companies can borrow in the same way as individuals, but only for purposes covered by their objects. They can use current assets as security by creating floating charges in addition to creating fixed charges over fixed assets.	Partners have unrestricted powers of borrowing in terms of amount and purpose. They cannot create floating charges, but can mortgage fixed assets.
(h)	Both in their formation and in their subsequent trading and other activities, companies are subject to a number of statutory rules of procedure and supply of information available to the public.	Partnerships may be created informally and need not disclose any information to the public about their affairs.
(i)	The dissolution of a company usually entails a formal liquidation.	Partnerships can be dissolved by mere agreement of the partners, but the creditors have first claim on the assets and some general legal principles apply.

2 Types of registered company

2.1 Introduction

The Companies Act 1985 permits the registration of various types of company, as illustrated by the following diagram.

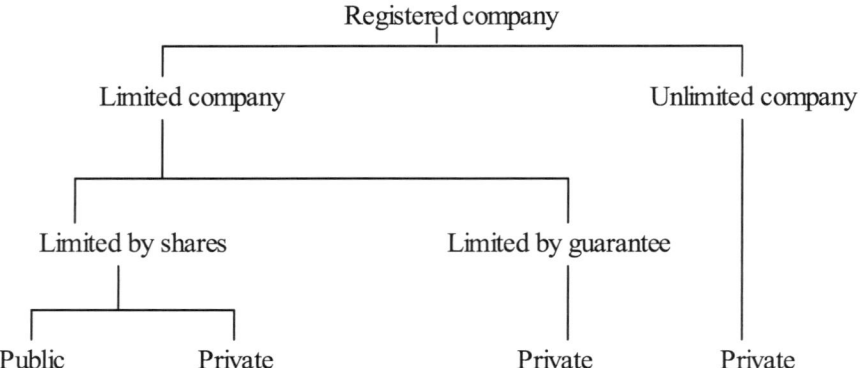

2.2 Companies limited by shares

In a case of a company limited by shares, the liability of a member to contribute to the company's assets is limited to the amount, if any, unpaid on their shares. Once the shares are fully paid there is, in general, no further liability, i.e. if the company becomes insolvent the shareholders are not required to make any further contribution to discharge its debts.

Companies of this type are the normal model used for business operations where there is a real risk of commercial loss. Limited liability is particularly useful where the shareholders leave the management of the company in the hands of its directors and have no immediate control over its financial situation and day to day transactions.

Companies limited by shares may be public or private.

2.3 Companies limited by guarantee

The member's liability is again limited, but to a sum that is agreed at the outset and which is recorded in the memorandum of association. If the company is wound up, the members will have to contribute the amount agreed.

In practice these companies are rare and tend to be used only for clubs and other non-profit making organisations, such as trade or research bodies. Such associations reckon to cover the cost of their services by charges or levies on those who use them and therefore have no need to raise share capital by the issuing of shares. They do, however, have the general advantage of corporate status and each member's guarantee is a form of reserve fund to be called upon in the case of crisis.

A guarantee company must be private unless it also has a share capital. In certain circumstances a company limited by guarantee may dispense with the word 'limited' at the end of its name.

2.4 Unlimited companies

In the case of an unlimited company, there is no limit on the liability of its members to contribute to its assets if it goes into liquidation.

Unlimited companies are not required to file their accounts at the Companies Registry (unless the company is in a group containing a limited company).

An unlimited company must be private.

2.5 Public companies and private companies

The Companies Act 1985 defines a public company as a company limited by shares (or limited by guarantee and having a share capital) being a company:

- the memorandum of which states that the company is to be a public company

- in relation to which the provisions of the Companies Act (as to the registration or re-registration of a company as a public company) have been complied with – in particular the requirement relating to a minimum authorised share capital of £50,000.

The Companies Act 1985 defines a private company as any company which is not a public company: thus private companies are the residual category of company.

A private company may be limited or unlimited, but a public company must be limited.

The differences between a private company and a public company include the following:

	Private Limited Company (Ltd)	Public Company (plc)
(a)	Can exist with one member	Must have at least two members
(b)	Can have a sole director	Must have at least two directors
(c)	No age limit for directors	Special procedure needed to appoint a director over 70
(d)	No compulsory qualification requirement for the Company Secretary	Company Secretary must be qualified, e.g. as an accountant or lawyer or chartered secretary
(e)	No minimum authorised share capital	Minimum authorised share capital of £50,000
(f)	Name must end with the word 'limited' (or the abbreviation 'Ltd' or the Welsh equivalent)	Name must end with the words 'public limited company' (or the abbreviation 'plc' or the Welsh equivalent)
(g)	No restriction on commencing business once a certificate of incorporation granted	Cannot commence business until it has received, in addition to the certificate of incorporation, a trading certificate
(h)	May not advertise its securities as being available for public subscription	May raise capital from the public subject to compliance with the prospectus requirements of the Financial Services Act 1986

		Private Limited Company (Ltd)	**Public Company (plc)**
(i)		No restriction on the type or amount of consideration receivable on the issue of shares	Many restrictions by the Companies Act 1985, e.g. the need for any non-cash consideration to be independently valued
(j)		The Companies Act 1985 rules regarding dividends, purchase and redemption of shares, loans to directors, etc. are less strict	The Companies Act 1985 applies stricter rules
(k)		Can dispense with some of the administrative requirements of the Companies Act 1985 by elective resolution (unanimous vote of members), e.g. can resolve not to hold Annual General Meetings	Elective regime not applicable
(l)		If small or medium-sized can file abbreviated accounts	Must always file full accounts

As stated above, a newly incorporated public company needs to obtain a trading certificate. As a pre-condition, the company must allot shares up to at least £50,000. Because of this necessary hiatus period (i.e. the company exists but cannot trade) it is rare in practice to incorporate as a public company. It is more common to incorporate initially as a private company and then at a later stage to re-register as public.

Private companies are very much more numerous than public companies although the financial resources of the latter are larger.

2.6 Public listed companies

A company that wishes its shares to be regarded as a medium for public investment must apply to the Stock Exchange for it to grant official listing for its securities.

The main advantage to the company of listing is that it facilitates the raising of new finance. This should be balanced against the following possible disadvantages:

- the cost and time of meeting additional disclosure requirements

- increased scrutiny by investors, the press and the public

- the likelihood that the company's management will be put under more pressure than before to pay dividends.

2.7 Small and medium-sized private limited companies

All private companies must as a general rule prepare annual accounts, have them audited, lay them before the members in a general meeting, send them to every member, and file their accounts with Companies House. However, the Companies Act 1985 provides filing modifications for certain small and medium-sized private limited companies.

A small company is defined as one that meets at least two of the following qualifying conditions:

- its turnover must not exceed £5.6 million

- its balance sheet total must not exceed £2.8 million

- its average number of employees must not exceed 50.

The corresponding conditions for a medium-sized company are:

- turnover must not exceed £22.8 million

- the balance sheet total must not exceed £11.4 million

- the average number of employees must not exceed 250.

A small company is required to file a modified form of its balance sheet together with the associated auditors' report, but no profit and loss account nor directors' report. An audit may also be dispensed with.

A medium-sized company is required to file its balance sheet, auditors' report and directors' report, but it may file a modified form of its profit and loss account.

All private companies (of whatever size) may, by elective resolution, dispense with the usual statutory requirement to lay the accounts before the members in a general meeting.

2.8 Single member private limited companies

The Companies (Single Member Private Limited Companies) Regulations 1992 (CSMPLCR) allows a private limited company to have only one member.

2.9 Welsh companies

A company is Welsh if its registered office is stated in its memorandum to be in Wales. If it is a private company it may use the word cyfyngedig (cyf) instead of limited (Ltd) in its name, and if a public company, the words cwmni cyfyngedig cyhoeddus (ccc) instead of public limited company (plc).

2.10 Overseas companies

A company incorporated outside Great Britain that establishes a place of business in Great Britain is called an overseas company. A place of business in this context includes a share transfer or share registration office. However, a company that only employs agents within Great Britain and has no office, has not established a place of business.

Such companies are, at least to some degree, regulated by UK company law. They must, for example, file accounts with the Registrar of Companies and must maintain an address within the jurisdiction where official communications, e.g. writs, can be sent.

2.11 Community Interest Companies

The Companies (Audit, Investigations and Community Enterprise) Act 2004 created a new type of company, the Community Interest Company (CIC), for those wishing to establish social enterprises.

The CIC is intended to be used primarily by non-profit-distributing enterprises providing benefit to a community, such as childcare, social housing, leisure and community transport.

To ensure that they use their assets and profits for the community interest, CICs will be restricted from distributing profits and assets to their members. This is known as an 'asset lock'.

3 Corporate personality

3.1 Salomon v Salomon

A company is a legal person, i.e. it is an entity in its own right – this is the doctrine of incorporation. Recognition that a company has legal personality independent of its members was established by the House of Lords in *Salomon v Salomon*.

Salomon v Salomon & Co Ltd (1897)

Facts: Mr Salomon had carried on a successful business as a sole trader. In 1892 he formed a company; in those days the minimum number of shareholders was seven and he had one share issued to himself, his wife and five of his children; his wife and children held their shares as his nominees. He then transferred his business to the company at a value of over £39,000. This price was in excess of the true value, but as Salomon owned the company no one was thereby defrauded. He took the price partly in 20,000 £1 shares, partly in cash withdrawn from the business in the course of transfer, and partly in a £10,000 debenture issued by the company and secured by a floating charge on its assets. The nature of a floating charge will be explained later in this text; the effect was that whoever held the debenture had a claim to the assets (to the extent of £10,000) in priority to the claims of any other creditor of the company. So Salomon became a secured creditor of his own one man company.

The business of the company did not prosper. Salomon pledged his debenture to one Broderip who lent him £5,000 in cash, which Salomon in turn paid over to the company. Eventually the company became insolvent; if the debenture were repaid in full there would be nothing left for the other creditors.

In the lawsuit which followed, the unsecured creditors advanced two main arguments:

- the sale transaction was a sham and so Salomon was still the owner of the business and liable for its debts

- the company was irregularly formed because six of the seven shareholders were mere nominees of Salomon.

Held: it was held that:

- the business was owned by and its debts were liabilities of the company, not of Salomon personally

- although Salomon owned beneficially all the issued shares of the company he (and Broderip as his successor) could also be a secured creditor with enforceable rights against the company in that capacity.

A rather more extreme example of the effect of the doctrine of incorporation arose in *Lee v Lee's Air Farming*.

Lee v Lee's Air Farming Ltd (1960)

Facts: This case concerned an aerial crop-spraying business. Mr Lee owned the majority of the shares (all but one) and was the sole working director of the company. He was killed while piloting the aircraft.

Held: Although he was the majority shareholder and sole working director of the company, he and the company were separate legal persons. Therefore he could also be classed as an employee, with rights against the company when killed in an accident in the course of his employment.

3.2 The veil of incorporation

The legal consequence of the doctrine of incorporation, namely that a company is a separate legal entity from its members, is expressed by saying that there is a veil of incorporation drawn down between the company and its members.

This legal separation and the concept of a company as an artificial entity means:

- **Perpetual succession** – a company is not dependent for its legal existence on the existence of members or directors: thus changes in membership (whether through death or otherwise) do not affect the legal existence of the company.

- **Ownership of property** – the company itself owns its own property, not the members or directors.

Macaura v Northern Life Assurance (1925)

Facts: M owned a forest. He formed a company in which he beneficially owned all the shares and sold his forest to it. He, however, continued to maintain an insurance policy on the forest in his own name. The forest was destroyed by fire. Could M claim on the policy?

Held: he could not since the property damaged belonged to the company, not him, and as shareholder he had no insurable interest in the forest.

This consequence of the doctrine of incorporation, that the property of the company belongs to the company and not the shareholders (nor directors) means that it is perfectly possible for members (and directors) to be convicted of theft from the company.

- **Limitation of liability** – since a company is itself legally the party to contracts it makes, it and it alone can be sued for breach of contract (or sue on a contract). It follows that members are not liable to creditors for the company's debts. Further a member is able to contract with the company (the contract is contained in the memorandum and articles) to limit their liability to contribute to the company's debts.

- **Separation of ownership and management** – because the company, as a commercial enterprise, is distinct from its members as proprietors it must have its own management in the form of a board of directors.

- **The company can sue and be sued in its own name** – the company as a legal person will sue if a wrong is done to it. Individual shareholders cannot generally sue in such circumstances and the decision as to whether the company will sue or not rests with the members collectively in a general meeting or with the board of directors.

- **Transfer of ownership** – where a company has issued shares, ownership of the company can be split or transferred without affecting the company. Many private companies restrict transferability of shares.

4 Lifting the veil of incorporation

4.1 Introduction

The principle that a company is a person separate from its members and also from the directors and others who manage it can produce unsatisfactory results in particular circumstances. Company law, therefore, recognises a number of exceptions to the principle. In those exceptional contexts, the company is treated as in some degree identified with its members or managers as if there were no distinction between them. Those exceptions are described as lifting the veil of incorporation.

Where the veil is lifted, the usual result is either that some other person is made to share liability for the company's debts or the assets, liabilities, profits and losses of the company are attributed to its shareholders.

4.2 Statutory examples

(a) **Minimum number of members** – if the number of members of a company (other than a private limited company) falls below two and this situation continues for six months, the remaining member, if they are aware of the situation, is liable (jointly and severally with the company) for the company's debts contracted after the six months. This is extremely rare.

Note: Private limited companies may have a single member.

(b) **Company name: s349 Companies Act 1985** – if any officer, e.g. a director or secretary, issues or signs, on behalf of the company, a bill of exchange or order for goods on which the company's name is incorrectly stated or is omitted, they are liable if the company itself defaults. The principle can be seen in the case of:

Penrose v Martyr (1858)

Facts: a company secretary 'accepted' a bill of exchange drawn on the company on which its name was incorrectly written. The company defaulted.

Held: the secretary was personally liable on the bill.

Minor spelling mistakes may not attract liability. In *Jenice v Dan (1993)* 'Primekeen Ltd' was written as 'Primkeen Ltd'.

(c) **Trading certificate** – where a public company trades or exercises borrowing powers before it has been issued with a 'trading certificate' the directors are jointly and severally liable to indemnify the other party in respect of any loss suffered by them as a result of the failure to obtain the certificate.

(d) **Group accounts** – if a group exists, a parent company must prepare group accounts consolidating the balance sheets and profit and loss accounts of it and its subsidiary undertakings.

Thus the veil is lifted between the individual entities within the group so that investors (and others) can judge the financial position of the group as a whole.

(e) **Fraudulent trading** – under s213 Insolvency Act 1986, if the court finds that the business of a company has been carried on with intent to defraud, it may declare any persons, e.g. directors, who were knowingly parties to the fraud liable for all or any debts and other liabilities of the company.

(f) **Wrongful trading** – under s214 Insolvency Act 1986, if in the winding up of an insolvent company a past or present director (or shadow director) knew or ought to have known, before the commencement of the winding up, that there was no reasonable prospect that the company could avoid insolvent liquidation, and failed to take every step to minimise the loss to the company's creditors, then the court may declare on the application of the liquidator that the person is liable to make such contribution as the court thinks fit.

Re Produce Marketing Consortium Ltd. (No. 2) (1989)

The company, after trading successfully for nine years, built up an overdraft, had a continuing trading loss and had an excess of liabilities over assets. In

February 1987 the directors recognised that liquidation was inevitable, but carried on trading until October 1987 arguing that this period of trading minimised loss to creditors while allowing an orderly disposal, for value, of the company's goods.

The court required them to contribute £75,000 to the assets of the company. It was held that:

- they should have known that liquidation was inevitable in July 1986 had the company produced timely internal accounts

- while trading on to dispose of assets was justifiable, the directors had done more than dispose of assets and so had failed to minimise losses.

4.3 Case law examples

(a) **Nationality** – in times of war it is illegal to trade with the enemy. It may be possible to lift the veil of incorporation so as to impute to a company the same nationality as its members.

Daimler v Continental Tyre & Rubber Co (1916)

Facts: the defendant, a UK incorporated company, was owned by five individuals and a company incorporated in Germany. Only one individual was British and he held one share.

Held: the claimants need not discharge the debt to the defendants since effective control of the latter was in enemy hands and hence to do so would be to trade with the enemy.

(b) **Mere facade (sham or puppet companies)** – the House of Lords stated that it is appropriate for the courts to lift the veil of incorporation only where special circumstances exist indicating that it is a mere facade concealing the true facts. This indicates the present reluctance of judges to lift the corporate veil.

Gilford Motor Co v Horne (1933)

Facts: a restraint of trade clause was binding on a former employee. He set up a company in an attempt to circumvent its provisions. He claimed that the company could not be bound by the restraint clause because it was a separate legal person from himself and not a party to the contract between himself and his former employer.

Held: the company was a sham and an injunction was granted against the former employee and the company.

(c) **Agency** – a source of difficulty has been in relation to groups where each company according to the doctrine of incorporation is a separate legal entity, i.e. there is a veil of incorporation between the companies.

However, there has been a number of cases where courts have been asked to lift the veil between the holding company and its various subsidiaries with the aim of benefiting the group by obtaining higher rates of compensation, e.g. on the compulsory purchase of premises.

The argument here is that the subsidiary is acting as an agent of its principal, the holding company.

Smith, Stone & Knight Ltd v Birmingham Corporation (1939)
Facts: SSK, a paper manufacturer, had a wholly controlled subsidiary, BW, which carried on a waste-paper dealing business operating from premises owned by SSK. On compulsory purchase of the premises the

court was asked to lift the veil between SSK and BW to enable BW to claim compensation as owner-occupier.

Held: the veil would be lifted on the basis that BW was running the waste-paper business as agent for SSK. The main fact that led the court to this conclusion was that SSK controlled the business on a day-to-day basis through its nominees (who were also directors of SSK) on BW's board.

Activity 1

For what reasons would the companies below have their veils of incorporation lifted?

(a)   Jim Brown, the company secretary of Lamplight Ltd orders some bulbs and signs the order form 'for and on behalf of Lighting plc'. The company later defaults on the order.

(b)   Sally is an accountant with Merger and Merger. Her contract of employment contains a restrictive covenant stating that when she leaves the firm she cannot induce her clients to move with her. Sally sets up Sal's Accounting Ltd and takes some of the clients, claiming that it is not she but her company that is dealing with the former clients.

(c)   Louise and Phil are the only two members of Harry plc. Phil sells all of his shares to Louise. Eight months later Harry plc enters into a contract with Exe Ltd.

Feedback to this activity is at the end of the chapter.

5   Company registration

5.1   Off-the-shelf companies

When a person has decided to incorporate their activities they can either form a new company or buy one 'off-the-shelf', i.e. buy an existing company. There are companies that specialise in forming companies, not intending the company to operate, which are then available for purchase; the share(s) are simply sold to the new owner and the director(s) and company secretary are changed from nominees of the person who registered the company to the new owner and their nominees. An off-the-shelf company costs £100 to £150 and for many small companies it is the preferred route to incorporation.

5.2   Registration documents

A person who wishes to form a company is required to deliver to the Registrar of Companies certain documents and to pay a fee. In practice, however, prior to submission of the requisite documentation they would check the proposed name against the index of existing company names to ensure that it is not the same as an existing name and, if the name contains a restricted word, obtain consent to its use from the body designated by the Secretary of State.

To form a company it is necessary to deliver to the Companies Registry the following documents:

*   **Memorandum of association** signed by at least two persons (one for a private limited company) called the subscribers and dated. The signatures of the subscribers must be witnessed by a third person. Each of the subscribers undertakes to subscribe for one or more shares of the company.

- **Articles of association** signed, dated and witnessed as for the memorandum (and by the same subscribers) or a statement that in lieu of special articles the company will adopt all or part of Table A.

- **Directors, secretary and registered office** (Form 10). The name, address and other particulars of the first directors and secretary, with their consent to act in that capacity, must be given on a form signed by the subscribers to the memorandum. The same form also gives the first address of the registered office. All these particulars take effect from the date of incorporation.

- **Declaration of compliance** (Form 12). This is a sworn declaration made either by a person who is named as a director or secretary of the company, or by a **solicitor** engaged in the formation of the company. The declaration is to the effect that the requirements of the Companies Act relating to formation have been complied with.

A registration fee is payable on presentation of the application.

5.3 Duties of the Registrar

On receiving the prescribed documents, it is the duty of the Registrar of Companies (acting through their staff) to examine the documents and satisfy themselves that:

- the relevant requirements of the Companies Act 1985 have been complied with

- the memorandum and articles of association do not infringe the Companies Act 1985

- the objects of the company set out in the memorandum are lawful

- the name of the company is not contrary to the provisions of the Companies Act 1985

- in the case of a public company, that the company's share capital as stated in its memorandum is not less that the authorised minimum.

5.4 Certificate of incorporation

If the Registrar is satisfied that the registration requirements and the above points have been complied with, they must issue a certificate of incorporation, which is conclusive evidence that:

- the relevant requirements of the Companies Act have been complied with

- the company is either a private or a public company as stated in the certificate.

The procedure between the delivery of the documents and the issue of the certificate usually takes about two weeks. On due notice in advance the Registrar will issue the certificate on a pre-selected date, such as 1 January, so that a company can be formed on a timetable basis.

The Registrar's certificate is conclusive evidence that the company has been validly incorporated on the date stated in the certificate.

Activity 2

If a trader was considering acquiring an 'off the shelf' company, as opposed to incorporating a new company, what are the likely advantages and disadvantages of this approach?

Feedback to this activity is at the end of the chapter.

5.5 Certificate of entitlement to do business

Although every company is in existence as a legal person as from its date of incorporation, a public company cannot do business or exercise any borrowing powers unless it has obtained from the Registrar a 'certificate of entitlement to do business' (more commonly called the trading certificate).

To obtain the trading certificate, the public company must deliver to the Registrar a statutory declaration in the prescribed form signed by a director or secretary stating:

- The nominal value of the company's allotted share capital is at least £50,000

- Each allotted share is paid up to at least one-quarter on the nominal value and the whole of any premium

- The preliminary expenses of the company and who has paid, or is to pay, them

- Any benefits given, or intended to be given, to promoters.

If a public company that does not have a trading certificate:

- does business or exercises borrowing powers, the company and any officer in default commit a crime punishable by a fine

- enters into a transaction with a third party, the directors are jointly and severally liable with the company to the third party on the transaction

- has been in existence for more than one year (whether or not it has done business or borrowed money), this is a ground for its winding up under s122 Insolvency Act 1986.

6 Promoters

6.1 Who is a promoter?

A promoter is a person who undertakes to form a company with reference to a given project and to set it going, and who takes the necessary steps to accomplish that purpose: *Twycross v Grant* (1877).

There is no statutory definition of a promoter. However, it is clear that a promoter will include those who raise the capital, appoint solicitors, directors etc. The promoters are usually also the first directors. The Companies Act 1985 does specifically exclude from the definition a person who acts merely in a professional capacity, e.g. a solicitor or accountant who advises on the law or accounting rules.

6.2 Promoters' duties

The law does not prohibit a promoter from making and retaining a profit from their promotion, but it does require them to disclose their profit from the promotion either:

- to a board of directors of the company independent of themselves

- to existing and intended shareholders.

The principle here is that a promoter, although they are neither trustee for nor agent of the company, stands in a fiduciary position in their dealings with it. This is a professional position of trust and competence. Under that principle, the company must be aware that it is buying the promoter's property or property in which they have an interest. If with that knowledge, imparted to shareholders or to an independent board of directors, the company completes the purchase it has by implication agreed that the promoter may obtain at its expense whatever benefit they may secure.

Summary

On completion of their studies, students should be able to:

- explain the differences between public and private companies and establishing a company by registration and purchasing 'off the shelf'

- explain the main advantages and disadvantages of carrying on business through the medium of a company limited by shares.

Self-test questions

Types of registered company

1   What are the two forms of limitation of liability? (2.1, 2.2 and 2.3)

2   Are the accounts of an unlimited company open for public inspection? (2.4)

Corporate personality

3   What is the ratio of the case of *Salomon v Salomon and Co Ltd*? (3.1)

4   What is the 'veil of incorporation'? (3.2)

Lifting the veil of incorporation

5   What is meant by 'lifting the veil'? (4.1)

Company registration

6   List the documents that must be forwarded to the Registrar in order to incorporate a company. (5.2)

7   On what date does a company legally come into existence? (5.4)

8   What type of newly incorporated company requires a trading certificate? (5.5)

Promoters

9   Define a promoter. (6.1)

Multiple-choice questions

Question 1

Which one of the following is not an example of an artificial legal person?

A   The chairman of a public company

B   A nationalised industry organised as a public corporation

C   A company limited by guarantee

D   A private company with only two shareholders

Question 2

Which of the following statements is/are true about a private company?

(i)   A private company is a company that does not qualify under the Companies Act to be a public company

(ii)   A private company is an incorporated business

(iii)   A private company is not required by law to file annual accounts at Companies House

(iv)   The shareholders of a private company cannot benefit from limited liability

A   (i) and (ii) only

B   (ii) and (iii) only

C   (i), (iii) and (iv) only

D   (i), (ii) and (iii) only

Question 3

Having decided to form a private company, on 1 April Mary and Kavita sent the required documents to the Registrar of Companies. Two weeks later, on 15 April, they received the certificate of incorporation dated 8 April. They were later informed that the company had been registered on 1 May. Which was the date of incorporation?

A   1 April

B   8 April

C   15 April

D   1 May

For the answers to these questions, see the 'Answers' section at the end of the book.

Practice question

Clipse Ltd

Walter is employed as managing director of Clipse Ltd, whose main object is to retail office equipment. His contract of employment contains a clause that states that in the event of his leaving the employment of Clipse Ltd he will not solicit their customers for a period of two years. He resigns his employment and together with his wife Jean forms a new company, Desks Ltd, whose main object is also retailing office equipment. Bill is a salesman employed by Desks Ltd. He is given customer lists by Walter and immediately begins soliciting Clipse Ltd's customers.

In order to raise cash for his new business, Walter enters into a contract to sell his house to Wilf for £50,000. Bill, who has always admired the house, approaches Walter and makes him an offer of £60,000. Walter transfers ownership of the house to Desks Ltd, and on behalf of the company enters into negotiations to sell the house to Bill.

Advise Clipse Ltd and Wilf on any action they can take.

For the answer to this question, see the 'Answers' section at the end of the book.

Feedback to activities

Activity 1

(a)   An officer has wrongly signed an order for goods as illustrated by the case of *Penrose v Martyr*.

(b)   Sal's Accounting Ltd will be regarded as a 'bubble' or 'puppet' company as in *Gilford Motor Co v Horne*.

(c)   The membership of the company has fallen to less than the statutory minimum of two for more than six months.

Activity 2

The principal advantages are as follows:

(a)   Speed – the company is already in existence. All that is required is to transfer existing shares to the new owners.

(b)   Cheapness – a single fee is paid to the formation agent. The constitutional documents have already been drafted, and there is no additional fee payable to the Registrar. Any necessary changes to the constitution can easily be organised.

The principal disadvantages:

(a)   The objects and articles of the company may not be entirely appropriate for the new owner (although use of s3A Companies Act 1985 and Table A are likely to make this less of a problem).

(b)   There is a requirement to ensure the change of share ownership and directors etc. is properly recorded.

Chapter 17

COMPANY ADMINISTRATION AND FINANCE: MEMORANDUM OF ASSOCIATION

Syllabus content

Company administration and finance

- The procedure for registering a company, the advantages of purchasing a company 'off-the-shelf', and the purpose and contents of the memorandum and articles of association

- Corporate capacity to contract

The memorandum of association is one of the two constitutional documents that a company must have (the other is the articles of association).

The most important clause is the objects clause. This sets out the type of business the company may engage in and therefore its capacity to make contracts.

Contents

1   The memorandum

2   The company name

3   Corporate capacity: pre-incorporation contracts

4   Corporate capacity: objects clause

1 The memorandum

1.1 Memorandum and articles of association

Every company is required to have a written constitution in the form of two documents. The memorandum of association defines the essential components of the structure of the company, partly for the information of those who do business with it. The second document is the articles of association (or Table A adopted in place of self generated articles) which is the code of internal regulations applicable to the company and its members in their dealings with each other.

The various clauses of the memorandum cannot be altered, except as specified by the Companies Act 1985 (CA85). The articles are, in principle, alterable by the members by special resolution but this general power is subject to some restrictions.

1.2 Contents of the memorandum

The mandatory clauses of the memorandum of a public company limited by shares state the following matters:

- the name of the company, which must end with the words 'public limited company' (plc) or the Welsh equivalent

- that the company is a public company

- the situation of the company's registered office

- the objects of the company

- that the liability of the members is limited

- the nominal amount of the authorised share capital (at least £50,000) divided into a specific number of shares of specific value

- after the main clauses of the memorandum comes a declaration of association, which must be signed by a minimum number of subscribers, i.e. two; they must each agree to take one or more shares – their signatures must be witnessed by a witness who signs as such; the date of signature must also be inserted.

The Secretary of State, by statutory instrument, has prescribed model forms for a company's memorandum. The model for a public company is Table F.

TABLE F

A PUBLIC COMPANY LIMITED BY SHARES

MEMORANDUM OF ASSOCIATION

1. The company's name is 'Western Electronics Public Limited Company'.

2. The company is to be a public company.

3. The company's registered office is to be situated in England and Wales.

4. The company's objects are the manufacture and development of such descriptions of electronic equipment, instruments and appliances as the company may from time to time determine, and the doing of all such other things as are incidental or conducive to the attainment of that object.

5.   The liability of the members is limited.

6.   The company's share capital is £5,000,000 divided into 5,000,000 shares of £1 each.

We, the subscribers of this memorandum of association, wish to be formed into a company pursuant to this memorandum; and we agree to take the number of shares shown opposite our respective names.

	Names and Addresses of Subscribers	Number of shares taken by each Subscriber
1.	James White, 12 Broadmead, Birmingham.	1
2.	Patrick Smith, 145A Huntley House, London Wall, London EC2.	1
		—
	Total shares taken	2
		—

Dated   XX-X-20XX

Witness to the above signatures,
Anne Brown, 13 Hute Street, London WC2.

Where the company is a private company limited by shares, the memorandum must be in a similar form, but there are four differences:

- the name of the company must end with the word 'limited' (Ltd) or the Welsh equivalent

- the second clause, i.e. that the company is public, is omitted

- there is no minimum share capital requirement

- the association (or subscription) clause needs only one subscriber – Companies (Single Member Private Limited Companies) Regulations 1992.

The model for a private company limited by shares is contained in Table B.

In the memorandum of a guarantee company, the amount that members may be required to contribute on a winding up to pay its debts must be stated.

1.3   Name clause

The name in the name clause of the memorandum is the legal corporate name of the company. There are restrictions on the use of any name other than the proper corporate name and change of name.

1.4   Public company clause

Only companies registered as public companies must include this clause in their memorandum. A public company may re-register as a private company if, *inter alia*, the company passes a special resolution altering the company's memorandum so that it no longer states that the company is to be a public company. Conversely, when a private company wishes to become a public company it must pass a special resolution altering the memorandum so as to include a statement that it is a public company.

1.5 Registered office clause

The next clause of the memorandum states that the registered office of the company is situated in England and Wales, or Wales, or in Scotland, as the case may be. This fixes the domicile and nationality of the company (but not its residence, e.g. for tax purposes, which can be in another country). The exact address is not given in this clause. This clause cannot be altered otherwise than by Act of Parliament.

1.6 Objects clause

The Companies Act 1985 requires the objects clause to set out expressly the business (or businesses) of the company.

The objects clause is intended to provide a measure of protection for investors in that they are aware of what type of business they are investing in.

1.7 Liability clause

In the case of a company limited by shares or by guarantee, the memorandum states that the liability of members is limited. As has been seen, this means limited to the unpaid part of their shares.

There is no liability clause in the memorandum of an unlimited company.

1.8 Capital clause

This clause of the memorandum of a company limited by shares must state:

- the total amount of the share capital that the company is authorised to issue

- how that amount is divided into shares of specified value, e.g. the share capital of the company is £100 divided into 100 shares of £1 nominal value each.

There may be more than one class of shares. It is possible, but not necessary or usual, to specify here the rights attached to, for example, preference shares. These are called class rights. Class rights are usually given in detail in the articles.

No minimum share capital is required for a private company, but a public company must have a minimum authorised share capital of at least £50,000.

The capital clause can be altered, if so authorised by the company's articles, for the following purposes:

- to increase the authorised capital

- to decrease authorised capital, i.e. to cancel shares that have not been issued

- to consolidate or sub-divide shares into different nominal values (the overall nominal amounts may not be altered)

- to convert fully paid shares into stock or vice versa.

The alteration must be done by the company in a general meeting. In the absence of an alternative majority specified in the company's articles, this will be by ordinary resolution (simple majority).

KEY POINT

No minimum share capital is required for a private company but a public company must have a minimum authorised share capital of at least £50,000.

1.9 Alteration of the memorandum

Only the registered office clause and the association and subscription clause cannot be altered in some way subject to special rules of procedure.

If, in addition to the compulsory clauses, the memorandum contains any other clause:

- If that clause is entrenched, i.e. expressed as unalterable, it cannot be altered by any act of the members of the company. For example, prohibition on payment of dividends may be entrenched in this way. If it is alterable only by a specified procedure, that procedure is obligatory and has precedence over the statutory rule.

- If the clause defines the rights of a class of shares and specifies a procedure for alteration (or refers to a procedure in the articles) the procedure must be followed. If no procedure is stated, it can only be altered by agreement of all members.

- If there is no restriction on alterations, the clause (unless it relates to share rights) can be altered in the same way and to the same extent as if it had been part of the articles, i.e. by special resolution. instead of the memorandum, but subject to the same procedure for objection by a 15% minority and appeal to the court as are given on an alteration of the objects clause, with the exception that debenture holders cannot apply for cancellation.

1.10 Companies Bill 2006

The Bill proposes the following changes to the formation of a company:

The Memorandum will become much shorter than at present. It will simply be evidence that one or more persons wish to form a company and, where applicable, that they will take at least one share each.

The declaration of compliance will be replaced by a statement of compliance. This may be made in paper or electronic form and need not be witnessed. It will be an offence to make a false statement of compliance.

If the company is to have a share capital, the application must contain a statement of the company's initial shareholdings and a statement of capital. This statement must contain:

- the total number of shares
- their aggregate nominal value
- particulars of the rights attached to each class, the total number of shares of that class and their aggregate nominal value
- the amount paid up on each share and the amount unpaid, if any.

2 The company name

2.1 Choice of name

The name in the memorandum of association is the company's legal name in which it will contract and sue and be sued.

A company shall not be registered under the Companies Act 1985 by a name:

- that includes otherwise than at the end of the name any of the following words and expressions limited, unlimited, or public limited company or their Welsh equivalents or abbreviations of any of those words or expressions

- that is the same as, or too like, a name appearing in the index of names, which the Registrar is required to keep

- the use of which by the company would in the opinion of the Secretary of State constitute a criminal offence

- that in the opinion of the Secretary of State is offensive.

2.2 Detail on this area

- **Final words** – a private company must have as the final word in its name 'Limited' or 'Ltd'; a public company must have as the final words in its name 'public limited company' or 'plc'.

It is an offence for a person who is not a public company to trade under a name that includes the words 'public limited company'. Similarly, a public company must not imply that it is a private company in circumstances in which the fact that it is a public company is likely to be material.

- **Name same as another** – the Registrar is required to keep an index of the names of existing companies, incorporated and unincorporated bodies and limited partnerships. It is this index that promoters of a company check against to ensure that the proposed name of the company they intend to form is not 'the same' as that of an existing company.

- **Illegal words** – a company shall not be registered by a name if, in the opinion of the Secretary of State, the use of the name by the company would be a criminal offence. Certain statutes have prohibited the use of certain words which are recognised as being associated with charitable or other organisations. Thus it is unlawful to use the words 'Boy Scouts', 'Girl Guides', 'Red Cross' or to represent oneself as a building society when not registered as such.

- **Consent of Secretary of State required** – consent of the Secretary of State is necessary to register with a name likely to give the impression that the company is connected in any way with the government or any local authority. In addition there is a long list of words that may only be used in company names with the consent of the Secretary of State or, in some cases, of a specified Department of State or public authority. Thus consent of the Secretary of State is required to use the words 'England', 'Ireland', 'Scotland', 'Wales', or 'Great Britain', 'British', 'Queen', 'International', 'European', 'association', 'chartered', 'council', 'society', 'group' and 'trust'.

2.3 The tort of passing off

Acceptance of a name by the Registrar of Companies does not relieve those concerned of liability under other branches of the law.

There is the risk of a passing off action by some other person on the ground that the company is, by the use of its name, leading the public to believe that the company's products are those of the person who makes the complaint i.e. that their business goodwill is being damaged. In a suitable case, the court may restrain the company from trading under its registered name and order that damages be paid to the person whose business has suffered loss. This is not an action under company law, but seeking redress for a civil wrong under the law of tort.

2.4 Change of name

By Secretary of State

- Where a company has been registered by a name that is the same as or, in the opinion of the Secretary of State, too like a name appearing or which should have appeared at the time of the registration in the index of names kept by the Registrar, the Secretary of State may within 12 months of that time, in writing, direct the company to change its name within such period as they may specify.

- The Secretary of State has an additional power within five years of registration to order an existing company to change its name on the grounds that the company presented misleading information for the purpose of being registered with a particular name.

- The Secretary of State may also direct a change of name if it is so misleading as to the nature of its activities as to cause harm to the public. There is no time limit within which the Secretary of State must act, but the company has a right to appeal to court. The name must then be changed within six weeks of the order of the Secretary of State.

In *Association of Certified Public Accountants of Britain v Secretary of State for Trade and Industry* (1997), the Secretary of State successfully petitioned the court for an order that the Association should change its name. The court ruled that the use of words such as 'certified accountant' in the company's name could mislead members of the public into thinking the association's members had a particular level of expertise, whereas membership of the association did not require any objective evidence of competence.

By the company

It happens more frequently that a company, of its own initiative, decides to change its existing name to some other. The company changes its name by passing a special resolution to that effect and presenting a signed copy of the resolution to the Companies Registry (with a fee). The change of name takes effect a few days later when the Registrar issues the certificate of change of name. They may refuse to do so and in that case the resolution has no legal effect.

A change of name by a company does not affect any rights or obligations of the company or render defective any legal proceedings by or against the company, and any legal proceedings that might have been continued or commenced against it under its former name may be continued or commenced against it under its new name.

2.5 Procedure for changing a company's name

The procedure is contained in s28 Companies Act 1985 :

- Call an Extraordinary General Meeting (EGM)

- Give those members who are entitled to attend and vote at the meeting a minimum of 21 days' notice that a special resolution to change the name is to be moved at the meeting

- Pass the special resolution (with a minimum of 75% of the votes that are cast being cast in favour)

- Send the special resolution and the new memorandum of association (containing the new name clause) to the Registrar of Companies within 15 days of the passing of the resolution

- The Registrar will issue a new certificate of incorporation containing the new name.

2.6 Business Names Act 1985

Providing that the company complies with the above rules, it is free within the provisions of the Business Names Act 1985 to adopt some other name (trade name) under which to carry on business.

Where the company is using a trade name it must:

- State in legible characters on all business letters, invoices and receipts issued in the course of the business and written demands for payments of debts arising in the course of the business its corporate name and an address for service of documents

- In any premises where the business is carried on and to which the customers of the business or suppliers of any goods or services to the business have access, display in a prominent position so that it may easily be read by such customers or suppliers a notice containing such name and address

- Provide its name and address for service immediately, in writing, to any person with whom anything is done or discussed in the course of the business and who asks for such.

Failure to comply with the provisions of the Business Names Act 1985 is an offence.

Activity 1

What, if any, objections are likely to be made to the following proposed company names?

(a) Ministry of Defence Suppliers plc

(b) The Ace Trading Company

(c) Whiplash Personal Services Ltd

(d) The International Trading Company Ltd

(e) The Small Trades Bank plc

(f) Smith Brothers Ltd

Feedback to this activity is at the end of the chapter.

2.7 Companies Bill 2006

Under the provisions of the Companies Bill 2006, a company can be ordered to change its name if an applicant can show that the name was chosen with the principal intention of seeking to obtain money from them or preventing them using the name where it is one in which they have previously acquired reputation or goodwill.

The current list of prohibited names is to be widened to include any name that suggests a connection with the Scottish administration, Her Majesty's Government in Northern Ireland or any public authority specified by regulations issued by the Secretary of State.

At present a company can only change its name by special resolution or following a direction by the Secretary of State. In future, a company will also be able to change its name by whatever means are provided in its articles.

These changes apply to an existing company changing its name as well as to the proposed name of a new company.

3 Corporate capacity: pre-incorporation contracts

3.1 Position at common law

A pre-incorporation contract is one made by a person on behalf of or purporting to be the company at a date prior to that on the company's certificate of incorporation,

A company cannot be bound by a contract that was made on its behalf by any person (including a promoter) before the company itself had been formed. At the time when the contract is made, the company is non-existent; it cannot after its formation ratify a contract to which it could not have been a party when the contract was made.

Kelner v Baxter (1866)

Facts: A, B and C entered into a contract with the claimant to purchase goods on behalf of the proposed Gravesend Royal Alexandra Hotel Co. The goods were supplied and used in the business. Shortly after incorporation the company collapsed.

Held: as the Hotel Co was not in existence when the contract was made it, was not bound by the contract and could not be sued for the price of the goods.

Kelner v Baxter shows that a company is not bound by a contract merely because it later performs it, e.g. by accepting the goods or services. The company will be liable if it makes a fresh contract after the company is formed; but there must be clear evidence that it intended to do so. Simply acting on the contract is not enough to establish the existence of a new contract.

3.2 S36C Companies Act 1985

S36C Companies Act 1985 provides that where a contract purports to be made by a company, or by a person as agent for a company, at a time when the company has not been formed, then subject to any agreement to the contrary the contract shall have effect as a contract entered into by the person purporting to act for the company or as agent for it and they shall be personally liable on the contract accordingly.

3.3 Possible solutions

There are a number of possible ways in which a promoter could get round the problem of the company being unable to enter into or ratify a pre-incorporation contract:

- The promoter could bring the negotiations to the point of agreement, but postpone any binding contract until the company is formed.

- The promoter could buy an 'off-the-shelf' company. Fully formed and legally constituted companies can be purchased on a 'ready-made' basis. This is the easiest solution.

- The promoter could agree that there will be no personal liability on their part once the company has been formed and taken over the obligations. S36C Companies Act 1985 appears to allow this as it does state that the promoter will be liable unless otherwise agreed.

- Purchase an 'option'. An option is a contract to keep an offer open to a specified person. Thus if, for example, the promoter wished to buy a factory/land for the company that cost £1 million, they would not wish to take on potential liability for that amount. However, the seller may be prepared to grant them an option, i.e. a promise that they will offer the factory to the company at the stated price as soon as it is formed. To bind the seller, the promoter will have to pay something for the option, but the price they pay will be considerably less than the full purchase price of the factory.

- The promoter could agree a term of the contract that either party may rescind if the company is not formed within a specified period of time. On rescission the parties will be restored to their pre-contractual positions.

- The promoter could include a term in the contract that states the company can, after its incorporation, enforce the contract.

Under the Contracts (Right of Third Parties) Act 1999, where a contractual term confers a benefit on the company and expressly identifies the company, the company can enforce it even if it does not exist at the time the contract is made.

3.4 Summary

Prior to the certificate of incorporation:

- the company does not legally exist

- the promoters are personally liable on all contracts entered into (even if in the name of the company)

- the company cannot ratify (formally adopt by way of an ordinary resolution of the members) a contract made before it is incorporated

- contracts are known as pre-incorporation contracts.

After the certificate of incorporation:

- the company is now a separate legal entity (it can form contracts in its own name, but cannot ratify pre-incorporation contracts)

- the promoters (usually) become the first directors and can now bind the company in contract

- the company may enter into a novation/assignment to contractually replace the pre-incorporation contract.

Activity 2

On 1 June a promoter acquires a mining lease. On 3 June they send off the incorporation documents to the Registrar. On 4 June they enter into a contract to acquire mining equipment for the company. The same day the registrar signs the certificate of incorporation for the 'Acme Mining Company plc'. The certificate is dated 5 June. On 8 June they sell the mining lease to the newly formed company at 100% profit.

Describe the status of the contracts entered into on 4 June and 8 June?

Feedback to this activity is at the end of the chapter.

4 Corporate capacity: objects clause

4.1 The *ultra vires* concept

DEFINITION

In company law '*ultra vires*' is used to describe transactions entered into by a company that are not within the capacity of the company as delimited expressly or impliedly by the company's objects clause.

The memorandum of association of every company must state the objects of the company. This requirement was intended to be satisfied by a short statement of the type of business that the company was formed to undertake. (See Table F in which the objects are set out very briefly.) However, modern practice is very different and the objects clause of most companies is at least two or three pages long with many sub-clauses.

The objects clause defines and limits the activities that the company is permitted to undertake. It defines the contractual parameters within which the company can contract.

Anything not authorised expressly or impliedly by the objects clause is *ultra vires* the company (the converse of *ultra vires* is *intra vires*). Literally, the words *ultra vires* mean 'beyond the powers'.

Ashbury Railway Carriage v Riche (1875)
Facts: the objects clause of the company set out the purpose of the company as the making and selling of railway carriages. The company entered into a contract to purchase a concession for constructing a railway.

Held: the contract was *ultra vires* and beyond the capacity of the company.

In addition to the matters set out expressly in the objects clause, a company has implied powers to do things incidental or consequential to carrying out the stated matters. For example, the implied powers of a trading company will include the power to borrow for the purpose of business, and to pledge its assets as security for loans. Other implied powers include powers to employ staff, pay wages, gratuities and pensions, to sell assets and to institute or defend legal proceedings. However, it is common for an objects clause to expressly list powers as well as objects.

Rolled Steel v British Steel Corporation (1985)

Facts: the objects clause contained a number of sub-clauses:

(A) To carry on business or businesses as exporters and importers of, and manufacturers of, and dealers in, and buying and selling agents for, iron, steel, copper, bronze, aluminium, lead, tin, zinc and other metal goods of all descriptions …

(K) To lend and advance money or give credit to such persons, firms or companies and on such terms as may seem expedient … and to give guarantees …

Held: clause A contained an object. Clause K contained two powers (to loan money, to give guarantees). Since the objects clause allowed guarantees, any guarantee was *intra vires* the company, albeit only a power and despite the fact that the particular guarantee resulted in no benefit to the company's actual business of steel retailing.

4.2 Alteration of the objects clause

In practice, a company that makes extensive changes in the nature of its business will be advised to bring its objects clause into line with the new situation by exercising the statutory power of alteration. A lender may stipulate that the borrower's objects clause shall be altered to the satisfaction of their advisers as a precondition of their loan.

The powers of alteration are of much practical importance and application where the inadequacy of the existing objects clause is realised before the transaction takes place, but alteration will not operate retrospectively to make an *ultra vires* transaction *intra vires*.

A company may, by special resolution, alter its objects clause.

- Objection to the alteration may be made by members holding at least 15% of the issued shares or of some class of shares or certain debentures, who did not vote in favour of the resolution.

- Any objection must be made by application to the court within 21 days of the passing of the resolution.

- The court has the power to confirm or cancel the proposed alteration or to impose a compromise. It might, for example, require the company to adopt some name suitable to its altered objects or to give security to debenture holders. In particular, the court is empowered to provide for the purchase by the company of members' shares and the consequent reduction of capital and can make the necessary alterations to the memorandum and articles.

The company must wait 21 days to see whether objection will be raised. It then has 15 days in which to file at the Companies Registry a copy of the memorandum as amended.

4.3 Effect of an *ultra vires* transaction

Introduction

At common law an *ultra vires* transaction is void. However, s35 Companies Act 1985 provides that an *ultra vires* transaction is not void simply for being *ultra vires*.

S35 Companies Act 1985: A company's capacity is not limited by its memorandum

The effect of s35 on *ultra vires* contracts is as follows:

- Once the contract has been made, neither the outsider nor the company may challenge it on the ground that it is *ultra vires*.

- The directors commit a breach of duty for which the company may sue them. The members could choose to relieve the directors from liability by special resolution.

- The company may, by special resolution, ratify an *ultra vires* transaction and thereby enforce it against a third party, even though the directors are committing a breach of duty.

- A member may obtain an injunction to prevent the directors from entering into an *ultra vires* transaction.

- If the third party to the *ultra vires* contract is a director of the company, it is voidable at the instance of the company.

Failure of the substratum

Where a company is not carrying on any business authorised by the objects clause, a member can petition the court for a winding up order on the grounds that as the substratum of the company has failed it is just and equitable to bring the company to an end: s122(g) Insolvency Act 1986 (IA86). This might provide a member with an alternative remedy to an injunction if a company is committing an *ultra vires* act that is evidence of failure of the substratum.

Re German Date Coffee Co (1882)

Facts: there was failure to carry out the object of making coffee from dates by means of a German patent (although the company did manufacture it with a Swedish patent).

Held: the company would be wound up.

This is most unlikely to occur nowadays given the width of objects clauses.

For a member to succeed under s122(g) Insolvency Act 1986 all the main objects of the company must have failed.

4.4 Format of an objects clause

A company may choose to state (often in very great detail) its objects and its powers or it may state that its object is to carry on business as a general commercial company. This means:

- the object of the company is to carry on any trade or business whatsoever

- the company has power to do all such things as are incidental or conducive to the carrying on of any trade or business by it.

Activity 3

Stephen is setting up a private limited company for the purpose of the repair, and retailing of tyres and all other associated activities. He has heard of the *ultra vires* doctrine and is concerned to draft the memorandum to ensure that any legal difficulties are kept to a minimum.

How would you advise him?

Feedback to this activity is at the end of the chapter.

4.5 Companies Bill 2006

Under the changes proposed in the Companies Bill 2006 it will be possible to form a company without an objects clause. Directors will therefore be able to commit any lawful act.

The directors of an existing company will continue to be bound by their company's objects clause, unless and until it is changed by the members.

Summary

On completion of their studies, students should be able to:

- explain the purpose and legal status of the memorandum and articles of association

- explain the ability of a company to contract.

Self-test questions

The memorandum

1   List the clauses that must be contained in the memorandum of a private limited company. (1.2)

2   List the clauses that must be contained in the memorandum of a public limited company. (1.2)

3   What type of resolution is normally necessary to increase authorised capital? (1.8)

The company name

4   How does a company change its name? (2.5)

Corporate capacity: pre-incorporation contracts

5   Who is liable for a pre-incorporation contract? (3.2)

Corporate capacity: objects clause

6   What is the meaning of the phrase *ultra vires*? (4.1)

7   How can a company alter its objects clause? (4.2)

8   What is the purpose of the objects clause and what is the effect of breaching it? (4.1 and 4.3)

9   What is the effect of a 'general commercial company clause'? (4.4)

Multiple-choice questions

Question 1

The capital clause in the memorandum of association of a company limited by shares sets out

A   The total amount of authorised capital

B   The total amount of authorised capital and its division into shares of fixed amount

C   The total amount of issued capital

D   The total amount of issued capital and its division into shares of fixed amount

Question 2

What is the minimum number of subscribers to a public limited company's memorandum of association?

A   1

B   2

C   7

D   20

Question 3

What type of resolution is required to be passed in order to alter the objects clause of a company's memorandum of association?

A   An extraordinary resolution

B   An ordinary resolution

C   An ordinary resolution with special notice

D   A special resolution

For the answers to these questions, see the 'Answers' section at the end of the book.

Practice question

Question 1: Plum Pie Ltd

(a)   The directors of Plum Pie Ltd wish to change the name of the company to Apple Pie Ltd.

What procedure should they adopt, and what requirements must be satisfied?

(b)   Bubble Ltd wishes to trade as South Birmingham Pigeon Breeders.

What requirements must be satisfied?

(c)   Don plc has as its main object the business of travel agents, but there are subsidiary objects, including one that authorises the company 'to borrow money' and another that permits the company 'to carry on any business which the directors consider to be profitable'. The travel agency has closed and the directors have now approached Money Bank for a loan to build a factory for the manufacture of shoes. Discuss the position of the bank.

(d)   How, and to what extent, may a company alter its objects clause, and what are the rights of a shareholder who disagrees with an alteration?

Question 2: ABC Ltd and XYZ plc

ABC Ltd and XYZ plc were both formed on the same day, each with two directors and £100,000 nominal value of issued share capital.

Required:

(a)   Delete as appropriate and fill in the gaps.

Both companies *do/do not* require the value of issued share capital to be £100,000. *ABC Ltd/XYZ plc/Both companies* must have a minimum of ………………………. to be incorporated.
………………………. needs at least one director and a ………………………….

who *must/need not* be qualified.   **(5 marks)**

(b)   Delete as appropriate and fill in the gaps.

ABC Ltd/XYZ plc also requires a …………………………. before it can commence trading or borrow. To do so before this is issued would have the following consequences:

(i)

(ii)

(iii)

(iv)

(7 marks)

(c)   The memorandum of association filed by ABC Ltd will contain certain clauses, for example:

(i)

(ii)

(iii)

(iv)

(4 marks)

(Total: 16 marks)

For the answers to these questions, see the 'Answers' section at the end of the book.

Feedback to activities

Activity 1

(a)   Permission would be required for this name as it suggests a connection with government.

(b)   There is no apparent reason why the word 'limited' is not in the name.

(c)   This is likely to be perceived as an offensive name.

(d)   The word 'International' is included in the list of words for which permission is required.

(e)   Calling a company a bank, unless it is one as defined by the Banking Acts, is an offence.

(f)   There may be a problem if an existing company has a name similar or the same as this.

Activity 2

(a)   Contract 4 June.

This is a pre-incorporation contract. It is dated prior to the date on the certificate of incorporation of the company.

However, it is a valid contract. It is just that it is not enforceable by or against the company. If the supplier failed to provide the equipment, the company, as a third party, would not be successful in any action against the supplier.

It would make no difference that the company had ratified the contract.

(b)   Contract 8 June

On the facts given it would appear that the promoter has made a profit out of the promotion of the company without disclosing the fact to the shareholders or the board of directors. This is a breach of fiduciary duty.

The contract is therefore a voidable contract, which can be rescinded by the company, as long as the company does not delay and can restore the mining lease to the supplier in the same condition, it will recover any monies paid out.

Activity 3

The doctrine of *ultra vires* means that any transactions entered into that are not permitted by the company's objects clause are in principle void. These days the effect on a third party, or even the company, has been largely nullified by the Companies Acts.

However, acting *ultra vires* is a breach of the director's duty to manage the company in accordance with the constitution.

Stephen should therefore be advised to register with the object of carrying on business as a 'general commercial company', which allows it to carry on any trade or business whatsoever.

Chapter 18

COMPANY ADMINISTRATION AND FINANCE: ARTICLES OF ASSOCIATION

Syllabus content

Company administration and finance

- The procedure for registering a company, the advantages of purchasing a company 'off-the-shelf', and the purpose and contents of the memorandum and articles of association

The articles are one of the two critical documents of incorporation and are examined on a fairly regular basis.

Contents

1 Table A

Table A is a model or standard set of articles laid down in the Companies Acts.

A company limited by shares may either have its own special articles or, alternatively, it can adopt or allow Table A to apply wholly or in part.

There are the following alternatives:

- a company may have its own articles and expressly exclude Table A from applying

- a company may expressly adopt Table A with or without alterations and exclusions

- in any other case, Table A applies to the extent that any articles of the company fail to provide for matters covered by Table A.

Note that a company is governed by the Table A in force when it was registered, not necessarily the current version.

2 Form of articles

If a company has its own articles they must be:

- printed

- divided into paragraphs and numbered consecutively

- signed (if they are the original articles delivered to form the company) by each subscriber to the memorandum whose signature on the articles must also be dated and witnessed.

3 Legal effect of articles

3.1 The articles as a contract

The memorandum and articles, when registered, bind the company and its members as if they have been executed under seal by the members and the members had agreed to observe them .

The articles are in all respects enforceable by the company against its members.

Hickman v Kent or Romney Marsh Sheepbreeders Association (1920)

Facts: the company's articles included a clause to the effect that all disputes between the company and its members were to be referred to arbitration. A member brought court proceedings against the company.

Held: the proceedings were stayed. The company could enforce the arbitration clause against a member.

The articles are enforceable by the shareholders against the company.

Pender v Lushington (1877)

Facts: the articles provided for one vote per ten shares, with no member to have more than 100 votes. A member with more than 1,000 shares transferred the surplus to a nominee and directed him how to vote. The chairman refused to accept the nominee's votes.

Held: the right to vote was enforceable against the company.

However, the contract is enforceable only when it relates to matters arising between the company and its members as members.

Eley v Positive Government Security Life Assurance (1876)

Facts: the articles provided that Eley should be solicitor to the company.

Held: this was not a right given to him as a member and he could not rely on the articles as a contract for professional services.

The right to be a director of a company has also been held to be an outsider right.

Rayfield v Hands (1960)

Facts: the articles required the directors to be members, i.e. to hold qualification shares and to purchase shares from any member who wished to sell.

Held: this was enforceable against the directors in their capacity as members.

S14 Companies Act 1985 states that the articles of association form a contract between company and members, and members between themselves, even if they do not in fact sign the articles.

They are contractually binding and the individual articles are the terms of the contract. However, the articles have no effect as a contract between the company and a person who is not a member, even if they are named in the articles and given apparent rights against the company. In *Eley's* case above, Eley's membership was irrelevant to his claim; as solicitor he had no claim – he was attempting to enforce a non-member's right.

Activity 1

State whether the following provisions in the articles would be enforceable under s14 in each situation.

(a) Member's right to vote

(b) Member's right to attend general meetings

(c) Pre-emption rights in favour of existing shareholders on a proposed transfer of shares

(d) Member's right to receive a dividend

(e) An arbitration clause against the company by a director/shareholder being sued by the company for breach of director's duty

(f) An article requiring directors to purchase the shares of a member who wishes to sell

Feedback to this activity is at the end of the chapter.

4 Alteration of articles

4.1 Procedure and restrictions

A company has a general power to alter its articles by passing a special resolution. This general power, however, is subject to overriding restrictions as follows:

- The alteration must neither conflict with the memorandum nor with the Companies Act or other relevant laws.

- The number of shares that a member is bound to subscribe for (and the amount payable on their shares) may not be increased without their consent. Any rights of a class of shares may only be altered in accordance with the relevant rules and procedure contained in the memorandum or articles.

- The alteration may not override an order of the court.

- The alteration must be for the benefit of the company.

- No contract extraneous to the articles can prevent a company from altering its articles but the company is liable for damages if, in altering the articles, it commits a breach of any such contract.

4.2 Alteration for the benefit of the company

When there is a conflict between members over a proposed alteration, the question that may arise is whether the majority are seeking an unfair advantage for themselves or merely exercising their right as a majority to make changes for the benefit of the company, even if a minority thereby loses some advantage.

The general test of validity is whether the alteration is proposed in good faith for the benefit of the company as a whole. This test includes two elements (good faith and benefit) but it is a single principle:

Greenhalgh v Arderne Cinemas (1950)

Facts: the issue was the removal from the articles of the members' right of first refusal of any shares that a member might wish to transfer; the majority wished to make the change in order to admit an outsider to membership, in the interests of the company.

Held: the benefit to the company as a whole was held to be a benefit that any individual hypothetical member of the company could enjoy directly or through the company and not merely a benefit to the majority of members only. The test of good faith did not require proof of actual benefit, but merely the honest belief on reasonable grounds that benefit could follow from the alteration. In several cases the court has held that actual and foreseen detriment to a minority affected by the alteration was not in itself a sufficient ground of objection if the benefit to the company test was satisfied.

An alteration to remove a fraudulent director has been upheld.

Shuttleworth v Cox (1927)

Facts: the purpose of the alteration was to remove from office a director who had repeatedly failed to account to the company for money in his hands.

Held: the alteration was valid.

Alteration to remove members by enforcing a transfer of their shares will not be upheld unless restricted to cases where there is clear benefit to the company and compensation is payable.

Sidebottom v Kershaw Leese & Co (1920)

Facts: the alteration was to expel a member who carried on a business in competition with the company.

Held: it was a valid alteration.

Effectively, only an alteration to forfeit shares without compensation is likely to be struck down under this requirement.

An alteration, which is otherwise valid, may be made with retrospective effect.

Allen v Gold Reefs of West Africa (1900)

Facts: Z held fully paid up and partly paid up shares in the company. The company's articles provided for a lien for all debts and liabilities of any member upon all partly paid shares held by the member. The company by special resolution altered its articles so that the lien was available on fully paid up shares as well.

Held: that the company had the power to alter its articles by extending the lien to fully paid shares.

However, it cannot deprive members or directors of accrued rights, e.g. to dividend or to remuneration.

4.3 Breach of contract

If the proposed alteration of the articles (or of the memorandum) will put the company in breach of another contract, the company cannot by injunction be restrained by the other party to the contract from exercising its statutory power to alter its articles, but the other party may sue for damages for breach of contract.

Southern Foundries v Shirlaw (1940)

Facts: alteration of the articles to empower the holding company to remove the managing director of the subsidiary from his office of director. He thereby ceased to be managing director in breach of the company's contract to employ him in that capacity.

Held: the alteration was valid, but the company was in breach of the service contract and liable for damages.

4.4 Summary

Articles can always be altered by special resolution of the members of the company in a general meeting.

This is subject to the following limitations that an alteration of the articles:

- cannot conflict with the memorandum

- cannot conflict with company law

- cannot be illegal

- cannot alter class rights

- cannot override an order of the Court, and

- cannot be otherwise than for the best interests of the company.

5 Companies Bill 2006

In future, all of a company's key internal rules will be set out in the articles.

The Secretary of State will prescribe draft model articles for each type of company. However, at the time of going to print, only the draft model articles for private companies had been published. The model articles are intended to be user-friendly and are therefore written in plain English. They are extremely short in comparison with the current model articles; this is partly because some of the regulations have been moved into the primary legislation.

5.1 Proposed changes

The draft model articles for private companies make a number of changes to the current version of Table A, including the following:

- It will be possible for board decisions to be taken following exchanges of emails on different days. (At present, all participating directors must be able to hear each other and speak to each other at all times. This means that a conference telephone call is the minimum requirement.)
- A director who is or may be suffering from a mental disorder no longer automatically ceases to be a director.
- An undischarged bankrupt cannot be a company director, but a person who makes an arrangement or composition with his creditors can be a director unless the articles prevent it.
- There is nothing in the draft model articles to prevent directors paying both interim and final dividends without the approval of the shareholders.

5.2 Adoption and entrenchment

On incorporation, companies will be free to adopt, modify or exclude the appropriate set of model articles. It will normally be possible to alter the articles by special resolution. However, some or all of the articles could be entrenched. Entrenchment can only occur at the time the company is formed, or subsequently if all the members agree, and will make it impossible to alter the articles unless more rigorous requirements are met. Companies House must be notified when articles are entrenched and when entrenchments are removed.

5.3 Existing companies

Companies already in existence will continue to be bound by their existing memorandum and articles. However, they may (by special resolution) choose to change their memorandum and articles to adopt some or all of the new provisions.

Summary

On completion of their studies, students should be able to:

- explain the purpose and legal status of the memorandum and articles of association

Self-test questions

Table A

1   What are the three alternative ways for a company to devise the articles? (1)

Legal effect of articles

2   What is the legal effect of the articles? (3.1)

3   Why could the members enforce the articles in Pender v Lushington but not in Eley's case? (3.1)

Alteration of articles

4   How do you alter the articles? (4.1)

5   What is the principal case law test of whether the alteration is valid? (4.2)

6   Can an alteration of articles have retrospective effect? (4.2)

7   Can the existence of a separate contractual obligation prevent an alteration of the article? (4.3)

Multiple-choice questions

Question 1

Which one of the following statements is correct?

A   The articles of association set out the external regulations governing the conduct of the company

B   The articles of association is the only document submitted to the Registrar of Companies in the process of company formation

C   The articles of association give details of the director's powers and shareholders' voting rights

D   The articles of association must state the company's name and the objects for which the company is formed

Question 2

The provisions of Table A apply automatically unless excluded or modified by the articles of association in the case of:

A   Private companies limited by shares only

B   Public companies limited by shares only

C   All companies limited by shares

D   All limited companies

For the answers to these questions, see the 'Answers' section at the end of the book.

Practice questions

Question 1: Aire Ltd

The articles of association of Aire Ltd provide that Donald and Charles are to be employed as sales manager and accountant respectively at salaries of not less than £10,000 pa until they attain the age of 65 years. They have both been so employed for many years and are now in their late fifties.

(a)   Advise Donald who has received notice from the company purporting to discharge him. He does not wish to leave.

(b)   Advise Charles who has offered his resignation, which has been rejected by the company.

Question 2: Beta Ltd

John has for several years asked numerous awkward questions at the annual general meetings of Beta Ltd and has become very unpopular with the board. One of the directors has suggested that the articles of association be altered to enable a majority of the members of the company to buy out John's shareholding at a fair value as certified by the company's auditor.

What principles would be applied by the court in deciding whether such an alteration was valid?

Feedback to activities

Activity 1

(a)   Yes – *Pender v Lushington.*

(b)   Yes – this is a right given to a member in that capacity.

(c)   S14 has been interpreted to allow the enforcement of pre-emption rights on transfer by member against members.

(d)   Yes – this is the same as (a) and (b).

(e)   No – the director would be seeking to enforce the clause in his capacity as director not member. See *Eley v Positive Government Security Life Assurance.*

(f)   It depends on whether the articles require the directors to be shareholders as well. See *Rayfield v Hands*.

Chapter 19

COMPANY ADMINISTRATION AND FINANCE: MEETINGS

Syllabus content

Company administration and finance

- Board meetings: when used and the procedure at the meeting

- Annual and extraordinary general meetings: when used and the procedure at the meeting including company resolutions and the uses of each type of resolution

It is important to understand the main procedures at board meetings and general meetings in order to be able to advise shareholders how to exercise their rights as shareholders. Knowledge of the different types of resolutions affects all areas of company law.

Contents

1   Board meetings

2   General meetings

3   Calling a meeting

4   Conduct of meetings

5   Companies Bill 2006

1 Board meetings

1.1 Procedure for calling the meeting

There are very limited rules for the calling and conduct of board meetings. Unless the articles otherwise provide, any director may call a board meeting.

The meeting must be called at a reasonable time and place.

No minimum period of notice is required.

The notice need not state the business to be transacted at the meeting.

1.2 Procedure at the meeting

The board meeting may expressly or by custom establish a quorum, i.e. the minimum number of persons required to be present.

If no quorum is fixed, Table A provides a quorum of two.

The board has the power to appoint a chairman. Table A gives the chairman a casting vote.

Unless the articles otherwise provide, each director present has one vote. A resolution is carried where a majority of votes are cast in its favour.

1.3 Minutes

Minutes of board meetings must be kept. If signed by the chairman, the minutes are *prima facie* evidence of the proceedings.

Directors have the right to inspect the minutes of meetings.

2 General meetings

2.1 The importance of rules about meetings

The ultimate control of the company rests with its members in a general meeting. There are, therefore, rules to ensure that there is at least one meeting in every year and that additional meetings be called when required and must be called on the requisition of a sufficient number of members. Adequate notice must be given to members of any meeting that is to be held and minimum attendance (the quorum) is required to transact business. The conduct of meetings is regulated both by general law and by special rules on company meetings.

Decisions at meetings are taken by majority vote on resolutions. For some decisions a 75% majority is required of the votes cast.

2.2 Types of meeting

The two important types of general meeting are the annual general meeting (AGM) and extraordinary general meeting (EGM).

As a rule, a general meeting is one in which all shareholders may take part and which decides on matters binding the whole membership.

Class meetings may be held by particular classes of shareholder and decide matters relating to that particular class, e.g. for a variation of class rights: the rules of procedure are much the same as those of general meetings.

There may also be class meetings of debenture-holders or other creditors.

2.3 Annual General Meetings (AGMs)

(a)   Every company must hold a first AGM within 18 months of incorporation and thereafter no more than 15 months apart and once in every calendar year.

(b)   If the company fails to hold an AGM within the prescribed time the Department of Trade and Industry, on the application of any member, may order it to be held. The Department of Trade and Industry can give directions for holding the meeting and may fix the quorum at one member only.

(c)   The following business is usually transacted at an AGM:

   (i)   consideration of accounts and reports of directors and auditors

   (ii)   declaration of a dividend

   (iii)   election of directors in place of those retiring

   (iv)   appointment of auditors and fixing their remuneration.

Table A does not prescribe the business to be conducted at an AGM. Accordingly, full details of the business have to be set out in the notice convening the meeting. Some companies' articles, however, set out the above as 'ordinary' business with the intention that full details are not necessary in the notice convening the meeting.

Appointment of auditors must be made at the meeting that considers the accounts; this is usually the AGM. The articles will typically require some non-executive directors to retire at each AGM, with the right to offer themselves for re-election. Accordingly, items (i)–(iv) are the standard minimum agenda for an AGM. Other business can be taken as well.

A private company can elect, by elective resolution, (a resolution of which not less than 21 days' notice has been given and to which all members who are entitled to attend and vote agree) to dispense with the holding of an AGM. However, any member of the company may, by notice to the company not later than three months before the end of the year, require the holding of an AGM in that year.

2.4 Extraordinary general meetings (EGMs)

A general meeting that is not an AGM is an EGM.

There is no limit on the number of such meetings in a year or the intervals between them. But as convening a meeting entails formalities and sometimes expense, the directors convene such meetings infrequently. Non-urgent matters, i.e. technical amendment of the articles, can often conveniently be taken as an addition to the business of the next AGM.

2.5 Persons able to convene meetings

(a) **Directors** – the articles usually authorise the directors to call an EGM whenever they think fit.

Where it becomes known to any of the directors of a public company that there has been a serious loss of capital, i.e. if the company's net assets are half or less than its called up share capital, the directors must convene an EGM to consider whether any, and if so what, measures should be taken to deal with the situation.

(b) **Members** – members also have a statutory right to require the directors to convene an EGM. To be valid, the requisition must be signed by members holding at least one-tenth of the issued and paid up shares carrying voting rights. If the company has no share capital, members having at least one-tenth of the rights to vote at general meetings must sign the requisition.

The requisition must state the objects of the meeting and be signed by the requisitionists and deposited at the registered office. If, within 21 days of the deposit of the requisition, the directors have not convened the meeting, the requisitionists, or a majority of them (in voting rights) may themselves convene a meeting to be held within three months of that date. In that case the company refunds their costs to the requisitionists and may recover them from the defaulting directors.

The directors can, in theory, defeat the requisition by convening the meeting for a date that lies a long way ahead (there is no maximum period of notice – however Table A provides that it must be held within eight weeks of receipt of the requisition) but the court's powers, referred to below, could then be invoked. The Companies Act 1989 plugs this loophole by providing that directors are deemed not to have duly convened a meeting if they convene a meeting for more than 28 days after the date of the notice convening the meeting.

Members may also have the power to call an EGM themselves.

Unless the articles otherwise provide, two or more members holding at least one-tenth of the share capital (even if it has no voting rights), or if there is no share capital, 5% of the members (even without voting rights) may call a meeting. In practice, articles usually have the effect of excluding these extended rights which are, therefore, of little importance.

(c) **Department of Trade and Industry** – if default is made in holding the annual general meeting, the Department of Trade and Industry may, on the application of any member, call such a meeting and give such ancillary or consequential directions as it thinks expedient.

2.6 Class meetings

Class meetings are not meetings of the company but of a class of its shareholders usually for the purpose of considering a proposed variation of class rights. The articles may require that decisions in order to be binding on the class shall be taken by extraordinary resolution requiring a three-quarters majority.

The provisions of the articles relating to general meetings usually apply in relation to class meetings in connection with the variation of the rights attached to a class of shares. However:

- The necessary quorum at any such meeting (other than an adjourned meeting) shall be two persons holding or representing by proxy at least one-third in nominal value of the issued shares of the class in question, and at an adjourned meeting one person holding shares of the class in question or their proxy.

- Any holder of shares of the class in question present, in person or by proxy, may demand a poll. A poll is one vote per share, as opposed to the usual show of hands.

3 Calling a meeting

3.1 Introduction

A meeting will not be properly held unless proper notice has been given to persons entitled to receive it. The question of notice is usually determined by the articles but is subject to statutory provisions, in particular that notice must be served on every member in the manner required by Table A, except insofar as the company's articles have made alternative provision.

3.2 Length of notice of meetings and resolutions

The statutory minimum:

- 21 days' written notice for an AGM

- 14 days' written notice for an EGM (seven days if it is an unlimited company), except that if a special resolution is to be moved, 21 days' notice is required for an EGM.

The articles can impose a requirement of longer but not shorter notice. Many articles provide that in reckoning the period notice is deemed to be given 48 hours after posting; that day and the meeting itself are excluded from the period. Where clear notice rules of this kind apply a notice must be posted, e.g. on Monday for a meeting to be held on a Thursday (two or three weeks later).

The notice requirements can, however, be waived:

(a)   in the case of an AGM if so agreed by all the members entitled to attend and vote

(b)   in the case of an EGM by a majority of members holding not less than 95% of the voting shares or (if there is no share capital) by 95% of the members having the right to attend and vote.

A private company may by elective resolution (see below) elect to substitute another percentage in (b) for 95%, but this may not be below 90%.

3.3 Persons entitled to receive notices

The articles will usually state who is entitled to receive a copy of the notice. If they do not, Table A applies and the persons entitled to receive the notice are every member; the personal representative of a deceased member provided they themselves would have been entitled to notice; the trustee of a bankrupt provided the member would have been entitled to notice and the auditor.

The general law is that failure to give notice, even to one member entitled to it, invalidates the meeting. It is usual to provide that accidental failure to give or non receipt of notice shall not invalidate the proceedings.

3.4   Contents of a notice

The business of an AGM need only be specified in the notice in general terms, e.g. 'to elect a director' is sufficient notice even if the meeting unexpectedly elects a different candidate from the director offering himself for re-election.

In the case of other business, sufficient detail must be given in the notice to enable a member to be aware of what is proposed. Thus a proposal on directors' fees must disclose the exact amount involved. This duty is nowadays discharged by setting out in the notice the full and exact text of the resolution to be moved. But for an ordinary resolution this is a matter of practice and not a rule of law.

If the notice includes a special or extraordinary resolution, the text of the resolution must be set out in full because the statutory definition of such a resolution makes this necessary.

In every case the notice must state that a member entitled to attend and vote may appoint a proxy or proxies to attend and vote on their behalf. An AGM and a special or extraordinary resolution must be specified as such.

The date, time and place of the meeting must be given.

Whether any notice given is satisfactory, depends on the requirements of the statute and of the articles and, generally speaking, on whether in the particular circumstances it is reasonably adequate to enable an ordinary member to decide whether or not they ought to attend the meeting to safeguard their interests.

3.5   Circulation of members' resolutions and statements

Members have a statutory right to require the company:

- to give to members entitled to receive notice of the AGM, notice of any resolution that is to be moved by them at the next AGM

- to circulate to members entitled to receive notice of any general meeting any statement of not more than 1,000 words on any resolution or business to be discussed at that meeting.

To have such a right the members must be either of the following:

- members having at least 5% of the total voting rights of all members entitled to attend and vote

- at least 100 members holding paid up shares to an aggregate of at least £10,000 (i.e. £100 average).

The members must deposit a copy of the requisition, signed by the requisitionists, not less than six weeks before the meeting (if a resolution is to be put on the agenda of the AGM), or a week (in the case of a statement to be circulated). However the directors cannot defeat the requisition by calling an AGM after the deposit of the requisition.

The members must bear the expense involved.

The intention is to give members an opportunity to put forward views or proposals that the directors may not favour. It is rarely used in practice. Firstly, directors have the advantage with circulars as they have better opportunity to prepare them and, if prepared for the benefit of members, to finance their circulation from company funds (but they must be truthful).

Secondly, when there are rival appeals for the votes of members at a forthcoming meeting, the opposition prefer to issue their circulars direct to members rather than give the directors the advantage of seeing them in advance.

If a company fails to comply, the member may seek an order of the court permitting the resolution to be moved at the appropriate meeting.

3.6 Special notice

Special notice should be clearly distinguished from a special resolution.

Special notice, when required, is given to the company by a member at least 28 days before the meeting. It is notice that the member intends to move a resolution at the meeting.

If the company, i.e. the directors, agree or are by law required, to include the resolution (of which special notice has been given) in their notice of the meeting, the company includes the resolution in a 21 days' notice issued to members to convene the meeting if the motion is put before an AGM, or 14 days if the motion is to be put before an EGM. But unless the member who gave the special notice has the minimum support described above, the directors are entitled to refuse to include the resolution in their notice of the meeting and it cannot then be moved.

Pedley v Inland Waterways Association (1977)

Facts: the claimant was a shareholder in the defendant company. He sent notice to the company that he wished to propose at the next AGM the removal of the directors of the company. The notice was headed 'Special Notice' and, as required, was given more than 28 days before the AGM. The company secretary wrote to the claimant, saying that as the resolution did not have the necessary support, the company did not have to include the proposal in the agenda. The claimant claimed that support for the inclusion of his resolution was unnecessary and issued a claim form against the company.

Held: the company was under no obligation to give notice to its members of the claimant's resolution. Without the necessary support, a shareholder did not have the right to compel the inclusion of a resolution in the company's agenda.

If, after receiving a special notice, the directors call a meeting for a date which is less than 28 days later, the special notice is still treated as valid.

The purpose of these complex rules is to give to directors, members and any individual (director or auditor) concerned ample warning of the proposer's intentions.

Special notice is only required for resolutions of three types:

(a)   to remove a director from office or to appoint a substitute in their place

(b)   to elect a director aged seventy or more where that age limit applies

(c)   to remove an auditor from office or to appoint any auditor other than the retiring auditor

In cases (a) and (c) where the special notice of an intended removal is received by the company, a copy of it must be sent forthwith to the director or auditor concerned.

Activity 1

Produce a table showing the type of meeting that can be called, the period of notice required and the percentage of shareholders required to approve a waiver of the notice period.

Feedback to this activity is at the end of the chapter.

4 Conduct of meetings

4.1 Introduction

The following are the main requisites of a valid meeting:

- it must be properly convened by notice

- a quorum must be present

- there should be a chairman who should discharge their duties in a proper manner

- if the meeting is to reach decisions, resolutions and any amendments should be proposed for discussion and then put to the vote in a proper manner.

4.2 Quorum at meetings

DEFINITION

A quorum is the minimum number of persons whose presence is requisite in order that a meeting may validly conduct business.

A quorum is the minimum number of persons whose presence is requisite in order that a meeting may validly conduct business.

If the articles do not make special rules for a quorum, then two members personally present is the quorum for a meeting of a company. Articles often provide that proxies may be counted in the quorum.

In general one member cannot constitute a quorum. But there are some exceptions:

(a)   One member can be a quorum for a class meeting if they hold all the shares of the class and the regulations allow it.

(b)   If a meeting is ordered by the Department of Trade and Industry or by the court, the quorum may be fixed at one member.

(c)   At an adjourned class meeting the quorum shall be one person holding shares of the class.

(d)   The quorum can be one member where the company is a single member private limited company.

One member who attends in their own right and as proxy for another does not constitute a quorum of two members present in person or by proxy; they are still one member and that is insufficient.

In practice the directors themselves will often be shareholders and the numbers of them present will assure a quorum. Problems can arise when a company has, for example, only two members and one refuses to attend to prevent a valid meeting being held. Case (b) above affords a solution.

Where the articles provide that a quorum shall be present when the meeting proceeds to business, it has been held that the meeting can validly continue even after part of the quorum originally present has withdrawn. Most companies' articles, though, require a quorum throughout.

4.3 Resolutions – introduction

The business of the meeting is conducted by the putting of, voting on and passing or not of resolutions.

For the business to be properly conducted, each resolution must be properly put, any amendment properly put, discussed and voted on and the resolution (as amended if this is the case) properly discussed and voted on. It is therefore necessary to know:

- the types of resolution and requirements for each to be properly put to the meeting

- moving and discussion of resolutions

- amendments

- voting.

4.4 Types of resolution

The different types of resolution are:

- **Ordinary resolution** – an ordinary resolution is passed by a simple majority of votes cast (this is more votes in favour of the resolution than against). The period of notice required depends on the type of meeting at which the resolution is moved (21 days for an AGM and 14 days for an EGM). In two cases only, i.e. the removal of a director from office and the removal of an auditor, an ordinary resolution is expressly specified by law. It is also required wherever the law does not call for a special cr extraordinary resolution. References to 'a resolution' mean an ordinary resolution.

- **Special resolution** – a special resolution requires at least a three-quarters majority and notice of at least 21 days.

  Special resolutions are prescribed for a number of important company decisions, e.g. an alteration of the articles and reduction of share capital.

- **Extraordinary resolution** – an extraordinary resolution is one passed by at least a three-quarters majority of votes cast at a meeting convened by a notice specifying the intention to propose the resolution as an extraordinary resolution. The period of notice can, therefore, be 14 days. It is used, among other things, to begin a voluntary winding up on grounds of insolvency, and, at class meetings, to vary class rights.

4.5 Written resolution

For private companies, a written resolution signed by all members entitled to vote will be as valid as a resolution passed in the normal way. In addition, the articles of association of any company, public or private may provide that instead of a meeting, a decision of the members may be taken by a written resolution duly signed by all members entitled to attend and vote. This is a common practice in private companies if the number of members is small and it is not convenient to hold a meeting. It appears that such an article will apply to all types of resolutions, ordinary, extraordinary and special.

Written resolutions have effect notwithstanding anything in the company's memorandum or articles. Thus any resolution, whether normally requiring a general meeting or a class meeting, can be passed as a written resolution.

Such a resolution, which must be contained in a document or series of documents, must be signed by all shareholders who would have been entitled to attend and vote at the meeting. The date of the resolution will be the date upon which the last signature is appended. The resolution must be entered in the minutes.

An auditor or a director may not be removed from office by written resolution.

The directors and secretary of a private company have a duty to send the company's auditors a copy, or otherwise inform them of the contents, of any written resolution. Breach of this duty is a criminal offence, although it is a defence to prove either that it was not practicable to comply with the requirement or that the accused believed on reasonable grounds that a copy of the resolution had been sent to the auditors or that they had otherwise been informed of its contents. Breach of this duty does not affect the validity of any resolution that has been passed.

The articles of association (e.g. Article 53 Table A) may provide that a decision may be taken by a written resolution duly signed by all members entitled to attend and vote. Written resolutions can only be used by **private** companies.

A **written** resolution can be used to pass any resolution except than to remove an auditor or director from office.

4.6 Voting – show of hands/poll

In votes on resolutions, the majority required is of votes cast. Members who do not vote are disregarded. The majority is required both on a show of hands and, if a poll is held, on a poll.

In the first instance, voting will be on a show of hands. This will be a rough guide as it will generally be on the basis of one vote per person, whatever the size of their actual shareholding and voting rights.

The standard practice is:

- first to take a vote on a show of hands in which each member present in person has one vote regardless of the number of their shares; proxies are not usually entitled to vote on a show of hands

- then if a poll is properly demanded (this is a rare occurrence – see below) to take a vote on a poll in which voting rights depend on shareholdings and proxies are entitled to vote. A vote on a poll overrides a previous vote on the same point by a show of hands.

Voting rights are specified in the articles; one vote for each ordinary share is normal. But there may be non-voting ordinary shares and or preference shares carrying the right to vote only in special circumstances.

The chairman's declaration of the result of a vote on a show of hands is conclusive unless either a poll is properly demanded or their declaration is manifestly wrong (e.g. carried by eleven to ten in a case where a 75% majority is obligatory).

The articles may prescribe the rules for demanding and holding a poll. The right to demand a poll cannot be totally excluded by the articles, except on the election of a chairman and the adjournment of the meeting. Furthermore, the articles may not set the minimum support required to obtain a poll at a higher level than five members entitled to vote, or any number holding at least 10% of the total voting rights or of the paid up shares carrying votes. Table A provides that a poll may be demanded by the chairman, at least two voting members or members representing not less than 10% of total voting rights. A proxy has the same right to demand a poll as the member whom they represent. These rules are to safeguard a minority against restrictive provisions in the articles designed to make it difficult to obtain a poll.

Subject to any provisions of the articles the chairman may decide, when a poll is properly demanded, whether it should be held at once or later when the necessary arrangements have been made.

When a poll is held at a later date and not at the meeting itself, members may only send in proxies during the interval if the articles permit this to be done.

Where there is to be a vote on a poll the first step (apart from deciding when it should be held, i.e. forthwith or later) is to appoint scrutineers (a task often given to the auditors). Members either sign voting lists for or against the resolution or hand in signed voting cards. The scrutineers check the signatures against the register of members and report the result to the chairman who declares it.

4.7 Proxies

The expression 'proxy' is used both to denote a person authorised to vote on behalf of a member and the paper or proxy card that gives them that authority.

Members of any company have important rights, which override any contrary provisions of the articles. These are:

(a)   Every member entitled to attend and vote at a meeting of a company having a share capital may appoint a proxy to attend and vote on their behalf:

(i)   a proxy need not be a member of the company, e.g. a member can appoint their solicitor to be their proxy

(ii)   in the case of a private company, the proxy has the right to speak at the meeting

(iii)   in the case of a public company only, the member may appoint more than one proxy, e.g. a bank nominee company holding shares for several different customers might wish to appoint one proxy to vote for and one against a resolution in accordance with the instructions given by each beneficial owner.

(b)   Every notice issued to convene a meeting must specify the right to appoint one or more proxies and that a proxy need not be a member.

(c)   Proxies may be deposited at any time up to 48 hours before the meeting begins, i.e. the articles may fix a shorter but not longer time.

(d)   If the company issues proxy cards, i.e. invites proxies, it must issue them to all members and not only to some, i.e. to drum up support from its selected supporters.

The same rules apply to class meetings.

4.8 The chairman and procedure

The chairman's role is a crucial one. Therefore, it is essential that there should be a chairman to preside over the meeting. The articles usually provide that the chairman of the board of directors, failing them another director or failing that, one of the members present chosen by them, shall act as chairman.

The chairman has a general duty to act in good faith in the interests of the company as a whole and in fairness to all sections of opinion present. If the chairman fails to conduct the meeting properly – the meeting and any purported resolution passed thereat is void.

Byng v London Life Assurance (1988)

Facts: a general meeting was called to pass a special resolution to approve a merger. The merger had aroused some opposition and critical press comment and as a result far more members attended than could be accommodated in the venue. Adjacent rooms for the overflow were taken with audio-visual links, but these did not work. The chairman opened the meeting even though members were still pressing to get in. After one member proposed a vote of no confidence in the board, the chairman decided to move the meeting to another venue at a later time. Far fewer members were able to attend at this later time and at this different venue, but the chairman went ahead and the special resolution was carried.

Held: in the chaotic circumstances, the meeting was not effective to pass the resolution.

In conducting the meeting the chairman should take it through its business in an orderly fashion, ensuring that one particular resolution at a time is proposed for discussion and that members relate what they say to the item then before the meeting. The chairman must maintain order and for that purpose may require members to desist from making irrelevant or provocative remarks. When the chairman judges that all points of view have been adequately expressed, they may put the resolution then under discussion to the vote and declare the result. The chairman has a casting vote only if the articles give them one.

Subject to any provisions of the articles, the chairman may adjourn the meeting if the meeting agrees or if they consider it necessary to adjourn to avoid disorder. If they adjourn the meeting improperly before its business is concluded, the meeting may elect another chairman and continue.

4.9 Adjournment and dissolution

Meetings may be adjourned and the business completed at a later date. Motions for closure of discussion, adjournment or dissolution of the meeting may generally be passed by ordinary resolution.

Where a resolution is passed at an adjourned meeting it is deemed to have been passed on the date it was in fact passed and not deemed to be passed at an earlier date.

4.10 Minutes of meetings

- **Retention** – a company is required to maintain minutes of its general meetings to be entered in a minute book. Such minutes are usually a brief formal record of resolutions passed. A company must also keep minutes of board meetings.

- **Signing** – the minutes are usually signed by the chairman of the meeting or of the next succeeding meeting. Signed minutes are evidence of the proceedings but it is permissible to call other evidence, if any exists, to rebut the minutes.

- **Inspection** – the minute book of general meetings must be kept at the registered office and must be open to inspection by members.

4.11 When a meeting need not be held

Meetings may be dispensed with where a written resolution has been passed. Note also the right of a private company to dispense with having an AGM by elective resolution.

These provisions are important as they are an attempt to reduce the burden of regulation on private companies.

4.12 Registration and publicity

Details of, and resolutions in, meetings are generally the private concern of the company and its members. However, certain resolutions that may affect third parties must be registered. Thus, a signed copy of certain resolutions must be filed at the Companies Registry. Resolutions to be filed include:

- all special resolutions

- all extraordinary resolutions

- all resolutions to increase or decrease authorised share capital

- all resolutions of class meetings (agreeing to vary class rights)

- resolutions for voluntary winding up.

Note that an ordinary resolution, unless it falls within these categories, does not have to be filed.

Such resolutions are thereafter annexed to the articles and become part of the company's public documents.

4.13 The elective regime

The elective regime permits private companies unanimously to dispense with certain formalities. Elective resolutions allow the company:

- to fix the duration of the authority of the directors to allot shares, which may be longer than five years

- to dispense with the requirements to lay accounts and reports before the company in general meeting

- to dispense with the requirement to hold an annual general meeting

- to dispense with the requirement to appoint auditors annually

- to reduce the majority required to consent to the holding of a general meeting of the company at short notice from members holding 95% to not less than 90% in nominal value of shares having the right to attend and vote at a general meeting.

An elective resolution can be revoked by ordinary resolution.

Activity 2

Produce a table showing the different types of resolution, the notice period (if any), the percentage of votes required to pass them and if a copy of the resolution has to be forwarded to the Registrar.

Feedback to this activity is at the end of the chapter.

5 Companies Bill 2006

5.1 Notice periods

In future, companies must hold AGMs within six months of the day following the accounting reference date.

The minimum period of notice for the AGM of a public company will remain at 21 days. The minimum period of notice for all other meetings in all companies will be 14 days. However, the articles may specify longer periods.

5.2 The elective regime

The elective regime will be the norm in all private companies. However, if the members do not want the elective regime to apply, they will be able to change the constitution to this effect.

5.3 Resolutions

A valid resolution in a private company may be passed at a meeting of the members or as a written resolution. However, a valid resolution in a public company may **only** be passed at a meeting of the members.

Unanimous agreement to a written resolution will no longer be required. Instead, the level of support that would have sufficed at a meeting will be required.

A written resolution may be proposed and circulated by the directors. It may also be requisitioned by the members and, if so, it must be circulated by the directors. Members can requisition a resolution if they hold 5% of the total voting rights or such lower percentage as may be specified in the company's articles. They may also supply a statement up to 1,000 words long to be circulated with it.

- Members may vote on the hard copy of the resolution or by electronic means, if permitted. Once a member has signified their agreement to a written resolution, they cannot withdraw their agreement.
- The period for agreeing a written resolution will be the period specified in the company's articles. If no period is specified, it will be 28 days.
- The company's articles cannot remove the ability of a private company and its members to propose and pass a statutory resolution as a written resolution.

5.4 Members' statements

The Bill makes the following changes to the existing law:

- When the statement relates to a resolution or other matter to be dealt with at a public company's AGM and is received before the company's financial year end, the shareholders will not be required to cover the costs of circulating the statement.
- The shares relied on to trigger the circulation of a statement must carry rights to vote on the relevant resolution rather than just at the meeting.
- Requests in electronic form will be permitted.

5.5 Proxies

Members of all companies will have the right to appoint more than one proxy. All proxies will be able to attend, speak and vote at a meeting.

Every notice calling a meeting must contain a statement informing the member of their rights to appoint one or more proxies and any more extensive rights conferred by the company's articles.

A proxy may be elected as chairman of a general meeting by resolution of the members passed at the meeting.

5.6   Quoted companies

Quoted companies will be required to disclose on a website the results of all polls taken at a general meeting.

Members of quoted companies holding 5% of the voting rights (or 100 members each holding on average £100 of paid-up capital) will be given the right to require an independent report of any poll taken, or to be taken, at a general meeting. The members' request must be made within one week of the meeting where the poll is taken. Members may make their request in advance of the meeting if they wish, but unless the company's articles already require all votes to be taken on a poll, members may need to take steps to ensure that a poll is called.

The company will be required to publish the report on its website.

Summary

On completion of their studies, students should be able to:

*   explain the use and procedure of board meetings and general meetings of shareholders

*   explain the voting rights of directors and shareholders and identify the various types of shareholder resolutions.

Self-test questions

General meetings

1   When must a company hold AGMs? (2.3)

2   What is the usual business conducted at an AGM? (2.3)

3   Who can convene meetings? (2.5)

Calling a meeting

4   How can shareholders compel the inclusion of a resolution on the agenda of an AGM? (3.5)

5   For what three purposes is special notice of a resolution required? (3.6)

Conduct of meetings

6   What is the quorum for a company meeting? (4.2)

7   What is the difference between voting on a show of hands and voting on a poll? (4.6)

Multiple-choice questions

Question 1

What majority is needed and what notice is required for a special resolution of a company limited by shares?

A   Seventy-five percent of those voting in person or by proxy at a general meeting called with not less than 21 days' notice of the proposed resolution

B   Over 75% of those voting in person or by proxy at a general meeting called with not less than 21 days' notice of the proposed resolution

C   Seventy-five percent of those voting in person or by proxy at a general meeting called with not less than 28 days' notice of the proposed resolution

D   Over 75% of those voting in person or by proxy at a general meeting called with not less than 28 days' notice of the proposed resolution

Question 2

What minimum length of notice must be given to shareholders in a limited company who are entitled to attend and vote at an extraordinary general meeting summoned to pass an ordinary resolution?

A   7 days

B   14 days

C   21 days

D   28 days

Question 3

An extraordinary general meeting of a company may be validly held at short notice provided consent is given by the holders of:

A   a simple majority of the voting shares

B   a majority holding 75% of the voting shares

C   a majority holding 95% of the voting shares

D   100% of the voting shares

Question 4

How many members of a company limited by shares are required to requisition an extraordinary general meeting?

A   Members carrying not less than 10% of the paid-up capital of the company that carries the right of voting

B   Members carrying not less than 15% of the voting rights

C   Either members carrying not less than 5% of the paid-up capital of the company that carries the right of voting or 100 members

D   Either members carrying not less than 10% of the voting rights or 100 members

For the answers to these questions, see the 'Answers' section at the end of the book.

Practice questions

Question 1: Dozy plc

The directors of Dozy plc have not called an annual general meeting of the company for nearly two years and a shareholders' committee has been formed. It wishes to call a meeting in order to remove the directors.

Advise the committee how it may proceed to call a general meeting or to have one called.

Question 2: Fork Ltd

Fork Ltd has a fully paid up share capital of £10,000 divided into 10,000 £1 shares. The two directors, Bill and Ben, each hold 150 shares. The remaining 9,700 shares are held by six other shareholders. These six shareholders requisition an EGM of the company to pass a vote of no confidence in the board of directors.

(a)   Say why these shareholders are in a position to make a valid requisition.

(b)   What are the requirements of a valid requisition?

(c)   If Bill and Ben ignore the requisition, what further action can the shareholders take?

For the answers to these questions, see the 'Answers' section at the end of the book.

Feedback to activities

Activity 1

Meeting	Days notice	% required to waive notice
AGM	21	100
EGM	14 (or 21)	95*
EGM of unlimited company	7 (or 21)	95*

* Private company can reduce this figure (but not below 90%) by passing elective resolution.

Activity 2

Type of Resolution	Notice period (days)	% of those voting to pass	To the Registrar?
Special	21	75	Yes
Ordinary	14	Majority	Sometimes (e.g. increase of authorised share capital)
Extraordinary	14 or 7	75	Yes
Elective	21	100	Yes
Written	–	100	Sometimes

Chapter 20

COMPANY ADMINISTRATION AND FINANCE: RAISING OF SHARE CAPITAL

Syllabus content

Company administration and finance

- The rights attaching to the different types of shares and the purposes and procedures for issuing shares

The two main sources of finance for a company are share capital and loan capital. In this chapter the legal rules on types of shares and their issue are covered. This includes rules on the amount of share capital that can be issued, who has authority to do so, to whom it can be issued and what forms payment may take.

Contents

1   Types of shares

2   Public subscription

3   Issue of shares

4   Companies Bill 2006

1 Types of shares

1.1 The nature of a share

The share capital of a company is divided into shares that are units defining the shareholder's proportionate interest in the company.

A share is the interest of the shareholder in the company measured by a sum of money, for the purpose of liability in the first place and of interest in the second, but also consisting of a series of mutual covenants.

The main elements and characteristics of a share are:

- it gives a right to receive dividends declared on that class of shares

- unless it is a non-voting share, it carries a right to vote at general meetings; such rights are usually defined in relation to shares, e.g. one vote for each share

- on a liquidation or reduction of capital, a share defines the right to receive assets distributed to members of that class

- where there is liability, e.g. to subscribe capital, it is measured by reference to shares: if £1 shares are issued at par, the liability is to pay £1 for each share

- various rights of membership are given by the Companies Act 1985 and by the memorandum and articles of association in terms of shares, e.g. the right to requisition the holding of a general meeting or to receive notice

- subject to any restrictions of the articles of association, a share is transferable by its nature.

1.2 Calls

Shareholders in a public company are legally bound to pay 25% of the nominal value of each share on application for allotment and the remaining instalments as specified in the contract for the shares. If the contract contains no stipulation, the company may make calls for the benefit of the company in order to raise unpaid capital from shareholders. Calls must be made in the manner provided by the articles. Shareholders are of course liable up to the full amount of the unpaid nominal value of their shares on a winding up. The articles of association often empower the company, if acting in good faith, to forfeit the shares of a member who fails to fulfil their obligations to pay calls.

1.3 Classes of shares

In the absence of contrary provision in the memorandum or articles, it is presumed that the rights of all shareholders are equal. These include rights to equal liability to calls (where shares are not fully paid up) dividends (however much is paid up on each share), attendance and voting at meetings and return of capital on an authorised reduction of a winding up.

If a company has more than one class of share, the shares will be differentiated by reference to special rights of the shares of each class.

Class rights will generally consist in one or more rights distinguished from rights of other classes as follows:

- in respect of dividends paid out of profits

- in respect of assets distributed on a winding-up or a reduction of capital

- in respect of voting rights.

The exact mix is a matter for determination by the company and its members when the class of shares is created. In appropriate cases shares can be given other rights, e.g. the right to appoint one or more directors.

Some of the common different types of shares are:

- **Ordinary shares (the equity)** – typically these carry normal rights without special definition. If there is only one class it need not be explicitly described as ordinary.

- **Preference shares** – these carry rights, e.g. with respect to dividends or on winding up, in preference to other shares.

- **Redeemable shares** – these carry a right by the company to redeem (ie buy back) the shares. As this would reduce the capital of the company, there are strict rules about the issue and redemption of such shares. These rules are covered in the next chapter.

- **Deferred or founders' shares** – these rank after ordinary shares for dividend and sometimes return of capital. They may have additional voting rights. In a typical case such shares were taken by promoters in recognition of their special position. They are now not often found.

- **Non-voting shares** – these can be of any class.

1.4 Preference shares

Preference shares are shares that carry rights in preference to other shares. The usual preferences given are:

- payment of dividend

- return of capital on winding up of the company.

The shares may also be subject to restrictions, e.g. voting rights.

Dividend

A preference share generally confers the right to receive a dividend up to a specified amount before any dividend is paid on the ordinary shares.

The preferential dividend is deemed to be cumulative unless expressly described as non-cumulative. Cumulative means that the preference shareholder will be entitled to arrears in dividend if not paid out in one year before any payment can be made to the ordinary shareholders by way of dividend.

The right to a preference dividend is exhaustive. Thus, if the preference dividend is paid in full there is no further right to dividend unless there is an express right, i.e. to participate equally with ordinary shares as soon as the latter have received a dividend of a specified amount. Such shares are called participating preference shares and rank as equity share capital.

If a company goes into liquidation with arrears outstanding of preference dividends, the right to receive arrears (other than any dividend already declared) lapses unless the articles provide that the arrears shall be paid out of the assets available in winding up. They have no claim on any reserves that could have been applied in paying their dividends. If dividend arrears are payable on liquidation, payment may come from the assets of the company even if before liquidation they represented capital and not profits capable of distribution as dividends.

Capital

Preference shares are usually given priority in any return of capital. That priority right is exhaustive, i.e. they are entitled to be repaid capital, but not to participate in any surplus assets.

However, preference shares do not have any priority over ordinary shares in return of capital unless expressly so provided. If not provided, they rank *pari passu* (equally) with ordinary shares in bearing their proportion of any deficiency of paid up capital.

Re Saltdean Estates (1968)

Facts: the company had ordinary and preference shares, the preference shareholders having priority on the return of capital. The company proposed to reduce capital (with the court's permission) by way of returning capital, i.e. nominal value, to them to eliminate the class.

Held: the preference shareholders had received what their class right entitled them to – repayment of nominal value before the ordinary shareholders. They were not entitled to more.

Activity 1

A company has an issued ordinary share capital of £50,000 and a preference share capital of £25,000 with priority on a winding up.

On a winding up, how much does each class receive assuming the company has net assets available for contributories amounting to:

(a)   £20,000

(b)   £135,000.

Feedback to this activity is at the end of the chapter.

1.5   Terminology

The term 'share capital' is used to describe the capital of a company represented by shares.

It is important to be able to differentiate between:

- Authorised share capital – the maximum amount of share capital that a company is authorised by its memorandum to issue, e.g. £100 divided into 100 shares of £1 each. This will be contained in the capital clause.

- Issued or allotted share capital – the nominal amount of the share capital actually issued at any time, e.g. £100 authorised capital, of which 50 £1 shares have been issued.

This represents the liability of the members of the company. They are liable to the extent of the nominal (par) value of their shares, which means that the company is entitled to use the full amount of the sum received for the shares in order to satisfy claims against it.

Issued share capital may be:

- **Paid up capital** – the amount so far paid on partly-paid shares, e.g. 50 £1 shares for which 50p has been paid is a paid up capital of £25.

- **Called capital** – the amount that the company has called on the shareholders to contribute.

- **Uncalled capital** – this is unusual. Shares are generally fully paid, particularly as shares are often worth more than their nominal amount. S101 Companies Act 1985 requires shares in a public company to be paid up at least as to 25%. Where it exists, the company may resolve that uncalled capital be treated as reserve capital, i.e. capital that is only to be called up on a winding up.

Thus, a company may have the following structure of its share capital:

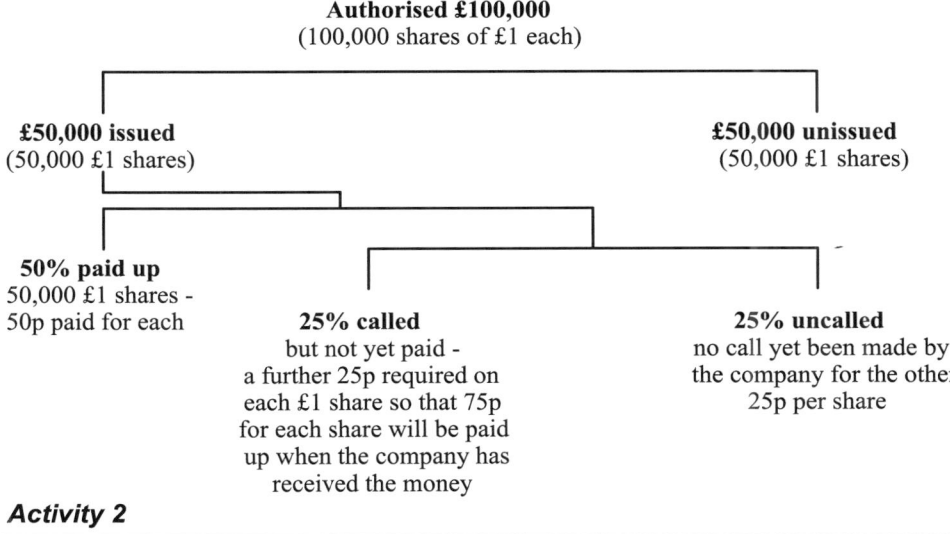

Authorised £100,000
(100,000 shares of £1 each)

£50,000 issued
(50,000 £1 shares)

£50,000 unissued
(50,000 £1 shares)

50% paid up
50,000 £1 shares -
50p paid for each

25% called
but not yet paid -
a further 25p required on
each £1 share so that 75p
for each share will be paid
up when the company has
received the money

25% uncalled
no call yet been made by
the company for the other
25p per share

Activity 2

A company has 250,000 50p shares in issue with 30p paid up. The remainder has been called. What is the paid up capital?

Feedback to this activity is at the end of the chapter.

2 Public subscription

2.1 Introduction

It is illegal for a private company's securities (shares or debentures) to be advertised as being available for public subscription. Thus it is public companies only which can raise capital by public subscription.

2.2 Methods of public subscription

There is a variety of ways in which capital can be obtained from the public by the issue of shares.

- **Direct invitations to the public (also called offers for subscription)** – a large company of well-known financial standing may be able to attract sufficient subscriptions from the public by issuing a prospectus and inviting subscriptions for shares directly.

  To ensure that the issue of shares is a success, and that all the shares issued are sold, the company will usually arrange underwriting. This is an agreement with the issuing house that it undertakes to subscribe for all the shares that are not otherwise sold. Underwriters usually spread the risk by sub-underwriting agreements. The underwriters and sub-underwriters are paid a commission for their services.

- **Offers for sale** – an offer to the public may be made in an indirect way by selling the shares directly to an issuing house (an institution whose function is to float off company shares) for the issuing house to resell them directly to the public by issuing a prospectus and inviting applications.

- **Placings** – a company may place shares with an issuing house, either for it to buy and resell to selected clients or to act as the company's agent in finding clients to subscribe for the shares.

The issue may be at a fixed price or it may be on a tender basis, i.e. persons are in effect being asked to put in written bids for shares. Usually there is a minimum price and the issue price reflects the average price of tenders (or of the higher tenders if the issue is over-subscribed).

3 Issue of shares

3.1 Authorised capital

A company can only issue available unissued shares. If there are none or not enough it will be necessary to create additional shares by an increase of share capital. This entails an alteration of the capital clause. There must be authority in the articles for the purpose of increase. Thus it may be necessary to alter the articles (by special resolution) to give the company power to increase its authorised share capital, which it would then exercise by ordinary resolution.

One of the changes being introduced by the Companies Bill 2006 is that it will no longer be necessary for a company to have an authorised maximum share capital. Shareholders can still choose to set a limit on the amount of the share capital by inserting a suitable provision in the constitution, but they will not be required to do so. Note, however, that an existing company will continue to be bound by its authorised share capital unless and until an alteration is made by the members.

3.2 Authority of directors to allot shares

Directors may not allot relevant securities (i.e. all shares except subscriber shares and employee shares, but including convertible securities) without first obtaining authority from the shareholders. Such authority may be general or specific, conditional or unconditional, but it can only exceed five years in the case of a private company that has passed an elective resolution extending the period beyond five years or for an indefinite period.

The authority must state the maximum amount of relevant securities that may be allotted under it and the date on which it will expire, which must usually be not more than five years from:

(a)   in the case of an authority contained in the company's articles at the time of its original incorporation, the date of that incorporation

(b)   in any other case, the date on which the resolution is passed.

However, such an authority (including an authority contained in the articles) may be revoked or varied by the company in a general meeting.

The authority may be renewed by the company in a general meeting for a further period not exceeding five years.

A resolution of a company to give, vary, revoke or renew such an authority may be an ordinary resolution. A copy must be forwarded to the Registrar within 15 days.

In general, the directors of a company must have the authority of the shareholders to allot shares. An unauthorised allotment is a criminal offence.

A director who knowingly and wilfully contravenes, or permits or authorises an allotment without obtaining the shareholders' authority is liable to a fine, but the validity of any allotment is not affected.

3.3 Pre-emption rights (statutory)

The allotting of additional shares of the same class may lead to a reduction in the value of the existing shares, but it is not regarded as a variation of class rights such that the special rules relating to variation and objection would apply.

Therefore, to safeguard the position of existing shareholders, no company can allot equity securities without first offering them *pro rata* to existing equity shareholders on the same or more favourable terms than it is proposing to offer them to other people. The shareholders must be given 21 days in which to decide whether to accept or reject the offer.

There are a number of exceptions to this requirement, *inter alia*:

- Where the securities are part of an employees' share scheme.

- Where the securities are to be paid for otherwise than wholly in cash.

- In the case of a private company, this requirement may be excluded by a provision in the memorandum or articles.

- Where general authority has been given to the directors to allot shares, the directors may be given, by special resolution or by the articles, discretion to exclude or modify the statutory pre-emption rights.

- By special resolution the statutory pre-emption rights may be excluded or modified in relation to a particular allotment. The directors are required to circularise the members before the meeting justifying the proposal.

An allotment in contravention of the rule regarding pre-emption rights is not invalid but the company and every officer of it who knowingly authorised or permitted the contravention are jointly and severally liable to compensate any person to whom an offer should have been made for any loss, damage, costs or expenses that the person has sustained or incurred by reason of the contravention (there is a two year limitation period).

3.4 Issue for an improper purpose

As with all powers exercised by directors, they must be exercised for the purpose for which they were conferred – the proper purposes rule. The prime purpose of an issue of shares is that the company is in need of further finance. Any other purpose is at least questionable.

Case law has concluded that it would be an improper purpose to issue shares to:

- defeat a take-over bid

- facilitate a take-over bid

- prevent the removal of directors

- secure the passing of a special resolution or

- deprive a shareholder of their special voting weight.

The courts have not, however, concluded that the only proper purpose of an issue of shares is the need to raise finance. It was recognised in *Clemens v Clemens* that it might be a proper purpose to issue shares to employees and directors in order to given them an equity interest in the company's fortunes, but not to prevent the company being taken over.

If the directors do make an issue for improper purposes, the issue is voidable. It may be ratified by the company provided no votes are exercised by the members to whom the shares were improperly issued. Exceptionally, ratification is not allowed if it would constitute fraud on the minority.

Hogg v Cramphorn (1967)

Facts: the directors of a company learned of a proposed take-over bid, which they genuinely believed would not be to the benefit of the company. In order to defeat the bid, they issued 5,000 shares to be held on trust for the company's employees.

Held: the issue was an improper exercise of directors' powers and thus invalid. However, the court ordered a general meeting of the company to be held so that consideration could be given to ratifying the issue. The 'new' shares would not be allowed to vote.

Howard Smith Ltd v Ampol Petroleum Ltd (1974)

Facts: A and B owned 55% of the issued share capital of M Ltd between them. They made an offer for all the share capital of M Ltd. At the same time another company, X Ltd, made a similar offer. Although the directors of M Ltd favoured X Ltd's offer, there was no chance that it would succeed because A and B as majority shareholders of M Ltd would vote to reject offers from any other source. In order that X Ltd's offer would stand the greatest chance of success, the directors of M Ltd issued $10 million worth of shares to X Ltd, thereby converting A and B's holding into a minority one.

Held: The issue was an improper exercise of directors' powers and therefore invalid since the sole motive was to enable a take-over to succeed, which the majority shareholders were otherwise in a position to block.

Bamford v Bamford (1970)

Facts: in order to fight off a take-over bid the directors of X Ltd issued five million shares to B Ltd for cash. The shareholders who supported the take-over complained and the directors called an extraordinary general meeting of the company, which approved and ratified the directors' action. B Ltd did not vote.

Held: although the issue of shares by directors to defeat a take-over bid was an improper exercise of their powers, the issue would remain valid because it had been ratified by the company in general meeting.

3.5 Partly paid shares

A public company must not allot a share unless at least one-quarter of the nominal value and the whole of any premium is paid up. Shares may be issued on the basis of payment either by instalments at fixed dates (so that a company raises money for an expanding business or long-term project by stages as required) or by instalments (calls) when demanded by the company. The directors are usually given the power under the articles of association to make such calls. They must use this power for the benefit of the company as a whole, e.g. they cannot make calls exclusively on shareholders other than themselves.

A company may by special resolution decide that part of the amount payable on its shares shall only be called up for payment when the company is wound up. This creates reserve capital and it is rather similar in the result to a company limited by guarantee. Reserve capital in this sense should be clearly distinguished from capital reserves, which are quite a different thing.

Forfeiture and surrender of shares on failure to pay subscription moneys on shares or for sums owing to the company are possible if the articles contain appropriate provisions.

3.6 Issue of shares at a discount on their market value

In general it is for the directors to fix the price at which shares are to be issued and, particularly in the case of rights issues to existing members, it is common practice to issue shares at a discount to the market value in order to encourage take-up.

As with all powers of directors, they have a fiduciary duty to exercise it in the interest of the company as a whole: shares issued to friends and relatives of directors at below market value may be questioned as a breach of fiduciary duty.

3.7 Issue of shares at a discount on the nominal value

A company may not issue its shares for a consideration which is less then the nominal value of the shares. If a company did enter into a contract to issue shares at a discount, it could not enforce it against the allottee, but if they took the shares they would be liable to pay the amount of the discount as unpaid share capital and interest on that amount at 5%. Not only is the allottee liable to make good the discount, but so are subsequent holders of the shares while they hold them.

This rule does not apply to debentures that may be issued at a discount unless they carry an immediate right of conversion into shares on such terms that in effect a right to take shares at a discount is given through the debentures.

The ban on issue of shares at a discount can be inconvenient if the market price of a company's shares has fallen below par and the company wishes to raise cash by the issue of additional shares.

3.8 Issue of shares at a premium

A company is always free to issue shares at a premium, e.g. to obtain £2 each for £1 shares. No special power in the articles is required nor is any other sanction required. If it is possible to issue shares at a premium, the directors should do so (to secure a benefit to the company). As stated above, unless the shares are offered entirely to existing shareholders as a rights issue, failure to obtain the best price may be evidence of a breach of duty by the directors.

Share premium account

Any premium obtained must be treated as equivalent to capital and safeguarded accordingly. This is effected by requiring the premium to be credited to a share premium account, which can only be distributed to members under the same procedure as in a reduction of share capital. The share premium account can also be applied for certain capital purposes, however, such as:

(a)   to pay up bonus shares to be issued as fully paid to members

(b)   in writing off preliminary expenses, or expenses, commission or discount incurred in the issue of shares or debentures

(c)   in paying the premium (if any) on redemption of debentures.

Note that a share premium account cannot be used for a bonus issue of debentures.

With reference to public companies, there is a further restriction on the use of the share premium account. A public company must not make a distribution of profit by way of dividend if to do so would reduce its net assets below the aggregate of its called up share capital and undistributable reserves. The share premium account is an undistributable reserve for the purposes of this section.

A shareholder who pays a premium for their shares obtains no rights to the premium in the hands of the company. Their dividends are calculated by reference to the par value of their shares. On a liquidation or return of capital, no extra sums are payable to those shareholders who subscribed for their shares at a price above par value.

3.9   Payment for shares – cash or kind

Shares are normally paid for in cash, although the full issue price need not necessarily be received on allotment.

The company may agree with subscribers that they shall pay for their shares in kind, e.g. by transferring property or even rendering services to the company instead of paying cash. In any case, a company should obtain property or services of a value at least equal to the nominal value of the shares.

Private companies are free to determine whether the value of what is received is in fact adequate. If a company chooses to acquire property at a rather high price and in payment allot shares of a nominal value equal to that price, the decision of the directors cannot generally be challenged. But if the consideration is patently inadequate or it is clear on the face of the documents that it is illusory or fraudulent, the courts might query the adequacy of the consideration. This is an application of the contractual rule – consideration must be valuable and sufficient but need not be adequate. Hence, it is easy to evade the rule that shares cannot be issued at a discount by issuing them for non-cash consideration.

However, a public company may not:

(a)   issue subscribers' shares other than for cash

(b)   allot shares for consideration, which includes an undertaking that may be performed more than five years after the allotment

(c)   accept in payment for its shares performance of services for the company

(d)   allot shares for non-cash consideration unless:

    (i)   the consideration for the allotment has been independently valued

    (ii)   a report with respect to its value has been made to the company by a person appointed by the company during the six months preceding the allotment of shares

    (iii)   a copy of the report has been sent to the proposed allottee.

3.10 Bonus issues

A bonus or capitalisation issue of shares is effected by appropriating some part of the company's reserves (including share premium account or capital redemption reserve fund) to paying-up unissued shares in full and then distributing those shares as a bonus to shareholders, e.g. if a company has an authorised share capital of £200,000, but has issued only £100,000, it can capitalise £100,000 from its reserves to issue the remaining 100,000 shares as fully paid on the basis of one new share for each share already held.

This is not the same as the company issuing shares without receiving consideration for them. The reserves are shareholders' funds and the effect of the transaction is to reduce the reserves in providing consideration for the shares. The individual shareholder is, of course, no better off since they own the same proportion of the increased issued share capital as before. Power under the articles is required to make an issue of this kind.

3.11 Rights issue

In a rights issue the shares are offered to existing shareholders (in proportion to their shareholding) usually at less than the current market value of the shares.

For example, a company whose £1 shares stand at, say, 190p each, may offer new shares at, say, 170p on the basis of one new share for every four shares already held.

3.12 Application for shares and allotment of shares

The subscribers to the memorandum of association must agree to take at least one share each. The company when formed enters their names in its register of members as holders of those shares and requires the subscribers to pay the money due on those shares.

In other cases a company will generally obtain from potential shareholders a written application for shares to be issued to them. The directors of the company then pass a resolution to allot and issue the shares to the applicants. A letter of allotment is written to inform the applicants that shares have been allotted to them. If payment (in cash or kind) has not already been made for the shares it will then become due.

The allottee has a contractual right to have their name entered on the register of members.

Activity 3

Why might bonus shares be issued by a company?

Activity 4

The three directors of Court Ltd, F,G and H, each hold one third of the company's issued share capital. It has been decided to issue 50,000 further ordinary shares to X in order to purchase his business. The company has sufficient authorised capital, but neither the articles nor any existing resolutions make provision for issue of shares. What is necessary for this allotment to be legal?

Feedback to these activities is at the end of the chapter.

4 Companies Bill 2006

4.1 Private companies

It will no longer be an offence for a private company to offer its securities (both shares and debentures) to the public. Instead it may be compulsorily wound up or compelled to re-register as a public company.

If a private company intends to become a public company, it will be able to make a public offer of its securities before it has completed the formalities of re-registration. However, it must undertake to re-register as a public company in no more than six months from the making of the offer to the public. Acts done in good faith in anticipation of re-registration will not be treated as breaching the prohibition on offers to the public, even if the re-registration arrangements do not ultimately succeed.

The Bill also removes the requirement that there must be prior authorisation in order for the directors to allot shares. This is subject to the condition that after the allotment there will only be one class of shares. However, if the members wish, they may use the articles to restrict the right of the directors to allot shares.

4.2 Public companies

Prior authorisation of an allotment will be required for the directors of public companies

In addition, a public company must not allot shares unless all the shares offered are taken up or the offer is made on the basis that it will go ahead even if all the shares offered are not taken up.

4.3 Return of allotment

In future, the return of allotments sent to the registrar must be accompanied by a statement of capital. This shows the total subscribed capital at the date to which the return of allotments is made up and ensures that the public register contains up-to-date information on a company's share capital.

4.4 Share premium account

In future, companies will be unable to use the share premium account to write off preliminary expenses or to write off any expenses incurred, commission paid or discount allowed in respect of an issue of debentures or in providing for the premium payable on a redemption of debentures.

They will continue to be able to use it to write off any expenses incurred or commission paid in connection with the share issue giving rise to the premium.

4.5 Exercise of members' rights

New provisions are aimed at the situation where the beneficial owner of shares holds them through an intermediary. For example, a fund manager holds shares on behalf of the owner of an Individual Savings Account.

Members will be permitted to amend the company's articles to enable another person to be identified as being entitled to exercise all or any specified rights of the member. Rights may include the right to attend and vote at meetings or to receive the annual accounts. However, the right to transfer shares must remain with the member whose name is on the register.

Conclusion

This chapter considered the law surrounding the issue of share capital by a company and therefore the chapter commenced with an explanation of the nature of shares, the distinction between share and loan capital and the terminology surrounding share capital.

Issues of shares by companies in general were then considered. This included the rules on allotment of shares and the authority required by the directors of a company in order to be able to issue shares. Shares may be issued at a premium, thereby setting up a share premium account, but not a discount. Shares may also be issued for non-cash consideration, but in the case of public companies there are several rules for such a situation. The distinction between a rights issue and a bonus issue was also considered.

Summary

On completion of their studies, students should be able to:

- explain the nature of different types of share, the procedure for the issue of shares, and acceptable forms of payment

- explain the repercussions of issuing shares for an improper purpose.

Self-test questions

Types of shares

1   What two priority rights are commonly given to preference shares? (1.4)

2   What is the difference between authorised and issued share capital? (1.5)

Public subscription

3   What are the various methods of issuing shares to the public? (2.2)

Issue of shares

4   Where must authority be in order to pass an ordinary resolution to increase authorised capital? (3.1)

5   What can be the effect of shareholders not having pre-emption rights? (3.3)

6   What is the one-quarter rule? To what type of company does it apply? (3.5)

7   What are the allowed uses of the share premium account? (3.8)

8   List the special statutory rules regulating payment for shares issued by a public company. (3.9)

Practice questions

Question 1: Rakolite plc

Rakolite plc wishes to raise capital in order to finance expansion of its activities and is considering the following alternative methods of attracting capital in a highly competitive market by public issue:

(a)   A series of debentures with a nominal value of £1. The debentures will be issued at 80p. The debentures are redeemable at nominal value on 1 January 2012.

(b)   A series of debentures with a nominal value of £1 also to be issued at 80p and redeemable at nominal value on 1 January 2012. One of the terms of issue is that debenture holders will be entitled at any time after 1 July 2008 to convert their debentures into fully paid £1 ordinary shares.

(c)   A series of debentures with a nominal value of £1 also to be issued at 80p and redeemable at nominal value on 1 January 2012. One of the terms of issue is that debenture holders will be entitled at any time after 1 July 2008 to convert their debentures into fully paid ordinary shares with a nominal value of 75p.

Advise Rakolite plc on the legal validity of the above proposals.

Question 2: A Ltd

The directors of A Ltd, which was incorporated last month, propose to issue £1 shares of the company in exchange for 50p shares of B Ltd on the basis of a straight one-for-one exchange of shares.

State the relevant legal rules if the net asset value of the shares of B Ltd at the time of the exchange is:

(a)   £1.25 per share

(b)   75p per share.

None of the existing members of A Ltd wish to purchase additional shares.

Would your answer differ if A were a public limited company?

For the answers to these questions, see the 'Answers' section at the end of the book.

Feedback to activities

Activity 1

(a)   Preference shareholders   –   £20,000

      Ordinary shareholders   –   nil

(b)   Preference shareholders   –   £25,000

      Ordinary shareholders   –   £110,000

Activity 2

250,000 shares at 30p each, £75,000.

Activity 3

Bonus shares might be issued in order to reduce the market value of the shares, e.g. a company has 200,000 shares in issue with a market value of £5 each, total market value, £1 million. If a bonus issue of 300,000 shares is made then there are 500,000 shares in issue, total market value still £1 million. This has theoretically reduced the value of one share to £2.

Activity 4

The shares can only be allotted if the members (i.e. F, G and H) pass a resolution in a general meeting giving themselves as directors the authority to issue the shares. This must specify the maximum amount of shares that may be allotted and must be for a period of not more than five years.

The consideration for the shares is a business, therefore not cash. As Court Ltd is a private company there is no necessity for an independent valuation to be made of this non-cash consideration.

There is no need to pass a special resolution disapplying the statutory pre-emption rights since, although the shares are equity securities, they are not being issued for cash.

Chapter 21

COMPANY ADMINISTRATION AND FINANCE: MAINTENANCE OF SHARE CAPITAL

Syllabus content

Company administration and finance

- The maintenance of capital principle, the purposes and rules for which shares may be issued, redeemed or, purchased and the provision of financial assistance for the purchase of its own shares

The law provides rules on the maintenance of capital in order to prevent a company reducing its capital by returning it to members, whether directly or indirectly. Capital of limited companies is regarded as a guarantee, or buffer, fund for creditors.

Contents

1   Introduction to capital maintenance

2   Increase and reduction of capital

3   Redemption of redeemable shares

4   Purchase of own shares

5   Permissible capital payment

6   Financial assistance for the acquisition of own shares

7   Distributions of profit

8   Companies Bill 2006

1 Introduction to capital maintenance

1.1 Introduction

The liability of the members of a company limited by shares is restricted to the nominal value of the shares issued to them. If the company is prosperous it will have assets worth more than the nominal value of its issued share capital out of which to satisfy claims against it. If it falls on hard times it may have lost capital so that the sum total of its assets is less than its issued share capital; and if its shares are paid up, no money may be obtained by making calls on the members. The law does not seek to avoid all the consequences necessarily attendant on the speculative ventures it encourages by permitting limited liability companies, but it does take steps to safeguard the capital to which outsiders are entitled to look. The rules on maintenance of capital prevent the company from reducing its share capital by obtaining less than the value of the shares on issue (it cannot issue shares at a discount) or by returning capital to members. The rules do not prevent the company from using the capital to trade (that is what it is there for).

The capital that a limited company must maintain as a guarantee or buffer fund for creditors includes not only share capital, but also the share premium account and capital redemption reserve. Loan capital, i.e. borrowings, is not subject to maintenance.

It is important to note that while share capital must be maintained, the actual cash or assets subscribed can be used by the company – the creditor's buffer is an accounting fund, not real money.

1.2 Rules on capital maintenance

Once capital has been raised it must be maintained. The law attempts to achieve this by:

(a) Forbidding a company from acquiring its own shares.

   There are a number of exceptions to this maintenance rule, in particular:

   (i) reductions of capital

   (ii) redemption of redeemable shares

   (iii) purchase of own shares

(b) Forbidding a company from giving financial assistance for the acquisition of its own shares.

(c) Forbidding a company from making distributions except out of distributable profits.

2 Increase and reduction of capital

2.1 Increase of capital

A company may alter its capital clause to increase its authorised share capital, if so authorised by its articles, by passing an ordinary resolution. Clearly there are no difficulties for the maintenance principle produced by increasing authorised capital.

2.2 Other capital changes

Subject always to appropriate powers existing in the articles, a company may:

- Consolidate or divide its shares, e.g. £1 shares can be consolidated into half the number in £2 shares or divided into twice the number in 50p shares. However, the proportions of amounts paid and unpaid must remain the same where shares are partly paid, e.g. if before sub division every £1 share was 50p paid then the new shares of 50p must be treated as 25p paid. Since the overall nominal values remain the same, this alteration does not contravene the maintenance principle.

- Convert its shares or some of them into different classes of shares with special rights, e.g. preference shares can be converted to ordinary and *vice versa*. But if any of these shares are already issued, the consent of the class must be obtained by following a special procedure called variation of class rights. This though would not contravene the maintenance principle as again capital is not reduced.

2.3 Diminution of capital

A company may cancel unissued shares in the same way as it can increase its unissued shares. This is not a reduction in capital as, although the company had the power to issue shares, it had not actually done so.

2.4 Reduction of capital

If a company wishes to reduce its issued share capital it must pass a special resolution to reduce and obtain the approval of the court.

But a public company cannot reduce its capital below the statutory minimum unless it is first re-registered as a private company, or the court otherwise directs.

The price of limited liability is a restriction on the return to members of money subscribed as share capital. A reduction of share capital can effect such a repayment. The restrictions, however, extend to all methods of reducing share capital with or without repayment of money etc.

There are three possible modes of reduction:

(a) Cancellation wholly or in part of liability on issued shares not fully paid up, e.g. if a company had an issued capital of 50 £1 shares with 50p paid, the unpaid sum of 50p on each share could be cancelled. This would reduce the authorised and issued capital by £25 leaving 50 shares of 50p fully paid as the reduced issued capital. The resources of capital available to pay the company's debts are thereby reduced.

(b) Cancellation of some part of the paid up value of the issued shares that is lost or unrepresented by available assets, e.g. if a company had an authorised, issued and fully paid capital of £100 in £1 shares, it could cancel, say, 50p per share and reduce its authorised issued and fully paid capital to £50 in 100 issued shares of 50p. The £50 cancelled in this way would permit a corresponding reduction in, for example, a debit balance on the profit and loss account in the balance sheet.

(c) Repayment to members of some part of the paid up value of their shares that is in excess of the needs of the company, e.g. taking the same initial situation as in (b) above, the company might repay to members 50p per share in cash and so reduce its capital to £50 in 100 shares of 50p. In this case the asset side of the balance sheet would be reduced by £50 in cash paid out to members.

In cases (a) and (c), where the effect is to reduce the actual or potential fund available to meet the company's debts, the creditors would have grounds for objection and accordingly they are given a right to object.

2.5 Procedure for reduction of capital

(a) The company must have power in its articles to reduce its capital. If necessary the articles must be altered to this effect before proceeding to stage (b) below, but the alteration may be made at a prior stage of the same meeting.

(b) The company must pass a special resolution setting out the terms of the reduction.

(c) It then applies to the court for an order confirming the reduction (the resolution is not effective until confirmed).

(d) The court is then required to consider the position of creditors of the company in cases (a) and (c) of paragraph 2.4 above and may do so in any other case. But the court has a general discretion as to what should be done.

If the company has more than one class of shares, the court will also consider whether the reduction is fair between classes. In this it will have regard to the rights of the different classes in a liquidation of the company since a reduction of capital is by its nature similar to a partial liquidation.

Summary

Reduction of capital directly affects two groups of people:

* **The shareholders** – the company must have the power in its articles to reduce capital and the members must agree to the reduction by passing a special resolution.

* **The creditors** – where reduction reduces the fund available to pay unsecured creditors, protection is afforded to them by the court. The court has to agree to the reduction and can vary, cancel or allow it with conditions.

3 Redemption of redeemable shares

DEFINITION

Redeemable shares are those which, under their contractual terms of issue, must be bought back by the company at a certain time.

Redeemable shares are those which, under their contractual terms of issue, must be bought back by the company at a certain time.

A company limited by shares or limited by guarantee and having a share capital may, if authorised by its articles, issue shares that are, or at the option of the company or the shareholder, are to be liable, to be redeemed. However:

* no such shares may be issued at any time when there are no issued shares of the company that are not redeemable

* redeemable shares may not be redeemed unless they are fully paid

* the terms of redemption must provide for payment on redemption

* the articles must, at the time of issue, set out the terms of redemption.

In general, redemption may only take place by using the proceeds of a fresh issue, and/or distributable profits. Any premium payable on redemption must also be paid out of the company's distributable profits.

On redemption out of the profits of the company, the company is required to establish a capital redemption reserve equivalent to the amount by which the company's issued share capital is thereby reduced. Such fund is a capital fund, though it may be used to pay up unissued shares for the purpose of a bonus issue.

Shares are treated as cancelled on redemption, reducing the company's issued share capital.

A company that has issued shares up to its maximum authorised capital is allowed to issue fresh shares for the purpose of redeeming an existing issue of redeemable shares.

Private companies may redeem shares out of capital where so authorised by their articles. The procedure to be followed, called a 'permissible capital payment', is covered later in this chapter.

Activity 1

A limited company has in issue 100,000 £1 redeemable preference shares, partly paid up to 75p. The terms of redemption allow redemption at any time and the company also has in issue 400,000 50p ordinary shares. Can the redeemable preference shares be redeemed immediately?

Feedback to this activity is at the end of the chapter.

4   Purchase of own shares

A company limited by shares or limited by guarantee and having a share capital, which it is authorised to do so by its articles, may purchase its own shares. The shares may be redeemable shares or they may not be.

However, a company may not purchase any of its shares if, as a result of such purchase, there would no longer be any member of the company holding shares other than redeemable shares; and any such purchase must be in accordance with the provisions set out in the Companies Act.

The rules on the financing of the purchase are the same as the rules on financing of redeemable shares (see above).

The shares purchased are treated as cancelled.

The procedure followed depends on whether it is a market purchase or an off-market purchase.

- **Market purchases, i.e. on the stock exchange** – prior approval by an ordinary resolution is required for the purchase of a number of shares within a specified price band (i.e. the resolution must state the maximum and minimum price that may be paid) and within a specified time, not greater than eighteen months. Thus the approval is general rather than specific.

- **Off-market purchases, i.e. not on stock exchange** – this requires a special resolution of the company authorising it to make the contract to purchase (not the purchase itself). For a public company, such approval must be limited to a contract mad e within a period of no more than 18 months from the date of approval.

  The contract must be available for inspection for at least 15 days before the meeting (at the company's registered office) and at the meeting itself. The name of the vendor must be made clear as vendors may not vote with the shares concerned on the resolution and failure to abstain may invalidate the resolution. They can, however, vote with any other shares owned.

(Where a company has purchased its own equity shares, but has not cancelled them by the balance sheet date, the shares are referred to as treasury shares.)

Activity 2

X plc wishes to purchase 600 of its shares. The current market value of such a block is £8,000. X plc has distributable profits amounting to £6,000.

Can it achieve its aims?

Activity 3

A public company purchases, out of distributable profit, 20,000 of its own £2 ordinary shares at a price of £3 each. What amount must be transferred to capital redemption reserve?

Feedback to these activities is at the end of the chapter.

5 Permissible capital payment

5.1 Redemption and purchase of own shares – additional provisions for private companies

A private company limited by shares or limited by guarantee and having a share capital, if authorised to do so by its articles, may redeem or purchase its own shares out of capital through a permissible capital payment, but only to the extent that its distributable profits (and proceeds of a new issue, if any) are insufficient.

A payment out of capital will not be lawful, however, unless:

- The directors of the company make a statutory declaration specifying the amount of capital required and stating that having made full inquiry into the affairs and prospects of the company they have formed the opinion that the company will not thereby become insolvent and will still be able to continue to carry on business as a going concern. Such declaration must be supported by and have annexed to it an auditors' report.

- A special resolution approving the payment out of capital is passed within the week immediately following the date on which the directors make the statutory declaration.

- Within the week immediately following the date of the resolution for payment out of capital, and having delivered a copy of the statutory declaration and the auditors' report to the Registrar, the company must cause to be published in the London Gazette and in an appropriate newspaper (or give notice in writing to that effect to each of its creditors) a notice detailing its intention and actions and bringing to the attention of creditors the statutory rights of objection.

- The payment out of capital must be made not earlier than five nor more than seven weeks after the date of the resolution.

  During the five weeks before payment any member, other than one who voted in favour of the resolution, or any creditor may apply to the court for cancellation of the resolution. On the hearing of such an application the court may make such an order as it thinks fit.

Activity 4

A Ltd wishes to purchase 200 of its £1 ordinary shares at 25p above par. It has distributable profit amounting to £190 and is not proposing to fund the purchase by a new issue.

What is the amount of permissible capital payment?

Feedback to this activity is at the end of the chapter.

6 Financial assistance for the acquisition of own shares

6.1 The rule

It is unlawful for a company to give financial assistance, directly or indirectly, for the acquisition of its own shares. The assistance is unlawful whether it is given before, at the same time or after the acquisition. It is similarly unlawful for a subsidiary to give financial assistance for the acquisition of shares in its holding company.

The Companies Act defines financial assistance very broadly to include:

- a gift

- an indemnity

- a guarantee or security for a third party loan

- a loan

- assuming by assignment a third-party loan or security

- the release or waiver of an obligation

- any other financial assistance whereby the net assets of a company are materially reduced.

6.2 Effect of a breach of prohibition

In the event of a breach of the prohibition on the giving of financial assistance, the Companies Act 1985 states that:

- the company is liable to a fine

- every officer in default is liable to a fine and/or imprisonment

- the transaction is unlawful.

Case law has established:

- Any guarantee or other security issued in connection with the transaction is void.

- If the company provides financial assistance in the form of an unlawful loan it cannot sue on the contract to recover the loan because the contract is illegal.

- The company may sue its directors for breach of duty because they have wrongfully dissipated the company's assets in breach of their fiduciary duty.

- The company may sue other persons involved in the transaction (particularly the person who received the assistance) for breach of trust. A person will be liable as a constructive trustee to return the money or compensate the company for its loss if:

- they knowingly receive company property, in breach of the prohibition

- they knowingly participate in a dishonest design on the part of the directors to mis-apply company property.

6.3 Exceptions

The following exceptions are designed to exclude from the prohibition certain transactions that the law regards as legitimate.

(a) If the company's principal purpose in giving the assistance is not that of financing an acquisition, or the giving of the assistance for that purpose is but an incidental part of some larger purpose of the company, then, always provided that the assistance is given in good faith in the interests of the company, the transaction is a lawful one.

(b) Where the lending of money is part of the ordinary business of the company, the loan will be lawful. In order for the loan to be in the ordinary course it must be at the free disposition of the borrower.

(c) It is lawful to provide, in good faith in the interests of the company, money for the purchase of shares under an employee share scheme. The scheme may include salaried directors.

(d) Where loans are made to employees (other than directors) to enable them to purchase fully paid shares.

In the exceptions (b), (c) and (d), assistance given by a public company must either not reduce net assets, taken at book value, or in the alternative, be provided out of distributable profits.

6.4 Relaxation of the restrictions for private companies

A private company may give assistance for the acquisition of shares in itself or in its (private) holding company, providing that either the net assets are not reduced thereby, or, if they are, the assistance is provided out of distributable profits.

The statutory procedure, which must be followed, requires the following:

- The directors must make a statutory declaration. It must describe the assistance to be given, identify the recipient and declare that the company is solvent. Solvency here means that the company will be able to pay its debts as they fall due within the following year or, if it is intended to wind up within the next 12 months, that the company will be able to pay its debts within 12 months of commencement of winding up.

- A report by the auditors must be annexed to the declaration. The report must state that the auditors have enquired into the state of affairs of the company and are not aware of anything to indicate that the opinion of the directors as to solvency is unreasonable.

- A special resolution must be passed by the company (except where it is a wholly owned subsidiary) within the week following the statutory declaration.

- The statutory declaration and report must be filed together with the special resolution within 15 days after the passing of the resolution (or within 15 days of the declaration if no special resolution is necessary).

- The assistance must be given not earlier than four weeks after the resolution (unless all members voted for the resolution) and not later than eight weeks after the statutory declaration (unless the court orders otherwise after objection has been made).

The purpose of the four weeks' hiatus period after the special resolution is to enable objection to be made to the court by members who did not vote for the resolution, provided they are holders of at least 10% by nominal value of any class of issued share capital.

Activity 5

A company X Ltd controls all the shares in Y Ltd. X Ltd wishes to sell its shares in Y Ltd and the employees of Y Ltd wish to set up a new company Z Ltd in order to purchase the shares. The employees wish Y Ltd to agree to allow its assets to be used as security for a bank loan to Z Ltd in order to buy the shares in Y Ltd. Does the law permit this?

Feedback to this activity is at the end of the chapter.

7 Distributions of profit

7.1 Profits available for dividend: rules for all companies

DEFINITION

Profits available for dividend are accumulated, realised profits so far as not previously utilised (whether by distribution or capitalisation) less the accumulated, realised losses, so far as not previously written off.

All companies are prohibited from paying dividends except out of profits available for that purpose.

Profits available for dividend are accumulated, realised profits so far as not previously utilised (whether by distribution or capitalisation) less accumulated, realised losses, so far as not previously written off.

This definition permits the distribution as dividend of a capital profit, i.e. a surplus over book value realised on sale of a fixed asset. But the key words are:

- **accumulated** – which means that the balance of profit or loss from previous years must be brought into account in the current period

- **realised** – which prohibits the inclusion of unrealised profits arising from the revaluation of fixed assets retained by the company.

There are the following supplementary rules.

- If fixed assets are revalued and as a result more has to be provided for depreciation than would have been necessary if the original value had been retained, the additional depreciation may be treated as part of the realised profit for dividend purposes.

- If a provision is made in the accounts it is to be treated as a realised loss unless it is merely a diminution in value of fixed assets or of all fixed assets other than goodwill appearing on revaluation.

7.2 Profits available for dividend: additional rules for public companies

DEFINITION

Undistributable reserves are:

- share premium account
- capital redemption reserve
- unrealised profits

In addition to the rules set out above, a public company may not pay a dividend unless its net assets are at least equal to the aggregate amount of its called-up share capital and undistributable reserves. It may not pay a dividend so as to reduce its net assets below that aggregate amount. If, for example, the share capital plus undistributable reserves is £1 million and the net assets are £999,999, no dividend may be paid; if the net assets are £1,000,001, the dividend is limited to that amount which would leave the net assets at £1 million, i.e. £1.

(less unrealised losses unless previously written off)

- any other reserve that the company is prohibited from distributing by any statute or by its memorandum or articles of association.

Undistributable reserves are:

- share premium account

- capital redemption reserve

- unrealised profits (less unrealised losses unless previously written off)

- any other reserve that the company is prohibited from distributing by any statute or by its memorandum or articles of association.

7.3 Consequences of making an unlawful distribution

If a member of a company receives a dividend that is wholly or in part paid in breach of the rules and they either know (when they receive it) or have reason to believe that it is paid in breach of the rules, they are liable to repay to the company all or so much of it as is paid in breach of the rules. There is no time limit for this liability.

Activity 6

A company had a balance on its profit and loss account reserve at the beginning of its accounting year of losses of £3,000. During the year the company made trading profits of £7,000 and revalued its fixed assets by £5,000. What are the profits available for distribution?

Feedback to this activity is at the end of the chapter.

8 Companies Bill 2006

8.1 Private companies

Private companies will no longer be prohibited from providing financial assistance for the purchase of their own shares. In addition, they will be able to use a new and simpler system of reducing their share capital that does not involve the court. The new system involves:

- a solvency statement signed by all the directors

- a special resolution of the members.

The reduction no longer has to be authorised by the articles.

The following requirements in respect of redeemable shares have been removed:

- The requirement for the company's articles to authorise a proposed allotment of redeemable preferences shares.
- The requirement that the terms of redemption must provide for payment on redemption. Instead, subject to agreement between the company and the shareholders, the amount may be paid later than the redemption date.

8.2 All companies

The directors will be able to determine the terms, conditions and manner of a redemption of redeemable shares. Prior authorisation by the members is required, which may be given by the articles or by a resolution.

A company's articles will no longer need to give authorisation for the purchase of its own shares. However, the members, if they wish, may restrict or prohibit a company from purchasing its own shares by including a provision to this effect in the articles.

Conclusion

A limited company may not generally buy its own shares as this will reduce its creditors' buffer. However, there are certain situations in which the acquisition of shares by a company is lawful.

If a company provides financial assistance for purchase of its own shares, this will only be lawful if it is a private company and follows a certain statutory procedure or, if a public company, the provision of finance falls within a number of exceptional circumstances.

The rules regarding the profits available for distribution are essentially that only accumulated realised profits less accumulated realised losses are available for distribution.

Summary

On completion of their studies, students should be able to:

- explain the maintenance of capital principle and the procedure to increase and reduce share capital.

Self-test questions

Introduction to capital maintenance

1   What capital constitutes a buffer fund for creditors? (1.1)

Increase and reduction of capital

2   List the three possible ways of reducing capital. (2.4)

Redemption of redeemable shares

3   Must redeemed shares be cancelled? (3)

Purchase of own shares

4   What type of resolution is needed for:

    (a)   a market purchase of a company's own shares? (4)

    (b)   an off-market purchase of a company's own shares? (4)

Permissible capital payment

5   How is the amount of a permissible capital payment calculated? (5.1)

Financial assistance for the acquisition of own shares

6   What is meant by financial assistance? (6.1)

7   List the circumstances where financial assistance is lawful. (6.3)

Distributions of profit

8   Define profit available for dividend. (7.1)

9   Explain the net assets test that applies to public companies. (7.2)

Multiple-choice question

Question 1

To enable a company to reduce capital, the shareholders must sanction the reduction by:

A   Ordinary resolution with the usual notice

B   Special resolution with the usual notice

C   Ordinary resolution with special notice

D   Special resolution with special notice

For the answer to this question, see the 'Answers' section at the end of the book.

Practice questions

Question 1: Zed Ltd

Zed Ltd has an authorised share capital of £100,000 in £1 ordinary shares, of which 60,000 have been issued and are fully paid. The company intends:

(a)   to cancel the 40,000 unissued shares

(b)   to repay in cash 50p per share to the holders of the 60,000 issued shares.

What is the procedure for effecting each of these changes? The company's articles of association are in the form of Table A.

Question 2: Seasky Ltd

Seasky Ltd has an issued share capital of £150,000 divided into 100,000 ordinary shares and 50,000 10% preference shares all of £1 each. The terms of issue of the preference shares are that they may be redeemed at par at the option of the company at any time after 31 December 20X3.

The board wishes to exercise the option to redeem because the company has surplus cash.

Explain to the board the legal requirements with which the company must comply.

Question 3: Esk Ltd

Esk Ltd incurred trading losses during each of the four years of its existence and its net assets only represent one half of the nominal value of its issued share capital. In the fifth year it made a profit, which the directors now wish to distribute as a dividend.

Explain whether a dividend can be paid. Would your answer differ if Esk were a public company?

For the answers to these questions, see the 'Answers' section at the end of the book.

Feedback to activities

Activity 1

No, as only fully paid shares can be redeemed.

Activity 2

Yes, but only if it first makes a fresh issue of shares raising at least £2,000 in order to fund the purchase. A public company may only use distributable profit and/or proceeds of a fresh issue for purchase (or redemption) of own shares.

Activity 3

£40,000. (20,000 shares at £2 nominal value.)

Activity 4

	£
Purchase price (200 × 1.25)	250
Less: All distributable profit	(190)
Permissible capital payment	60

Activity 5

The security for a bank loan on Y Ltd's assets would be classed as financial assistance to purchase its own shares. However, as Y Ltd is a private company it may give this assistance for the acquisition of shares in itself providing that the net assets are not reduced or if they are then the reduction is out of distributable profits, and provided the statutory procedure is followed.

Activity 6

£4,000. Profit for the year £7,000 less accumulated losses of £3,000. The unrealised profit on the revaluation of fixed assets is excluded.

Chapter 22

COMPANY ADMINISTRATION AND FINANCE: LOAN CAPITAL

Syllabus content

Company administration and finance

- The ability of a company to borrow money and the procedure to be followed

- Unsecured loans, and the nature and effect of fixed and floating charges

This chapter looks at borrowing by the issue of debentures, concentrating in particular on secured borrowings. The distinction between the fixed and the floating charge, their relative priorities and the different remedies on default available to the chargee are covered. The publicity requirements for charges and their validity are also considered.

Contents

1 Raising loan capital

1.1 Borrowing powers of a company

In addition to capital raised by the issue of shares, companies may need to borrow. This may be done in several ways, such as the issue of debentures (secured or unsecured) or obtaining an overdraft or loan from the bank. Obtaining goods on normal trade credit is not usually treated as borrowing.

A trading company has an implied power to borrow for purposes incidental to its business. In practice the memorandum is likely to include in the objects clause an express power to borrow. A non-trading company can only borrow if it has an express power. If the power to borrow is implied, it is limited to borrowing for purposes incidental to the company's business. If the power to borrow is express then borrowing for a purpose other than to fulfil an object will be *intra vires* the company, but an abuse of the directors powers.

Borrowing is a contract to repay the loan. Even if it is within the company's powers it can still be unenforceable against the company if the directors or other representatives of the company borrowed on its behalf without being authorised to do so. The directors' powers to borrow may be limited in amount by the articles. But if they exceed their powers, the company can ratify the borrowing by ordinary resolution in a general meeting and it may be prevented from denying that the directors had authority. Borrowing powers are usually exercised by the board; however, an individual director may be expressly authorised to exercise the company's borrowing powers. In the absence of express authority, a single director other than a managing director has little implied authority to borrow.

1.2 Nature of a debenture

The term debenture is used to denote the document issued by a company setting out the terms of a loan; such loans are usually medium or long-term borrowings.

A debenture is defined in company law as including debenture stock, bonds or other securities of a company, whether constituting a charge on the assets of the company or not, i.e. it may be secured or unsecured.

An ordinary mortgage of freehold land by a company is a secured debenture.

1.3 Debentures and shares compared

Both debentures and shares are commonly grouped together as securities.

Holdings in company debentures or loan stocks are dealt with on the Stock Exchange under similar procedures to share dealings. The same prospectus rules apply to both. But there are essential distinctions between the two:

- a debenture-holder is a creditor; a shareholder is a member of the company

- a company may freely purchase its own debentures

- interest on a debenture is a debt that may be paid out of capital if there are no profits. It is an expense for tax purposes (unlike a dividend, which is payable out of taxed profits)

DEFINITION

A debenture is defined in company law as including debenture stock, bonds or other securities of a company, whether constituting a charge on the assets of the company or not, i.e. it may be secured or unsecured.

KEY POINT

Both debentures and shares are commonly grouped together as securities.

- debentures may be issued at a discount, e.g. £100 nominal for £95 cash, but not if they carry an immediate right to convert into shares so as to confer a right to acquire shares at a discount.

Debenture-holders and shareholders are both providers of finance to a company. Shareholders are members whose dividends are appropriations of profit whereas debenture-holders are creditors and their interest is an expense of the company.

1.4 Registered debentures

The more common form of debenture is a registered debenture. This will state that the monies and interest are payable to the person named in the debenture (the registered holder). Title to the debenture depends on the holder's name being entered in a register maintained by the company. Transfer is effected in the same way as shares are transferred (i.e. a proper instrument must be delivered to the company).

1.5 Issue of debentures

Debentures are subject to many of the rules that apply to shares. In particular, an offer of debentures to the public is subject to the same general prospectus requirements as for an issue of shares. An offer of debentures to the public by a private company is an offence.

Debentures may be issued at a discount, unlike shares. But the rule against the issue of shares at a discount may not be evaded by issuing debentures with an immediate right of conversion into shares on such terms that the shares will have been issued for less consideration than their par value.

If debentures are issued at a premium, i.e. for more than their nominal value, there is no restriction on the use of the premium when received, but it would normally be transferred to capital reserve. If the debentures are issued at a discount or on terms requiring a premium to be paid on redemption the discount or premium may be charged to the share premium account.

Where identical debentures are issued as a series but to different lenders, possibly on different dates, it is usual to exclude the normal principle of priority of the earlier over the later claim by providing that they shall all rank *pari passu*. This may be so even if the amounts subscribed by the lenders are unequal.

Where a convertible debenture is issued, additional restrictions are imposed:

- the directors must be authorised by the company in general meeting or by its articles to make the issue

- the company must not allot any such securities unless it has offered them first to existing members or debenture-holders on equal or more favourable terms.

The restrictions are necessary anti-avoidance provisions in view of the additional restrictions on the allotment of shares.

1.6 Redemption of debentures

Unless the debentures are perpetual, the company is bound to repay the debentures by the specified final date for redemption and may by the terms of the debenture have the option to repay within some specified period before the final date.

The terms of the debenture may require the company to make an annual payment into a sinking fund for eventual redemption or alternatively to redeem a proportion of the outstanding debentures each year. Unless the debentures prohibit it, the company is free to purchase its own debentures in the market.

When debentures have been redeemed the company is free to re-issue them unless the articles or any contract (i.e. the terms of the debentures) prohibit re-issue or the company has by some formal act, e.g. a resolution passed in a general meeting, shown an intention to cancel the redeemed debentures. Where debentures have been issued, e.g. to a bank, to secure advances made from time to time on the current account, the debentures are not treated as redeemed by reason only of the company's account going into credit.

Debentures can be issued at a premium or at a discount. They may also be redeemed at a premium in which case the premium may be charged to the share premium account.

KEY POINT

Debentures can be issued at a premium or at a discount.

Activity 1

Can X Ltd make an offer of debentures to the public?

Feedback to this activity is at the end of the chapter.

2 Fixed charges and floating charges

2.1 Introduction

A lender to a company may obtain security in the form of a personal guarantee of a director or shareholders. Otherwise the lender is likely to demand security in the form of a charge over its assets if their bargaining position enables them to insist upon it.

A company that has either an express or implied power to borrow also has an implied power to charge its assets as security for the loan.

DEFINITION

A fixed charge is created by the procedure appropriate for mortgaging property of that particular type, e.g. a mortgage of land by deed, a mortgage of shares of another company by transfer to the mortgagee.

2.2 Fixed charge

A fixed charge is created by the procedure appropriate for mortgaging property of that particular type, e.g. a mortgage of land by deed, a mortgage of shares of another company by transfer to the mortgagee.

The essential feature of a fixed charge is that, if properly created it, attaches from the moment of creation (the company cannot deal with the property without the lender's consent) to the property in question and (subject to registration) gives the holder of the charge an immediate security over the property in priority to subsequent claimants.

2.3 Floating charge

A fixed charge over fluctuating assets is obviously inappropriate as the company's freedom to dispose of its stock-in-trade, for example, is essential if it is to carry on its business efficiently. On the other hand, if it cannot create a suitable security interest over such assets, it is deprived of the means of raising a loan secured by the use of what is likely to be a substantial part of its assets. This difficulty has been overcome by the invention of the floating charge.

DEFINITION

A floating charge has been defined in *Re Yorkshire Woolcombers Association* as having three characteristics.

- it is a charge on a class of assets present and future, e.g. if it applies to stock in trade or book debts it comprises whatever assets of that class the company may own at the moment of crystallisation

- the class of assets will change from time to time in the ordinary course of the company's business

- the company may carry on its business and dispose of the assets in the course of business until the charge crystallises.

A floating charge does not attach to the property until the charge crystallises (this means that it fixes onto certain property). Until crystallisation of the charge, the company is free to dispose of assets subject to it: the person to whom the assets are transferred takes them free of the charge. It is also possible for the company, while still owning the assets subject to the floating charge, to create fixed charges over them in priority to the floating charge. A floating charge has been defined in *Re Yorkshire Woolcombers Association* as having three characteristics:

- it is a charge on a class of assets present and future, e.g. if it applies to stock in trade or book debts it comprises whatever assets of that class the company may own at the moment of crystallisation

- the class of assets will change from time to time in the ordinary course of the company's business

- the company may carry on its business and dispose of the assets in the course of business until the charge crystallises.

It is the last point of the definition that makes the crucial distinction between fixed and floating charges. The type of charge that has been created is not determined by the nature of the property over which it is created but rather by the degree of freedom accorded to the company to deal with the charged property in the course of its business.

Siebe Gorman v Barclays Bank (1979)

Facts: the company created a charge over book debts. The charge provided that the company could not charge or assign these debts and had to pay the proceeds into an account with the chargee bank, which the company could not operate without the consent of the bank.

Held: this was a fixed charge: the absence of the ability to use the book debts in the normal course of business deprived the charge of the character of being floating.

Re Brightlife Ltd (1987)

Facts: the company created a charge over book debts. The company retained the freedom to pay the proceeds into its bank account and use them in the normal course of its business.

Held: the charge was a floating charge.

A floating charge may also be expressed to apply to the company's undertaking and property: it then comprises the fixed as well as the current assets.

However, there are limitations on the value of the floating charge, in that if the company's fortunes fall so drastically that it has little property in its possession then there is little on which the floating charge can fix.

2.4 Crystallisation of floating charges

A floating charge crystallises in any of the following circumstances:

- the liquidation of the company

- if an administrator is appointed

- if an event occurs which by the terms of the debenture causes the floating charge to crystallise. Thus the debenture may contain provisions, e.g. that the charge will crystallise if the company fails to keep the property subject to the charge repaired/insured or (very important for floating charge holders) if the company fails to keep stock levels sufficiently high (i.e. of a value equal to or more than the amount of the loan).

There is some doubt as to whether crystallisation will occur automatically on the occurrence of the event specified or whether that happening merely permits the debenture-holders to take action to bring about crystallisation, e.g. by giving notice of their decision, and that crystallisation will only occur when the debenture-holders take action. The general view is that automatic crystallisation is possible.

Activity 2

Is a charge on a company's undertaking and property a fixed or floating charge?

Feedback to this activity is at the end of the chapter.

3 Registration of charges

3.1 Registration at Companies House

KEY POINT

A charge may become invalid on failure to register it at the Companies Registry.

A charge may become invalid on failure to register it at the Companies Registry. This rule is to enable other creditors to discover the existence of the charge by searching the file at the Companies Registry before making a loan or otherwise giving credit to the company.

If the prescribed particulars are not delivered to the Registrar within 21 days of creation of the charge then the charge is void. Note that the underlying debt remains valid; only the charge is void.

The duty to register is on the company and failure is an offence by the company or any officer at fault. However, because the creditor may be prejudiced by failure to register, the charge may be registered by him.

3.2 Procedure for registration

The original instrument of charge and the prescribed particulars (a form showing date of creation, property charged, amount secured and name of chargee) are delivered to the Registrar of Companies who returns the original instrument and sends to the company and the chargee (the lender) a copy of the particulars and the note made by them of the date particulars were delivered. Any person may require the Registrar to provide a certificate of the date on which the particulars were delivered. Such a certificate is conclusive evidence that the particulars were delivered no later than the date stated in the certificate.

3.3 Failure to register

The effect of failure to register is that the charge, but not the debt secured, becomes void where commencement of insolvency proceedings or acquisition of the interest occurs after the creation of the charge (whether before or after the end of the 21 days). The loan becomes repayable immediately, notwithstanding any fixed period in the loan agreement. Thus the creditor becomes an unsecured creditor in a liquidation or an administration.

Where particulars are delivered late, the charge is not void, unless at the date of delivery the company was unable to pay its debts or became so because of the transaction, and insolvency proceedings began within:

- two years (floating charge to a connected person)

- one year (floating charge to non-connected person) or

- six months (fixed charges).

After this time it is void against the administrator or liquidator. Insolvency proceedings include making an administration order or commencement of liquidation.

Where particulars are inaccurate or incomplete, the charge is void to the extent of the error or omission. However, the chargee may apply to the court for an order that the charge is effective against the administrator or liquidator on the grounds that the error in the particulars did not mislead or prejudice an unsecured creditor. The chargee may also apply for an order that the charge is effective against a person who acquired an interest in the property on the grounds that they did not rely on the particulars.

The Companies Act 1985 specifically provides that a person taking a charge over a company's property shall be taken to have notice of any matter requiring registration and disclosed on the register at the time the charge is created.

3.4 Register of charges

The company must maintain a register of charges at its registered office. The register is open to inspection by members and creditors.

Activity 3

A bank is considering making a loan to H plc. H plc has offered a floating charge over the assets and undertaking of the company. What steps should the bank take to ensure that the assets and undertaking of H plc are not already the subject of a charge?

Feedback to this activity is at the end of the chapter.

4 Priority of charges

4.1 Priority of charges generally

The following rules apply, provided that any registration requirements have been duly satisfied:

(a) A fixed charge attaches to the property at the moment of creation. It will generally take priority over any subsequent fixed charge of the same property and over a floating charge created at any time.

This is so even if the fixed charge was created after the floating charge unless:

(i) the floating charge prohibits the creation of subsequent charges with priority over itself

(ii) the holder of the fixed charge had actual notice of the restriction, i.e. registration *per se* does not constitute notice of the prohibition.

(b) A floating charge attaches to the property only when it crystallises. It will generally take priority (by order of creation) over a subsequent floating charge, but be postponed to any fixed charge.

In general a fixed charge has priority over a floating charge on the same assets no matter when the two charges were made. The only exceptions to this are if the fixed charge is not properly registered or if the floating charge is specifically stated to rank above all later created charges.

4.2 Priority of floating charges

When a floating charge crystallises, the debenture-holders entitled to the benefit of the charge have priority over the relevant assets except to the following extent:

(a) The holders of any fixed charge on the company's assets have priority over a floating charge on the same assets:

  (i) the owner of goods let to the company under a hire-purchase agreement retains title to them and has priority over the floating charge

  (ii) the seller of goods may reserve title to goods until they have received payment from the buyer. If the reservation of title clause is effective, the property in the goods will not pass until the buyer pays, until such time the seller may claim their own goods back.

(b) The company's preferential debts, even if unsecured, are to be paid out of assets subject to a floating charge, insofar as any other assets not subject to the charge are insufficient. This rule applies even if the company is not in liquidation

(c) Special situations:

  (i) a judgement creditor probably has priority if at the time the charge crystallises they have been paid or the company's goods have been seized and sold

  (ii) a landlord may retain goods of the company (and the subsequent proceeds of sale) seized in course of distraining for rent before the floating charge crystallises.

Activity 4

Z Ltd creates a floating charge on its undertaking and property on 1 June 209X. On 30 November 209X a fixed charge is attached to Z Ltd's factory building, which it owns. Which charge takes priority?

Feedback to this activity is at the end of the chapter.

5 Validity of charges: Insolvency Act 1986

A floating charge created in favour of an unconnected person within 12 months prior to the commencement of winding up or the making of an administration order is invalid unless it is proved that the company was solvent immediately after the creation of the charge. If this condition is not met such a floating charge will be invalid except to the extent of money, goods or services advanced to the company at the same time as, or after, the creation of the charge.

Where the floating charge is in favour of a connected person of the company, e.g. a director, their relatives and other companies within the group, the period within which the charge is vulnerable is two years and there is no need to show that at the time the charge was created that the company was insolvent.

6 Debenture-holders' remedies

6.1 Introduction

A debenture-holder is in a contractual relationship with the company. The terms of the contract are fixed when the debenture is issued and are not variable subsequently, except on normal contractual principles. Therefore the debenture-holder is entitled to seek a remedy for action taken by the company in breach of contract.

6.2 Unsecured debentures

If the debenture is unsecured, any action to enforce payment of principal or interest is limited to an action for debt or steps are taken to have the company wound up or to apply for an administration order, i.e. the normal remedies of an unsecured creditor.

6.3 Secured debentures

If, however, the debenture is secured, the debenture-holder has the normal rights of an unsecured creditor and in addition they may enforce their security in the following ways:

(a) If their debenture is issued under the common seal of the company they have a statutory power to sell the property or to appoint a receiver of its income in specified circumstances of default.

(b) The debenture-holder can resort to any express power given by the debenture to be exercised on the occurrence of any one of specified happenings or defaults of the company. Typical instances of events on which the power is exercisable are default in payment of principal or interest; commencement of winding up; appointment of a receiver (by another secured creditor); ceasing to carry on business; breach of various restrictions imposed by the debenture, such as a substantial disposal of assets without the debenture-holder's consent. If the company is a holding company, many of the restrictions will be expressed to apply to its subsidiaries also.

(c) They can in the last resort apply to the court for an order for:

   (i) sale

   (ii) delivery of possession

   (iii) foreclosure

   (iv) appointment of a receiver of the property subject to the charge.

   The court will order sale or appoint a receiver only in three cases:

   • when the principal or interest is in arrears

   • when the company has gone into liquidation

   • when the security is in jeopardy.

   The last of these situations is generally established by showing that:

   • other creditors are about to seize assets in execution of a judgement for debt or are about to petition for a compulsory winding up

   • the company has ceased or is about to cease to carry on its business or to transfer its assets to its shareholders or some other person.

The fact that the assets on realisation would not repay the debenture in full has been held insufficient.

Since a forced sale of assets is often an uncompromising means of realising the security, the secured creditor is most likely to appoint an administrator. The administrator may be able to restore the financial position of the company and discharge the secured debt, by sale or otherwise. If they are unable to do so, administration may be a preliminary to the company going into liquidation.

7 Receivership – the old rules

7.1 Appointment

The rules concerning the ability to appoint an administrative receiver have been changed by the Enterprise Act 2002. However, the old rules continue to apply to lending arrangements in existence prior to the enactment of the new Act.

An administrative receiver is appointed to:

- get in the assets charged

- collect income due on them

- realise the assets

- pay the proceeds to the debenture-holders.

The receiver can be appointed as a receiver and manager so that they have the additional power of carrying on the company's business.

The appointment is a sign that the company is or may be in financial difficulty. Accordingly, every invoice, order or business letter of the company must state that a receiver has been appointed. Notice of the appointment must also be given to the Companies Registry within seven days by the person who made or applied for it. The appointment causes any floating charge to crystallise unless this has already occurred.

7.2 Control of assets/position of directors

On taking up their appointment, the receiver assumes control of the assets subject to the charge. The powers of the directors with regard to those assets are in suspense so long as the receiver is in control.

The administrative receiver has the power to dispose of any company asset that is subject to a charge, other than the one under which they are appointed, as if it were not subject to a charge. To do so they must apply to the court for leave, which will be granted if the court is satisfied that the sale is likely to promote a more advantageous sale of the asset and the proceeds will be used to pay the sums secured by the charge.

8 Enterprise Act 2002

8.1 Introduction

The Enterprise Act removes the ability of floating charge holders to appoint an administrative receiver, unless the lending arrangement was in existence prior to the enactment of the Enterprise Act.

In order to understand this change and the reason for it, it is necessary to understand the distinction between an administrative receiver and an administrator.

An administrative receiver was a receiver appointed by the holders of a floating charge that extended over substantially the whole of the company's property. The receiver primarily owed their duties to the floating charge holders, rather than to the company's creditors as a whole.

By contrast, an administrator manages the company's affairs with a view to realising the maximum value for all of the creditors.

Under the rules prior to the Enterprise Act 2002, there was a potential conflict between the interests of the secured creditors and the remaining creditors and shareholders. The holders of a floating charge had an effective veto over the appointment of an administrator. In addition, the actions of the administrative receiver, whilst looking after the interests of the secured creditors, could potentially prejudice the viability of the company.

The Enterprise Act 2002 aims to facilitate the rescue of viable companies by shifting the balance in favour of the administration procedure that accounts for the interests of all the creditors of a company, not just the holder of the floating charge. Essentially, this means that administration will now become the principal means of enforcement for lenders with security over all or substantially all of a company's assets.

8.2 Payments by the receiver/administrator

The statutory order of application of a company's assets is now as follows:

(a) Creditors secured by fixed charge obtain payment out of their charged asset.

(b) Preferential debts, including:

 (i) Wages and salaries of employees due in respect of the four months ended on the date of liquidation, up to a maximum of £800 in any one case.

 (ii) Accrued holiday remuneration of an employee due on termination of their employment before or at the date of liquidation. There is no limit on this.

(c) Creditors secured by floating charge out of their charged asset.

(d) Ordinary unsecured creditors. This category includes any debt not included elsewhere.

(e) Post-liquidation interest. This is interest at a set rate on all the above categories of debt. Should there still be assets at this stage, the company is solvent.

(f) Adjustment of rights of contributories. This is the procedure for distributing the remaining assets amongst the members: in general, the order would be:

 (i) deferred debts, e.g. debts due to members as members such as dividends declared, but not paid, before the date of liquidation

 (ii) return of nominal value to preference shareholders

 (iii) return of nominal value to ordinary shareholders

 (iv) any remaining surplus then goes to ordinary shareholders.

Activity 5

A bank has made a long-term loan to F Ltd. The loan is secured by a combination of a fixed charge over the company's property and floating charges over the other assets. F Ltd is defaulting on the interest payments. What are the remedies available to the bank?

Feedback to this activity is at the end of the chapter.

Conclusion

Debenture-holders and shareholders are both providers of capital to a company. However, whereas shareholders are members of the company, debenture-holders are simply creditors.

There are various different types of debentures and only a public company may offer debentures to the public. Debentures may be issued at a discount or at a premium and the terms of the debenture will specify the date and amount of redemption of the debentures.

Debentures will generally be secured by either a fixed or a floating charge on the assets of the company. Such charges must be registered at the Companies Registry and the company itself must keep a register of charges at its registered office.

If the company does not pay the interest or capital repayments on the loan then the secured debenture-holder has a number of options that may result in the appointment of a receiver/administrator to the company.

Summary

On completion of their studies, students should be able to:

- explain the ability of a company to take secured and unsecured loans, the different types of security and the registration procedure.

Self-test questions

Raising loan capital

1   How is a debenture defined? (1.2)

Fixed charges and floating charges

2   What is a fixed charge? (2.2)

3   What are the three characteristics of a floating charge? (2.3)

Registration of charges

4   When must a charge be registered with the Registrar? (3.1)

5   What is the effect of failure to register? (3.3)

Debenture-holders' remedies

6   What rights of action does a holder of an unsecured debt have? (6.2)

Receivership – the old rules

7   What powers does an administrative receiver have? (7.1 and 7.2)

Enterprise Act 2002

8   What is the order of application of a company's assets? (8.2)

Multiple-choice question

Question 1

In relation to company charges, which of the following is correct?

A   A private company cannot create fixed charges

B   A public company cannot create floating charges

C   Both private and public companies may create fixed and floating charges

D   All business organisations can create fixed and floating charges

For the answer to this question, see the 'Answers' section at the end of the book.

Practice question

Flannel Ltd

Flannel Ltd acquired a substantial loan from ABCD Bank plc. Flannel Ltd is required to give a fixed charge over its factory premises and adjoining land. In addition, the company must grant a floating charge over a significant proportion of its stock.

Required:

(a)   Delete as appropriate and fill in the gaps.

The charge mentioned in relation to the stock *could/could not* have been created had the organisation been a partnership. The advantages of a fixed charge to Flannel Ltd include the fact that a major ……………………….. can be utilised as ………………….. The main disadvantage is that it cannot be …………… without ………………………..   **(5 marks)**

(b)   Explain the major advantage and disadvantage of a fixed charge to a lender. *(Your answer must not exceed 35 words.)*   **(5 marks)**

(c)   Complete the sentence.

A floating charge can be defined as …. *(Your answer must not exceed 10 words.)*   **(5 marks)**

(d)   Fill in the gaps.

If the charges are not registered with the Registrar within ……………………….. the charge is ……………………….. and the directors

…………………………..

The charge over the factory would have to be registered with ……………………….. also.   **(5 marks)**

For the answer to this question, see the 'Answers' section at the end of the book.

Feedback to activities

Activity 1

No, because X Ltd is a private company.

Activity 2

A floating charge.

Activity 3

The bank should initiate a search at Companies House to determine whether there are any charges already registered over H plc's assets. Any charges not registered will be void against the bank.

Activity 4

The fixed charge has priority, providing that the floating charge does not prohibit the creation of the fixed charge and the holder of the fixed charge was not given actual notice of that prohibition.

Activity 5

(a)   Sue for breach of contract

(b)   Threaten to present a winding up petition

(c)   Apply to the court for an administration order

(d)   Appoint a receiver

Chapter 23

COMPANY ADMINISTRATION AND FINANCE : THE BOARD

Syllabus content

Company administration and finance

- The appointment, retirement and removal of directors and their powers and duties during office

- The division of powers between the board and the shareholders

Contents

1 Appointment of directors

2 Qualification and disqualification of directors

3 Service contracts of directors

4 Removal of directors

5 Powers of directors

6 Liability of the company for acts of directors (and others)

1 Appointment of directors

1.1 Introduction

The members are free to decide, in the articles, on the way in which the company is to be managed, e.g. by a board of directors, managers, a managing committee, etc. Normally, it will be by a board of directors elected by the general meeting (and most likely according to the provisions of Table A).

The term 'director' includes any person occupying the position of director by whatever name called.

The test is one of function not of title: the terms governors, managers or trustees are occasionally used in articles instead of directors. Similarly the mere description of someone as a director (e.g. where an employee is referred to as an associate director) will not necessarily make them one for these purposes.

Shadow directors

Certain provisions of the Companies Act apply to persons who are not appointed directors but who are shadow directors.

A shadow director means a person in accordance with whose directions or instructions the directors of the company are accustomed to act. However, a person is not a shadow director by reason only that the directors act on advice given by them in a professional capacity.

The meaning of the terms 'director' and 'shadow director' was extensively considered in the case of *Re Hydrodan* (1994). In the case Millett, J divided directors up into:

- *de jure* directors (validly appointed directors)

- *de facto* directors (those who assume to act as directors without having been validly appointed or at all), and

- shadow directors (who are not directors).

He considered that the three terms did not overlap, and that to establish that a person is a shadow director it is necessary to prove the following:

- who the company's directors are (whether *de jure* or *de facto*)

- that the person alleged to be a shadow director directed those directors how to act

- that those directors acted in accordance with such instructions

- that the directors were accustomed so to act.

Judicial interpretation of this section has been very narrow and it is unlikely that a person will be regarded as a shadow director unless all the directors nearly always act on their instructions.

Executive and non-executive directors

A distinction is drawn in practice – though not by the law – between executive directors and non-executive directors. A non-executive director's function is to attend board meetings, whilst the executive director's function includes not only attendance at board meetings but also day-to-day responsibility for the management of the business. In their capacity as an executive, such a director will often be a full-time employee of the company. The Cadbury Report on

---

DEFINITION

The term 'director' includes any person occupying the position of director by whatever name called.

DEFINITION

A shadow director means a person in accordance with whose directions or instructions the directors of the company are accustomed to act. However, a person is not a shadow director by reason only that the directors act on advice given by them in a professional capacity.

corporate governance recommends that the boards of all listed companies consist of both executive and non-executive directors and further recommends that non-executive directors' functions should be clearly set out and should include a supervisory role over the executive directors.

1.2 Numbers

A public company must have a minimum of at least two directors and a private company one, as long as this one is separate from the company secretary. The maximum number of directors is usually fixed by the articles, but there is no requirement that there shall be a specified maximum nor is there any statutory limit on the number.

Table A specifies a minimum of two directors. It does not specify a maximum number.

The secretary of the company may also be a director, but a sole director may not also be secretary.

1.3 Method of appointment

The first directors are either named as such in the articles or alternatively the articles give authority, usually to the subscribers to the memorandum, to appoint the directors. The documents delivered to the Registrar to secure incorporation of a new company must include particulars of the first directors and their signed consent to act as such. They are not the first directors unless this is done.

The appointment of subsequent directors is regulated by the articles. If Table A is adopted, the main points are:

• At each annual general meeting one-third of the non-executive directors (to the nearest whole number) retire, but are eligible for re-election. A managing director or other executive director, or any director for whom the articles make specific provision, e.g. X is to be director for life, and any director retiring under the rule below is disregarded in arriving at the numbers to retire. Those longest in office since their last election should retire first. The chairman, unless also a managing director, is subject to normal retirement by rotation.

• The board of directors has power to appoint a new director either to fill a vacancy or as an addition to their number (subject to any maximum permitted number). A director so appointed holds office only until the next annual general meeting at which they retire and are eligible for re-election.

When directors of a public company are elected in a general meeting, the appointment of each director must be voted on separately, unless the meeting previously agrees without any dissentient to waive the rule. A procedural defect in the appointment of a director does not usually invalidate the acts of that director (or of the board of which they are an apparent member); but there must have been a purported appointment.

Activity 2

List the principal ways by which directors may be appointed to office.

Feedback to this activity is at the end of the chapter.

1.4 Age qualification

A public company and a private company that is a subsidiary of a public company are subject to s293 Companies Act 1985, which provides that:

- no person is capable of being appointed a director if at the time of their appointment they have attained 70 years of age

- a director must retire at the AGM next following their seventieth birthday.

These provisions do not apply:

- if they are excluded by the articles

- if the director's appointment was made at a general meeting by passing an ordinary resolution of which special notice that stated their age was given.

S294 Companies Act 1985 imposes a duty on the directors to disclose their ages to the company.

Under the provisions of the Companies Bill 2006, the maximum age of 70 will be abolished, and there will be a minimum age of 16 throughout Great Britain. Existing directors under the age of 16 will lose office when the Bill takes effect.

It will, however, remain possible for the articles to specify minimum ages (which must be over 16) and maximum ages.

2 Qualification and disqualification of directors

2.1 Who may be a director

Generally, any person may be a director. In addition, a company may be a director of another company, in which case it is usual to appoint an individual to represent it at board meetings.

A director need not be a member of the company.

There are certain situations in which a person will not be entitled to be a director of a company. These situations are ones where the same person holds more than one office, thereby infringing the rule that a company must have a minimum number of directors, as explained above.

Certain persons, because of their own conduct or characteristics, may not act as directors. These break down into several categories:

- **disqualification by age**

- **disqualification because not a member** – the law does not require a director to be a member, but the articles may

- **other grounds for disqualification** – the articles may so provide

- **statutory disqualification** – under the Company Directors Disqualification Act 1986 (CDDA 86).

2.2 Share qualification

There is no rule of law that a director must also be a member of the company. However, the articles may impose such a requirement, i.e. a share qualification clause to ensure that as they have a stake in the company they will work harder for it.

2.3 Articles

The articles often provide that a director shall cease to hold office if they become insolvent or insane or are absent from board meetings for a specified minimum period (usually six months) without leave: see Table A, which provides that a director will cease to hold office on a resolution of the board if they are absent from board meetings for more than six consecutive months without permission of the directors.

2.4 Company Directors Disqualification Act 1986 (CDDA)

The Company Directors Disqualification Act 1986 contains provisions whereby the court can or must make an order disqualifying a person for a specified period from being:

- a director

- a liquidator or administrator

- a receiver or manager

- in any way, whether directly or indirectly, concerned in the promotion, formation or management of a company.

The period of disqualification runs from the date of the order and depends on the grounds on which the order was made and the court making the order.

The Company Directors Disqualification Act 1986 groups the grounds for disqualification into three groups:

- ss2–5 relating to misconduct (from Companies Act 1985)

- ss6–9 relating to unfitness (from Insolvency Act 1986)

- ss10–12 relating to various grounds (from Companies Act 1985 and Insolvency Act 1986).

2.5 Grounds for disqualification – general misconduct

(a)   S2 Company Directors Disqualification Act 1986 empowers a court to make a disqualification order against a person who is convicted of an indictable offence in connection with the promotion, formation, management or liquidation of a company or with the receivership or management of company property. The maximum period of such an order is 15 years. The court making the order may be the court convicting them or the court winding up the company.

Case law indicates that the courts are taking a very broad view of 'in connection with ... management'. Thus, a director of a building company, who was convicted of offences under the Health and Safety at Work Act 1974 in relation to an unsafe building site operated by the company, was also disqualified under the Company Directors Disqualification Act 1986. Another example arose where a director (who was the chairman and a qualified accountant), having been convicted of insider dealing and sent to prison for 18 months under what is now the Criminal Justice Act 1993, was then disqualified under the Company Directors Disqualification Act 1986 for 10 years.

(b)   (i)   S3 Company Directors Disqualification Act 1986 empowers a court that is winding up a company to make a disqualification order against its directors if it appears that they have persistently defaulted in their duty to file documents or notify the Registrar of

Companies as required by the Companies Act 1985. Persistent default will be conclusively proved by showing that the person has been adjudged guilty of three or more defaults in the previous five years in respect of the duty to file accounts and make returns, etc.

The maximum period for an order under this section is five years.

(ii) S5 Company Directors Disqualification Act 1986 empowers a court that convicts a person of a summary offence in relation to persistent default of their duty to file documents or notify the Registrar of Companies as required by the Companies Act 1985 to make an order disqualifying that person for a maximum period of five years. This is basically the same as the power under s3 given to a court winding up a company.

(c) S4 Company Directors Disqualification Act 1986 empowers the court winding up a company to make a disqualification order if it appears that the person has been guilty of an offence of fraudulent trading whilst the company is a going concern, or any fraud in relation to the company.

The maximum period of disqualification is 15 years.

2.6 Grounds for disqualification – unfitness

(a) Under s6 Company Directors Disqualification Act 1986 the court must make a disqualification order against a person if it is satisfied that:

(i) they are or have been a director of a company that has at any time become insolvent (whether while they were directors or subsequently)

(ii) their conduct as a director of that company (taken alone or with their conduct as a director of any other company or companies) makes them unfit to be concerned in the management of a company.

A shadow director is regarded as a director for this purpose.

The application to the court is made by the Secretary of State (or the Official Receiver as directed by the Secretary of State) where it appears to the Secretary of State to be expedient in the public interest that such an order should be made. It must be made within two years of the company winding up or going into administration, unless the court gives leave for a later application.

There is a duty on the Official Receiver, a liquidator, an administrator or an administrative receiver to report to the Secretary of State if they consider that a director's conduct in relation to the company, considered individually or taken together with their conduct as director of another company, makes them unfit to be concerned with the management of a company. In addition, the Secretary of State or Official Receiver may require any of these people to furnish them with information and documents relating to the director's conduct as they may reasonably require to decide whether or not to apply for a disqualification order.

Sch1 Company Directors Disqualification Act 1986 sets out various criteria to be considered by the court in determining the unfitness of a director. These include any breach of fiduciary duty and general misfeasance.

A disqualification order under s6 will last for a minimum of two years and a maximum of 15 years.

(b)   S8 Company Directors Disqualification Act 1986 provides for disqualification following investigation of a company by the Department of Trade and Industry. The court may make the order if it is satisfied that the person's conduct in relation to the company makes them unfit to be concerned in the management of a company.

A shadow director is regarded as a director for this purpose.

An application under this section may be made whether the company is insolvent or not and the court has a discretion as to whether it makes an order or not.

There is no minimum period of disqualification but there is a maximum of 15 years.

2.7   Other cases of disqualification

(a)   S10 Company Directors Disqualification Act 1986 provides that the court may make a disqualification order against any person against whom it makes an order to contribute to the company's assets under s213 Insolvency Act 1986 (fraudulent trading) or s214 Insolvency Act 1986 (wrongful trading).

There is no minimum period for an order under s10. The maximum period is 15 years.

(b)   S11 Company Directors Disqualification Act 1986 provides that it is an offence for an undischarged bankrupt to be a director of or otherwise concerned in the management of any company without leave of the court.

(c)   S12 Company Directors Disqualification Act 1986 provides that, where a person fails to make any payments as required by an administration order, the court may make a disqualification order against that person not exceeding two years. An administration order is an order providing for the administration by the county court of a debtor's estate.

2.8   Consequences of contravening a disqualification order

*   S13 Company Directors Disqualification Act 1986 – any person who acts in contravention of a disqualification order or while an undischarged bankrupt is guilty of an offence – the maximum penalty is two years' imprisonment and or a fine.

*   S14 Company Directors Disqualification Act 1986 – where a company is guilty of an offence under s13 any person who consented to or contributed to the company so acting is also guilty of an offence and may be prosecuted.

*   S15 Company Directors Disqualification Act 1986 – provides that anyone who is involved in the management of a company while disqualified (under a disqualification order or while an undischarged bankrupt) or who acts or is willing to act on the instructions of a person who is disqualified shall be personally liable for the company's debts incurred during the time they act.

The Secretary of State maintains a register of disqualification orders that is open to public inspection: s18 Company Directors Disqualification Act 1986.

Activity 2

What are the principal restrictions on appointment to or continuation in office as a director?

Feedback to this activity is at the end of the chapter.

3 Service contracts of directors

3.1 Introduction

A person who acts as a director may be:

- An officer of the company only – a director may serve in an office other than that of director although they cannot be an auditor and if they are the sole director they cannot be the company secretary.

- An officer and an employee of the company under a contract of service – thus, they might be a director of and also a lecturer employed by the company. This is fairly clear. What is less clear is where they are an officer and an employee of the company in their capacity as director. Thus, a person who is a director (an officer) may also be the managing director (an employee).

- An officer and an independent contractor of the company under a contract for services – thus, a person who is a director (an officer) may also be the finance director who merely provides occasional services and therefore in law can be an independent contractor, as they merely provide services as opposed to actually being in the service of the company as an employee under a contract of service.

Whether or not a director has a contract for services or a contract of service (the latter meaning they are an employee) is important for employment law, but in company law the importance is limited to liquidation; money due under a contract of service is a preferential debt, but money due under a contract for services is an ordinary debt.

What is important for company law is whether or not the director has a contract (the general term service contract is now used to cover both types) as there are statutory rules on the length of service contracts. In addition, whether or not a director has a service contract is relevant to remuneration and any claim for damages on dismissal (remember that the articles are not a contract between the company and a director in that capacity).

3.2 Who negotiates directors' service contracts?

This is dealt with by the company's articles.

Table A allows the board to enter into an agreement with any director for their employment by the company on such terms as the board thinks fit. The director concerned may not vote on their contract at the board meeting nor may they be counted towards the quorum.

3.3 Long-term service contracts

A company cannot include a term in a director's service contract that it should continue for more than five years during which time it cannot be terminated by the company by notice or can only be terminated in specified circumstances, without first obtaining the approval of the shareholders in a general meeting by an ordinary resolution. If a clause is included in the contract in contravention of the section, it is void and the contract is deemed to contain a clause entitling the company to terminate it at any time by giving reasonable notice. The Cadbury Report recommends that for listed companies the period should be reduced to three years.

3.4 Contracts of service to be open for inspection

The company is required to keep at its registered office (or other appropriate place) a copy of the service agreements of all its directors and directors of its subsidiaries who are employees (or a written summary if there is no contract in writing). There is an exception for directors who work wholly or mainly abroad and where the unexpired period of the contract is less than 12 months. Members of the company have a statutory right of inspection.

4 Removal of directors

4.1 Introduction

A director may cease to hold office in various ways:

- Directors may be removed from office by disqualification arising under statutory provisions or under the terms of the articles set out above.

- If the articles provide for the removal of a director for other reasons, removal according to those provisions will be effective.

- A director may relinquish office by resignation or by not standing for re-election.

Note also that:

- If appointed under a fixed term contract, expiry of the term means termination of the directorship.

- Winding up and administration does not necessarily operate to terminate directors' contracts of employment, although they lose their powers to act. An administrator has power under the Insolvency Act 1986 to appoint and remove directors.

- The appointment of a receiver out of court by debenture-holders does not necessarily terminate directors' contracts of employment, at least so long as the role and function of the receiver is not inconsistent with the continuation of those contracts.

4.2 Removal of directors under s303

The articles generally provide for how to remove a director, but in addition s303 Companies Act 1985 lays down a statutory rule. This statutory power cannot be excluded, but it may be possible to circumvent it by weighted voting rights.

Bushell v Faith (1970)

Facts: a provision in the articles tripled the votes of shares held by directors on a resolution to remove a director. Parliament only required an ordinary resolution and made no provision as to how the resolution could be obtained or defeated, although it was pointed out that such an article as the one in question was sometimes necessary in a family company in order to reduce repercussions from family quarrels in the boardroom and in general meetings.

Held: the provision was upheld. The ratio of the case probably limits the application of this principle to private companies.

S303 does not carry with it the power to deprive a director of compensation for dismissal to which they are otherwise entitled. This will depend upon whether they have a right to compensation arising from a contract of employment with the company, as distinct from any right solely as a member under the articles (assuming the director is a shareholder).

Managing directors often have contracts of service and rights over and above those of directors in general.

Articles may enable the directors to appoint a managing director on such terms as they think fit.

Removal of a director may found a claim by that director for breach of a service contract.

Southern Foundries Ltd v Shirlaw (1940)

Facts: a managing director was appointed under a contract with the company for ten years but, after the articles had been changed empowering his removal as director, he was dismissed.

Held: the House of Lords awarded him damages for wrongful dismissal since the alteration of the articles, although effective, constituted a breach of his contract of service. It was contrary to the agreement that he should serve for ten years, which became impossible when he lost his directorship. Note that at this time there were no restrictions on the length of service contracts.

Dismissal of a director of a small partnership type company may give rise to the compulsory winding up of the company.

Ebrahimi v Westbourne Galleries (1973)

Facts: Mr Ebrahimi had been in business with a colleague for 25 years, the last ten as a company. He agreed to transfer some of his shares to his colleague's son, who then combined with his father to dismiss Mr Ebrahimi from the board.

Held: the company would be compulsory wound up on the ground that it was just and equitable under s122(g) Insolvency Act 1986.

Alternatively to winding up, a director may petition for relief from unfair prejudice under s459 Companies Act 1985.

4.3 Procedure for removal of a director

S303 Companies Act 1985 states that a director can be removed under this section by the passing of an ordinary resolution with special notice. Notice is given by the person(s) wishing to remove the director.

This person(s) should give a minimum of 28 days' notice to the company. The company must then inform the director forthwith.

The company should then give notice to all members who are entitled to attend and vote at the general meeting. This notice is:

- a minimum of 14 days if the motion to remove is to be voted on at an Extraordinary General Meeting (EGM)

- a minimum of 21 days if the motion to remove is to be voted on at an Annual General Meeting (AGM).

The director has various rights to protest their removal (this is the purpose of the special notice provision). They may require the company to circulate their written representations (they must be read out at the meeting if there was no time for prior circulation). They must be allowed to attend and vote at the meeting.

If a director is deprived of the rights to protest their removal, their removal is not valid under s303. Exceptionally in *Bentley-Stevens v Jones* (1974) a director who was not allowed to protest his removal was held validly removed because those denying him his rights had ordinary resolution control of the company.

Removal of directors is an important area of the syllabus. The most examinable part of this subject is the procedure under s303 Companies Act 1985.

The key points to remember are:

- removal under this section requires an ordinary resolution

- special notice is given to the director(s) who is/are to be removed. This is to give time to write to all members who will be involved in the vote at the general meeting

- a director can block the passing of the ordinary resolution to remove them by having 50% of the voting power

- the company may not be able to afford to remove the director if they have a long term service contract which, if breached, will entitle them to the balance of the salary owing to them under the fixed term.

Activity 3

The directors of Northgate Forest Football Club want one of their number to step down from the board. They believe that the director concerned, named Read, has been supplying the media with confidential information about the state of health of their ailing manager, Brian Clogg.

Set out the advice you would give to Read, who is reluctant to resign.

Feedback to this activity is at the end of the chapter.

5   Powers of directors

5.1   Introduction

Companies invariably delegate extensive powers of management to their directors.

Table A states that 'subject to the provisions of the Companies Act, the memorandum and the articles and to any directions given by special resolution, the business of the company shall be managed by the directors who may exercise all the powers of the company'.

Two points to remember:

- **Acts *ultra vires* the company** – the company can obviously only delegate such powers as the company itself may have, i.e. the directors are not competent to engage in *ultra vires* transactions. They may, however, do anything that the company in a general meeting could do.

- **Directors acting for an improper purpose** – directors can only validly exercise their powers in the interests of the company and for the purposes for which the powers are conferred, unless the company in a general meeting authorises what they have done or intend to do. Anything done by directors which, although *intra vires* the company, is not done for an authorised purpose, is an unauthorised act and may not be binding on the company.

The delegation of powers is to the directors collectively, i.e. acting as a board of directors the board may, of course, be authorised by the articles to sub-delegate powers to an individual director, e.g. by appointing them to be managing director or by express delegation of powers to a director or to a committee of directors. In either case, such delegation is possible only if authorised by the articles since the directors are themselves delegatees of the company.

An individual director has no direct authority from the company to act on its behalf except, perhaps, to sign documents as a director (for which a single director's signature suffices unless the articles require more than one).

Two types of legal problem may arise in connection with directors' powers:

- the company in a general meeting may wish to exercise or control the directors in the exercise of their powers

- the company may deny that the directors or a single director were authorised to commit the company in some transaction with an outsider.

5.2 Authority

Authority to act so as to bind the company stems from the agreement of the members of the company, the shareholders. Authority issues from them in two basic ways:

- from the articles of association

- from decisions in a general meeting (in which there may be participation by others afforded the right to vote, e.g. debenture-holders).

To a large extent, in practice, the decisions of the general meeting in large public companies will coincide with the wishes of the directors since the directors will control the proxy voting machinery. In other cases, it may be important to decide the effect of the division of power between the general meeting and the board of directors.

The general view appears to be that powers delegated to the board by the articles cannot be exercised by the members in a general meeting; and nor can the general meeting instruct the board in the exercise of their delegated powers.

Breckland Group Holdings v London & Suffolk Properties Ltd (1989)

Facts: C held 51% of the company's voting shares and instructed solicitors to commence an action in the company's name against six defendants (including the company's managing director).

Held: where a company's articles vest the right to commence legal proceedings in the company's name in the board: the board, alone, and not the general meeting, is able to exercise that right. Thus C could not cause the company to commence litigation and accordingly the solicitors had no claim against the company for their fees.

Shaw v John Shaw (1935)

Facts: the company's board (acting by a majority of its directors) resolved that the company commence litigation against two errant directors. A shareholders' meeting resolved, by ordinary resolution, that the action be discontinued.

Held: the ordinary resolution could not overrule the board's decision.

The opening words of Article 70 subject the powers of the directors to manage the company to:

- provisions of the Companies Act

- provisions of the memorandum and articles

- directions given by special resolution (except that no such direction shall invalidate any prior act of the directors).

The provisos are clear cut:

- Certain powers are expressly reserved to members in general meeting by the Companies Act itself. These powers include alteration of the memorandum, articles and share capital, removal of directors and a decision to voluntarily wind up the company.

- The memorandum or articles may expressly reserve powers to the members in a general meeting. Thus, under Table A, appointment of directors, declaring of dividends and decisions to capitalise profits are specifically reserved to members (subject to some conditions).

- Directions given by special resolution; the shareholders may direct the board as to their actions.

Thus, the members are not solely without power to control directors whose actions are not in accord with members' wishes.

5.3 Ultimate control lies with the general meeting

- The general meeting may remove the directors (s303 Companies Act 1985 – by ordinary resolution) and appoint a board more in sympathy with its wishes.

- It may withdraw the powers by altering the articles by special resolution.

Neither of these will invalidate authorised acts already done by the directors, but will ensure (hopefully) more unity in the future.

5.4 How directors' powers are exercised

It should be clear that the directors only have such powers as are delegated to them, and that the articles will usually delegate wide powers to the board of directors. Unless there is then a power to sub-delegate, all decisions and actions must be by the board collectively.

5.5 Managing director (MD)

The articles may permit the appointment of an MD (or more than one) and delegation to them of any of the powers of the board to be exercised by them either collaterally with or to the exclusion of the board. Note that it is the function of the board, and not the general meeting, to appoint a managing director.

The board may be authorised to delegate any or all of its powers to the MD, who will thus have complete control over their exercise until their authority is revoked. In such a case, the general meeting, the board and the MD will each have exclusive jurisdiction over their respective spheres of power.

An MD is something more than a director with management functions. They are deemed to have general powers as an individual to commit the company to contracts. However, they are the board's delegate only; thus they have no power to exercise those residual powers of the shareholders.

An MD's appointment ceases if they cease to be a director. If they have a separate service agreement providing for their employment as MD, their removal from office as director may be a breach of contract: *Southern Foundries v Shirlaw*; but they cannot prevent, by injunction, an alteration of articles, or the passing of an ordinary resolution by the company removing them from office.

Activity 4

Identify the possible recourses of the general meeting if the board of a company refuses to undertake a commercial project that has been approved by a resolution of the meeting.

Feedback to this activity is at the end of the chapter.

6 Liability of the company for acts of directors (and others)

6.1 Introduction: agency in company law

There are certain circumstances in which a company may incur liability (i.e. for contracts, torts and crimes). This may be because the company itself has committed an act or, more likely, an act will be done on behalf of the company by an employee or agent. Whether or not such an act will make the company liable depends on the power of the company to act in such a situation (the *ultra vires* rule and its exceptions) and on whether or not the person acting is capable of binding the company.

The issue is basically one of the law of agency. A principal (here, the company) will be liable for the acts of its agent if the agent has acted within either:

(a)   the actual scope of the authority conferred on them by their principal prior to the transaction or by subsequent ratification, or

(b)   the apparent scope of their authority. This last is based on representations by the principal. It is based on estoppel.

       (i)   Thus, if a person has been appointed to the office of Managing Director, they will appear to a third party to have authority to bind the company in all contracts connected with the management of the company. Similarly, other agents will have apparent authority from what is usual to their position or office. Remember that a non-executive director has no usual authority by virtue of that office.

(ii)   Thus, if the company holds a person out as occupying a particular office or position, it will then be estopped from denying to a third party who relies on the representation that the person has authority usual to that position. This doctrine of holding out is illustrated by the leading case of:

Freeman & Lockyer v Buckhurst Park Properties (1964)

Facts: Kapoor, a property developer, and Hoon, formed a private company that purchased Buckhurst Park Estate. The board of directors consisted of Kapoor and Hoon and a nominee of each. The company's articles gave the company power to appoint an MD, but none was appointed. Kapoor, however, acted as such. He instructed the claimants, a firm of architects, to do work for the company, which was completed. The company refused to pay claiming that Kapoor had no authority to bind the company to this type of transaction.

Held: Kapoor had been held out as having apparent authority to enter into this transaction by those having actual authority to commit the company in this way, i.e. the board. The company is, therefore, estopped from denying to anyone who has entered into a contract with an agent in reliance upon such apparent authority that the agent had authority to contract on behalf of the company.

A third party cannot rely on apparent authority when they know, or perhaps ought to know, of the lack of actual authority.

6.2 Personal liability

Although the third party cannot sue the company on a transaction that is outside the scope of the agent's actual or apparent authority, they may sue the agent personally for breach of warranty of authority and thereby recover damages for any loss.

In addition, if an agent acts outside their actual authority, they commit a breach of duty and the principal could sue them and, in a serious case, dismiss them.

6.3 Transactions beyond the board's powers

A transaction might be beyond the powers of the board for several reasons.

* The transaction is *ultra vires* the company as delimited by its memorandum.

* The transaction, although *intra vires* the company, is an abuse by the directors of the company's powers.

* The transaction was beyond the directors' powers as set out by the company's articles or by the general meeting. Nowadays articles of companies will commonly delegate all the company's powers to the board, but in the past it was extremely common for articles to subject the exercise of borrowing powers by the board to the sanction of the members in general meeting.

Unless the members have ratified the contract, at common law it is not binding on the company.

S35A Companies Act 1985 now provides considerable protection to third parties. It provides that, in favour of a person dealing with the company in good faith, the power of the board to bind the company or authorise others shall be deemed to be free of any limitations in the company's constitution including by resolution or agreement by members. It further states:

- a person deals with a company if they are party to any transaction or other act to which the company is a party

- a person shall not be regarded as acting in bad faith by reason only of their knowledge that an act is beyond the powers of the directors under the company's constitution

- a person shall be presumed to have acted in good faith unless the contrary is proved.

S35B states:

- a party to a transaction with a company is not bound to enquire as to whether it is permitted by the company's memorandum or as to any limitation on the powers of the board of directors to bind the company or authorise others to do so.

However, the provision does not affect any right of a member of the company to bring proceedings to restrain the doing of an act that is beyond the powers of the directors. Thus, prior to the directors acting, a member could seek an injunction to prevent the directors from acting beyond their powers, but could not do so once they had acted. The provision does not affect the liability of the directors to the company for acts done beyond their powers.

6.4 Invalidity of transactions involving directors

S322A Companies Act 1985 provides that where a company enters into a transaction to which the parties include a director or person connected with a director of the company or its holding company and the board has exceeded the limitation in its powers under the company's constitution, the transaction is voidable by the company. This provision therefore modifies the rules in s35A Companies Act 1985 when a director or connected person contracts with the company and renders the contract voidable. 'Connected person' is defined as for substantial property transactions, essentially close relatives, companies under the directors' control, etc.

S322A Companies Act 1985 provides that the transaction will cease to be voidable if:

- the restriction is no longer possible

- the company is indemnified for any loss suffered

- a *bona fide* purchaser for value without notice of directors exceeding their authority acquires rights on the subject matter of the transaction

- the company in a general meeting ratifies the transaction by ordinary or special resolution.

However, s322A Companies Act 1985 also provides that whether the transaction is avoided or not, any director or connected person who was a party to it and any director of the company who authorised it is liable to account to the company for any gain or indemnify the company for any loss.

Summary

On completion of their studies, students should be able to:

- explain the procedure for the appointment, retirement, disqualification and removal of directors and their powers and duties during office.

Self-test questions

Appointment of directors

1   Who is a shadow director? (1.1)

2   How many directors must a company have? (1.2)

3   What is the age qualification for directors and when does it apply? (1.4)

Qualification and disqualification of directors

4   What are the grounds for disqualification under the Company Directors Disqualification Act 1986? (2.5–2.7)

Service contracts of directors

5   How long is a long-term service contract? (3.3)

6   Where must directors' service contracts be kept? (3.4)

Removal of directors

7   How is a director removed from office under s303 Companies Act 1985? (4.2 & 4.3)

Powers of directors

8   Where are the directors' powers stated? (5.2)

Liability of the company for acts of directors (and others)

9   In what circumstances is a third party protected by s35A Companies Act 1985? (6.3)

Multiple-choice questions

Question 1

A director may be removed from office under section 303 of the Companies Act 1985 by:

A   Ordinary resolution with the usual notice

B   Special resolution with the usual notice

C   Ordinary resolution with special notice

D   Special resolution with special notice

Question 2

Which of the following statements is correct?

A   A managing director is an agent of the company

B   A managing director is an agent of the board

C   A managing director is an agent of the shareholders

D   A managing director is not an agent

For the answers to these questions, see the 'Answers' section at the end of the book.

Practice question

Susan and Shirley

Susan and Shirley were business partners for many years. On 1 April 20X5 the business was incorporated. Susan now has 51% of the shares and Shirley, 49%; both were named in the company's Articles as directors and both have a service contract. Susan would like to remove Shirley from the board because of a personal disagreement. Susan wishes to run the company alone.

Required:

(a)   Delete as appropriate, and fill in the gap and complete the sentence.

Shirley *can/cannot* be removed from her office under ....because .... *(Your answer must not exceed 20 words.)*

(5 marks)

(b)   Fill in the gaps and delete as appropriate.

Removal would be by .... with .... These require consent by .... of those entitled to vote. Susan *can/cannot* therefore remove Shirley. The notice required for the meeting would have to be .... **(5 marks)**

(c)   If Shirley is removed from office, the company *will/will not* be in breach of contract and she *will/will not* be entitled to sue for lost earnings as in the case of .... **(3 marks)**

(d)   Explain how Shirley's case may be helped if she can persuade a court that this was a 'quasi-partnership'. *(Your answer must not exceed 40 words.)*

(7 marks)

For the answer to this question, see the 'Answers' section at the end of the book.

Feedback to activities

Activity 1

(a)   Co-opted by board.

(b)   By members in a general meeting by ordinary resolution.

Activity 2

(a)   Where the director is a sole director and is also the company secretary.

(b)   Where the director of a public company is over 70 years old.

(c)   Non-compliance with a share qualification clause in the articles.

(d)   Disqualification by the articles.

(e)   Disqualification under the Company Directors Disqualification Act 1986.

Activity 3

Assuming the articles are in the form of Table A, there is no provision whereby the board of a company can require a director to vacate their position provided they attend board meetings.

By Table A, a director may resign by notice, or by 'not standing for re-election when they are required to do so' (for example under the retirement by rotation provisions of Table A).

The usual method of removing a director from office is to utilise the procedure of s303. This requires the general meeting to pass an ordinary resolution of which special notice has been given. The notice must be given at least 28 days before the meeting, and the director concerned has a right to circularise the company with a statement, as well as to speak at the meeting, in their support.

If Read were to be removed under this procedure (or under any other procedure set out in the articles, if they are not in the form of Table A), he may well have a claim against the company for wrongful and/or unfair dismissal, if he is an executive director: *Shirlaw v Southern Foundries Ltd.*

Activity 4

(a)   Remove the board under s303.

(b)   Alter the articles by special resolution to make the board subject to the direction of the general meeting.

(c)   If the articles are in the form of Table A, pass a special resolution to direct the board.

(d)   It may be possible to bring an action under s459 of Companies Act 1985 on the basis of 'unfair prejudice' or s122 of Insolvency Act 1986 (to wind the company up on the just and equitable ground), although the court will probably need evidence of more than just a disagreement with the company's commercial policy.

Chapter 24

COMPANY ADMINISTRATION AND FINANCE: DIRECTORS' DUTIES

Syllabus content

Company administration and finance

- Directors' powers and duties

- Fraudulent and wrongful trading, preferences and transactions at an undervalue

This chapter considers the duties that every director owes to their company deriving from both the common law and statute. The accountability of directors and to whom they are accountable is one of the contentious issues of corporate governance.

Contents

1 Nature of the duties of directors

1.1 The director's roles

Firstly, the directors of a company are persons of some importance with a definite place in the constitutional structure of the company. It is they who, in practice, control the company and upon whom the fortunes of the company largely depend. But this does not mean that they can treat the company as their own.

Secondly, the directors have certain duties that they are obliged to fulfil. These derive from the various roles that a director has within the company.

- **Director as an employee** – although a director may be an employee, they need not necessarily be one, so their duties are not necessarily related to a contract of service. Generally speaking, an employee's duty of fidelity may impose lesser obligations than the director's duties of good faith.

- **Director as an agent** – they will be in the position of an agent (although the precise nature of the agency will depend upon the particular circumstances) and so will owe the duties of an agent. But their relationship with the company cannot be determined solely by reference to the law of agency, especially as they do not necessarily have all the rights of an agent.

- **Director as a trustee** – the quasi-trusteeship position of a director has great significance with reference to breach of duty in that if a director in breach of fiduciary duty misapplies company assets, they commit a breach of trust and under trust law principles become liable to restore the misapplied property. The same liability attaches to any person who knowingly assists in a breach of trust or who knowingly receives company assets misapplied in breach of trust. This principle was earlier seen in operation when considering the effect of a company giving unlawful financial assistance for the acquisition of its own shares.

The position of director is not, however, wholly analogous to that of a trustee. A trustee must be cautious and safeguard the trust property; the director, however, is engaged in a speculative undertaking and the likelihood of their having to take risks is such that their obligation to refrain from negligence is far less onerous than that of a trustee.

1.2 To whom are the duties owed?

KEY POINT

Generally, directors owe duties to the company as a whole and this includes the members as a collective body.

There are potentially a number of individuals or bodies to whom the director owes duties; the company, the members, the employees, the creditors, the board. These shall be dealt with in turn.

The company

The general rule is that directors owe their duties to the company as a whole. This has traditionally been taken to mean to the shareholders as a collective body, which includes present and future shareholders.

The directors may take account of their own interests as shareholders and of the interests of particular sections of shareholders; they are not required to think of the company as an entity that is completely distinct from its members. S309 Companies Act 1985 requires them to have regard to the interests of employees and members, but their duty is to the company.

The members

The directors owe no general duty to individual members.

Percival v Wright (1902)

Facts: some shareholders wrote to the secretary of a company asking if he knew of anyone wishing to purchase shares in the company. After negotiations, the shareholders sold their shares to the chairman of the company and two directors. Subsequently, the claimants discovered that during the negotiations the board had been engaged in talks with another party concerning a takeover of the company, at a price that was considerably more than they had obtained for their shares. The attempted takeover did not take place. The shareholders wished to have the sale of their shares set aside on the basis that the directors should have disclosed the negotiations with the bidder.

Held: the directors must act *bona fide* for the interests of the company, but they are not in a fiduciary position in relation to individual shareholders. Therefore the individual shareholders had no action against the directors. (Presumably the company itself could have sued if the actions of the directors had caused a loss to the company.)

The same principle was applied in *Scottish Co-operative Wholesale Society v Meyer* (1958) where the majority shareholder in a holding company had appointed its nominees as the majority of the directors of the subsidiary and it was stated by the House of Lords that their first duty was to the subsidiary, the company of which they were directors, and not to the holding company, the majority member and their nominator.

However, despite the general rule, particular circumstances may give rise to a duty owed by directors to particular shareholders, for example where they are authorised to act as agents for particular shareholders in relation to the sale of their shares.

The employees

S309 Companies Act 1985 insists that the directors have regard to the interests of the company's employees as well as to the members. However, the duty is to the company. There is no duty to the employees and any breaches of the directors' duties are enforceable by the company as the proper claimant, so not surprisingly this is regarded as unlikely to be enforced.

The creditors

The law does not recognise a duty to others, e.g. creditors, customers, or (for example, in environmental matters) to the community, but there are numerous provisions designed to protect such persons and in practice it will generally be in the interests of the company that its relations with creditors, etc. should be harmonious and that the company should be of good repute.

A director appointed by holders of debentures under a power in the debentures owes their duties primarily to the company and not to the debenture-holders. This might appear to detract from the protection given to debenture-holders, in that their appointee will not be obliged merely to promote their interests, unless it is remembered that the appointee should be able to see, by their membership of the board, that the affairs of the company are properly conducted and in the manner presumably expected by the debenture-holders.

The board

It might be argued that the directors are responsible to the board of directors of which they are a member and which may have initially secured their appointment as directors. But, although directors may derive power from their activities as a board (their authority to bind the company generally depends on whether or not they act as a board) their duties are not owed to the board, i.e. to themselves. Thus, they cannot control the extent and exercise of their duties, or excuse breaches of them, by board decisions.

A further aspect of this is that although directors exercise their powers collectively as a board, their duties are owed individually.

Summary

Each director owes a duty to the company. The significance of this is that since the company is a legal entity it is the company who sues. This is an aspect of the rule in *Foss v Harbottle* (1843) which, in general, prevents a member suing where wrongs have been done to the company.

1.3 Acting in the interests of the company as a whole

Directors are bound to carry out their duties (to exercise the powers and discretion given to them) but the means by which they do so will not generally be specified. They are, however, obliged to adhere to their overriding duty of good faith and to act in what they consider to be in the interests of the company as a whole.

- **Who decides what is in the best interests of the company?**

  The test here is subjective, i.e. did the directors themselves honestly believe that they were acting in the best interests of the company? If so, their judgement will not be impugned even if the outcome shows or the opinion of the court is that they showed bad judgement.

  As an example, a director and controlling shareholder must not procure a service agreement for themselves entirely to provide a pension for their widow: *Re Roith* (1967). He was held to be in breach of duty because he had given no thought to the benefit of the company.

  Similarly in *Bishopsgate Investment Management Ltd v Maxwell (No 2)* (1994) – summary judgement was given against Ian Maxwell (one of Robert Maxwell's two sons, the other being Kevin) who, as director of Bishopsgate, signed stock transfer forms transferring shares, forming part of the company's pension fund for employees, to another company controlled by Robert Maxwell. Judgement was given against Ian mainly because he had given no thought to the benefit of Bishopsgate, merely by signing because Kevin told him to do so.

- **What are the interests of the company as a whole?**

  This is really another aspect of the problem posed above, i.e. to whom is the duty owed and what happens if there are conflicting duties?

Directors must take account of the interests of the company. This requires taking account of all relevant interests (whether of shareholders, creditors, employees, etc.) in deciding what is in the overall interests of the company. However, since the employees and creditors rarely have the ability to sue the directors, most directors will give priority to the rights of shareholders.

A number of statutory provisions of the Insolvency Act 1986 are designed to protect creditors (notably the fraudulent and wrongful trading provisions of s213 and s214 Insolvency Act 1986 under which the liquidator can take action against errant directors). Although such action by the liquidator is theoretically taken by them on behalf of the company, it is the creditors who stand to benefit where the company is insolvent.

In summary, although directors owe their duties to the company and it is the company that sues them for breach, whether or not they are in breach of their duty will entail consideration of their treatment of members, employees and perhaps creditors.

1.4 In what capacity do directors owe duties?

Directors owe duties whilst acting in the capacity of director – thus, for example, at a board meeting each director must exercise their vote in the interests of the company and not, for example, in their own personal interest.

The position is different at general meetings where, if a director is a member, they will be voting, not in their capacity as a director but in their capacity as a member.

2 The fiduciary duty of directors

2.1 Introduction

Every director has a fiduciary duty to act in good faith for the benefit of the company as a whole.

Although there is one overriding fiduciary duty it has a number of different, but overlapping applications.

2.2 Duty to exercise powers for the proper purpose (the proper purposes rule)

Although the directors themselves must decide how to exercise their powers, and although actions taken by them outside their powers may be ratified by the company in general meeting, this does not permit the directors to exercise their powers other than for the purposes for which they are given.

Obviously, the exercise of a discretion may require the taking account of many factors and the influence of mixed motives. But the directors will be justified if their main purpose is a proper one.

The most common instance of challenge of directors' exercise of powers for a proper purpose is the issue of shares by directors for the purpose of creating additional votes at a general meeting in order to resist a takeover bid or otherwise to affect voting control. The power to issue shares is given to directors by the articles for the purpose only of raising additional capital or acquiring assets that the company needs for its business. The issue of shares for any other purpose, even if the directors honestly believe that to do so is in the interests of the company, is a breach of their duty. A number of illustrative cases were given in Chapter 20.

2.3 Duty to avoid a conflict of interest

A director may be in a position where there is a conflict between their duty to the company and their own personal interests. For example, they become a director of a company that provides training to accountants while working as an independent tutor teaching at rival colleges. There is a general rule that this should not be allowed. Thus, a director must not do or omit to do something if that gives rise to a conflict, or might reasonably be expected to give rise to a conflict, between the duties of their office and either their private interest or any duties they owe to any other person. The possibility of such a conflict arises in a number of circumstances:

- where a director is in a position to compete with the company

- where a director makes a profit from their position as director

- where a director contracts with the company. Here there are:

- general rules that relate to any contract
- specific rules about transactions of substantial value
- specific rules on loans and other forms of credit being given to a director

- where a director owns shares or debentures in the company and as a result of their position has information that gives them an advantage in dealing in the shares or debentures.

These shall be dealt with in turn.

2.4 Not to compete with company

(a) **Competing businesses** – a director should not compete with the company of which they are a director and, despite the possible advantages of having non-executive directors who are involved with other businesses, they should not serve as a director of another company, at least where they have a contract of employment with the first company.

Other problems of conflict of interest can arise where:

(i) a director is appointed to the board as a nominee of some outside interest, e.g. a major loan creditor

(ii) a director of company A is also a director of company B, which is a competitor of company A.

There is apparently no objection in principle to making either arrangement, but there is a very real conflict of interest if at any time the director has to (or chooses to) advance the interest of the other party whom they represent rather than that of the company. It has been said that if such a situation develops, the director must either put the interest of the company first or resign the directorship. It is an uncertain area of law and much depends on the facts of the case.

(b) **Confidential information** – they should not abuse the confidence placed in them by disclosing to others, or using for their own purposes, confidential information obtained by virtue of their being in office as a director.

2.5 Profits obtained from the position of director

One potential breach of duty concerns the making of profits, which the director would not have made if they were not a director.

Directors may actively divert property or opportunities to themselves that would otherwise have gone to the company. The law will not allow them to keep the benefits and provides that it is a breach of their fiduciary duty to obtain any benefit from their office without the company's consent, given by the articles or a resolution in general meeting. They are accountable to the company as constructive trustee for any such profit.

Cook v Deeks (1916)

Facts: the shares of a railway company, T, were held in equal shares by four people who also constituted the board. The company carried out several large construction contracts for the Canadian Pacific Railway Co. Three of the directors, hearing that there was a new contract coming up, obtained it in their own names to the exclusion of the company and formed another company, D, to carry out the work. They then passed resolutions by virtue of their shareholding approving the sale of plant by T to D and declaring that T had no interest in the new contract with the Canadian

Pacific. The fourth director, Cook, brought an action against the others claiming that the benefit of the contract properly belonged to T and the directors could not use their voting power as shareholders to vest it in themselves.

Held: the opportunity to obtain the new contract came to the directors whilst acting as directors of T, the contract belonged in equity to the company and the directors could not retain the benefit of it for themselves. Moreover, the directors could not use their voting control to appropriate the interest and property of the company.

Thus, the directors could not keep the benefit of the contract, even though it had been ratified by the general meeting, as it had been their own voting power that had resulted in the ratification.

Another situation occurs where the directors have acted openly and honestly, but still obtained a benefit from their position. The rule appears to be strict and to depend on the mere making of a profit from the position as director, regardless of the motives or the consequences for the company.

Regal (Hastings) Ltd v Gulliver (1942)

Facts: Regal owned a cinema. The directors wished to acquire the leases of two other cinemas with a view to selling the whole as a going concern. Regal had insufficient funds to purchase the leases and the directors were unwilling to purchase in their own names, thereby making themselves personally liable without limit. So they formed a company, Amalgamated, with a capital of 5,000 £1 shares. Regal subscribed for 2,000 shares and the directors and their friends subscribed for the rest. Eventually the three cinemas were sold as a going concern by a sale of the shares in both companies. The directors made a profit on the sale of their shares in Amalgamated. The company sued for the recovery of this profit.

Held: the directors used their opportunities and special knowledge as directors to make a secret profit for themselves. They were accountable to the company for the profits made. In their decision the House of Lords recognised that the directors, as controlling shareholders, could have passed a resolution in general meeting to approve the retention of their profit. But they had not done so. Thus, the (potential or actual) breach of duty may be authorised or ratified by the general meeting, provided the effect of this is not to permit fraud on the minority shareholders as in *Cook v Deeks* (1916).

Ostrich Farming Corp Ltd v Wallstreet (1998)

Facts: Ostrich Farming Corp Ltd encouraged the public to invest in ostrich farming and made extravagant claims as to the profits to be made. The ostriches were bought at an inflated price from Wallstreet plc, a business with which the directors had close connections. This enabled profits of over £3 million to be made by the directors.

Held: there was a clear breach of fiduciary duty and the directors were liable to account for the secret profits.

The fiduciary duty can survive even after the director has left the company.

IDC v Cooley (1972)

Facts: Cooley, the managing director of IDC, had been negotiating a contract on behalf of the company, but the third party wished to award the contract to him personally and not to the company. Without disclosing his reason to the company (or its board) he resigned in order to take the contract personally.

Held: he was in breach of fiduciary duty as he had profited personally by use of an opportunity that came to him through his directorship: it made no difference that the company itself would not have obtained the contract. He was therefore accountable to the company for the benefits gained from the contract.

Cooley's case has, however, been distinguished in:

Island Export Finance v Umunna (1986)

Facts: U was managing director of IEF and in 1976 he secured a contract for it from the Cameroon postal authorities. In 1977 he resigned from IEF due to general dissatisfaction with it and subsequently obtained orders from the Cameroon postal authorities for his own company. IEF sued him for breach of fiduciary duty.

Held: he was not in breach of fiduciary duty. There were two main reasons behind the decision. First, that while U may have in a general way contemplated that Cameroon authorities might be a good source of business for his own company on resignation, the exploitation of the opportunity was not his primary or indeed an important motive for his resignation. Second, neither when U resigned nor when he obtained the orders was IEF actively pursuing further business with the Cameroon authorities: at most it had a hope of obtaining further orders, but that could not in any realistic sense be said to be a maturing business opportunity of IEF.

There is a *dicta* to support the view that if a company *bona fide* for good business reasons rejects a corporate opportunity then a director who takes the opportunity personally is not in breach of fiduciary duty.

2.6 Contracts with the company

The general rule

A director should not generally contract with their company, otherwise they might be dismissed as a director; they must account for profits; and the company may avoid the contract (it need not do so). It is immaterial that the contract is made on fair terms and after full disclosure, unless the articles permit contracting.

Aberdeen Railway v Blaikie (1854)

Facts: the defendant company entered into a contract to purchase a quantity of chairs from the claimant partnership. One of the directors of the company was also a member of the partnership at the time of contract.

Held: the director was interested in both sides of the bargain. Therefore, he could not make the best bargain for the company. No question should be raised as to the fairness of a contract so entered into. The company was entitled to avoid the contract.

This situation necessarily exists where the director contracts directly or has an interest (e.g. as director or shareholder of another company) in a contract with their company.

Exceptions to the rule

- **Articles allow** – the practical inconvenience of the strict principle is such that the articles usually permit directors to be interested in certain specified types of contract and to retain any profit realised from such contracts, provided they disclose the nature and extent of their interest to the board. There are also standard provisions prohibiting directors from voting on and being counted for quorum purposes at board meetings considering contracts in which they may be interested.

- **Approval by general meeting of members** – the company in a general meeting can, after full disclosure of the terms of the contract, approve it and exempt the director from the rule.

3 Statutory intervention

3.1 Introduction

In general, any statutory provision must be complied with in addition to the common law fiduciary duty. It is important to realise, in relation to breach of each statutory provision, whether it provides for civil remedies or criminal penalties (or both) as examination questions will often require students to make the distinction.

3.2 Part X Companies Act 1985 Enforcement of Fair Dealing by Directors

Directors to disclose interests in company contracts: s317 Companies Act 1985

A director who is interested directly or indirectly in a contract or proposed contract with their company must declare the nature of their interest at a meeting of the directors. The disclosure should be made at the first meeting at which the proposed contract is considered by the board or when the director's interest first arises (if later). In *Guinness plc v Saunders* (1990) it was stated that board means a full board, not merely a committee of the board. Even where the company only has one director, they must declare their interests to themselves, and ensure this is recorded in the minutes of the board meeting. A director may, however, give a general notice that they are a shareholder of another company or a partner of a firm and so are interested in any future contract made with it. It is only the nature of the interest and not all the material facts that have to be disclosed. A director who fails to comply with the section is liable to a fine and the contract may be voidable (this issue has not yet been decided).

This provision enables the board to comply with their statutory duty of disclosing in the annual accounts detailed particulars of transactions or arrangements with the company in which a director had directly or indirectly a material interest.

Substantial property transactions: s320 Companies Act 1985

A company shall not enter into an agreement:

- whereby a director of the company or its holding company or a person connected with such a director is to acquire one or more non-cash assets of the requisite value from the company

- whereby the company acquires one or more non-cash assets of the requisite value from such a director or a person so connected

unless the arrangement is first approved by an ordinary resolution of the company in general meeting and, if the director or connected person is a director of its holding company or a person connected with such a director, by a resolution in general meeting of the holding company.

The definition of connected persons of a director is complex, but can be summarised as follows:

- spouse, children (under 18) or stepchildren
- a company in which the director or their connections control at least 20% of the equity or votes
- a trustee of a trust from which the director or their connections may benefit
- a partner or director of any of their connections.

A non-cash asset is of the requisite value if at the time the arrangement in question is entered into its value is not less than £2,000 (£5,000 following the Company Law Reform Bill) but, subject to that, exceeds £100,000 or 10% of the amount of the company's assets, whichever is less.

Should the resolution not be obtained, the transaction is voidable unless:

- restitution is no longer possible or the company has been indemnified for loss or damage suffered by it, or

- any rights have been acquired *bona fide* for value without actual profit.

The section further provides that the director and any person connected with them in contravention of s320 and any director who authorised the arrangement is liable:

- to account to the company for any gain that they have made, and

- jointly and severally with any other person liable under the section to indemnify the company for any loss or damage.

Note that s320 extends to persons connected with the director.

4 Duty of care and skill of directors

4.1 Introduction

Unlike the above elaborate rules, the standard of competence required of company directors is fairly simple. Directors as such are supervisors rather than working executives (they may, of course, double both roles as director employees) and it would hardly be practicable to prescribe professional standards of qualification.

4.2 The duty

The standard of care and skill required of a director has been described in:

Re City Equitable Fire Insurance Co (1925)

Facts: The company was in liquidation and it was discovered that there was a shortage of funds due mainly to the deliberate fraud of the Managing Director (MD), for which he had been convicted. The company's articles excluded the officers of the company from liability in respect of the acts, defaults or neglects of others. The liquidator brought an action against the other directors of the company, who had acted honestly throughout, for negligence.

Held: the points established were:

(a) A director need not exhibit in the performance of their duties a greater degree of skill than may reasonably be expected from a person of their knowledge and experience. Directors are not liable for mere errors of judgement.

(b) A director is not bound to give continuous attention to the affairs of the company. Their duties are of an intermittent nature to be performed at periodical board meetings and at meetings of any committee of the board upon which they happen to be placed. They are not, however, bound to attend all such meetings, though they ought to attend whenever, in the circumstances, they are reasonably able to do so. (In *Re Cardiff Savings Bank* (1892), a director who attended only one board meeting in 38 years was held not liable in negligence for mismanagement that had occurred during that time.)

(c) In respect of all duties that, having regard to the exigencies of business, and the articles of association, may properly be left to some other official, a director is, in the absence of grounds for suspicion, justified in trusting that official to perform such duties honestly. In *Dovey v Cory* (1901), it was held that a director of a joint stock banking company was entitled to rely on the judgement and advice of the general manager of the bank.

Such duties are, in practice, even less onerous than the wording might suggest. It has been said that a director must do their best without having to be competent. Certainly one cannot say whether a person has been guilty of negligence unless one can determine what is the extent of the duty that they are alleged to have neglected. This requires consideration of the nature of the company's business and of the manner in which the company's work is distributed among officials.

Different expectations will be made of different directors, e.g. of executive and non-executive directors, the latter being potentially useful in being able to bring to the board a breadth of knowledge and experience that the company's own management may not possess and in increasing the element of independence and objectivity in board decision-making.

A leading case on directors' negligence is:

Dorchester Finance Co Ltd v Stebbing (1989)

Facts: the company was a money-lending company and had three directors, Parsons, Hamilton and Stebbing. All three had considerable accountancy and business experience (Parsons and Hamilton were chartered accountants). No board meetings were ever held and Parsons and Hamilton left all the affairs of the company to Stebbing. Parsons and Hamilton did, however, turn up from time to time and sign blank cheques on the company's account, which they left Stebbing to deal with. Stebbing loaned the company's money without complying with statutory regulations applying to money-lending such that the loans were unenforceable.

Held: all three were liable in negligence.

5 Fraudulent and wrongful trading

5.1 Fraudulent trading

If in a winding up it appears that the company's business has been carried on with intent to defraud creditors or for any fraudulent purpose, the court may declare that any persons who were knowingly parties to the fraudulent trading shall make such contribution to the company's assets as the court thinks proper: s213 Insolvency Act 1986.

It is necessary to establish dishonest intent. In *Re William C Leith Bros (1932)* it was said that if the directors carry on the business and cause the company to incur further debts at a time when they know that there is no reasonable prospect of those debts being paid, this is a proper inference of dishonesty. The court also added that if the directors honestly believed the debts would eventually be paid, there would be no intent to defraud.

R v Grantham (1984)

Facts: the directors ordered a consignment of potatoes on a month's credit at a time when they knew that payment would not be forthcoming at the end of the month when it was due.

Held: the directors were convicted of fraudulent trading.

A person is not liable for fraudulent trading where they have no dishonest intention.

Re EB Tractors Ltd (1986)

Facts: the directors caused the company to incur debts at a time when they would not be paid on the due date. They, however, showed that they thought the company would survive and the debts eventually paid.

Held: the directors' honest belief (although unrealistic) negated the intention to defraud: they were not liable.

The second point required to establish liability is that the person concerned shall be a party to the fraudulent trading.

In *Re Maidstone Buildings* (1971) it was established that a person is not party merely by reason of knowledge, they must take some active step, such as the ordering of goods.

The following are the possible consequences of fraudulent trading.

- The court may order the person liable to make such contribution to the company's assets as it thinks fit – s213 Insolvency Act 1986. The application is made by the liquidator.

- Criminal liability – the punishment includes not only an unlimited fine but also up to seven years' imprisonment. Criminal liability can lie whether or not the company is in liquidation.

- Fraudulent trading is a specific ground for disqualification under the Company Directors Disqualification Act 1986.

5.2 Wrongful trading

The provision of wrongful trading contained in s214 Insolvency Act 1986 is designed to remove one of the difficult obstacles to the establishment of being party to fraudulent trading – namely proving dishonesty. It applies only to directors, former directors and shadow directors.

Under s214 Insolvency Act 1986, a liquidator may apply to the court for an order that a director of a company that has gone into insolvent liquidation should make such contribution to the company's assets as the court thinks proper. The court will need to satisfy itself that, at some time before the commencement of the winding up, the director knew or ought to have known that there was no reasonable prospect that the company would avoid going into insolvent liquidation and that they were a director at that time.

The court will not make an order if it is satisfied that as soon as the director knew or ought to have concluded there was no reasonable prospect of avoiding insolvent liquidation, they took every step they ought to have taken to minimise the potential loss to the company's creditors.

The director is expected to reach those conclusions and take such steps as a reasonably diligent person would take. The legislation also expects such a director to have the general knowledge, skill and experience that may reasonably be expected of a person carrying out the same functions as were carried out by that director (objective test). In addition, it expects the director to use the general knowledge, skill and experience that they themselves have (subjective test), i.e. the director is expected to use their specialist knowledge and experience. This is far more onerous than the previous statement of a director's duty of skill and care.

When considering the director's functions, the court will have regard not only to those functions that they carried out, but also to those entrusted to them. This means that the director could be made liable for those actions they should have carried out but failed to.

The effect of this provision is that a director may be made personally liable for the debts and liabilities of the insolvent company if:

- they knew that it could not avoid insolvent liquidation and did not take all reasonable steps open to them to prevent its creditors from suffering greater loss than they would have suffered by an immediate cessation of the company's activities

- a reasonable director with the knowledge available to them would have concluded that the company could not have avoided insolvency and would have taken more effective steps to minimise the loss to creditors.

Anything obtained as a result of these provisions would go to the liquidator for the payment of the company's debts.

In *Re Produce Marketing Consortium* (1989), the first case heard under the new provision of wrongful trading, the court held that:

- Directors cannot rely on the fact that they were unaware of facts that they could and should have ascertained from documents, e.g. the accounts.

- The standard required is that of a reasonable director of that type of company, i.e. a higher standard is expected for directors of larger companies. However, certain minimum standards must be maintained.

- Here the directors had received the accounts two years late but had known that the company was in financial difficulty – they were ordered to pay £75,000 contribution.

<table>
<tr><td>

KEY POINT

Wrongful trading is not a criminal offence.

</td><td>

Wrongful trading is not a criminal offence, but it is a specific ground for the making of a disqualification order – CDDA86.

</td></tr>
</table>

5.3 Transactions at an undervalue and preference

The liquidator (or administrator) may apply to the court to set aside company transactions at an undervalue (s238 Insolvency Act 1986) or where the company gives a preference (s239 Insolvency Act 1986).

(a) A company enters into a transaction at an undervalue if the company makes a gift or otherwise enters into a transaction on terms that the company receives no consideration or insufficient consideration.

The transaction would not be set aside if it was entered into in good faith on the reasonable belief that it would benefit the company.

(b) A company gives a preference if it does anything to put a creditor in a better position in the event of the company's insolvent liquidation than they would otherwise be. The court will not make an order under s239 Insolvency Act 1986 unless the company was influenced by a desire to prefer the creditor. Thus, a payment made or charge created in favour of a creditor who is threatening legal proceedings might be a defence to an action under this section. If the preference is given to a connected person it is presumed that the company was influenced by its desire to give a preference.

The transaction or preference will only be set aside by the court if the company is insolvent and the transaction or preference was made within the relevant period, which is:

- any transaction at an undervalue or a preference to a connected person (as for invalidity of floating charge, except that employees are not connected persons under ss238 & 239) within two years of the onset of insolvency

- preferences to other persons within six months of the onset of insolvency.

The onset of insolvency is the commencement of the liquidation or presentation of the petition for an administration order.

The transaction or preference will not be set aside unless at the time it was made the company was not able to pay its debts or the company became unable to pay its debts as a result. The burden of proving this is on the person seeking to have it set aside, except where a transaction at an undervalue is alleged to a connected person in which case it is presumed.

S241 Insolvency Act 1986 gives the court wide powers in the orders it may make, e.g. release any security or invest property in the company. However, a *bona fide* purchaser for value without notice of the relevant circumstances who was not party to the transaction or preference is protected.

6   Companies Bill 2006

The Bill brings the existing common law duties of directors into statutory law. However, in interpreting and applying the new statutory provisions, regard should be had to the corresponding common law rules and equitable principles.

The statutory provisions differ from the current law in two respects:

- Transactions or arrangements with the company do not have to be authorised by either the members or by the board. Instead, interests must be declared.

- The board may authorise most conflicts of interest arising from third party dealings by the director. However, this authorisation is only effective if the director in question has not participated in the decision to authorise or if the decision would have been valid even without his participation.

Authorisation may be given by the directors in the following circumstances:

- Where the company is a private company and nothing in the company's constitution invalidates such authorisation. (In other words, the default position for private companies is that authorisation is permitted.)

- Where the company is a public company and its constitution includes provision enabling the directors to authorise the matter. (In other words, the default position for public companies is that a transaction is not permitted unless expressly permitted by the articles.)

Authorisation is not permitted in respect of the acceptance of benefits from third parties.

Summary

The director may be able to avoid the consequences of breach of duty in several ways:

(a)   The company may approve what the directors have done or intend to do by a resolution to that effect passed in a general meeting. If the directors are also shareholders they may cast their shareholders' votes in favour of a resolution to approve their action (and the retention of benefit obtained from it):

North West Transportation Co v Beatty (1887)

Facts: the company purchased a boat from one of its directors for a reasonable price. The purchase was ratified by a general meeting, including the votes of the director.

Held: every shareholder has a right to vote upon any question; the fact that this shareholder had a controlling shareholding and had an interest in the contract made no difference.

However, in this difficult area of law there are at least two limiting conditions:

(i)   If the irregular act to be approved is the issue of shares made for the improper purpose of altering the balance of voting power, the votes attached to the new shares may not be used in voting on the resolution: *Hogg v Cramphorn* (1967).

(ii)   If the directors are also controlling shareholders, they may not exercise their control to carry a resolution approving the transfer to themselves of property or profits that otherwise belong to the company: *Cook v Deeks (1916)*. But, they may apparently use their control to approve the retention of a personal profit that could not have accrued to the company: *Regal (Hastings) v Gulliver* (1967).

(b)   In the *City Equitable Case* (1925), the innocent directors were relieved of any possible liability by an exemption given to them by the articles. Such exemption may no longer be given in advance. Thus an article that provides that the directors will not be sued if they are in breach of duty will be void.

(c)   The court may exercise its discretion to relieve the directors, if they have acted honestly and reasonably and ought fairly to be excused. This section cannot be used to excuse wrongful trading – *Re Produce Marketing* (1989).

(d)   The director might be insured – s310 Companies Act 1985 does not prevent the company from insuring officers against liability.

On completion of their studies, students should be able to:

*   explain the procedure for the appointment, retirement, disqualification and removal of directors and their powers and duties during office.

*   explain the rules dealing with the possible imposition of personal liability upon the directors of insolvent companies.

Self-test questions

Nature of the duties of directors

1   To whom does a director owe their duties? (1.2)

The fiduciary duty of directors

2   What did the leading case of *Regal (Hastings) v Gulliver* establish? (2.5)

Statutory intervention

3   Define a substantial property transaction. (3.2)

Duty of care and skill of directors

4   State the propositions established in *Re City Equitable Fire Insurance*. (4.2)

Fraudulent and wrongful trading

5   What is fraudulent trading? (5.1)

6   Who can be liable for wrongful trading? (5.2)

7   What is a preference? (5.3)

Multiple-choice questions

Question 1

Directors owe fiduciary duties to:

(i)   The individual shareholder

(ii)   Shareholders as a whole

Which of the above is/are correct?

A   (i) only

B   (ii) only

C   Both (i) and (ii)

D   Neither (i) nor (ii)

Question 2

Under the Companies Act 1985, a director who is interested in a contract with the company must declare the nature of their interest:

A   At the first meeting of the directors of the company after the interest arose

B   At the first meeting of the company following the coming into existence of the interest

C   At a meeting of the directors of the company and at the first general meeting of the company following the coming into existence of the interest

D   Immediately, in writing, to the company secretary

Practice questions

Question 1: Griff plc

John is a non-executive director of Griff plc, a listed company. Shortly after attending a board meeting where arrangements were finalised for an agreed take-over bid for the company by Whale plc, John bought shares in Griff plc from Adam as a result of a direct approach from Adam. Once the bid was made public, John re-sold his shares at a profit.

You are required to advise Griff plc, Adam and Whale plc whether any or all of them have an action against John for recovery of the profit.

Question 2: Williams Ltd

Ellen and Freda are the only directors of Williams Ltd, each holding 20% of the company's issued share capital. The remaining 60% of the shares are held by their father, Bill, the founder of the company. Although Bill is no longer a director, he continues to exert considerable influence over the policy and management of the company.

For some time Ellen and Freda have been aware of a serious drop in turnover and profits. An extraordinary general meeting was called on 1 November 20X2 to discuss the situation, and Bill warned his daughters that insolvency appeared inevitable. They, however, remained convinced that the profitability of the company would be restored in line with the expected upturn in the economy generally. Bill was persuaded to support his daughters' desire to continue trading, in return for their promise to arrange for Williams Ltd to make an early repayment of Bill's unsecured loan of £10,000 over the following three months. Bill was repaid on 1 January 20X3.

On 1 June 20X3 Williams Ltd's bankers cancelled the company's overdraft facilities, and at an extraordinary general meeting on 20 June 20X3 the shareholders reluctantly passed a resolution placing Williams Ltd in creditors' voluntary liquidation.

You are required to discuss whether Ellen, Freda or Bill have acted in breach of company law, and if so, the possible consequences of the breach.

For the answers to these questions, see the 'Answers' section at the end of the book.

Chapter 25

COMPANY ADMINISTRATION AND FINANCE: THE RIGHTS OF MAJORITY AND MINORITY SHAREHOLDERS

Syllabus content

Company administration and finance

- The rights of majority and minority shareholders

This chapter looks at shareholders' rights as individuals.

Contents

1   Majority rule and minority protection

2   Statutory protection of the minority

1 Majority rule and minority protection

1.1 Introduction

The control of the company rests with the members acting through votes at general meetings or the directors to the extent that the powers to manage have been delegated to them. However, the members will have such control over the directors as are set out in the articles and provided by statute, in particular the right to remove directors or to alter the articles to remove the directors' powers.

The members' decisions are, usually, by simple majority. Thus, an individual member, or a group of members with a small percentage shareholding may be bound by decisions with which they disagree. In particular, in smaller companies the directors may also be the majority shareholders and thus the minority shareholders have virtually no control over the company's activities.

However, there are certain situations where minority shareholders may be able to influence the company's activities.

These circumstances can be divided into:

- Statutory protection given to the minority on various aspects of the general conduct of the company meetings

- Statutory provisions allowing institution of court proceedings – specific statutory minority protection

- Common law rules governing the institution of court proceedings in matters relating to the conduct of companies' affairs: exceptions to the rule in *Foss v Harbottle*

- The right of a member to petition the court if they prove the company's affairs are being conducted in a manner unfairly prejudicial to them – s459 Companies Act 1985

- The right to petition (to formally apply to) the court to have the company wound up on the ground that it is just and equitable in the circumstances (just and equitable winding up) – s122(g) IA 1986.

1.2 Conduct of company meetings

There are certain statutory provisions to protect the minority.

(a) Some changes of the company's constitution or affairs are considered sufficiently major that they require a 75% majority of votes cast. Thus, the holders of just over 25% of the voting shares have a veto in these cases. The important examples are to:

    (i) alter the objects

    (ii) alter the articles

    (iii) alter the name

    (iv) reduce the capital.

(b) There are some things that the company cannot do unless each member's consent is obtained.

    (i) The company cannot increase a member's liability unless they agree in writing.

    (ii) It cannot re-register as an unlimited company unless all the members agree.

(c)   Certain provisions give the members the power to call meetings or to require information to be circulated to members.

The powers are:

(i)   to require directors to call an EGM (if the members have 10% of paid-up voting capital)

(ii)   to require a resolution to be put to the AGM (if 5% of voting rights or 100 members)

(iii)   to require a statement to be circulated (if 5% of voting rights or 100 members).

The practical difficulty that confronts a shareholder of a large company is how to contact and co-operate with other dissatisfied members and also the expense of such action. By contrast, the directors representing the majority have the records, resources and organisation of the company under their control.

1.3   Institution of court proceedings – specific statutory minority protection

Certain provisions give members a right to object to the court, even though a resolution has been passed with the requisite majority. Thus:

- Members having 15% of voting shares and who did not vote in favour of the resolution can apply to the court to set aside an alteration of objects or class rights. Where additional clauses are entrenched in the memorandum, there is a right of appeal to the court if they are at all alterable.

- Members holding 10% of the issued share capital can apply to the court where a private company gives financial assistance for the purchase of its own shares.

- Members holding 5% of voting shares can apply to the court to set aside a resolution for re-registering a public company as a private company, but no person can apply who consented or voted in favour of the resolution.

- Any member may apply to the court to object to a private company making a permissible capital payment or to injunct an *ultra vires* transaction.

1.4   Institution of court proceedings – the rule in Foss v Harbottle

A breach of duty owed to the company may arise from statute, contract, tort or the fiduciary position of the party in breach. The duty may be owed by a third party, a director, or even perhaps by a member, e.g. in the unlikely case of their having to pay calls on shares not fully paid up. Since the duty breached is one owed to the company, which is a separate person in law, the company is the proper person to seek a remedy for the breach. In addition, as the majority of members may ratify or excuse a breach, it would be futile (in the absence of fraud or other inequitable conduct) for the minority to litigate against the wishes of the majority.

Foss v Harbottle (1843)

Facts: individual shareholders brought action against directors alleged to have misapplied company property.

Held: the company, as the victim of the alleged misdeeds, was the proper claimant to complain.

The rule, therefore, prevents each and every shareholder from taking whatever form of action they wish, in situations where the company itself, either by decision of the board or a resolution of the general meeting, can decide whether or not to take action.

The rule in *Foss v Harbottle* has two principles.

- In order to redress a wrong done to a company or to recover money or damages alleged to be due to the company, the action should *prima facie* be brought by the company itself.

- Where the majority does not wish the company to sue, the court will not generally permit the minority to sue on its behalf nor interfere in the internal management of the company.

These principles represent different aspects of the majority rule in company law, i.e. if the majority can do something, the minority cannot interfere.

These principles can, however, produce an unfair or unsatisfactory result. First, if a shareholder is unhappy with the conduct of the board and alleges that the board (or an individual director) is in breach of duty, there is a little chance of the board suing itself. Further, there is some uncertainty under the second proposition as to how far a majority should be permitted to authorise an irregularity that infringes the company's constitution.

Is the individual shareholder to be deprived by the company of insisting on their right to have its affairs conducted in accordance with the regulations? Can the company act capriciously in disregard of the interests of all but the majority shareholders? Can the directors, by decisions in board meetings and by their ability to control decisions of the general meetings, treat the company as their own and act as they wish, taking account only of their own interests?

1.5 The powers of the majority

The ordinary members participate in the running of the company by taking part in discussions and voting in general meetings. Resolutions passed in general meetings are, therefore, the practical result of the collective will of the various members – the majority decision displays the fact that more of the individual members, whatever their motives may be, have wanted one decision rather than another.

It is quite justifiable for the individual shareholders to exercise their votes in whichever way they wish, and to take their chance on whether the majority of the other voters agree with them or not. Their vote is their personal property that they can use as they wish, even if their action as a shareholder runs contrary to the path they must pursue in some other capacity, e.g. as a director (it being a separate issue whether or not they are in breach of any duties as a director and, if so, what the effects of the breach are).

Northern Counties Securities Ltd v Jackson and Steeple Ltd (1974)

Facts: a director had complied with an obligation to call a general meeting and to advise the members to vote for a resolution that had to be passed if the company were not to be in contempt of court. In his capacity as shareholder he voted against it.

Held: the director was entitled to vote in this way.

Accordingly, the exceptions to the rule in *Foss v Harbottle* may be summarised as a right of individual shareholders to raise objection:

- Where the individual rights of a member are infringed.

- Where action is taken in disregard of the company's articles or by some other irregularity, such as convening a general meeting by an inadequate notice.

- Where the transaction is a fraud on the company by those who control it, which includes, possibly, where the power of the majority is exercised in an unjust manner and not *bona fide* in the interests of the company as a whole. This exception is commonly called 'fraud on the minority'.

1.6 Infringement of a member's personal rights

The articles may give to each member personal rights that they can use almost as a form of property, e.g. their right to cast the votes attached to their shares. A member is generally entitled to enforce these rights against the company as personal rights (rather than on the company's behalf to protect its constitution). In *Pender v Lushington* (1887) the court enjoined the directors from acting on the basis of a resolution not having been carried because votes attached to the claimant's nominee shareholding were improperly rejected. The claimant sued in a representative capacity, but it was held that he could sue personally in respect of his individual right to have his vote recorded.

1.7 Irregularity in conduct of a company's business

It has been argued that every member has, by virtue of the rights and obligations binding the company and the members, a right to have the affairs of the company conducted in accordance with the regulations by which they have agreed to be bound. However, the individual member's right to participate is subject to the rules in the company's regulations as to how the company is to be run and to the general rules of company law. So, even where there is a potential irregularity of which they can feel justifiably aggrieved, they may be unable to take any action if it is something that could have or would be condoned or ratified by the general meeting. Taken a step further, this means that the court may restrain action on the part of shareholders to give the general meeting the opportunity of condoning the irregularity. In *Hogg v Cramphorn Ltd* (1987), the minority shareholder maintained a representative action in respect of a defensive issue of shares, but the case was adjourned to give the company the opportunity to ratify the issue.

However, situations where a successful action has been brought include:

Edwards v Halliwell (1950)

Facts: a trade union had increased its rate of subscription without altering its rules.

Held: the challenge was upheld. The proper procedure for altering the rules should be followed. (The decision was based on company law.)

1.8 Fraud on the minority by controlling majority

This is the most difficult area to produce comprehensive principles that have been established in different cases. It can be pleaded even if there is no infringement of a personal right, no irregularity in the conduct of the business and the transaction in question is *intra vires* the company.

If the majority have defrauded, or plan to defraud, the company of its property, any resolution passed to approve their action (by use of their votes) is invalid: *Cook v Deeks* (1916). This exception to the general principle of majority control is necessary to protect the company – and indirectly its minority shareholders – against a fraudulent majority.

To bring this exception into operation there must be:

(a)   misappropriation of the company's property or other fraudulent conduct

(b)   control of the company by those who misappropriate it.

Condition (a) was satisfied in the case cited above. Mere negligence of a controlling shareholder in disposing of the company's property to a third party is not enough. However, if the facts have not yet been fully established and the directors' negligence has yielded a profit at the company's expense to one of themselves, the court will allow the action to proceed so that the full facts may be elicited.

Daniels v Daniels (1977)

Facts: the claimants, minority shareholders in a company, brought an action against two directors and the company. They alleged that the company, on the instructions of the directors, who were also majority shareholders, sold the company's land to one of the directors (who was the wife of the other) for £4,250 and that the directors knew, or ought to have known, that was at an undervalue. Four years later the land was sold for £120,000. The directors claimed that there was no reasonable cause of action.

Held: the exception to the rule in *Foss v Harbottle,* enabling a minority shareholder to bring an action against a company for fraud where no other remedy was available, should include cases where, although there was no fraud alleged, there was a breach of duty by the directors and majority shareholders to the detriment of the company and the benefit of the directors. Accordingly, the minority had a cause of action.

In *Prudential Assurance v Newman Industries* (1982) the court held that day-to-day management control was sufficient control to satisfy (b) above.

Where there is no actual fraud, i.e. misappropriation to themselves of the company's property etc., the majority may use their votes to approve a transaction beneficial to themselves. They may also approve mere negligence on the part of the directors or the exercise by the directors of their powers for an irregular but not dishonest purpose.

It has also been held that if the majority exercise their rights merely to discriminate against the minority, this can be challenged in the courts and set aside.

2   Statutory protection of the minority

2.1   S459 Companies Act 1985 – Relief from unfair prejudice

Any member of the company who complains that the affairs of the company are being conducted in a manner unfairly prejudicial to the interests of some or all of the members (including themselves) may petition for an order under s459.

2.2   Who may petition?

Any single member may sue. It must be the petitioner who is being unfairly prejudiced; it is insufficient to plead that some other of the members are being unfairly prejudiced.

S459(2) Companies Act 1985 provides that the provisions apply to a person who is not on the register as a member of a company, but to whom shares in the company have been transferred (e.g. to the personal representatives of a deceased member).

However, by its express terms, s459 is limited to members, and so would not justify a petition by a debenture-holder, or other creditor or third party.

If, after an inspector's report or the production of documents, it appears to the Department of Trade and Industry that the company's affairs are being conducted in a manner unfairly prejudicial to any of its members, the Department may (either as well as or instead of petitioning for a winding up) petition for an order under s459.

It has been held that there is no requirement that the petitioner comes to court with 'clean hands', i.e. they acted fairly themselves. Such a requirement probably does exist where a petition is presented to wind up the company under the just and equitable ground in s122(g) Insolvency Act 1986. It does, however, appear that the petitioner's conduct for the purposes of s459 may be material in one of two ways:

- it might render the other side's conduct, even if prejudicial, not unfair

- it might affect the relief that the court might think fit to grant.

2.3 What is 'unfairly prejudicial'?

The courts give a very broad interpretation to the meaning of 'unfair'. The House of Lords case of *O'Neill v Phillips* (1999) stated that unfairness may arise in two ways:

- from the strict infringement of legal rights, e.g. breach of the articles

- from the unfair use of power that abuses the enjoyment of legal rights, e.g. the removal of a director for no valid legal reason.

A useful test to determine unfairness is to ask whether the exercise of the power in question 'would be contrary to what the parties, by words or conduct, would have actually agreed?'

The cases are varied and the court looks at all the circumstances.

Scottish CWS v Meyer (1959)

Facts: CWS was majority shareholder in a subsidiary company and through its nominees controlled the board. It was in the business interests of CWS to run down the business of the subsidiary and this they did by withholding supplies from it. M's shares in the subsidiary became virtually worthless.

Held: his petition succeeded.

Remedy: CWS to purchase M's shares at a fair value.

Re London School of Electronics (1986)

Facts: X and CTC were shareholders and directors in LSE, a company running a tutorial college. CTC diverted LSE's students to another company, which it controlled and when X complained it removed X from the board. X then retaliated by setting up a company to which he diverted students.

Held: X's petition succeeded. Unlike s122(g) Insolvency Act 1986, a petitioner is not barred from relief by the maxim 'He who comes to equity must come with clean hands'.

Remedy: order that respondents purchase petitioner's shares.

Re Elgindata (No 1) (1991)

Facts: (i) numerous complaints of bad management, and (ii) the MD used the company's assets for his personal benefit and for the benefit of his family and friends.

Held: petition granted on basis of (ii), but not (i): the court stating ... 'although, in an appropriate case, serious mismanagement of a company's affairs would constitute unfairly prejudicial conduct, the court would normally be very reluctant to accept that managerial decisions can amount to unfairly prejudicial conduct. It is not for the court to resolve differences of commercial judgement. It is not unfair for a member of a company to suffer the consequences of poor management of the company: it is one of the risks of investing in a company that its management may turn out to be not of the highest quality. The petitioners had no right to expect a reasonable standard of general management from the managing director.'

Remedy: order that respondents purchase petitioner's shares.

Re Cumana (1986)

Facts: oral agreement between the two shareholders that they would share the profits of their business ventures $\frac{2}{3} : \frac{1}{3}$. The one who was to get $\frac{2}{3}$ devised various schemes to cut the other out of his $\frac{1}{3}$: viz (i) he diverted the company's business to another controlled by himself, (ii) he caused the company to make a large rights issue that he knew the other shareholder could not afford to take up, (iii) he caused the company to pay him an excessive bonus and to make excessive contributions to his pension funds.

Held: all three complaints amounted to unfair prejudice.

Remedy: order that respondents purchase petitioner's shares.

Note: there was also an interim injunction to prevent the rights issue.

Re Bird Precision Bellows (1984)

Facts: X owned 26% of the shares in a quasi-partnership company and he was removed from his directorship by the majority.

Held: his petition succeeded.

Remedy: order for purchase of his shares by the majority at a fair value (here the court fixed this on a pro-rata basis without any discount to reflect the fact that the shares constituted a minority holding).

Re R A Noble (1983)

Facts: B and N set up a business on the basis that B put up the capital and N ran it on the understanding that N would consult B on major matters. B petitioned on the basis that he was not informed of or adequately consulted on important matters.

Held: the petition was dismissed. The evidence showed that the situation arose largely because of B's lack of interest (he had confined himself to vague questions at social occasions).

Re a company, without notice Kremer (1989)

Facts: breakdown in the relationship between the members of a small private company because the petitioner (one of the member-directors) had, due to old age, lost his business acumen. The articles gave power to force the transfer of shares in such circumstances.

Held: the petition of the expelled member was dismissed.

Re H R Harmer (1959)

Facts: H (aged 77) and his wife controlled 78.6% of the voting capital (but only about 10% of the share capital). H took the view he was entitled to disregard board decisions because he controlled so many voting shares.

Held: the petition of his two sons (the directors and other shareholders) succeeded.

Remedy: court altered articles to appoint H president for life (an office carrying no rights or duties) and further ordered him not to interfere in management decisions.

Failure to comply with company law, e.g. absence of general meetings or failure to produce accounts, have been held to be unfairly prejudicial.

The wealth of cases on s459 can be summed up by *Re Saul Harrison plc (1995)* where the Court of Appeal denied a remedy to the minority shareholders. The court ruled that it is not enough for shareholders to disagree with management; if the actions of the board are lawful there must be some clear reason for judicial intervention.

2.4 Powers of the court

The court has a free hand in making such orders as it thinks fit for giving relief in respect of the matters complained of once it is satisfied that a petition under the section is well founded. For example, the court may:

- Regulate the conduct of the company's affairs in the future.

- Require the company to refrain from doing or continuing an act complained of by the petitioner, or to do an act that the petitioner has complained it has omitted to do.

- Authorise civil proceedings to be brought in the name and on behalf of the company by such person or persons and on such terms as the court may direct.

- Provide for the purchase of the shares of any members of the company by the other members or by the company itself and in the case of a purchase by the company itself, the reduction of the company's capital accordingly. The problem here is that where a minority is disposing of its shares, the price is usually discounted to take account of the fact that the vendor does not have control. On occasion it may be that the court orders that the respondents purchase the shares from the petitioner. This is rare but it occurred for example in:

Re Nuneaton Borough Association Football Club (1991)

Facts: the petitioner was allotted 24,000 shares in the company at a time when its authorised capital was only 2,000 (and 1,700 had earlier been allotted to the respondent). The petition was on the basis that he had bought something that did not exist.

Held: his petition succeeded.

Remedy: the court ordered that he buy out the respondent's shares. The fair value was the open market value of a controlling holding.

In *Re Bird Precision Bellows Ltd* Nourse J considered that it was erroneous to assume that a minority shareholder in a quasi partnership company was selling freely. If the sale was not from a willing vendor, the shares should be valued on a pro rata basis with no element of discount.

2.5 'Just and equitable' winding up

It may be that the person complaining of the behaviour of the majority wishes to get their capital out of the company to invest elsewhere or start in business on their own or with other persons. An application under s459 Companies Act 1985 may result in an order that their shares be purchased. Alternatively, they may apply for the company to be wound up completely and their capital returned to them. In this case they would apply to the court under s122(g) Insolvency Act 1986 that the company be wound up. The justice and equity depend on all the circumstances of the case. Considerations that may incline the court to wind up include: changes in personal relationships that have rendered the operation of a small company unfair to the petitioner.

Ebrahimi v Westbourne Galleries (1973)

Facts: the company was formed in 1958 to take over a business founded by N. From 1945, however, the business had been carried on in partnership with E, sharing the management and profits equally. When the company was formed N and E were the only shareholders and directors, holding 500 £1 shares each. Soon N's son, G, was made a director and N and E each transferred 100 shares to him. Soon there were disputes and N and G passed an ordinary resolution in general meeting removing E from office. E petitioned for a winding-up order on the just and equitable ground: s122(g) Insolvency Act 1986 .

Held: the company would be wound up on the just and equitable ground. The company was founded on the basis that the character of the association would remain, i.e. a matter of personal relation and good faith. This had failed and thus by analogy to partnership law the court would order a winding up.

Other examples are:

(a)   That the substratum of the company has gone, i.e. that the principal object or objects of the company cannot ever or can no longer be achieved.

Re German Date Coffee Co (1882)

Facts: the memorandum of the company stated that its object was the working of a German patent to manufacture coffee from dates. The company failed to acquire the German patent, but acquired a Swedish one and established works in Hamburg where it manufactured coffee from dates without a patent. Some shareholders withdrew from the company when they discovered that a German patent would not be obtained. The large majority wished the company to continue, but two shareholders petitioned the court for a winding up order on the basis that as the main object for which the company had been formed was impossible to carry out, it was just and equitable to wind the company up.

Held: the whole substratum of the company was gone, the business was to make coffee from dates using a German patent in Germany and not to enter into business generally; the shareholders were entitled to say that they did not enter into the company on these terms, and so the company ought to be wound up.

It is necessary that all the main objects and not merely some of them should now be unattainable.

Re Kitson (1946)

Facts: a company was formed with the objects to purchase a particular engineering business and carry on the business of general engineering.

The company did not acquire the business. Some shareholders petitioned to have the company wound up.

Held: the substratum had not failed as the company also had as an object the carrying on of a general engineering business.

(b)   That a state of deadlock exists in the management of the company. This situation is most likely to occur when the company has a small number of directors who are also the majority shareholders.

(c)   Where the company is like a small partnership based on mutual trust and confidence and that trust and confidence is broken, the court might consider it just and equitable to wind the company up: *Ebrahimi v Westbourne Galleries* (1973).

(d)   If the company was formed for some fraudulent purpose: *Re Walter Jacob Ltd.* (1989) – share pushing.

There are legal problems with s122(g) Insolvency Act 1986 that are not the case with s459 Companies Act 1985.

(a)   Under s122(g) Insolvency Act 1986 'He who comes to equity must come with clean hands'.

(b)   Case law shows that a petitioner must have an interest in the winding up of the company, e.g. it is most likely that there will be surplus assets.

(c)   A contributory shall not be entitled to present a petition unless the shares in respect of which they are a contributory or some of them:

(i)   were originally allotted to them

(ii)   have been held by them and registered in their name for at least six months during the 18 months before the commencement of the winding up

(iii)   have devolved upon them through the death of a former holder.

(d)   The court has a discretion to refuse winding up on the ground that the petitioner acted unreasonably in not pursuing an alternative remedy.

Re A Company (1983)

Facts: the petitioner had refused an improved offer to buy his shares, even though the facts of the case came within the above.

Held: winding up was refused and the court ordered that his shares be valued for purchase.

There are also non-legal considerations, such as the fact that it might be financially disadvantageous to the petitioner to have the company wound up. For all these reasons the petitioner may prefer s459 Companies Act 1989 as an alternative to s122(g) Insolvency Act 1986 .

(e)   This is a final and extreme remedy and the court will not grant it unless nothing else is available.

Summary

On completion of their studies, students should be able to:

- identify and contrast the rights of shareholders with the board of a company.

Self-test questions

Majority rule and minority protection

1   What is the effect of the rule in Foss v Harbottle? (1.4)

2   What two matters must normally be shown in order for a shareholder to bring themselves within the 'fraud on the minority' exception to the rule in Foss v Harbottle? (1.8)

Statutory protection of the minority

3   What powers does the court have in relation to giving relief from unfair prejudice? (2.4)

4   List the restrictions on a petition by a member for just and equitable winding up. (2.5)

Practice question

Enid

Enid is a minority shareholder in Dine plc. She is concerned about a number of activities relating to the directors of the company and comes to you for advice.

Two of the directors, Whine and Moan, will no longer speak to each other and all communication has to be through the remaining director, Peace. Prior to incorporation the business was a partnership with the three current directors as partners.

One of the causes of disagreement between Whine and Moan is that Whine caused a rights issue to take place knowing that Moan had no money to take up the new shares. Whine's motive may have been to gain a controlling stake in the company.

Required:

(a)   Fill in the gaps and delete as appropriate.

Enid may have limited options in terms of what she can do about these facts. The rule in ……………………….. stipulates that if a wrong is done to the company then only the company may sue. It *does/does not* appear that a wrong has been done to the company here. If the director's actions were ………………………..or specifically fraudulent these would always provide exceptions to the above rule.   **(3 marks)**

(b)   Fill in the gaps.

Enid could ………………………... under ………………………... and ask for Dine plc to be ………………………... as this is just and equitable.

(3 marks)

(c)   If Whine were to use his controlling interest to remove Moan, a court could be persuaded that this is a …………………………..and a member-director has been removed from office as in …………………………..., as this is ……………………… . This *would/would not* be likely to be successful since the Insolvency Act 1986 …. *(Your answer must not exceed 15 words.)*

(5 marks)

(d)   Explain, citing case law, what Whine's behaviour with the rights issue might amount to.   *(Your answer must not exceed 30 words.)*

(5 marks)

(Total: 16 marks)

For the answer to this question, see the 'Answers' section at the end of the book

.

Chapter 26

COMPANY ADMINISTRATION AND FINANCE: COMPANY SECRETARY

Syllabus content

Company administration and finance

- The qualifications, powers and duties of the company secretary

The chapter considers the position of the company's chief administrative officer: the Company Secretary.

Contents

1   Role and qualifications

Every company must have a secretary and the role cannot be doubled with that of sole director. The post may be held by another company or by joint secretaries; any formal act of a secretary may in their absence be performed by a deputy or assistant.

In a public company, the secretary is required to be a person with the requisite knowledge and experience to discharge the function of a secretary and who holds a relevant qualification, such as:

- having had three of the previous five years acting as company secretary of a public company

- being a member of a recognised body

- being a barrister, advocate or solicitor admitted in the UK

- being any other person who appears to the directors as being capable of discharging those functions.

Recognised bodies are the Institute of Chartered Accountants in England and Wales, the Institute of Chartered Accountants of Scotland, the Institute of Chartered Accountants in Ireland, the Association of Chartered Certified Accountants, the Institute of Chartered Secretaries and Administrators, the Chartered Institute of Management Accountants and the Chartered Institute of Public Finance and Accountancy.

No formal qualifications are required to be the company secretary of a private company.

2   Appointment and removal

The articles usually provide for the appointment of a company secretary by the directors.

Table A provides that the secretary shall be appointed by the directors for such a term, at such remuneration and upon such conditions as they may think fit, and any secretary so appointed may be removed by them.

3   Duties

KEY POINT

There are no specific duties imposed on the Company Secretary by the Companies Act 1985.

There are no specific duties imposed on the Company Secretary by the Companies Act 1985 (although various documents, such as the annual return, require the signature of a director or secretary). Their duties, therefore, are whatever the board chooses to entrust to them. These duties might include:

- Preparing for, attending and taking action after meetings of the board of directors and also general meetings. These tasks will include preparation of notices and agenda, or working papers and information summaries and of minutes of the proceedings.

- Maintaining the statutory registers (though the register of members of a large company is now often entrusted to professional registrars using computers); this includes dealing with share transfers and the issue of share certificates.

- Witnessing, i.e. signing as witness (together with a director) the company seal when applied to documents.

- The generation and delivery of returns of all kinds to the Companies Registry.

- Preparation of the numerous returns required by government departments and official bodies.

Depending on the size of the headquarters staff, the secretary may also be the chief accounting officer, have charge of staff employment and pension matters, obtain legal advice from solicitors, confer with the auditors and deal with the Stock Exchange.

4 Status

A company secretary may be a director, but is not automatically a director and if not a director they will not be a member of the board. However, the secretary is an officer and often is also an employee of the company.

The statutory register of directors must also include the secretary's particulars. The first appointment of the secretary and any subsequent change must be notified to the Companies Registry. The secretary must give their written consent in the notification.

5 Liability

Many sections of the Companies Act 1985 impose criminal liability on officers in default. A company secretary is an officer and if the board has entrusted them with discharging such statutory duties and they fail, the company secretary is liable as an officer in default. In addition, some sections of the Companies Act 1985 (notably in relation to delivery of the annual return) specifically impose criminal penalties on them by name.

At common law they, as officer and/or employee, will owe a fiduciary duty and a duty of care and skill to the company.

If they acts as agent for the company and makes a contract for which they have no authority, they, like any agent, will be personally liable to the third party in damages for breach of warranty of authority.

6 Authority

Like all of the company's agents, the secretary will bind the company to third parties in contract where they act within their authority, actual or apparent.

Lord Denning in *Panorama Developments v Fidelis Furnishing Fabrics* stated:

'He is an officer of the company with extensive duties and responsibilities. This appears not only in the modern Companies Acts, but also by the role which he plays in the day-to-day business of companies. He is no longer a mere clerk. He regularly makes representations on behalf of the company and enters into contracts on its behalf which come within the day-to-day running of the company's business. So much so that he may be regarded as held out as having authority to do such things on behalf of the company. He is certainly entitled to sign contracts connected with the administrative side of a company's affairs, such as employing staff, and ordering cars, and so forth. All such matters now come within the ostensible authority of a company's secretary.'

Panorama Developments v Fidelis Furnishing Fabrics (1971)

Facts: Bayne was company secretary of the defendant. Without authority from the directors he ordered from the claimants, a car hire firm, self-drive limousines stating that they were for the business purposes of the company. In fact he used the cars for his personal purposes. The company refused to pay for the cars.

Held: the contract was binding on the company since hiring of cars was usual to the office of company secretary.

Although Lord Denning in his speech seemed to imbue the office with authority to make contracts within 'the day-to-day running of the business' it is questionable whether this extends beyond the administrative side of the business to commercial activities. In the same year, the Court of Appeal stated '… it is established beyond all question that a secretary, while performing the duties appropriate to the office of secretary, is not concerned in the management of the company. Equally, I think he is not concerned in carrying on the business of the company' – *Re Maidstone Buildings* (1971).

Case law has held the following to be not within the usual authority of the office of company secretary:

- borrowing of money

- summoning a general meeting

- registering a transfer of shares (ie making an entry in the register of members)

- commencing litigation in the company's name.

7 Companies Bill 2006

7.1 Private companies

The position of company secretary will become voluntary.

The duties that company secretaries currently undertake will continue to be required, but directors can choose to carry them out themselves.

In future, anything required to be sent to the company secretary may be sent to the company itself.

7.2 Public companies

It will remain compulsory for all public companies to have a company secretary.

The Secretary of State can issue a direction requiring a public company to appoint a company secretary within a specified period. Failure to comply will be an offence.

The required qualifications amend the present requirements in two respects:

1. they do not include the qualification of having held the office of the company's secretary (or assistant or deputy secretary) on 22nd December 1980

2. there is no requirement for the company secretary to be a 'natural person'.

Only a public company will be required to have a register of secretaries. Only a public company will be required to notify details to Companies House.

Summary

On completion of their studies, students should be able to:

- explain the qualifications, powers and duties of the company secretary.

Self-test questions

Role and qualifications

1 Are there any statutorily required qualifications for the Company Secretary of a private company? (1)

Liability

2 To whom and why might a company secretary be liable in damages for breach of warranty of authority? (5)

Chapter 27

ETHICS AND BUSINESS

Syllabus content

Ethics and business

- Values and attitudes for professional accountants

- Legal frameworks, regulations and standards for business

- Nature of ethics and its relevance to business and the accountancy profession

- Rules-based and framework approaches to ethics

- Personal development and life-long learning

- Personal qualities of reliability, responsibility, timeliness, courtesy and respect

- Ethical principles of integrity, objectivity, professional competence, due care and confidentiality

- Concepts of independence, scepticism, accountability and social responsibility

- The CIMA and IFAC *Codes of Ethics for Professional Accountants*

Contents

1 Introduction

Accountants have a duty to observe the highest standards of conduct and integrity, and to uphold the reputation of their profession. To help them achieve this duty, accountants are expected to comply with both the terms and the spirit of any laws, regulations and standards for business.

The framework of laws, regulations and standards that apply to accountants exist as a means of ensuring public trust in the profession.

In the UK, the Financial Reporting Council (FRC) is the independent body responsible for regulating corporate reporting and governance. It consists of a number of operating bodies, the two most relevant here being:

- the Professional Oversight Board, which reviews how the professional accountancy bodies regulate their members

- the Auditing Practices Board, which issues guidance on the application of auditing standards.

2 The CIMA and IFAC Codes of Ethics

CIMA's *Code of Ethics for Professional Accountants* is based on the IFAC *Code of Ethics*, issued in June 2005. IFAC stands for International Federation of Accountants, which is the global organisation for the accountancy profession. The IFAC *Code of Ethics* was developed with the help of input from CIMA and the global accountancy profession.

The IFAC *Code of Ethics* applies to all bodies that are members of IFAC. It can be downloaded free from the IFAC website at www.ifac.org. Although members may establish their own codes, the standards that they impose may not be less stringent than the IFAC *Code of Ethics*. CIMA's own *Code of Ethics for Professional Accountants* reflects its status as a Chartered Institute and is used as a basis for reviewing cases under CIMA's disciplinary procedure.

CIMA's *Code of Ethics for Professional Accountants* is in three parts.

- Part A sets out the fundamental principles of professional ethics and provides a framework for application of those principles.

- Part B deals with professional accountants in public practice. It covers the issues that they face in relation to their clients, such as marketing their services, custody of client assets and fees.

- Part C deals with professional accountants in business. It covers the reporting of financial and other information that may be relied on by third parties.

3 Fundamental principles

KEY POINT

CIMA's *Code of Ethics for Professional Accountants* lists five fundamental principles:

• integrity
• objectivity
• professional competence and due care
• confidentiality, and
• professional behaviour.

CIMA's *Code of Ethics for Professional Accountants* lists five fundamental principles, with which its members are expected to comply:

• integrity

• objectivity

• professional competence and due care

• confidentiality, and

• professional behaviour.

3.1 Integrity

Accountants should be straightforward and honest in all their professional and business relationships.

3.2 Objectivity

Accountants should not allow bias, conflict of interest or the undue influence of others to override their professional or business judgements. For example, a threat to objectivity may be created when a professional accountant in public practice:

• competes directly with a client

• has a joint venture or similar arrangement with a major competitor of a client

• performs services for clients whose interests are in conflict or the clients are in dispute with each other.

3.3 Professional competence and due care

Professional competence may be divided into:

• attainment of professional competence

• maintenance of professional competence through continuing professional development.

Due care or diligence encompasses the responsibility to act in accordance with the requirements of an assignment, carefully, thoroughly and on a timely basis. Accountants should also take steps to ensure that those working under their authority have appropriate training and supervision.

A threat to professional competence and due care is created if the fee quoted is so low that it may be difficult to perform the engagement in accordance with applicable technical and professional standards for that price.

3.4 Confidentiality

Accountants should respect the confidentiality of information acquired as a result of their professional and business relationships. They should not disclose any such information to third parties without proper and specific authority, unless there is a legal or professional right or duty to disclose.

Accountants are or may be required to disclose confidential information in the following situations:

- When it is permitted by law and authorised by the client or the employer.

- When it is required by law, for example:

  - production of documents in the course of legal proceedings

  - disclosure to the appropriate public authorities of infringements of the law.

- Where there is a professional duty or right to disclose, which is not prohibited by law, for example:

  - to comply with the quality review of the professional body

  - to respond to an inquiry or investigation by a member body or regulatory body

  - to protect the professional interests of a professional accountant in legal proceedings

  - to comply with technical standards and ethics requirements.

In deciding whether or not information should be disclosed, accountants should consider:

- whether the interests of all parties could be harmed if the client or employer consents to the disclosure of information

- whether all the relevant information is known and substantiated

- the type of communication that is expected and to whom it is addressed.

Note that the need to comply with the principle of confidentiality continues even after the end of relationships between the accountant and a client or employer.

3.5 Professional behaviour

Accountants should comply with all relevant laws and regulations and avoid actions that discredit the profession. They should not:

- make exaggerated claims for the services they are able to offer, the qualifications they possess, or experience they have gained

- make disparaging references or unsubstantiated comparisons to the work of others.

4 Independence, accountability and responsibility

4.1 Independence

It is in the public interest and, therefore, required by the *Code of Ethics*, that members of assurance teams and their network firms be independent of assurance clients.

Independence requires both:

• independence of mind – this permits the expression of a conclusion without being affected by influences that compromise professional judgement

• independence in appearance – the avoidance of facts and circumstances that are so significant that a reasonable and informed third party would reasonably conclude a firm's integrity, objectivity or professional scepticism had been compromised.

In considering the significance of any particular matter, qualitative as well as quantitative factors should be taken into account. A matter should be considered clearly insignificant only if it is deemed to be both trivial and inconsequential.

As it is impossible to list every situation in which independence could possibly be compromised, the *Code of Ethics* provides a conceptual framework that requires firms and members of assurance teams to identify, evaluate and address threats to independence, rather than merely comply with a set of specific rules, which may be arbitrary.

4.2 Accountability and social responsibility

Accountants need to be accountable for their actions. They owe this accountability to their employers, their clients, the profession and to the public at large.

The accountant's wider role may be referred to as social responsibility. It relates to the community.

5 Personal qualities

Accountants are members of a profession and have a duty to uphold high standards. The key virtues that accountants need to exhibit are:

• Reliability – accountants must be trustworthy and dependable.

• Responsibility – accountants must be responsible for their actions and decisions.

• Timeliness – accountants must deliver the agreed work at the agreed time.

• Courtesy – accountants must be polite towards others.

• Respect – accountants must have regard for the views and attitudes of others, even when they disagree with them.

As the regulation of the accountancy profession grows ever more complex, it is important that all accountants stay up to date with their knowledge. CIMA members are expected to meet CIMA's continuing professional development requirements.

6 Rules-based and framework approaches to ethics

6.1 Introduction

There are two different approaches to formulating a code of ethics:

• a rules-based approach

• a framework approach.

6.2 Rules-based ethics

A rules-based approach to ethics is sometimes referred to as a compliance approach. It explicitly sets out what individuals can and cannot do, and specifies the sanctions that will be imposed for non-compliance.

A rules-based approach works because it instils a sense of fear. Individuals comply because they are required to and because they fear the consequences. However, the main disadvantage of this approach is the fact that the rules cannot cover every particular situation and rules may become out of date as circumstances change.

6.3 Framework approach

KEY POINT

A framework approach to ethics provides a set of principles to help individuals arrive at the correct decision.

Its main advantage is that it can be applied more easily to new developments in business practice or to unique cases.

A framework approach to ethics provides a set of principles to help individuals arrive at the correct decision. It attempts to instil the idea of the 'correct' thing to do.

Its main advantage is that it can be applied more easily to new developments in business practice or to unique cases. However, its disadvantage is that it is left to the member to decide how best to deal with an ethical question within the framework laid down.

It is also much more difficult to monitor compliance than in a rules-based approach.

Summary

On completion of their studies, students should be able to:

- apply the values and attitudes that provide professional accountants with a commitment to act in the public interest and with social responsibility

- explain the need for a framework of laws, regulations and standards in business and their application

- explain the nature of ethics and its application to business and the accountancy profession

- identify the difference between detailed rules-based and framework approaches to ethics

- identify the need for continual personal improvement and life-long learning

- identify the need to develop the virtues of reliability, responsibility, timeliness, courtesy and respect

- explain the ethical principles of integrity, objectivity, professional competence, due care and confidentiality

- identify concepts of independence, scepticism, accountability and social responsibility

- explain the reasons why CIMA and IFAC each have a *Code of Ethics for Professional Accountants*.

Self-test questions

Introduction

1 What is the name of the independent body responsible for regulating corporate reporting and governance? (1)

Fundamental principles

2 What are the five fundamental principles listed in CIMA's *Code of Ethics*? (3.1-3.5)

3 In which situations may an accountant disclose confidential information? (3.4)

Independence, accountability and responsibility

4 What are the two different aspects of independence? (4.1)

Personal qualities

5 State three of the key virtues that accountants are required to have. (5)

Rules-based and framework approaches to ethics

6 What is the main advantage of a framework approach to ethics? (6.3)

For the answers to these questions, see the 'Answers' section at the end of the book.

Chapter 28

ETHICAL CONFLICT

Syllabus content

- Relationship between ethics, governance, the law and social responsibility

- Unethical behaviour

- Ethical dilemmas and conflicts of interest

This chapter considers how ethical conflicts can arise. It looks at the safeguards that can be put in place to eliminate or minimise conflicts and at how such conflicts can be resolved.

Contents

1   Ethics, governance, the law and social responsibility

2   Consequences of unethical behaviour

3   Threats

4   Safeguards

5   Ethical conflict resolution

1 Ethics, governance, the law and social responsibility

Ethics are the values and attitudes that underpin a business. They state the standards expected of the employees. Although it is not mandatory for employees and businesses to behave in an ethical way, they are expected to do so.

Governance refers to the way in which an organisation is run. It focuses on accountability. In the UK, companies are expected to abide by the *Combined Code* (see the following chapter). However, the *Combined Code* is not backed up by the force of law and there are no real sanctions that can be applied to companies that fail to comply.

By contrast, the law is mandatory. It must be obeyed and sanctions are imposed on businesses and individuals who fail to comply.

Social responsibility refers to how a company behaves towards the community in which it operates. It involves a consideration of the organisation's stakeholders. Stakeholders may have a financial relationship with the organisation; for example, they may be shareholders, employees, customers or suppliers. Alternatively they may have an interest in how the organisation behaves; for example, regulatory bodies, the media or pressure groups.

As far as the relationship between these factors is concerned, the law underpins all of them, as compliance is obligatory. It is sometimes said that ethics begins where the law ends; i.e. ethics may lead an individual to behave in a particular way even if they are not legally obliged to do so. Ethics therefore provides a framework for an organisation's governance and social responsibility.

2 Consequences of unethical behaviour

Although it is rarely mandatory to behave in an ethical fashion, adverse consequences frequently await those who behave unethically. The main consequence is loss of reputation which, in turn, may lead to a range of unwelcome outcomes:

- an individual may lose their job (and hence their income) or their position in the community

- a company may lose custom and be forced into liquidation

- a professional body may lose credibility and have its royal charter withdrawn.

The consequences may reach beyond those parties directly involved in the unethical behaviour. For example, if HM Revenue and Customs discover that one firm in a particular industry has been behaving unethically, it may conclude that other firms in the same industry have been behaving in the same manner. This may lead them to open investigations into some of those other firms. Similarly, if an accountant is found to have a client who has been behaving unethically, this may lead HM Revenue and Customs to investigate other clients dealt with by that accountant.

KEY POINT

The final sanction against unethical behaviour is legislation.

The final sanction against unethical behaviour is legislation. If organisations are unable to abide by their own voluntary ethical codes of behaviour, the government may feel obliged to step in and legislate to force them to behave appropriately.

3 Threats

3.1 Introduction

In the previous chapter consideration was given to the fundamental principles contained in CIMA's *Code of Ethics*. Accountants have an obligation to evaluate any threats to compliance with these fundamental principles.

The code lists five different types of threat:

KEY POINT

The code lists five different types of threat:
- self-interest
- self-review
- advocacy
- familiarity
- intimidation.

- self-interest
- self-review
- advocacy
- familiarity
- intimidation.

3.2 Self-interest threats

These may occur as a result of the financial or other interests of an accountant or of an immediate or close family member. The code lists some examples:

- having a financial interest in a client
- undue dependence on total fees from a client
- having a close business relationship with a client
- concern about the possibility of losing a client
- potential employment with a client
- a loan to or from a client or any of its directors or officers.

3.3 Self-review threats

These may occur when previous judgement needs to be re-evaluated. Examples given in the code include the following:

- the discovery of a significant error during a re-evaluation of the work
- reporting on the operation of financial systems after being involved in their design or implementation
- having prepared the original data used to generate records
- a member of the assurance team being, or having recently been, a director or officer of that client.

3.4 Advocacy threats

These may occur when an accountant promotes a position or opinion to the point that subsequent objectivity may be compromised.

3.5 Familiarity threats

These may occur when, because of a close relationship, the accountant becomes too sympathetic to the interests of others. Examples include:

- accepting gifts or preferential treatment from a client

- the long association of a senior member of the personnel of the assurance team with the assurance client.

3.6 Intimidation threats

These occur when an accountant is deterred from acting objectively by threats, actual or perceived.

4 Safeguards

4.1 Introduction

Once a threat has been identified, an accountant should consider what safeguards could be implemented to eliminate or minimise the threat. According to the code, safeguards fall into two categories:

- safeguards created by the profession, legislation or regulation

- safeguards in the work environment.

4.2 Safeguards created by the profession, legislation or regulation

The *Code of Ethics* gives several examples of such safeguards:

- educational, training and experience requirements for entry into the profession

- continuing professional development requirements

- corporate governance regulations

- professional standards

- professional or regulatory monitoring and disciplining procedures

- external review by a legally empowered third party of the reports, returns, communications or information produced by an accountant.

4.3 Safeguards in the work environment

Safeguards in the work environment may be firm wide or engagement specific. The *Code of Ethics* gives several examples of each type.

Firm-wide safeguards may include:

- leadership of the firm that stresses the importance of compliance with the fundamental principles

- leadership that establishes the expectation that members of the firm will act in the public interest

- documented internal policies and procedures requiring compliance

- using different partners and engagement teams with separate reporting lines for the provision of non-assurance services to an assurance client

- a disciplinary procedure to promote compliance with policies and procedures.

Engagement-specific safeguards in the work environment may include:

- involving an additional professional accountant to review the work done

- consulting an independent third party

- discussing ethical issues with those charged with governance of the client

- disclosing to those charged with governance of the client the nature of services provided and extent of fees charged

- involving another firm to perform or re-perform part of the engagement

- rotating senior assurance team personnel.

Certain safeguards may increase the likelihood of identifying or deterring unethical behaviour. The *Code of Ethics* suggests:

- an effective, well-publicised complaints system, enabling colleagues, employers and members of the public to draw attention to unprofessional or unethical behaviour

- an explicitly stated duty to report breaches of ethical requirements.

4.4 Applying safeguards

In deciding which safeguards to apply, an accountant should consider what a reasonable and informed third party, having knowledge of all relevant information, including the significance of the threat and the safeguards applied, would conclude to be unacceptable.

If an accountant cannot implement appropriate safeguards, they should decline or discontinue the specific professional service involved.

5 Ethical Conflict Resolution

5.1 Steps to resolve conflict

When an accountant is faced with a dilemma, such as a threat to one of the *Code of Ethics'* fundamental principles, there are a number of steps that should be followed as part of the resolution process:

KEY POINT

All alternative courses of action should be considered and the possible consequences of each should be weighed.

(a) the relevant facts should be gathered

(b) the ethical issues involved should be identified

(c) the fundamental principles relating to the matter in question should be determined

(d) any established internal procedures should be followed

(e) all alternative courses of action should be considered and the possible consequences of each should be weighed.

5.2 What if conflict cannot be resolved?

If an ethical conflict cannot be resolved satisfactorily by following the above procedure, the accountant should consider consulting with those charged with governance of the organisation, such as the board of directors or the audit committee.

It may be advisable to document the substance of the issue and the details of any discussions held or decisions taken.

If a significant conflict cannot be resolved, the accountant should obtain professional advice from the relevant professional body or legal advisors. However, they should be careful to avoid breaching the organisation's confidentiality.

If the conflict remains unresolved after exhausting all the above possibilities, where possible the accountant should refuse to remain associated with the matter creating the conflict and, if necessary, resign altogether from the engagement, the firm or the employing organisation.

Summary

On completion of their studies, students should be able to:

- explain the relationship between ethics, governance, the law and social responsibility

- describe the consequences of unethical behaviour to the individual, the profession and society

- identify situations where ethical dilemmas and conflicts of interest occur

- explain how ethical dilemmas and conflicts of interest can be resolved.

Self-test questions

Ethics, governance, the law and social responsibility

1   What is meant by social responsibility? (1)

Consequences of unethical behaviour

2   What are the possible consequences to an individual of unethical behaviour? (2)

Threats

3   What, according to CIMA's *Code of Ethics*, are the five different types of threat? (3.1)

Safeguards

4   Give three examples of safeguards created by the profession, legislation or regulation. (4.2)

5   What are the two categories of safeguards in the work environment? (4.3)

Ethical conflict resolution

6   What is the first step that should be taken to resolve an ethical conflict? (5.1)

For the answers to these questions, see the 'Answers' section at the end of the book.

Chapter 29

CORPORATE GOVERNANCE

Syllabus content

- The role and key objectives of corporate governance in relation to ethics and the law

- Development of corporate governance internationally

- The behaviour of directors in relation to corporate governance and duty of care towards their stakeholders

- The role of the board in establishing corporate governance standards

- Types of board structures and corporate governance issues

- Policies and procedures for best practice companies

- Rules-based and principles-based approaches to governance

- The regulatory governance framework.

Contents

1 Introduction

The term 'corporate governance' has not been defined by either legislation or the courts. However, it is generally understood to be the system by which companies are directed and controlled.

Although companies have always been subject to the strict provisions contained in the various Companies Acts, there has been a perceived lack of effective control over the directors of public listed companies. Many directors have been the recipients of excessive remuneration packages, and mis-management of some high-profile companies has led to their collapse.

The directors of UK listed companies are required to ensure that their company complies with the *Combined Code* on corporate governance. This is a code of best practice that covers matters such as the procedures by which directors' remuneration is fixed, the way in which they communicate with shareholders and the ways in which they safeguard the company's assets. Directors must include a statement in the annual report and accounts describing the procedures that they follow in order to comply with the *Combined Code*, and giving details of any non-compliance.

2 The interaction of ethics, corporate governance and company law

The interaction of ethics, corporate governance and company law was considered in the previous chapter. In terms of corporate governance, company law sets out the fiduciary duties that directors owe to their companies. If the shareholders consider that the directors are not acting in the best interests of the company, they have the power to remove them from office. However, in public companies, there is a huge number of shareholders and it is often difficult for them to organise themselves in order to take collective action. In addition, a large percentage of share capital tends to be in the hands of institutional investors. If problems arise, they are probably more likely to dispose of their shareholding rather than take an active role in controlling management.

Neither ethics nor corporate governance have the force of law. Ethics consists of those principles and standards that should be adopted and applied. However, there are no formal sanctions for failure to comply. The regulations and codes setting out the best-practice standards of corporate governance are also fairly toothless. Companies are merely required to disclose the extent to which they have complied with the codes and to give reasons for non-compliance. It is therefore possible for a company to comply with a code by explaining why it has not complied with it!

3 The history of corporate governance in the UK

3.1 The need for corporate governance

During the late 1980s a number of large UK public companies failed, some of them as a result of large-scale fraud by directors. These companies included Polly Peck, Maxwell Communications, and BCCI.

These failures reduced public confidence in financial reporting and auditing. Many people believed that company directors regarded accounting standards as a set of rules to be circumvented and 'creative accounting' was implicated in several company liquidations. For example, the accounts of Polly Peck showed that the company was apparently in a healthy position while in fact it was on the verge of collapse. Directors were putting auditors under increasing commercial pressure to accept the use of 'creative accounting' schemes.

These problems were addressed by the introduction of new standard-setting regimes for both financial reporting and auditing. There were other concerns about the accountability of directors, for example:

- There was no clear framework for ensuring that directors reviewed internal controls in their companies.

- There was a perceived lack of accountability for directors' remuneration, which in some cases was believed to be excessive. In addition, there was increasing public concern that financial statements did not adequately reflect directors' remuneration.

A general need was perceived for a strengthening of the systems of corporate governance used by UK companies.

3.2 The Cadbury Report

The Cadbury Committee was set up in 1991 by the Financial Reporting Council, the Stock Exchange and the accountancy profession to examine the reporting and control functions of boards of directors, and the role of auditors and shareholders. It was chaired by Sir Adrian Cadbury.

The Cadbury Report, entitled '*The Financial Aspects of Corporate Governance*', was issued in December 1992.

The Committee issued a code of best practice for company directors. Compliance with the code was voluntary. However, the London Stock Exchange Listing Rules required UK-incorporated listed companies to include a statement in their annual report and accounts as to whether they had complied with the code. Non-compliance had to be explained.

Broadly, the Cadbury Code recommended the following:

KEY POINT

The Cadbury Code recommended

- the roles of chief executive and chairman should not be held by the same person

- the board should consist of both executive and non-executive directors

- the establishment of a remuneration committee

- the establishment of an audit committee

- the roles of chief executive and chairman should not be held by the same person

- the board should consist of both executive and non-executive directors

- independence of the board (no financial connection with the company except fees and shareholdings)

- the establishment of a remuneration committee consisting wholly or mainly of non-executive directors. The committee's role being to deal with the appointment and remuneration of the executive directors

- service contracts in excess of three years to be approved by the shareholders in a general meeting

- the establishment of an audit committee with a majority of non-executive directors.

The Cadbury Committee also recommended that directors of listed companies should report on the effectiveness of the company's system of internal control. This requirement was incorporated into the *Combined Code* (see below).

3.3 The Greenbury Report

Early in 1995 the Confederation of British Industry (CBI) set up a committee to draw up guidelines on directors' remuneration. The committee was headed by Sir Richard Greenbury. This move was a response to increasing public concern that financial statements still did not adequately reflect management remuneration. The committee included members from the Institute of Directors, the National Association of Pension Funds and the Stock Exchange.

KEY POINT

The Greenbury Report set out a code of best practice in determining and accounting for directors' remuneration.

The committee reported in September 1995. The Greenbury Report set out a code of best practice in determining and accounting for directors' remuneration. Some of the main recommendations were as follows:

• directors should not be given discounted share options

• annual bonuses should not be pensionable

• all long-term incentive schemes should be approved by the shareholders

• executive directors' service contracts should not provide for notice periods in excess of one year.

All listed companies registered in the UK were required to comply with the Greenbury Code from 1995 onwards. They had to include a statement about their remuneration committee. Any areas of non-compliance were to be explained and justified.

3.4 The Hampel Report

In January 1998 another report on corporate governance was issued, this time from a committee under the chairmanship of Sir Ronnie Hampel. While both the Cadbury and Greenbury Reports concentrated on preventing abuses, the Hampel report was 'concerned with the positive contribution which good corporate governance can make'. Throughout, it aimed to restrict the regulatory burden facing companies and substitute broad principles where practicable.

As each company's circumstances are different, a 'one-size-fits-all' approach to corporate governance issues was rejected. Instead, each listed company was required to include in its annual report a narrative explaining how the broad principles of corporate governance had been applied.

KEY POINT

Directors must comply with the substance as well as the letter of all best practice pronouncements.

The general message of Hampel is that a board must not approach the various corporate governance requirements in a compliance mentality: the so-called 'tick-box' approach. Good corporate governance is not achieved by satisfying a checklist. Directors must comply with the substance as well as the letter of all best practice pronouncements.

3.5 Subsequent developments

KEY POINT

The Hampel Committee drew up a single Combined Code of Best Practice, incorporating the Cadbury, Greenbury and Hampel recommendations.

After publishing its report, the Hampel Committee drew up a single *Combined Code of Best Practice*, incorporating the Cadbury, Greenbury and Hampel recommendations. The London Stock Exchange has made the code compulsory for all listed companies. The provisions of the *Combined Code* are considered in detail later in this chapter.

The *Combined Code* was modified in 2003 following the Turnbull Report and the Higgs Report.

The Turnbull Report

The Turnbull Report, which was published in 1999, concluded that directors should:

- evaluate the likely risks facing a company

- ensure that effective safeguards and internal controls are put in place to prevent or minimise risk.

The Higgs Report

The Higgs Report was commissioned in response to the collapse of the American company Enron. It made the following recommendations:

- The role of chairman and chief executive should not be combined.

- The chairman's role is to provide leadership for the non-executive directors and to communicate shareholders' views to the board.

- A chief executive should not become chairman of the same company.

- A nomination committee (with a majority of independent non-executive directors) should recommend future executive and non-executive directors.

- Directors should be subject to a professional development programme and an annual evaluation of their performance.

- At least half the board of the top 350 listed companies must be independent non-executive directors.

- Smaller listed companies must have at least two independent non-executive directors.

4 The history of corporate governance internationally

4.1 Corporate governance in Europe

In the wake of continuing stock exchange mergers across Europe in 1999 and 2000, a problem arose because national corporate governance guidelines differed widely across Europe, but uniform rules were required for the new exchanges created, e.g. Euronext combining the exchanges of France, Holland and Belgium.

The European Association of Securities Dealers (EASD) issued a new set of guidelines in 2000 to act as a benchmark for companies. EASDAQ, the European stock market for high growth companies, has adopted the guidelines so that quoted companies must disclose the reasons if they do not comply.

In 2003, the European Commission decided that it would not formulate a separate code of European corporate governance. Instead, it would develop a common approach through the issue of directives.

A European Union Corporate Governance Forum was established in October 2004. It has 15 members and its overall objective is to co-ordinate the corporate governance approaches taken by member states.

4.2 Corporate governance in the United States

The Enron scandal and other such corporate scandals in the USA illustrated the failure of corporate governance codes to protect investors from unscrupulous directors. Voluntary codes were viewed as failing to protect against senior executives who sanctioned misleading accounting treatments, or audit committees that agreed misleading financial statements.

In 2002, the Sarbanes-Oxley Act in the USA introduced requirements relating to corporate governance into the federal law.

It extended protection to internal and external whistleblowers in publicly traded companies for the first time. The provisions:

- make it illegal to 'discharge, demote, suspend, threaten, harass or in any manner discriminate against' whistleblowers

- establish criminal penalties of up to 10 years for executives who retaliate against whistleblowers

- require board audit committees to establish procedures for hearing whistleblower complaints.

The Act makes no distinction between US and foreign private issuers listed in the USA. Thus there will be cross-border effects if companies want a listing in the USA. For example, chief executive officers and finance directors of foreign companies listed in the USA will have to sign 'oaths of honesty' certifications about the integrity of their company accounts.

4.3 Corporate governance elsewhere in the world

On an international basis, it is politicians under the auspices of international organisations such as the United Nations and the Organisation for Economic Co-operation and Development (OECD) who try to advance levels of corporate behaviour.

At the June 2000 meeting of the OECD, ministers from all the member countries plus Argentina, Brazil, Chile and Slovakia signed up to a new international code of conduct setting out international standards for multinational companies to follow in combating corruption, safeguarding consumer rights and promoting good labour practices. Each government is responsible for ensuring that multinational enterprises operating in or from their home country abide by the guidelines.

5 Best practice

5.1 Introduction

The final version of the Hampel *Principles of Good Governance and Code of Best Practice* (the '*Combined Code*') was published in 1998 and slightly amended in July 2003.

The Combined Code consists of 17 principles and, under the heading of each principle, a number of more detailed provisions.

The principles and provisions cover five topics:

- directors

- remuneration

- accountability and audit

- relations with shareholders

- institutional shareholders.

5.2 Directors

Every company should be headed by an effective board, which is collectively responsible for the success of the company.

There should be a clear division of responsibilities at the head of the company between the running of the board and the executive responsibility for the running of the company's business. No one individual should have unfettered powers of decision; hence the roles of chairman and chief executive should be split:

- the chairman should be responsible for the working of the board and the agenda for board meetings

- the chief executive should have full operational control and authority to carry out the policies determined by the board.

The board should include a balance of executive and non-executive directors (and, in particular, independent non-executive directors), such that no individual or small group of individuals can dominate the board's decision taking. The following persons cannot be regarded as independent:

- anyone who has been an employee of the company in the previous five years

- anyone who has had a material business relationship with the company in the previous three years

- anyone who has served on the board for more than nine years.

There should be a formal rigorous and transparent procedure for the appointment of new directors to the board.

The board should be supplied in a timely manner with information in a form and of a quality appropriate to enable it to discharge its duties. All directors should receive induction on joining the board and should regularly update and refresh their skills and knowledge.

The board should undertake a formal and rigorous annual evaluation of its own performance and that of its committee and individual directors.

All directors should be submitted for re-election at regular intervals, subject to continued satisfactory performance. The board should ensure the planned and progressive refreshing of the board.

5.3 Directors' remuneration

Levels of remuneration should be sufficient to attract, retain and motivate directors of the quality required to run the company successfully, but a company should avoid paying more than is necessary for this purpose. A significant proportion of executive directors' remuneration should be structured so as to link rewards to corporate and individual performance.

There should be a formal and transparent procedure for developing policy on executive remuneration and for fixing the remuneration packages of individual directors. No director should be involved in deciding their own remuneration.

5.4 Accountability and audit

Financial reporting

The board should present a balanced and understandable assessment of the company's position and prospects.

Internal control

The board should maintain a sound system of internal control to safeguard shareholders' investment and the company's assets.

KEY POINT

The board should, at least annually, conduct a review of the effectiveness of the group's system of internal controls

The board should, at least annually, conduct a review of the effectiveness of the group's system of internal controls and should report to shareholders that they have done so. The review should cover all material controls, including financial, operational and compliance controls and risk management systems.

Audit committee and auditors

The board should establish formal and transparent arrangements for considering how they should apply the financial reporting and internal control principles and for maintaining an appropriate relationship with the company's auditors.

5.5 Relations with shareholders

KEY POINT

A senior director should be identified and made available as a contact for shareholders.

There should be a dialogue with shareholders based on the mutual understanding of objectives. The board as a whole has responsibility for ensuring that a satisfactory dialogue with shareholders takes place.

The board should use the annual general meeting to communicate with investors and to encourage their participation. A senior director should be identified and made available as a contact for shareholders.

5.6 Institutional shareholders

Institutional shareholders should enter into a dialogue with companies based on a mutual understanding of objectives.

When evaluating companies' governance arrangements, particularly those relating to board structure and composition, institutional shareholders should give due weight to all relevant factors drawn to their attention.

Institutional shareholders have a responsibility to make considered use of their votes.

5.7 The Stock Exchange Listing Rules

The Stock Exchange Listing Rules require a listed company in the UK to include the following in its annual report and accounts:

- A narrative statement of how it has applied the principles set out in the *Combined Code*, providing an explanation that enables its shareholders to evaluate how the principles have been applied.

- A statement as to whether or not it has complied throughout the accounting period with the *Combined Code* provisions. A company that has not complied with the provisions, or complied with it for only part of an accounting period, must specify the provisions with which it has not complied, and give reasons for any non-compliance.

5.8   2006 Revisions

The Financial Reporting Council issued a new version of the code on 27 June 2006. The new version contains a small number of changes, such as:

- The restriction on a company chairman serving on a remuneration committee has been relaxed. However, it is still recommended that the chairman should not chair the committee.

- A 'vote withheld' option should be included on proxy forms so that investors can indicate reservations about resolutions that they do not wish to vote against.

- The recommendation that companies publish on their website the details of proxies lodged at a general meeting where votes are taken on a show of hands.

The Financial Services Authority will be consulting on these revisions before incorporating them into the Listing Rules. However, it is recommending that listed companies adopt the revised code on a voluntary basis from 1 November 2006.

Both the 2003 and 2006 versions of the *Combined Code* are available on-line at www.frc.org.uk/corporate/combinedcode.cfm.

5.9   The *Combined Code* and smaller companies

The *Combined Code* applies to all listed companies, whether they are large or small. The Hampel Committee decided not to draw a distinction between large and small quoted companies, although it recognised that smaller companies might have difficulty in complying with some of the provisions. The committee concluded that:

- any distinction based on size would be arbitrary

- high standards of governance are as important for smaller listed companies as for larger ones.

In practice, the *Combined Code* is not intended to be prescriptive. If the board of a small quoted company does not believe that a particular provision is appropriate, it should disclose this fact and the reasons for non-compliance. This enables readers of the annual report to consider the performance of the board based on the individual circumstances of the company.

6   Rules-based and principles-based approaches to governance

The *Combined Code* is a set of principles, rather than a set of rules. Directors are required to describe in their own words the way in which they have applied the general principles of corporate governance. There are several advantages to this approach.

- Because the directors report on the actual circumstances of their own company, in theory the report should be more meaningful than one based on specific detailed requirements.

- Requirements based on statute might be difficult to interpret, or be open to different interpretations.

A code of practice can be changed much more easily than statutory requirements. This means that the *Combined Code* can be updated to respond to changing conditions and changing expectations of shareholders and others.

There are, however, some potential disadvantages in having a *Combined Code* that consists of a set of principles rather than rules:

- describing procedures, as opposed to making specific disclosures, may be challenging for some boards

- there is a danger that the directors' statement might be drafted in such general terms that it becomes almost meaningless.

7 Board structures

7.1 Introduction

According to the *Combined Code*, the board's role is to provide 'entrepreneurial leadership'. It should:

- set the company's strategic aims, values and standards

- ensure that the necessary financial and human resources are in place for the company to meet its objectives

The two main types of board structure are unitary and two-tier.

7.2 Unitary board structures

The term 'unitary' board structure refers to the situation where there is one board that is responsible for both management and governance. This is the type of structure usually found in the UK and the USA.

A unitary board may consist wholly of executive directors or be a mixture of executives and non-executives.

The main problem with this type of structure is that the executive directors have two competing functions; namely, they are responsible both for managing the company and for supervising their own performance.

7.3 Two-tier board structures

Under a two-tier system, there is:

- a supervisory board with a chairman, and

- a management board with a chief executive.

This type of system is commonly found in France and Germany.

The management board is responsible for managing the company. It reports to the supervisory board. The supervisory board may also be responsible for appointing and removing the members of the management board.

In Germany, the shareholders are able to elect a certain number of the members of the supervisory board. Employees and trade unions are also represented on the board.

8   The effective of corporate governance on directors' behaviour

Korn/Ferry International, a worldwide executive search and leadership development firm, conducts an Annual Board of Directors Study. Their 2005 survey made a number of findings concerning the effect that corporate governance has on directors' behaviour:

- Of the directors who responded from the Americas, 72% said that Sarbanes-Oxley and its associated regulations had made their boards more cautious and 58% felt that the provisions should be repealed or overhauled.

- The corresponding figures from the UK in respect of the *Combined Code* were 61% and 28% respectively.

- Of the directors who responded from the Americas, 87% said that they expected to incur substantial compliance costs and there seemed to be unanimous agreement that these monies could be better spent elsewhere.

- The perceived risks in the current corporate governance environment have made directors worldwide more discriminating when it comes to accepting directorships. The majority of directors who responded from the Americas, Australasia, France and Switzerland stated that risk was a determining factor for would-be directors turning down boardroom seats.

- The burdens that the corporate governance regime places on directors were found to substantially increase the time commitments expected of them.

A summary of the findings can be found at http://www.kornferry.com/Library/Process.asp?P=Pubs_Detail&CID=1510&LID=1

Summary

On completion of their studies, students should be able to:

- define corporate governance

- explain the interaction of corporate governance with business ethics and company law

- describe the history of corporate governance internationally

- explain the effect of corporate governance on directors' behaviour and their duty of skill and care

- explain different board structures, the role of the board and corporate governance issues

- describe the types of policies and procedures that best-practice companies introduce

- explain the regulatory governance framework for companies.

Self-test questions

Introduction

1   What is meant by the term 'corporate governance'? (1)

The history of corporate governance in the UK

2   State three of the recommendations of the Cadbury Report. (3.2)

3   With which aspect of corporate governance was the Greenbury Report concerned? (3.3)

4   Which committee combined the findings of its own report together with the Cadbury and Greenbury Reports to form the Combined Code? (3.4)

The history of corporate governance internationally

5   Which Act was passed in the US to introduce corporate governance requirements into federal law? (4.2)

Best practice

6   According to the *Combined Code*, which persons cannot be regarded as independent? (5.2)

Rules-based and principles-based approaches to governance

7   What are the advantages of a principles-based approach to corporate governance? (6)

Board structures

8   What is meant by a unitary board? (7.2)

Chapter 30

ANSWERS TO MULTIPLE-CHOICE AND PRACTICE QUESTIONS

Chapter 1

Multiple-choice questions

1   The correct answer is **A**.

2   The correct answer is **B**.

3   The correct answer is **B**.

Practice question

Jane

(a)   As the word 'prosecuted' is used, this must be a criminal case.

(b)   **Act** – An Act of Parliament, also called a statute, is a primary source of law. It is made by Parliament itself. It commences as a Bill and, after passing through the House of Commons and the House of Lords, becomes law on the granting of Royal Assent.

   Regulations – a regulation, being a statutory instrument, is a type of delegated legislation. It is not made by Parliament itself but by someone else (here the Secretary of State) to whom authority to do so, for specified purposes and by specified procedures, has been delegated by Parliament.

   Directive – a directive is a blueprint for legislation, issued by the European Commission under authority of the Council of Ministers, addressed to member states. Under the Treaty of Rome, each member state then must implement the directive by transposing its contents into measures of national law within a set time period. Accordingly, a directive is not itself law.

   Relationship – the European Union (EU) directive required the UK Parliament to create legislation. Parliament complied with the directive by authorising the Secretary of State to make delegated legislation in the form of a statutory instrument. Parliament gave authority to the Secretary of State in the Health and Safety at Work Act (HSWA) 1974. It was therefore the HSWA 1974 that enabled the Secretary of State to make the regulation. The regulation is therefore subordinate to the HSWA 1974 and depends on that enabling Act for its very existence.

(c)   The jurisdiction of the European Court of Justice (ECJ) includes the function of interpretation of points of EU law when such a point is the subject of a reference by a national court. Thus a pre-requisite for such a reference to the ECJ is that Jane's case must involve some such point. Here, this would appear likely since the regulation was made in order to implement the contents of the directive and the English court would have referred to the directive when interpreting the wording of the regulation.

However, Jane may only compel a reference to be made to the ECJ once her case reaches the Judicial Committee of the House of Lords; in any lower court Jane may only request a reference as the lower courts have discretion whether or not to allow a reference.

Notes: When answering examination questions remember:

- to set out your answer in the format required by the question. Here the format is (a), (b), and (c).

- in your answer to address the question the examiner is actually asking (and not the question you would have liked them to ask!). This is particularly relevant in part (b) which actually asked you four things.

- always to explain (i.e. give reason(s) for) your answer. Thus in part (a) few marks would have been awarded for the following statement 'The court proceedings against Jane are criminal'. The marks were mainly given for identifying the use of the word 'prosecution' as the reason for your conclusion that the proceedings were criminal.

Chapter 3

Multiple-choice questions

1   The correct answer is **C**.

2   The correct answer is **B**.

3   The correct answer is **B**.

4   The correct answer is **C**.

Practice question

Bernice

(a)   High Court

judge

...on the balance of probabilities

(b)   negligent

... a duty of care, which he has breached by driving badly and this must cause foreseeable loss.

(c)   case law

precedent

...applying the 'reasonable man' test, that is whether the 'man on the Clapham omnibus' would have acted so.

(d)   Andrew may raise Bernice's contributory negligence; if proven her damages would be reduced in proportion to her blame.

Chapter 5

Practice questions

Question 1: Mark and Daniel

(a)   To be valid, Daniel's offer must satisfy the legal conditions for an offer:

    (i)   It must be a definite and unequivocal statement of willingness to be bound in contract to Mark. There can be little question on the facts that the offer to provide a room in a hotel for a fee is certain.

    (ii)   There must be a clear intention to be bound. Daniel must not be merely negotiating with Mark. Again there is little doubt that if Mark agrees to pay £75 per night there will be a contract.

    (iii)   The offer is made to a person. It is clearly made to Mark.

    (iv)   The offer must reach the person to whom it is made. It is the responsibility of the offeror to ensure that the offer reaches Mark. Daniel appears to have explained the terms to Mark and they have been properly communicated.

    (v)   The offer must be open when it is accepted by the offeree. There is no question, at this stage, that the offer is open. For the purposes of this part of the question the offer is open.

    As a result of all of the above elements being present, Daniel's offer to Mark is a valid one and it is capable of acceptance.

(b)   Mark is the offeree in this question. It is his legal responsibility to ensure that the acceptance is properly communicated to the offeror, Daniel. In this situation Daniel has specified a particular mode of acceptance, namely by first class post.

The facts here raise two issues:

    (i)   was the offer revoked by Daniel's actions, or was it still capable of acceptance by Mark?

    (ii)   as Mark did not accept in the way stipulated is his acceptance (i.e. by personal delivery) a reasonable acceptance?

    Dealing with the first issue. In order for Daniel's purported revocation to be effective it must reach the offeree before the acceptance is complete. Daniel has to ensure that Mark receives and understands the fact that the offer is terminated.

    In the case of *Byrne v Van Tienhoven* the Court held that the acceptance of the offer (by post) was effective before the revocation was complete. The offeror could not claim that there was not a contract. In the present case Mark did not receive the fax and so the revocation was not adequately communicated to him. He was still in a position to accept the offer.

    Dealing with the second issue. If a method of acceptance has been specified by the offeror the acceptance must be effected in this specific way or in a way that is equally quick, efficient and reliable. It must also be reasonable to have accepted in another way.

    It could be the case that Daniel requested that the offer be accepted by first class post because this is the way his bookings are always dealt with. Or it could be that he wants to receive the acceptance first thing in the morning. Either way this would mean that hand delivering the acceptance the next day is arguably not as efficient as the specified method and that the acceptance will not be adequate.

(c) It is the responsibility of the offeree to ensure that the acceptance is received. The acceptance will only be effective from the time the offeree properly communicates the acceptance to the offeror.

However, an exception to that rule is the postal rule. If acceptance by post is the chosen, obvious or reasonable method of acceptance the rule will apply. In this situation it is not only a reasonable method of acceptance but it is also chosen as the method of acceptance by the offeror. Where the rule applies the offer is deemed to be accepted, as long as the reply is properly addressed and posted, as soon as the letter is posted or placed into the hands of the relevant postal authorities: *Household Fire Insurance v Grant*.

On the first part of the facts Mark's acceptance will be complete as soon as his letter is posted regardless of the fact that the letter did not arrive.

However, on the second part of the facts; if Mark was at all aware of the postal strike it would not be reasonable for him to use this method of acceptance (even if stipulated by Daniel) and the postal rule would not apply. In this situation the offer would be accepted only when the acceptance is communicated to the offeror and if this is delayed by the strike there may be no contract here.

(d) Daniel specified that the acceptance should be in writing to be received by him the next day.

The postal rule will only operate when it is the chosen, obvious or reasonable way to accept the contract. To accept by second class post is not reasonable on these facts as it is unlikely that the letter will arrive, as required, by the next day.

If the postal rule does not apply the usual rule of acceptance prevails. This is that the acceptance will be complete as soon as it is clearly communicated to the offeror. The letter of acceptance does not arrive until the day after the day specified by Daniel, so the acceptance falls foul of the conditions laid down. There is no acceptance and so there is no contract for Mark to rely upon.

Question 2: A – sale of car

Offer and acceptance are necessary for a binding contract. An offer is a proposition made by one party to another with the intention of being bound. It needs to be distinguished from an 'invitation to treat' which is merely a preliminary proposition which cannot be accepted. The advertisement in the newspaper is merely an 'invitation to treat'. B has made an offer to buy at £4,500. This offer appears to have been rejected. Once an offer is rejected it no longer stands. In its place A has made an offer to sell the car to B for £4,800. This, it seems, is a standing offer as A has agreed that B should be able to test drive the car at the weekend. However, the agreement to hold the offer open is not supported by a consideration on the part of B, and as such it is revocable at any time up until acceptance. It is therefore necessary to decide whether B has accepted the offer so as to create a binding contract. Acceptance must be a final and unqualified assent on the terms of the offer. B has not made an unqualified acceptance of the offer to sell at £4,800 because his acceptance is subject to a satisfactory test drive at the weekend. Consequently there is no contract and as the standing offer was not supported by consideration on the part of B, A is at liberty to sell the car to X for £4,500.

Chapter 6

Practice question

Paul

Every simple contract must be supported by consideration. A simple contract is one not in the form of a deed. In each situation Paul will be legally bound by each promise only if consideration was given for it. Consideration may be defined as an act or forbearance, promised or actual.

(a)   Consideration must be valuable but need not be adequate. The word 'valuable' means that the consideration must be of some economic or monetary value such as a motor car and money. 'Need not be adequate' means that the consideration given by each party does not have to match in value – *Chappell v Nestle*. Thus £10 in return for an expensive car is consideration even though inadequate. Accordingly Paul is bound by his promise to Arthur.

(b)   Consideration must be sufficient. This means that what is offered as consideration must be capable in law to amount to consideration. In law past consideration is insufficient – *Re McArdle*. Consideration is past where it is wholly executed before the other party makes his promise. Thus Bernard's cleaning of the windows, having been done before Paul made his promise of payment, is past. Accordingly Paul is not bound by his promise to Bernard.

(c)   Performance of an existing duty is insufficient to amount to consideration. As in *Stilk v Myrick*, Charles is already contractually obliged to paint the house by a given date and the mere doing of this by Charles is insufficient unless some extra benefit is thereby conferred on Paul – *Williams v Roffey*. The given facts may not suggest any extra benefit, but it could be argued that getting the work done without worrying about legal actions or another decorator is a practical benefit.

(d)   Consideration must move from the promisee. This means that a party who wishes to enforce a promise must himself provide consideration – *Tweddle v Atkinson*. Thus David cannot enforce Paul's promise because David provided no consideration for it.

The doctrine of privity of contract states that only the parties to a contract can sue on it. Thus in order for Eric to enforce Paul's promise Eric must show that it was to him that Paul made the promise.

(e)   Since performance of an existing contractual duty is insufficient it follows that performance of less than a contractual duty is also insufficient. This is the basis of the rule in *Pinnel's* case (also called the rule in *Foakes v Beer*), which states that payment of a lesser sum does not discharge a debt of a greater amount. Although there are exceptions to the rule, the given facts do not here suggest any might be of relevance. Accordingly Paul is not bound by his promise of release.

Chapter 7

Multiple-choice question

The answer is **B**.

Chapter 8

Multiple-choice questions

1   The correct answer is **B**.

2   The correct answer is **D**. This situation is similar to the case of *Bisset v Wilkinson.*

3   The correct answer is **C**.

Practice question

Misrepresentation

An insurance policy is a special type of contract, a contract *uberrimae fidei* or of utmost good faith. Such contracts occur where one party is in possession of vital information that must be communicated to the other party so that they can assess the advisability of entering the contract. They are subject to different rules in misrepresentation and the general rule that silence will not amount to a misrepresentation does not apply. There is a positive duty on the insured to reveal all material facts to the insurance company. The material facts are those that will influence the insurance company in deciding whether to insure this person for this risk and, if so, what premium to charge. Thus in *London Assurance v Mansel,* failure to reveal the fact that he had been refused insurance was a misrepresentation by the insured and entitled the insurance company to rescind the contract. Thus, Mort's failure to reveal the three refusals will amount to a misrepresentation.

A second exception to the general rule that silence does not amount to a misrepresentation is where a half-truth is told, e.g. where silence distorts a positive statement, as in *Nottingham Brick v Butler* where a solicitor stated that he was unaware of any restrictive covenants on land, but failed to say that he had not checked the title deeds where such covenants would be revealed.

Mort's statement that he had been accepted by one insurance company is such a half-truth and thus amounts to a misrepresentation.

Chapter 9

Multiple-choice questions

1   The correct answer is **B**.

2   The correct answer is **C**.

3   The correct answer is **C**.

Practice question

F and W – Toaster

F v W.

F has no action in the law of contract against the manufacturer – she does not have a contract with the manufacturer.

F is advised that she may have a claim in contract against W on the basis of breach of the terms implied by the Sale of Goods Act (SGA) 1979. As the toaster has ceased to function after a week it is not of satisfactory quality within s14(2). The section clearly applies to F's situation as the seller is selling in the course of a business. The fact that W is not in any way at fault does not relieve him from liability as liability under the SGA 1979 is strict.

The term implied by s14(2) is a condition and therefore F prima facie has the right to repudiate the contract and recover her money.

However, it may be that F has lost her right to reject the toaster by virtue of s35 SGA 1979. A buyer cannot reject goods once they have been accepted and this section states that a person is deemed to have accepted goods when, after the lapse of a reasonable time, he retains the goods without intimating to the seller that he rejects them. In *Bernstein v Pamsons Motors* it was explained that 'reasonable time' meant enough time to try out the goods generally. It may be that the court considers a week more than long enough to try out a toaster. If this is so F cannot return the toaster to the shop and reclaim her money: her sole remedy is for damages to cover the cost of any repairs. In any event she will also have a claim in damages for the electric shock suffered.

Tutorial note: any exclusion clause in the contract between F and W would be void by virtue of s6(2) Unfair Contract Terms Act 1977 since F is dealing as a consumer.

W v manufacturer

W's claim is against the manufacturer, again for breach of the term implied by s14 SGA 1979.

As to the validity of the exclusion clause, the clause clearly fulfils the common law tests of incorporation into the contract and aptness of wording. Since the contract between W and the manufacturer is not a consumer transaction it will be valid if the manufacturer can prove that it is reasonable – s6(3) Unfair Contract Terms Act 1977. This involves the courts weighing up a number of factors i.e. the price and the bargaining position of the parties. Also of significance is the degree of knowledge of the exemption clause, and it is therefore necessary to question why W has only just discovered its existence. This could be a factor in his favour on finding the clause is unreasonable.

Again W's claim could be to repudiate the contract and/or to claim damages. It is unlikely that he is deemed to have accepted the goods because s34 and s35 SGA 1979 states that a buyer is not deemed to have accepted goods by treating them as his own (e.g. re-selling) until and unless he has had a reasonable opportunity of examining them: this is not normally the case where goods are packaged for immediate re-sale.

Chapter 10

Multiple-choice question

1   The correct answer is **C.**

Practice questions

Question 1: E's series of concerts

(a)   Depending on the precise circumstances, this situation will either give rise to a breach of contract on the part of D, in which case he will be liable to pay damages to E, or he will be able to rely on the doctrine of frustration. In the latter event D will be discharged from his duty to engage E, but will have to pay any expenses etc. that E may have incurred prior to the frustrating event: Law Reform (Frustrated Contracts) Act 1943. There will only be a frustrating event if the theatre is essential to the performance of the contract. This will only be the case if there is absolutely nowhere else for the concerts to be held. If there are other premises available, even if these are much more expensive to hire, the fact the contract becomes more difficult and expensive to perform is not a frustrating event.

(b)   E may be liable for breach of contract on the basis of non-performance of the contract. E may try to claim frustration on the grounds of personal non-availability. However, as he has been held guilty of drug smuggling, which has led to his non-availability, this would seem to be a case of self-induced frustration, which does not discharge E from the contract.

Question 2: Seville publications plc

The basic common law rule is that a contract is not discharged by partial performance; and that one who had not fully and perfectly fulfilled his contractual obligations cannot claim any payment for the part of the work he had completed. The authority for this basic proposition is *Cutter v Powell*. In that case, the widow of a seaman failed to recover even a proportion of the fee he was to have been paid for completing a voyage, he having died at sea.

This strict and sometimes unfair rule has been modified by a number of exceptions. For example, the widow in *Cutter v Powell* would now recover, under the doctrine of frustration of contract, a reasonable sum on a *quantum meruit* basis, to reflect the value of the benefit conferred by the proportion of the work actually completed by her husband. A similar approach is adopted where the contract has not been frustrated, but its completion has been prevented by the other party. Thus, in *Planché v Colburn,* an author was commissioned to write a series of articles for publication by instalments in a periodical. He undertook a substantial amount of work, only to be told by the publishers that they had decided to discontinue publication. They declined to pay him anything, on the basis that he had not completed the agreed work, although the reason for this was that they had stopped him. The court awarded him a reasonable sum for work done on the *quantum meruit* ('as much as it deserves') basis.

The facts outlined in the question are indistinguishable in substance from those in *Planché v Colburn*. Leporello should be advised accordingly. He should retain the £5,000 deposit pending negotiations upon what would be a reasonable payment for the work done. If he proposed to write, say, no less than 100,000 words and he has written 50,000, together with his planning and preparation, he has probably completed more than half the work, and on the basis of the contract price he should receive more than half of the £20,000 agreed. He should negotiate on these lines, but if litigation is necessary to enforce his claim, he should bear in mind that the court will award what it considers to be a reasonable sum for the work done and will not be bound to adhere to a proportion of the contract price.

Leporello might have in mind continuing work, finishing the book and demanding full payment. In *White & Carter (Councils) Ltd v McGregor* a similar approach in the case of an advertising contract succeeded: the court held that there was no need for the claimant to mitigate his loss in the case of such anticipatory breach of contract. The claimant completed the contract and recovered the full price. However, the *White & Carter* case seems to be an unusual decision based upon unusual facts; and it was made clear in *Clea Shipping v Bulk Oil* that the court will not automatically allow the full amount in such cases. Probably, Leporello should mitigate his loss by ceasing to write, at least until he has taken steps to try to arrange for another publisher to take the book. If he continues to write the book, he cannot, as the law stands, be sure of any damages for the work done by him after the publisher's breach of contract.

Chapter 11

Practice question

B Bros Ltd

(a)   damages

   Hadley v Baxendale, 1854

   Victoria Laundry v Newman Industries, 1949

   …any lost production that would arise 'in the ordinary course of things'. The Ozono related losses may be outside the 'contemplation of the parties' unless the Production Manager mentioned them.

(b)   The injured party has a duty to mitigate any loss suffered and should take steps to find an alternative market.

(c)   frustrated

   repayable

   …it equalled or was exceeded by any expenses incurred by the manufacturer before the frustrating event.

(d)   injunction

   equitable

   discretionary

   …to force the company to desist from selling to the People's Republic of Bazami.

Chapter 12

Multiple-choice questions

1   The correct answer is **D**. Independent contractors rank as unsecured creditors.

2   The correct answer is **D**.

3   The correct answer is **D**.

Chapter 13

Practice question

A, B, C & D

(a)   wrongfully

       damages

       without notice

       Employment Rights Act 1996

       one week

(b)   automatically unfair

       Employment Rights Act 1996

       Employment Tribunal

       is not

       higher

(c)   is not

       Vaux and Associated Breweries v Ward, 1969

       There was no change in the nature of the particular type of work being done.

Chapter 15

Multiple-choice questions

1   The correct answer is **D**. Answer A is not correct because of the Partnership Act 1890 definition of a partnership – 'the relationship which subsists between persons carrying on business in common with a view to profit'.

2   The correct answer is **C**. In law another word for partnership is firm. A partnership is not a legal person in its own right.

3   The correct answer is **A**.

Chapter 16

Multiple-choice questions

1   The correct answer is **A**.

2   The correct answer is **A**.

3   The correct answer is **B**. The certificate of incorporation is conclusive evidence of the date of incorporation.

Clipse Ltd

The restraint of trade clause in Walters contract with Clipse Ltd restrains Walter from soliciting Clipse's customers within a two-year period of his leaving Clipse's employ. Such a clause does not bind a company which is a separate legal entity, unless that company is a party to the agreement. Desks Ltd is not a party to the agreement, but is a company formed and partly owned by Walter who is bound by the clause. If it can be shown that the main purpose in forming the company was to avoid the application of the restrictive covenant, the court may lift the veil of incorporation and treat Walter and the company as one and extend the clause to the company. The case is similar to the *Gilford Motor Co v Horne*. It should perhaps be noted Clipse would also have to show that the restraint clause is valid for public policy reasons as there is a presumption against the validity of such clauses.

In land law there is a general principle that damages for a breach of contract of sale is an inadequate remedy and normally specific performance, i.e. an order to perform the terms of the contract, is awarded. This is on the basis that every piece of land is unique and damages will not be adequate compensation.

Specific performance, unlike damages, is an equitable remedy and will only be awarded by the courts in certain circumstances, in particular no order for specific performance will be made if this would affect the rights of a *bona fide*, (good faith), purchaser.

Walter is in breach of contract with Wilf and specific performance would normally be available against Walter. Walter has already transferred ownership of the house to Desks Ltd with a view to selling it to Bill. Walter has done this hoping to prevent an order of specific performance in Wilf's favour. If the company is a separate legal entity and is a *bona fide* purchaser it is unlikely that the court will disturb the transaction, despite Walter's ulterior motive. However, the court might equate the company and Walter and treat them as one to avoid a fraud being perpetrated on Wilf. Alternatively, the court might find that the company is not a *bona fide* purchaser, because there is no mention of the company having paid for the house. If this is the case, an order for specific performance could be made anyway without lifting the veil of incorporation.

It seems that the house has not yet been transferred to Bill but if it had been, unless Bill knows of the contract between Walter and Wilf, he would be a *bona fide* purchaser and no order for specific performance could be made against him.

Chapter 17

Multiple-choice questions

1   The correct answer is **B**.

2   The correct answer is **B**.

3   The correct answer is **D**.

Practice questions

Question 1: Plum Pie Ltd

(a)   A company may change its name on its own initiative by passing a special resolution (75% of those present and voting). However, the change does not take effect until the Registrar issues a certificate of incorporation under the new name, which will only be issued if the restrictions imposed when the company is incorporated have been complied with.

A company may not have a name that is likely to mislead the public as to its real status or activities or have offensive or criminal connotations. Certain words would also require Department of Trade approval.

The directors should first check that no company is registered with a similar name and then call an extraordinary general meeting of members, or put a resolution to the next AGM resolving that the name be changed. Plum Pie Ltd could then change its name to Apple Pie Ltd by passing a special resolution and applying for a new certificate of incorporation which would be granted provided the alteration was not misleading as to the company's activities.

(b)   A company is not obliged to trade under its own name. If it elects to carry on business under a different name, it must comply with the rules on 'business names'.

The Business Names Act (BNA) 1985 regulates the use of business names. A company is subject to these rules if it carries on business under a name that does not consist of its corporate name without any addition. It must state its company name on all business letters, written orders for goods or services, invoices, receipts or written demands for payment of debts and display its company name in a prominent position so that it may easily be read at all premises where the name is carried and to which customers or suppliers have access.

In addition, certain sensitive words may not be included in a company name without official approval. This prevents a company that has been refused a company name from getting around the bar by trading under a similar business name.

Bubble may therefore trade under a business name provided it displays all the required information. It may however require approval for its proposed name as the word 'breeder' is a regulated word that requires clearance from the Ministry of Agriculture. If approval is given, the company may then trade under its business name.

(c)   A company can only do those things stated in its objects clause or ancillary to those objects – otherwise it is acting *ultra vires: Ashbury Railway Carriage v Riche.*

Even if the contract is *ultra vires,* s35 Companies Act 1985 provides that an act done or promise given cannot later be challenged on the grounds that it is not within the objects clause and a third party will be able to enforce an *ultra vires* contract against the company. However, a member may restrain an action not yet taken and the company could sue the directors for breach of duty if the company is bound.

The question describes the other two objects as subsidiary. An inherently subsidiary power to borrow cannot be converted into an independent object. In *Rolled Steel* it was held that exercise of an express power for a purpose not ancillary to the objects would not be *ultra vires* but could be an abuse of power. A clause similar to the one that permits the company to carry on any profitable business was upheld in *Bell Houses v City Wall Properties*; thus the new activity might come within this clause and be *intra vires,* in which case the bank could sue to recover any loan made.

(d)   An alteration of objects may be made under s4 Companies Act 1985 by special resolution. A company may not alter its objects to validate retrospectively an *ultra vires* transaction (*Ashbury Railway Carriage Co v Riche*). The company can alter its objects clause for any reason and to any extent.

Holders of:

- 15% in nominal value of the company's issued share capital or any class thereof

- 15% in number of the company's members, if the company is not limited by shares

may object to the court within 21 days of the date of the authorising resolution. The court will do as it thinks fit.

Question 2: ABC Ltd and XYZ plc

(a)   do not

XYZ Plc

£50,000

ABC Ltd

company secretary

need not

(b)   XYZ plc

Trading certificate

(i)   It is a criminal offence by the company and its officers.

(ii)   Contracts with third parties are still binding on the company.

(iii)   Directors are personally liable on default by the company of three weeks or more.

(iv)   Winding up if no certificate within one year of incorporation.

(c)   Any four of the following:

(i)   Name clause

(ii)   Registered office clause

(iii)   Objects clause

(iv)   Capital clause

(v)   Clause stating that the company is public, if applicable

(vi)   Clause stating that the liability of the member is limited

(vii)   Declaration of association signed by subscribers.

Chapter 18

Multiple-choice questions

1   The correct answer is **C.**

2   The correct answer is **C.**

Practice questions

Question 1: Aire Ltd

The memorandum and articles of association are by s14 Companies Act 1985 a contract binding as if executed under seal between the company and its members and between the members themselves. But it is a contract binding only in respect of rights and obligations of members; only members are bound and then only in respect of membership matters.

In *Eley v Positive Government Security Life Assurance Co* the articles provided that Eley, who was a member, should be employed as the company's solicitor (without any time limit being specified). It was held that Eley could not enforce the articles as a contract of employment because this was not a right of membership. The company will rely on *Eley's* case and Donald will argue that the article in question and his long service are evidence of a contract to employ him to the age of 65. The court would have to decide which of the two conflicting precedents it preferred. If, as is probable, the court holds that the contract binds the company until Donald is 65, damages will be payable for premature termination by his dismissal.

The same principle applies to employer and employee. If Donald is subject to dismissal, Charles is entitled to resign (on reasonable notice). If Donald cannot be dismissed, Charles cannot resign.

Question 2: Beta Ltd

A company may alter or add to its articles of association by special resolution. However, an alteration must be exercised *bona fide* for the benefit of the company as a whole. This does not prevent a company altering its articles retrospectively. Thus in *Allen v Gold Reefs of West Africa* an alteration to give a company a lien on fully paid shares for debts due was held to be effective, even in respect of shares that were already issued and fully paid.

It is for the company itself, i.e. the shareholders, and not for the court to determine if the alteration could benefit the company, unless it is quite impossible for it to benefit the company.

Where there is a compulsory acquisition of a minority's shareholding, the courts will be very careful to scrutinise whether the alteration proposed is *bona fide*.

Thus in *Sidebottom v Kershaw Leese & Co. Ltd*, an alteration was made to the articles to provide for the acquisition of any shareholder's holding where he competed with the company's business. This was held to be a valid alteration.

However, in *Brown v British Abrasive Wheel* the court considered the alteration to provide for compulsory acquisition was not *bona fide*. A large majority of the shareholders wished to buy up the minority with a view to extending the capital. The minority refused to sell, and the majority then passed special resolutions altering the articles so as to enable the minority to be bought out. It was held that the alteration of the articles would be restrained as it was not for the benefit of the company.

It seems that on the facts of this case the alteration will fail as it is not proposed in the interests of the company, but to remove a shareholder who is 'a thorn in the side' of management.

Chapter 19

Multiple-choice questions

1   The correct answer is **A**.

2   The correct answer is **B**.

3   The correct answer is **C**.

4   The correct answer is **A**.

Practice questions

Question 1: Dozy Plc

The holders of at least 10% of the voting shares of a company may require the directors to call a general meeting. This is done by depositing at the registered office a requisition signed by the shareholders and stating the purpose for which the meeting is to be called. The directors must within three weeks of the deposit of the requisition call a meeting and the meeting must then be held within 28 days. If the directors do not convene the meeting the requisitionists, or a majority of them, may convene the meeting themselves for a date within three months of the deposit of the requisition. Their expenses are paid by the company and deducted from sums payable by the company to the directors.

As the purpose of the meeting is to remove the directors from office the requisitionists would also, in depositing their requisition, give special notice of their intention. This is notice to the company must be given 28 days before the meeting. The notice of the meeting would set out the resolution for removal of the directors. The directors themselves are entitled to receive a copy of the special notice from the company; to circulate 'representations' in their defence to members; and to be heard at the meeting itself.

Any members may under this procedure propose the removal of directors, but, unless there is some special provision in the memorandum and articles to the contrary, the directors can refuse to include the resolution in the notice covering the meeting unless the requisitionist(s) can muster at least one-twentieth of the voting rights or a hundred or more members holding at least £100 on average of the nominal share capital: *Pedley v Inland Waterways*. The resolution itself will be passed only if a majority of votes is cast in its favour at the meeting. The shareholders' committee must therefore have or obtain a majority of votes cast for their resolution.

Since no annual general meeting has been held for almost two years, the shareholders' committee could as an alternative procedure apply to the Department of Trade for an order that an annual general meeting be held. This might suit them if they lack the 10% support required to force the directors to call an EGM, but reckon to attract sufficient support when the meeting is convened to carry a resolution.

Tutorial note: If the company's name in the question had been Dozy **Ltd**, rather than Dozy **plc**, your answer should have included the possibility of the company having passed an elective resolution to dispense with the holding of AGMs.

Question 2: Fork Ltd

(a)   Shareholders holding at least one-tenth of the company's paid up share capital (with voting rights) have a right to requisition an EGM of the company.

(b)   The requisition must state the objects of the meeting and be signed by those requisitioning it. It must be deposited at the company's registered office. As the business of the meeting might lead to the dismissal of a director by ordinary resolution, the shareholders should give notice to the company that this is their intention, i.e. special notice requiring 28 days.

(c)   If the directors fail to call a meeting within 21 days of the requisition, the shareholders requisitioning the meeting may convene it themselves but must do so within three months.

The company will be liable to pay the reasonable expenses of the requisitionists in holding the meeting and the company is given the right to retain this sum from the remuneration normally given to the directors for these services.

Chapter 20

Practice questions

Question 1: Rakolite plc

(a)   Shares may not be issued at a discount but debentures may be. Debentures are not covered by the capital maintenance provisions.

(b)   The one exception to (a) is where debentures have an immediate right to be converted into shares. An issue of debentures at a discount would then be tantamount to an issue of shares at a discount, which is not permitted. In this case the option to convert is not immediate and thus does not fall within the exception. The issue will therefore be valid.

(c)   In this case the par value of any shares converted is 75p, therefore there is no suggestion at the time of issue of a discount, in fact the reverse is true. At the time of conversion it could be argued that the shares are issued at a premium, i.e. 80p is paid for a 75p share. If this is so, the difference of 5p per share must be transferred to the share premium account.

Question 2: A Ltd

(a)   It is assumed that the directors have the requisite authority from the shareholders to make this issue, and the issue is within the authorised share capital.

The issue of shares for a consideration other than cash, i.e. in this case in exchange for shares of B Ltd, is permissible but the return of allotment must have attached to it a copy of particulars of the contract of acquisition. Consideration to support a contract must be sufficient, i.e. of some monetary value, but need not be adequate and the parties to the contract are free to make their own bargain.

Where the net asset value of the company whose shares are acquired exceeds the nominal value of the shares issued (in this case by A Ltd) the excess should be treated as share premium. Thus, 25p per share should be placed in the share premium account.

(b)   In this case, the net asset value suggests that A Ltd is not obtaining full consideration for its shares. If that is so it would be issuing its shares at a discount on their nominal value, which is not permitted.

However, asset value is merely one indication of the value to be put on the shares of B Ltd. The merger of A and B may offer prospects of greater profitability for both companies. If the directors consider that the shares of B Ltd are worth an amount at least equal to the nominal value of the shares of A Ltd to be issued in exchange and enter the shares of B Ltd in their books at that value, their judgement, unless it is obviously not made in good faith and for sufficient reason, is unlikely to be set aside. In that case there is no issue of shares of A Ltd at a discount; there is an acquisition of assets (shares of B Ltd) at a possible over-value, which may be evidence of a breach of directors' duty, i.e. the duty to act in the best interest of the company.

If the company were a public company, on issuing the shares for a consideration other than cash, it must obtain an independent valuation of the proposed consideration. This requirement is dispensed with if the shares are issued in connection with a merger, which might be the case in this situation.

Chapter 21

Multiple-choice question

The correct answer is **B.**

Practice questions

Question 1: Zed Ltd

(a)   If its articles so provide a company may cancel any unissued shares. The procedure prescribed by the articles must be followed and a copy of any resolution (and also a copy of the memorandum showing the change in the share capital clause) must be filed at the Companies Registry. Under Table A unissued shares may be cancelled by ordinary resolution.

(b)   The repayment of part of money paid as subscription for issued shares is a reduction of share capital.

There must be authority in the articles and a special resolution must be passed in general meeting. Application is then made to the court for approval and the relevant financial information to show that the company can afford to repay £30,000 is provided. Creditors have a right to object if the reduction consists of a diminution of liability or a return of paid-up share capital, as in this case. The court is required to consider the effect of the repayment on the company's creditors. Unless some banker's guarantee or other adequate security is obtained to ensure that all existing creditors will be paid in full, the court will order an advertisement to be published and will consider any objections raised by creditors.

If the court is satisfied that the interests of creditors are safeguarded, it will make an order approving the reduction. The order is produced to the Registrar of Companies with a 'minute' setting out the details of the change of capital. The reduction takes effect and the cash may be paid out as soon as the court order is registered.

Question 2: Seasky Ltd

As a general rule, a company may not reduce its share capital by returning the capital to the shareholders. There are several exceptions to this, in particular a company may use the statutory reduction of capital procedure or the shares may be redeemed.

In this particular case, the company need not use the statutory procedure for reduction as the shares are expressly created as redeemable preference shares.

A company may, if authorised by its articles, issue shares that may be redeemed at the option of the company or its shareholders. Redemption may only be out of distributable profits of the company or out of the proceeds of a fresh issue of shares made for the purpose of redemption.

If a premium is payable on redemption, it must be out of distributable profits of the company.

Shares that are redeemed are treated as cancelled, thus reducing the company's issued share capital.

A capital redemption reserve must be created where the redemption has been financed otherwise than out of the proceeds of a fresh issue of shares. Where the redemption is solely out of the profits of the company, the amount transferred to the capital redemption reserve (from distributable profits) will be equivalent to the amount of share capital cancelled due to redemption. Where the redemption is partly out of profits the amount transferred to the capital redemption reserve will be computed as:

	£
Nominal value of shares redeemed	X
Less: Aggregate amount of proceeds of fresh issue of shares	X
Amount to capital redemption reserve	X

The capital redemption reserve is a quasi-share capital and may only be used for the issue of fully paid bonus shares.

Seasky would therefore require £50,000 of distributable profits to redeem all the redeemable preference shares and a transfer of this amount from distributable profits to capital redemption reserve would be required.

Note the company's capital remains at £150,000, which is now represented by 100,000 £1 ordinary shares and £50,000 in the capital redemption reserve.

As long as the company complies with the above requirements it may redeem the shares. The preference shareholders cannot claim that this is a variation of rights as the company is merely doing what it is permitted to do both by company law and its articles.

In addition, as a private company it may purchase shares with payment out of capital, but only to the extent that its distributable profit is insufficient, provided the proper procedure is followed, that is:

(a)   The directors of the company make a statutory declaration that the company will not thereby become insolvent and will still be able to continue to carry on business as a going concern. Such a declaration must be supported by an auditors' report.

(b)   A special resolution approving the payment out of capital is passed within the week following the statutory declaration.

(c)   Within the week immediately following the date of the resolution the company publishes in the London Gazette and in an appropriate newspaper a notice detailing its intention.

(d)   The payment out of capital is made not earlier than five nor more than seven weeks after the date of the resolution. Any creditor or any member who did not vote for the resolution may apply to court to have it cancelled. On the hearing of such an application the court may make such an order as it thinks fit.

Question 3: Esk Ltd

Dividends can only be paid out of profits available for distribution. These are defined as 'accumulated realised profits less accumulated realised losses'. Thus the directors of Esk must bring forward the previous trading losses and only if the profit of the fifth year is sufficient to wipe out the losses of the previous years, can they declare a dividend and then only of the excess.

Moreover, the directors of a company are obliged to consider the interests of the company, i.e. the shareholders and the employees. They should act in good faith in respect of both categories.

If Esk were a public limited company, there is an additional provision that the directors would have to consider. They can only pay a dividend out of profits available for distribution and only if net assets would not be reduced below the aggregate of the company's called-up share capital and its undistributable reserves. The undistributable reserves are made up of the share premium account, the capital redemption reserve fund, unrealised profits and any other reserves retained by the company. It is unlikely in this case that the profit made by the company could make up the capital and provide sufficient available profits for a legal distribution.

Chapter 22

Multiple-choice question

1   The correct answer is **C**.

Practice question

Flannel Ltd

(a)   could not

        asset

        security

        realised

        consent

(b)   A major advantage is that the company cannot realise the asset without the lender's consent; the major disadvantage is that the adequacy of the security depends on the charged property retaining its value.

(c)   …a charge on a class of assets, present and future.

(d)   21 days

        void (although late registration can be permitted)

        can be fined

        The Land Registry

Chapter 23

Multiple-choice questions

1   The correct answer is **C**.

2   The correct answer is **B**.

Practice questions

Question 1: Susan and Shirley

(a)   can

        Section 303 Companies Act 1985

        …this is possible despite any contract Shirley may have with the company or the provisions of the articles.

(b)   ordinary resolution

        special notice

        a simple majority

        can

        28 days

(c)   will

        will

        Southern Foundries v Shirlaw

(d)   Because the organisation was a partnership and contains the same members, Shirley may be able to petition the court under Section 122 Insolvency Act 1986 that the company be wound up on the grounds that it is just and equitable.

Chapter 24

Multiple-choice questions

1   The correct answer is **B**.

2   The correct answer is **A**.

Practice questions

Question 1: Griff plc

It is possible that Griff plc has an action against John for breach of fiduciary duty.

A director owes a fiduciary duty to their company to act in good faith for the benefit of the company. In particular, they may not make a personal profit out of their position or knowledge as director – *Regal (Hastings) v Gulliver*. They are accountable to the company for any such profit and they are accountable whether or not the company itself was able to make the profit: it is not a question of loss to the company. Accordingly it would seem that Griff plc may recover the profit John made on the share deals.

A director owes their fiduciary duty to the company, not to individual shareholders. In *Percival v Wright* (a case with the same material facts as the instant problem) it was therefore held that an individual shareholder could not sue to recover the profit the director had made on the share deal. Accordingly Adam has no action against John.

On the same principle, no fiduciary duty is owed by John to Whale plc and therefore it has no action against John for breach of fiduciary duty.

Question 2: Williams Ltd

The facts evidence a possible breach of s213 Insolvency Act 1986 (IA86) re fraudulent trading, s214 IA86 re wrongful trading, and S239 IA86 re preferences.

Fraudulent trading

Fraudulent trading occurs where the business of the company is carried on with intent to defraud creditors or for any fraudulent purpose. It is therefore necessary to establish dishonest intent. This will be inferred where a company carries on business and continues to incur liabilities where there is no reasonable prospect of those liabilities being met – *Re William C Leitch Bros*. Thus in *R v Grantham* two directors who ordered a consignment of potatoes on one month's credit at a time when they knew payment would not be forthcoming at the end of the month were found guilty of fraudulent trading. However, *Re William C Leitch Bros* established that because its directors were honestly of the opinion that the debts they caused the company to incur would eventually be paid they were not liable for fraudulent trading. The later case of *Re EB Tractors* confirms this contention. S213 identifies the persons liable for fraudulent trading as those knowingly party to the carrying on of business in the fraudulent way.

The facts of the question, which state that Ellen and Freda were convinced that the company would be restored to profitability, would seem to suggest that they genuinely believed its debts would be paid. Thus, although they were mistaken and possibly foolish, they did not have the necessary dishonest intent to constitute fraudulent trading.

As to Bill: the facts given state that he believed that insolvency was inevitable. He therefore has the necessary dishonest intent. However, the case of *Re Maidstone Buildings* established that a person is not a party to fraudulent trading solely by reason of knowledge, they must also take active steps to defraud, such as the ordering of goods. Thus if Bill, as stated, merely exerted influence over policy and management but did not actively manage the business he is not party to fraudulent trading.

Should it be the case the court decides that any one or all of Ellen, Freda and Bill are liable for fraudulent trading, the possible consequences are first, criminal (fine and/or imprisonment) and second civil liability. Under the latter, each will be liable to contribute to the company's assets such sum as the court thinks fit. The court would probably order the payment of a sum equal to the unpaid debts incurred during the fraudulent trading period. Additionally, fraudulent trading is a specific ground for the making of a disqualification order under the Company Directors Disqualification Act 1986.

Wrongful trading

Under s214 Insolvency Act 1986 persons potentially liable for wrongful trading are directors and shadow directors. Clearly Ellen and Freda, as directors, are within the ambit of s214. Bill will be if he can be classed as a shadow director, that is, a person in accordance with whose instructions or directions the board is accustomed to acting. More facts will be needed to ascertain whether Bill was in the habit of giving instructions that his daughters were in the habit of abiding by.

In order for a person to be liable for wrongful trading, the liquidator has the burden of proving the following two matters:

(a)   that the company is in insolvent liquidation – Williams Ltd is in creditors' voluntary liquidation and it is therefore very likely insolvent

(b)   that the person was a director (or shadow director) of the company at a time when they knew or ought to have known that there was no reasonable prospect of avoiding insolvent liquidation. The facts given clearly show Bill had this knowledge. As to Ellen and Freda, the question is whether they ought to have known. Unlike fraudulent trading, what they personally honestly believed is not material since s214 states that what a director ought to know and deduce is judged according to the standard of reasonably skilled, experienced and diligent directors. As shown in *Re Produce Marketing Consortium* the court will examine the history of the company to establish objectively whether there was a 'moment of truth' when the directors should have known insolvency was inevitable. The given facts tend to suggest Ellen and Freda were over-optimistic and either knew or ought to have known at an early stage that insolvent liquidation was a likely prospect.

S214 states that the person is not liable for wrongful trading if they can prove that they took every step with a view to minimising the potential loss to the company's creditors that they ought to have taken. Such steps would include such matters as cessation of business where continued trading is incurring losses, and taking expert advice on, for example, applying for an administration order sooner rather than later. Merely continuing to trade in the hope of better times is not such a step.

An action for wrongful trading may only be brought by a liquidator (it is not a criminal offence) and, in the same way as fraudulent trading, civil liability will result in the court ordering personal contribution to the company's assets and may result in disqualification.

Preference

A preference occurs where a company does anything or suffers anything to be done that puts a creditor in a better position in the event of insolvent liquidation than they would otherwise have been in. The repayment to Bill of his £10,000 loan is a preference.

The liquidator may set aside a preference in favour of a connected person of a company if they can prove that the preference took place within the two years immediately preceding the commencement of liquidation and at a time when the company was unable to pay its debts. Bill, being the father of the directors, is a connected person, he was paid on 1 January, commencement of liquidation was 20 June and the facts point to the company being insolvent on 1 January. The action to set aside the payment will be successfully resisted by Bill if he can prove that the company, in deciding to make the payment, was not influenced by a desire to better his position. His evidence appears very weak.

If, as seems likely, the liquidator can set aside the preference, the most likely result would be an order that Bill return the £10,000 to the liquidator. He would then rank for payment as the court so directs.

Chapter 25

Practice question

Enid

(a)   *Foss v Harbottle 1843*

         does not

         unlawful

(b)   go to court/sue

         section 122 Insolvency Act 1986

         put into liquidation

(c)   quasi-partnership

         Ebrahimi v Westbourne Galleries, 1973

         just and equitable

         would not

         …requires other reasonable remedies to be used before winding up is ordered.

(d)   This might be unfairly prejudicial conduct under section 459 Companies Act 1985; this case seems very like *Re Cumana* 1986 where such conduct was found.

Table of Cases

Index

PUBLISHING

FOULKS LYNCH

CIMA Publications

Please post your completed order form to:
Kaplan Publishing Foulks Lynch
Unit 2 The Business Centre,
Molly Millars Lane, Wokingham RG41 2QZ
Or fax it to: 0118 979 7455

For all queries relating to this order please call our helpline on 0118 989 0629

	Study Text £28.00	Workbook with CD £30.00	Exam Kits £16.00	Bitesize £10.00	Practice 4 Success CDs £25.00	Total Value
Certificate (New syllabus examinable from October 2006)	Quantity	Quantity	Quantity	Quantity	Quantity	
Paper C01 Fundamentals of Management Accounting	☐	☐	☐	☐	☐	
Paper C02 Fundamentals of Financial Accounting	☐	☐	☐	☐	☐	
Paper C03 Fundamentals of Business Mathematics	☐	☐	☐	☐	☐	
Paper C04 Fundamentals of Business Economics	☐	☐	☐	☐	☐	
Paper C05 Fund. of Ethics, Corporate Governance & Business Law	☐	☐	☐	☐	☐	

	Study Text £28.00	Exam Kits Nov 06 £15.00	Exam Kits May 07 £16.00	Pocket Notes £10.00	Practice 4 Success CDs £25.00	
Examination Date: Nov 06 ☐ May 07☐						
Professional	Quantity	Quantity	Quantity	Quantity	Quantity	
Paper P1 Management Accounting Performance Evaluation	☐	☐	☐	☐	☐	
Paper P2 Management Accounting Decision Making	☐	☐	☐	☐	☐	
Paper P3 Management Accounting Risk and Control Strategy	☐	☐	☐	☐	-	
Paper P4 Organisational Management & Information Systems	☐	☐	☐	☐	☐	
Paper P5 Integrated Management	☐	☐	☐	☐	☐	
Paper P6 Management Accounting Business Strategy	☐	☐	☐	☐	-	
Paper P7 Financial Accounting and Tax Principles	☐	☐	☐	☐	☐	
Paper P8 Management Accounting Financial Analysis	☐	☐	☐	☐	☐	
Paper P9 Financial Strategy	☐	☐	☐	☐	-	

TOPCIMA

Test of Professional Competence in Management Accounting (Study Text)	£28.00 ☐		The Knowledge*	£28.00 ☐

SUB TOTAL	£	
PLUS DELIVERY CHARGE (£5 FOR UP TO 10 BOOKS)	£	
TOTAL	£	

Cardholder Details

Name on card: ....

Address: ....

....

....

Telephone: ....

Delivery address (if different from above – a signature will be required)

Name: ....

Address: ....

....

....

Telephone: ....

Payment

1 I enclose Cheque/Postal Order/Bankers Draft for £.....................................

   Please make cheques payable to '**Kaplan Publishing Foulks Lynch**'.

2 Charge MasterCard/Visa/Switch/Delta no:

Valid from: | | | | Expiry date: | | | |

Issue no:
(Switch only) [   ]   Security Code: [   ]

Signature: .... Date: ....